Transport
Economics

Transport Economics

Theory, Application and Policy

GRAHAM MALLARD and
STEPHEN GLAISTER

palgrave
macmillan

First published 2008 by
PALGRAVE MACMILLAN
Houndmills, Basingstoke, Hampshire RG21 6XS and
175 Fifth Avenue, New York, N.Y. 10010
Companies and representatives throughout the world

PALGRAVE MACMILLAN is the global academic imprint of the Palgrave Macmillan division of St. Martin's Press, LLC and of Palgrave Macmillan Ltd. Macmillan® is a registered trademark in the United States, United Kingdom and other countries. Palgrave is a registered trademark in the European Union and other countries.

ISBN-13: 978–0–230–51687–8 hardback
ISBN-10: 0–230–51687–4 hardback
ISBN-13: 978–0–230–51688–5 paperback
ISBN-10: 0–230–51688–2 paperback

This book is printed on paper suitable for recycling and made from fully managed and sustained forest sources. Logging, pulping and manufacturing processes are expected to conform to the environmental regulations of the country of origin.

A catalogue record for this book is available from the British Library.

A catalog record for this book is available from the Library of Congress.

10   9   8   7   6   5   4   3   2   1
17   16   15   14   13   12   11   10   09   08

Printed and bound in China

Dedication

To Fay

Contents

Acknowledgements   xi
Introduction   xiii

Part I   Setting the Scene   1

1   The History of Transport in Europe   3
   1.1   Railways   3
   1.2   Roads and automobiles   6
   1.3   Shipping   10
   1.4   Aircraft   13
   1.5   Canals   16
   1.6   Lessons from History   17

2   The Importance of Transport in the UK and Europe   21
   2.1   Statistical importance   21
   2.2   Theoretical importance   29

Part II   The Theory of Markets: An Overview   33

3   The Demand for Transport   35
   3.1   Important definitions   35
   3.2   Determinants of demand   36
   3.3   The problem of the peak   41
   3.4   Elasticity of demand   49
   3.5   Market price   60
   3.6   Market welfare   61
   3.7   Markets in action: The effects of 11 September 2001 on
       the low-cost airlines   63
   3.8   The problem of rural demand   64

4   Markets, Costs and Revenues   67
   4.1   Important definitions   67
   4.2   Classification of costs according to their nature   68
   4.3   Classification of costs according to their scale   70

	4.4	Other types of cost important in transport economics	79
	4.5	Classification of revenue	80
	4.6	Profit maximisation and alternative objectives	83
	4.7	Market structures	90

5 **Competition and Contestability** **91**
	5.1	The assumptions and the model	91
	5.2	Normal and abnormal profit	92
	5.3	The adjustment mechanism	93
	5.4	Efficiency	94
	5.5	A fundamental model	96
	5.6	A transport case study: Tramp shipping	97
	5.7	Contestable markets	101

6 **Monopoly** **103**
	6.1	Definition and barriers to entry	103
	6.2	The model	107
	6.3	Price discrimination	110
	6.4	Yield management	115
	6.5	European competition policy	116
	6.6	Public service vehicle operations in Britain	119
	6.7	Natural monopolies	122

7 **Monopolistic Competition** **125**
	7.1	The model and outcomes	125
	7.2	Competition	126
	7.3	The road-haulage market in the European Union and Great Britain	127
	7.4	The taxi market in the City of Leicester	132

8 **Oligopoly** **137**
	8.1	Definition and model	137
	8.2	Location decisions	139
	8.3	The European air industry	141
	8.4	The global car industry	147

Part III   Market Failure in the Transport Sector: An Overview **149**

9 **Externalities** **151**
	9.1	Definitions and the model	151
	9.2	Missing markets	153
	9.3	A lack of ownership	156
	9.4	The transport sector and global warming	157
	9.5	Congestion as an externality	162
	9.6	The positive externalities of cycling	164
	9.7	Sustainable development and ethics	165

10   Public and Demerit Goods   **167**
   10.1   Public goods: The theory   167
   10.2   Galileo   168
   10.3   Street lighting   169
   10.4   Provision of roads   171
   10.5   The theory of demerit goods   173

11   Inequality, Poverty and Asymmetric Information   **177**
   11.1   Inequality and poverty   177
   11.2   Inequality in Europe   178
   11.3   The exacerbation caused by the transport sector   179
   11.4   Asymmetric information – The market for lemons   181

Part IV   Policy: An Overview   **183**

12   Privatisation and Deregulation   **185**
   12.1   Arguments in favour of privatisation and deregulation   186
   12.2   Arguments in favour of nationalisation and against
        deregulation   189
   12.3   Political risk and the need for governmental commitment
        in privatisation   190
   12.4   The methodology of privatisation   192
   12.5   The privatisation and deregulation of British rail   193
   12.6   The privatisation of British ports   201
   12.7   The privatisation and deregulation of British buses   202
   12.8   Competitive tendering in bus markets across Europe   208
   12.9   A summary of the experiences in Germany and
        Ireland   209

13   Project Appraisal: Cost–Benefit Analysis   **211**
   13.1   The need for, and types of, cost–benefit analysis   211
   13.2   The methodology of cost–benefit analysis   212
   13.3   Valuing non-marketed products   216
   13.4   Decision-making in practice   219
   13.5   The limitations of cost–benefit analysis   219
   13.6   The COBA model   220

14   Transport Investment   **225**
   14.1   Central or local government investment   226
   14.2   European Community investment   226
   14.3   Private investment and public–private partnerships   228
   14.4   The Channel Tunnel   229

15   General Forms of Government Intervention   **231**
   15.1   Introduction   231
   15.2   Command and control solutions   232
   15.3   Taxation   236
   15.4   Tradable permits   242

15.5   Case studies of the three options   245
15.6   Bureaucratic rent-seeking   246

16   Tackling Traffic Congestion   **249**
16.1   The situation   249
16.2   The principles behind road-user charging   250
16.3   Experiences and types of road-user charging   251
16.4   The methodology of road-user charging   253
16.5   How widely should charging be implemented?   272
16.6   The case for building more road capacity   272
16.7   Issues to be resolved to make road-pricing a practical
          national policy   273

Part V   The Future   **277**

17   Concluding Remarks   **279**
17.1   The major challenges ahead   279
17.2   Other trends   280
17.3   Words of perceived wisdom   280

Mathematical Appendix   **283**
M.1   A straight-line demand curve   283
M.2   A straight-line supply curve   284
M.3   Equilibrium   285
M.4   Substitute and complementary products   285
M.5   Elasticities   287
M.6   More sophisticated demand-and-supply analysis   288
M.7   Consumer surplus   290
M.8   Producer surplus   291
M.9   Total, marginal and average costs   292
M.10   Total, average and marginal revenue   294
M.11   Profit-maximising condition   295

Bibliography   297
Index   305

Acknowledgements

The authors would like to thank HMSO Licensing Division for permission to use data from the Office for National Statistics and the Department for Transport throughout the book; the European Commission Directorate-General for Energy and Transport for permission to use its data and research throughout the book; Clarkson Research Services for permission to use its data in Section 5.6; the Intergovernmental Panel on Climate Change for permission to use its data in Section 9.4; Alan Whittington of Professional Transport Services for the provision of information in Sections 6.6 and 7.3; the Oxford, Cambridge and RSA (OCR) Examinations Board for the provision of information in Sections 6.6 and 7.3; Leicester City Council for the provision of information in Section 7.4; Ryan and Adam Slatter for their valuable research assistance in Section 7.4; and four anonymous referees for their comments on a draft version of the text. The authors would finally like to thank Rees Jeffreys Road Fund, the Joseph Rowntree Foundation and the Esmee Fairbairn Foundation for their funding of research (commissioned by the Independent Transport Commission) that has formed the basis of Chapter 16.

In addition, Graham would like to thank (first and foremost) Fay for all of her love, encouragement and advice, and for her unwavering support, help and belief in him during the hard times. Without Fay, the book would never have been completed and Graham would be lost. It is to Fay that the book is dedicated. Graham would like to thank his wonderful family, particularly his parents, for all of their love and encouragement: Dereck and Jean; Janet, Paul, Adam and Ryan; Keith and Sally, and Nanna. Without his family, Graham would never have been in a situation to consider writing a book. Graham would also like to thank Stephen Glaister, Jaime Marshall and Geoff Harcourt for their enormous support, help and encouragement throughout this project. Without them, the proposal would never have progressed. Finally, Graham would like to thank his friends for their enormous support and encouragement: Ben Evans; Andy and Sally Mattches; David and Deborah Hargreaves; and Mark Vaughan-Shaw (whose laptop came in extremely handy during the final stages). Thank you.

Introduction

Transport economics is a subject that affects each one of our lives on a regular basis and in a significant way. For instance, here are some facts.

- The European Commission (June 2003) has estimated that 7500 kilometres of the road network in the European Union is blocked by traffic jams every single day.
- In the same report, the Commission has also estimated that at the main airports in the European Union some 35 per cent of flights are delayed by at least 15 minutes as a result of congestion.
- In 2003, private households in the European Union spent 748 billion euros, roughly 13.3 per cent of their total expenditure, on transport (EC, 2005).
- In 2003, there were over 7.5 million workers employed in the transport sector of the European Union (EC, 2005).
- The British government spent £13,241 million on the transport sector in the financial year 2002/2003 (ONS, 2004).
- In 2004, there were 49,807 fatalities on the roads of the European Union (EC, 2005).

These are just a few indicators of the importance of the transport sector to the European Union's economy and population; many more are assessed throughout this book. It is vital that economists have a solid understanding of this sector and are able to work within it, to the benefit of our society.

The transport sector also acts as an excellent case study of many economic concepts that are vital for any serious student of the subject. Through the study of transport economics, we can be enlightened about traditional and modern theories of the firm; sometimes controversial government policy tools, such as deregulation and privatisation; the market failures of market power, externalities, public goods, inequality and asymmetric information; the various possible solutions to these problems; and the methodology that underpins all large public investment decisions. Focusing on this single sector allows us to view these concepts through our own experiences of them, as well as to understand the history and future of this sector that affect us all so significantly.

This book has been written not only to open up important economic theories, but also to aid in the development of a wide range of crucial economic skills in a setting that is of everyday interest. By using this book to study the transport sector, one is able to develop one's ability and confidence in statistical and diagrammatical analysis; the design and evaluation of economic policies; simple, but fascinating, game theory; and investment appraisal. One is also able to develop one's own, thoroughly reasoned, views and conclusions about the state that our transport sector is in; the policies that governments should adopt to shape it; and the future that lies ahead for it.

There are two general approaches that can be taken when using this book to study transport economics. The first is the linear approach, in which one simply follows the structure of the book: Part I outlines the setting; Part II opens up the economic theories that underpin the transport sector, applying them to the transport sector of the European Union; Part III explores the theories and causes of market failure in the European transport sector; Part IV assesses the range of possible policies that can be used to correct these market failures; and finally Part V offers some concluding remarks. This first approach is the most thorough. The second is the horizontal (or thematic) approach, in which one studies transport economics by focusing on each mode of transport in turn. An outline as to how such study may be structured is suggested in Figure I.1. If this structure is adopted, it is important that the relevant theory sections are read alongside.

Economics is a subject that should always be challenged. The theories and practices expounded in this book have all been developed over time by able economists and it is important that serious students of the subject refer back to their original works. However, the theories and practices should not simply be accepted unquestioningly; they should always be freshly compared to the real world to assess whether they are still effective in its analysis. This is the only way that our understanding can be refined and improved; and, perhaps more importantly, the only

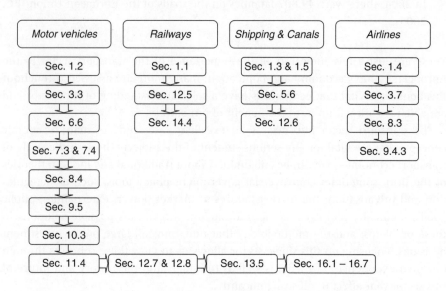

Figure I.1 A suggested horizontal study structure

way in which the subject can be guarded from widespread acceptance of ineffective and even harmful policies. As Joan Violet Robinson, an eminent Keynesian economist and a pioneer in theories of imperfect competition (Harcourt, 1995), commented, 'The purpose of studying economics is not to acquire a set of ready-made answers to economic questions, but to learn how to avoid being deceived by economists' (Joan Robinson, 1960).

Economics is also a subject that should be applied in a practical way in order to see the society in which we live improve. Traditionally the subject was that of *political economy*; it was only relatively recently that the two parts were separated. This has arguably done the subject a disservice as many students of it are simply intellectually curious about the solutions to set economic problems, rather than seeking to use theory in the development of policy beneficial to us all. It is intended that, throughout this book, readers will question how the functioning and outcomes of the transport sector can be improved. Surely this is the purpose of the subject?

This book has been designed primarily for transport economics courses at university level, but it is also of great use for able A-level students of the topic. It is hoped that it will be an invaluable text for students of transport economics, human geography and transport engineering, and for those who simply have an interest in the sector. For those who like to have economic claims supported by mathematical proofs, there is a mathematical appendix included at the end of the book, which takes students beyond the introductory level.

Transport economics is an exciting branch of this classical subject, which is crucial to the future of our way of life. We hope that you will find this book not only enjoyable, but also helpful in expanding your understanding of the subject in an interesting and relevant way.

Setting the Scene I

Ever since humans first walked the Earth, they have been engaged in transport: *the movement of people or goods from one place to another*. Until relatively recently, with the development of air travel, there have been two general forms of transport: land and sea.

At first, land transport was simply walking and carrying, until the development of the first vehicle: the sledge. These were constructed of wood and were drawn along by hand, allowing materials and other people to be moved. The earliest of these sledges that has so far been discovered was that in Northern Europe, dating back to 7000 BC. It is likely to have been used by hunter-gathering communities that populated the area at the time. Transport remained in this form for some 3000 years, until the domestication of cattle and the discovery that castrating a bull created the docile but incredibly powerful ox, in Southern Russia and Mesopotamia.

Sea transport was initially simply a matter of lashing logs and reeds together to form rafts, or using the hollowed-out trunks of trees. It was with the latter of these options that real development progressed, as the sides were increasingly extended; essentially the form that boats took until the introduction of metal hulls in the nineteenth century. It was again the civilisation of Mesopotamia, along with Egypt, that began to use sea transport extensively.

It is at this point that the different modes of transport began to emerge. The opening chapter of Part I takes up the development of each of the main modes of transport separately. It is intended to be a brief historical narrative of the development of transport in Europe, with particular focus on the UK. A multiple-volume work could be devoted to a thorough study of the economic history of transport and so this is not the purpose here. The general developments will be outlined, pausing at times and events from which particular economic lessons can be drawn. An appreciation of the development of transport is important for all students of transport economics, as it illuminates the factors that have shaped the sector to be as it is today. It forms the starting point of an understanding as to why transport economists are faced with the problems that exist in the early twenty-first century. This is the intention of the opening chapter, which concludes with a discussion of the overarching lessons that should be learnt from the preceding narrative. For case studies of these transport industries today, see the parts that follow.

Chapter 2 sets the scene in terms of how important the transport sector has come to be to the European economy today. This is first done by analysing a range of current statistics to assess the very practical impact that the sector has on factors such as employment, and household and government expenditure. The importance of the sector to the economic theories of the free market is then outlined, and it is argued that without a well-functioning transport system the free-market economy could not achieve a state of efficiency. This is so important that it underpins the very basis of current economics.

The History of Transport in Europe

1.1 Railways

1.1.1 Initial developments

The first railways were developed in Germany in the 1550s as wagons pulled along wooden rails by horses. This system was copied for use by the expanding British coal mines in the early 1600s, where wooden rails were laid down on which a single horse could draw 50–60 bushels of coal. These *tramroads* spread quickly throughout the Tyneside coalfield.

Iron-rails were first used in the UK around 1767. What is considered to be the world's first public railway was opened on 26 July 1803 in Surrey, south of London. It was a horse-drawn freight line connecting Wandsworth and Croydon which lasted for only 42 years. The first commercial passenger-carrying railway, which was also horse-drawn, was the Oystermouth Railway, which was authorised to carry passengers in 1807.

In the year following the opening of the Surrey Iron Railway, the first steam locomotive, which had been built by Richard Trevithick, was used at the Pennydarren Ironworks in Wales. However, it was not until 27 September 1825, and the opening of the Stockton and Darlington Railway, that steam locomotives were proved to be useful for public use. The railway was a single track, 25 miles in length, with a hundred passing loops and four branch lines leading to different collieries. Such networks were further developed with the opening of the Liverpool and Manchester Railway on 15 September 1830. This is considered to be the first modern railway as it was designed entirely for steam engines with cuttings and embankments rather than pulling-ropes to aid horse-drawn wagons up gradients. It was on this line that George Stephenson's *Rocket* was used.

These first railways were regarded as being a new type of toll-road, on which customers had to pay for the privilege of being able to use their own vehicles. Gradually, the owners saw the possibility of charging customers to use their vehicles instead. The financial possibilities spurred a *Railway Mania* with small investors rushing to establish small stretches of line. It was necessary to obtain an Act of

Parliament to build a line, and by 1845 there were over 1000 projects proposed. If a proposal was successful, the Act of Parliament allowed railway companies to exercise powers of compulsory land purchase, but some landowners charged excessive amounts and powerful landowners could even block such an act being passed in the first place. This forced railway companies to build sub-optimal routes, creating bends that would lead to the development of tilting-trains way into the future.

The railways were an essential part of the industrial revolution. They competed against the canal systems to be the main mode of freight transportation. The railways gained the upper hand as they could be built in areas that were unsuitable for the more traditional canal systems. Consequently, the railways grew rapidly and by the 1850s many steam railways had reached London. A metropolitan railway was built to connect the different terminals, the first section of which was completed in 1863. The first *metro* was born.

1.1.2 Increasing government intervention

At first, the government took a laissez-faire stance to the railways until the issue of safety became important. In 1840, the Act for Regulating Railways was passed, allowing the Board of Trade to appoint railway inspectors. By the end of the nineteenth century it was still not unusual for a hundred people to die on the British railways each year. Following a crash in Armagh that killed 80 passengers, an act in 1889 insisted on further safety measures with all passenger trains being required to have continuous automatic brakes.

By the 1890s electric power was practical, allowing the further development of underground railways in cities such as London and Paris. Most street railways were also electrified and became known as *trams*. In many European countries, these street railways expanded beyond city boundaries and actually connected cities, a notable example of that being Belgium.

In Britain, the Railways Act of 1921 amalgamated nearly all the railway companies into the *Big Four*, which consisted of the London, Midland and Scottish Railway; the Great Western Railway; the London and North Eastern Railway; and the Southern Railway. They all undertook strategies to rebuild their lines and their rolling stock, spurring a period of great competition between them. This truly was the golden age of the British railway. The act also introduced rail regulation in the form of the *Railway Rates Tribunal*, which was created to approve fare structures.

During the First World War, the railways were successfully taken under government control. Operating expenses were cut to a minimum and efficiency improved. By the cessation of hostilities, though, the railways were faced with growing competition from motor vehicles and road haulage. Prior to the war, the railways had enjoyed a monopoly in freight haulage and so the government had passed a legislation that turned them into *common carriers*, meaning that they had to transport any cargo that was offered to them at a nationally agreed price, which was below that to be profitable for the railways. Consequently, they had to cross-subsidise loss-making operations with profitable ones, causing them to raise prices.

Until 1957 when this obligation was removed, the railways suffered at a disadvantage to road haulage. The *Big Four* never ran a healthy profit: in fact, the LNER never made a profit at all.

1.1.3 Failures and lessons in Britain

The railway companies failed to respond effectively to the challenge that motor vehicles posed, belatedly adopting two strategies: reducing fares and attempting to obtain a foothold in the road market. The first of these was ineffective as, in general, it was uniformly implemented across all services rather than being tailored according to differences in profitability and costs, meaning that the net effect was a reduction in revenue. The latter response was initially focused on the passenger market. In 1928 the railway companies began to acquire financial interests in existing bus operators and, as noted in Aldcroft (1974), within three years they were associated with about 47 per cent of the buses on Britain's roads. The perfectly competitive nature of the road-haulage market at the time made it more difficult for them to employ a similar strategy in that and so they concentrated their response on purchasing and operating their own vehicles. By 1938, they owned approximately 2 per cent of the freight vehicles in operation. This was too-little-too-late and the passenger and freight motor-vehicle markets expanded at the expense of the railways.

The railway companies learned from their failure to stem the tide of competition from the motor industry and were determined to respond more quickly to the emergence of domestic civil aviation in the early 1930s. In March 1934, the four railway companies, along with Imperial Airways, established the Railway Air Services. This new operator was to compete directly with the emerging domestic airlines and was to be operated by Imperial Airways until it could purchase and manage its own craft. The company rapidly expanded its operations, focusing on the West Coast where the railway lines were under the greatest competition from the new airlines (the East Coast Main Line was subjected to very little competition from the skies). However, along with the other domestic airlines, the company made continual losses. The railway companies also invested in other airlines, acquiring a dominant interest in many but not owning many outright, and so were able to help consolidate the air industry to a certain extent.

During the Second World War, the four companies worked together and the network was used more than it had ever been before. Only necessary maintenance work was made, though, and so the network deteriorated greatly. In the UK the network was not damaged by bombing as much as in other European countries, which compounded the problem because it did not enjoy the rebuilding that occurred in these other countries after the conflict. It was clear that it could only be maintained by the private sector with great difficulty, and so with the Transport Act of 1947 it was nationalised.

By the 1950s the UK network was far behind those in Europe. Even in 1955 steam accounted for 87 per cent of the total miles travelled on the British network, compared to 10 per cent by electric power and the remaining 3 per cent by diesel.

It would be nearly 50 years after electric and diesel technology became feasible that it was extensively applied in Britain, whereas in mainland Europe it had been adopted much earlier. Even in the years following nationalisation the replacement policy was firmly in favour of steam locomotives. Why it took so long for the technology to be adopted in Britain has been debated and many possible explanations have been raised: the economic returns to electrification were doubtful; there was a lack of finance; and the competition from motor vehicles and air transport may have distracted railway companies from investing in new technology; but Aldcroft (1974) argues that the strongest factor was the comfort that the old technology afforded to the management, both before and after nationalisation. A modernisation plan of electrification and dieselisation was finally implemented. It cost over £1 billion at the time and largely failed as it misdirected funds towards activities that were no longer demanded from the system and as it rushed diesel locomotives into production before being fully tested.

In 1963, Richard Beeching published a report as head of the railway system, in which he proposed to close 5000 miles of track and 2363 small stations. These closures were mostly implemented but they failed to produce the desired savings or increase in profitability. The 1970s saw British Rail (a name that was adopted in 1968) introduce the high-speed diesel InterCity-125 trains, which attracted increasing numbers of passengers and an improvement in finances. However, by the 1980s much of the rolling stock was obsolete and approaching the end of its lifetime. The 1990s would see further dramatic changes.

1.2   Roads and automobiles

1.2.1   Early road vehicles and the Roman Empire

One of the earliest wheeled-wagons ever to be found was that near Zurich, dating back to 3000 BC. Within a century from when this wagon was being utilised, heavy-wheeled vehicles were in use across Europe, moving at a pace of around 2 miles per hour. It was during this time that they took on a regal status, being used primarily by heads of state.

Between 2000 BC and 1000 AD, the Roman Empire spread across Europe, building roads as the arteries of the empire. The Romans viewed the quick transportation of soldiers and goods as of the upmost importance and so countless soldiers and slaves were used in the construction of absolutely straight roads. Post-houses containing fresh horses were situated every 10 miles and lodgings for the travellers every 25 miles. By 1000 AD there were over 50,000 miles of such roads across the empire.

1.2.2   The expansion of public transport

The later contraction of the Roman Empire saw the deterioration of the European road network. It was not until the 1600s, when the surfaces began to be improved with paving stones, that the use of the roads once again increased. Horse-drawn carriages were available for hire in London in 1605 and by the second half of the century there were the first traffic jams. From 1640 onwards, public transport consisted of the stagecoaches which carried up to eight prosperous travellers inside, second-class passengers in an open basket at the back, and the least privileged on the roof with the luggage and a simple handrail for safety. It was during this time that the rich would send their young sons on the *Grand Tour* across Europe in private, well-sprung and comfortably upholstered carriages. It was on such a journey that the great economist Adam Smith was employed by Charles Townsend, a former Chancellor of the Exchequer, to guide his wife's son.

In 1782, John Palmer proposed to the government that mail should be carried in coaches. Two years later, the first mail coach ran from Bristol to London and within a year there was a network of such services to 16 other cities across Britain. By 1797 there were 42 routes, average speeds had increased to 10 miles per hour and Edinburgh could be reached from London in 3 days (it had been 12 days in 1750).

The early 1800s saw the road network improve considerably with the expansion of the turnpike system: toll roads that were administered by trusts, with users contributing to repair costs in proportion to their usage. In their peak, the turnpike trusts numbered over 1100 and administered some 23,000 miles of road. The trusts were inefficient, though, as there were no checks or limits on extravagance or borrowing; they failed to ensure particular repairs were made; they failed to establish a single nationwide system of roads; and certain individuals were given unjustifiable preferences.

The 1830s was the height of coaching, with the time required to travel from London to Edinburgh being cut to 42 hours and 33 minutes. By this decade the market was highly organised, with the fastest speeds being achieved on routes with the highest competition.

In terms of local public transport, there were two types of service in the early 1800s: hackney carriages and horse-drawn omnibuses. Up until 1830, the number of the former was regulated. In 1824/1825, there were some 1500 available for hire in the capital. However, after 1830, the number soared as the market was deregulated and it quickly became dominated by single-vehicle operations.

Horse-drawn omnibuses appeared in London in the late 1820s, having been copied from those in Paris that had operated successfully for many years. As with the hackney carriages, regulation was minimal and so many new single-vehicle operators entered the market. The difference between the markets was that associations of omnibus operators which acted collusively soon emerged.

In terms of private vehicles in Europe, the late 1700s and early 1800s saw the development of steam-power. Such vehicles were fashionable for a time and saw quick technological improvements until there was a backlash against them which included the British government passing laws that self-propelled vehicles on public roads must be preceded by a man on foot waving a red flag. This effectively killed further road developments and engineers largely turned their attention to the railways. The red flag law was not repealed until 1896.

1.2.3 Mass production and consolidation

At the end of the nineteenth century, the turnpike trusts were in decline (the last being abolished in 1895); hackney carriage and bus markets were booming; and the responsibility of maintaining the main roads had been transferred to county councils, thereby establishing the modern system of road administration. By this time the first automobiles with gasoline-powered internal combustion engines had been created. Commercial production of automobiles that utilised this power source was started in Germany by Daimler in the 1880s, shortly followed by Panhard et Levassor in France in 1889.

The motor vehicle was given legal recognition in the UK in 1903, along with regulations regarding licences, safe driving, identification and weight. Hundreds of small manufacturers competed with one another, driving innovation further and further on and the volume of vehicles higher and higher. Savage (1966) notes that in the UK there were 17,810 automobiles (excluding bikes) produced in 1904. By 1910 this number had increased to 107,635, by 1918 it was 330,518 and by 1922 it was 952,432, and still rising. It was during this time that the famous Ford Model T was created, ushering in a new era of mass production.

1.2.4 Buses

The first motor buses appeared in Britain around 1898. There was then rapid expansion in the market during the opening decade of the twentieth century as thousands of companies and individuals established operations, often only single-vehicle concerns. Severe competition led to wasteful and even hazardous conditions, with operators adopting strategies that encouraged dangerous driving. The conditions of the vehicles in terms of both mechanics and interior comfort also left a lot to be desired. Profits were low and losses were common.

After 1910, many of the technical difficulties were resolved and the competition began to stabilise. By the start of the First World War the market was beginning to be increasingly monopolistic, but the end of the war saw a new surge in entrants as soldiers that had been trained to operate vehicles during the war needed to find employment, the government sold wartime vehicles off cheaply, and in most areas anyone could establish a bus-operating business without a licence.

It was to address this that the Road Traffic Act was passed in 1930, introducing regulation into the market. Entry was restricted and it often protected existing concerns. The large companies steadily expanded at the expense of their smaller counterparts, but it was the local authorities that experienced the largest growth as they switched provision away from the tramways.

The effects of the regulation were, on the whole, positive: average fares declined over the 1930s; reliability and punctuality improved; the standard of the vehicles and of the operators' conduct also improved; and co-ordination between operators and the railway companies who invested in the market increased.

1.2.5   Freight transport

The early decades of the twentieth century saw tremendous growth in road freight. Despite the fact that there were no restrictions to entry into the market up until 1933, the vast majority of freight (some 80 per cent) was transported by the owners rather than by professional hauliers. As with the motor bus market there was severe competition between single-vehicle operations in the market, but this gradually gave way to consolidation as many of the weaker concerns were forced out. Rates varied according to service regularity, punctuality, insurance and the type of cargo, with companies increasingly specialising in either parcels or tonnage.

Road freight was generally less expensive than the railways and the service was often considered to be superior. Roads had the advantages of speed over small distances, reliability and flexibility, as well as being able to provide door-to-door services. Consequently, road freight expanded at the expense of the railways. This was made worse by the legal obligations placed upon the railways. Their fares were determined by the Railway Rates Tribunal and they had to be based on the value of the cargo rather than on the costs of transportation. This allowed the road companies to charge less for the goods of the highest value. The railways also had to publish their rates, which the road companies were able to use to their advantage and which meant that customers could demand comparable rates across the network. The road companies also largely focused on the routes that had been the most profitable for the railways. Overall, therefore, the railways were left with the least valuable cargoes on the least profitable routes. The railways responded by improving facilities and by purchasing interests in a handful of road-haulage companies. This failed to stem the tide, although in 1938 the railways still carried the largest share of traffic in Britain.

1.2.6   To today

By the 1930s most of the technology used in motor vehicles had been invented and throughout the 1950s speeds rose and they spread across the world. The market changed significantly in the 1960s as Detroit, the then leading centre of vehicle manufacturing in the world, began to fear foreign competition. Leading producers formed agglomerations to consolidate the market and to take advantage of economies of scale. By the 1970s the market contained far fewer producers, and manufacturers of small performance vehicles, such as BMW, Toyota and Nissan, began to increase market power due to the 1973 OPEC oil crisis, new emission regulations and the stagnation of the American industry.

Usage of motor vehicles has continued to increase, with such consumer expenditure largely accounting for the increasing expenditure on transport-related products and services. However, the health of the industry is no longer what it was.

1.3 | Shipping

1.3.1 The wooden era

From 3000 BC, the Mesopotamian and Egyptian civilisations extensively employed water-borne transport. The Egyptians exploited the wind to sail southwards down the Nile and then oarsmen to travel back again, a fact that is even depicted in the hieroglyphic symbols for travelling south and north.

The Phoenician civilisation, from 1100 BC onwards, developed two types of ship: one for transporting passengers and freight; and the other for military engagements. The second of these were to become known as *galleys* and were used to ram the ships of the enemy: a military tactic that was to remain until 1571.

Development of shipping was focused on warships, simply playing the role of adding to the banks of oarsmen. By 700 BC the Phoenicians were using biremes (two banks of oarsmen) but within 500 years another two banks were introduced (quinqueremes, first used by the Carthaginians but quickly adopted by the Romans). Cargo ships changed very little from those used by the Phoenicians. Even in the thirteenth century European cargo ships still had a single mast with a single square sail.

It was the Chinese who led further developments in the form of their *junks*. They introduced bulkheads to make the hull rigid and more watertight in rough seas; sternpost rudders, allowing more effective steering in deep seas (until this time the convention was to use a long oar projecting from the stern); and multiple masts, facilitating the use of larger vessels. These developments were gradually adopted by Europeans who, by the fifteenth century, had developed *caravels* which were used by the explorers Dias, Columbus and Magellan.

Smaller, but still significant, developments were made in the subsequent centuries until the seventeenth and eighteenth centuries when the East India companies of Europe invested in large ocean-going ships in order to engage in the profitable trade with India and the East Indies. Shipping continued in such wooden sailing ships, some of which were magnificent, until the development of iron steamships in the nineteenth century.

1.3.2 The iron era

The first iron boat was constructed in 1787 by John Wilkinson as a way of transporting the artillery equipment that his Shropshire-based business manufactured. It was a natural development as there were no railways, the roads were unsuitable for such large heavy loads, and the existing wooden hulled boats were unreliable for such cargoes. His business built many other metal barges for use on the River Severn but it would be more than another 40 years before iron steamships were constructed by the Laird brothers in Liverpool. The first ocean-going iron ship was the *Alburkah*, launched in 1832.

By the second half of the nineteenth century the shipping market had largely taken on its modern shape, being divided into two parts: *liner* services, which included all regularly scheduled services transporting relatively small cargoes on predetermined routes; and *tramp* services, which included all irregular services transporting larger cargoes at a daily rate per tonne. As shipping was the only form of international travel across the seas, the liner element included passenger services as well as those for freight.

1.3.3 British dominance

Britain established itself as the world's dominant shipping power in both of these sub-markets. It was also the dominant ship manufacturer, and the adoption of new techniques in ship building ensured that this supremacy was largely maintained until the First World War. In the early years of the twentieth century, British ships were transporting approximately half of the world's sea-borne trade.

From the second quarter of the nineteenth century onwards, Britain came under increasing competitive pressure, especially from Germany. Aldcroft (1974) notes that between 1890 and 1911 the British share of the total world fleet (in terms of tonnage) fell from 35.8 to 33.8 per cent, whereas that of Germany increased from 6.4 to 8.7 per cent. British dominance was especially challenged in the short-haul trades from home, Europe and Scandinavia.

Up until the First World War the shipping market was certainly not a freely competitive one. First, it was commonplace for governments to subsidise their fleets in a range of different ways. At this time, the maritime fleets were seen as being the flag carriers of the nations and, therefore, a part of national identities in a similar way in which the airlines were viewed in the second half of the twentieth century. The British government largely subsidised British lines covertly, paying them hugely inflated amounts for transporting mail. The German government employed three further types of subsidisation: direct payments to ship-owners for specific purposes; special railway rates for exported goods allowing the lines to undercut rivals; and special customs facilities for imported ship-building materials.

The subsidies granted by the French government warrant a brief consideration. It took a more centrally planned approach to its maritime fleet by granting navigational and constructional subsidies, the last of which were directed towards the construction of relatively inexpensive sailing ships. Consequently, at a time when most countries were replacing sailing ships with steam-powered vessels, France was actually expanding its sailing fleet. This was to be significantly disadvantageous to French shipping interests.

Secondly, by the twentieth century the shipping market was largely structured in collusive agreements (a second characteristic that it was to share with the airline industry in the second half of the twentieth century). The rise of competition had led to a whole series of agreements between shipping lines which, among other things, set prices, determined which ports different lines could access, and even pooled revenues for sharing between lines. This is known as the *conference system* and it generally left trade from the UK to the British lines, in return for their abstinence from trade from mainland Europe. The agreements were often broken, particularly by German lines. This occasionally led to rate wars but, more often than not, the British lines were prepared to overlook such transgressions to avoid harmful competition.

Thirdly, different lines from the same country often worked together against foreign competition, although this was less true of the British lines. It was rare, for instance, to see the German lines competing against one another. In fact, in the early twentieth century the ten largest German lines established a shipping union which had some 23,000 tonnes of shipping capacity to use in foreign competition.

1.3.4 The early twentieth century

During the First World War the British government took control of shipping as it did of the railways as well. The difference was that, after the hostilities had ended, the shipping industry was largely allowed to gradually go back to being privately run. The government maintained some control for a time, due to the requirements of adjusting back to a peace-time economy, but by the end of 1920 nearly all control had been relinquished.

As trade began to expand again, there was a boom in the shipping industry with rapid construction of new capacity. In fact, there was over-production which led to a subsequent crash in the market. There is an argument that had the government maintained a tighter control on the industry, the effects on British shipping companies of these problems in 1919–1920 could have been largely avoided.

1.3.5 The modern era

Since the Second World War, the structure of the shipping industry has experienced four major changes. The first was the demise of the passenger liner services. Prior to the war the majority of international travel that crossed the seas, especially trans-Atlantic journeys, still relied on the passenger sea-liners. The war marked the end of the age of these majestic ships and ushered in the age of civil aviation.

The second change was caused by the significant industrial changes of the time. Heavy industries began to source their raw materials from overseas, semi-manufactured products began to be traded in volume, and marketing systems became truly international. The effect of these changes was the emergence of a demand for the transportation of large cargoes of an unscheduled nature that had not existed before. In response, the tramp shipping market further divided into markets for *bulk* and *specialised* shipping.

The third change was to the way in which the market was shared between different shipping nations. The British fleet continued to decline relative to those of other countries. In 1939, the British fleet had accounted for 28 per cent of the world shipping tonnage but this fell to 11.5 per cent within 30 years. Britain was still the largest ship-owning country apart from the flags of convenience, but its dominance had been eliminated. In the decade following 1958, the tonnage of the world shipping fleet increased by 79 per cent; that of Norway doubled, the Greek fleet quadrupled, and those of Sweden, Denmark, Finland, Germany and Poland all grew more rapidly than that of Britain.

Finally, during the last decade of the twentieth century many of the major industries that owned their own shipping fleets, such as the oil and large liner companies, began to reduce the size of their fleets in preference for chartering the capacity that they required. As such, the importance of the tramp market has increased. It is also a sign of the competitiveness of the tramp market relative to the advantages to a company of owning its own fleet.

1.4 Aircraft

1.4.1 Taking to the air

Gliders and kites were the first forms of aircraft to be developed, but lighter-than-air flying airships were the first serious forms of aircraft. In June 1783, the brothers Joseph and Etienne Montgolfier lit a bonfire beneath a balloon made of canvas and paper, and observed as it inflated and rose into the air to a height of 3000 feet. In September of the same year, they repeated the exercise in front of King Louis XVI, this time with the balloon carrying three passengers: a sheep, a cock and a duck. This time it flew more than 2 miles and the passengers alighted unharmed. They repeated it for a third time in November with a larger balloon and with two human passengers. It travelled 6 miles in 25 minutes and also landed safely: the first (human) passenger aircraft.

The future for balloon transport was not to be with hot air, though. Earlier, in 1781–1782, scientists in England and Switzerland filled soap bubbles with hydrogen and watched as they rose to the ceiling. Jacques Alexandre César Charles harnessed this power and on 27 August 1783 his hydrogen balloon ascended to the same height as the Montgolfier balloon, but travelled 15 miles in 45 minutes before springing a leak and crashing. This balloon was more controllable than the earlier hot-air balloons, and in a second flight Charles reached 10,000 feet.

The first powered and controlled flight of an airship is considered to be that of Henri Giffard, who travelled 15 miles in France in 1852 with a steam-powered engine. Another important advance was in 1884, with *La France*, a French Army electric-powered airship covering 5 miles in 23 minutes.

During the nineteenth century, there were numerous advances in glider technology and achievement. By 1891, the modern hang-glider had been created, making flights of over 25 metres. The first self-propelled flight was that by Clément Ader's steam-powered *Eole*, which travelled 50 metres near Paris in 1890. In 1896, the American experimenter Langley made further advancements with his craft, reaching a distance of approximately 1460 metres.

It was the Wright brothers who designed a way of controlling such craft in flight. On 17 December 1903, they made the first controlled and powered flight. In the years that followed they made numerous public flights and by the end of 1905 they had made flights of over 39 kilometres in length. On 14 May 1908, they made what is accepted to be the first two-person aircraft flight.

The first aircraft to make routine controlled flights were non-rigid airships: *blimps*. In 1901, Alberto Santos-Dumont combined a balloon with an internal combustion engine and successfully flew his airship over Paris and around the Eiffel Tower. Designs of such *dirigibles* were advanced rapidly by the German count Ferdinand von Zeppelin.

Planes were quickly adopted for military use. The first country to do so was Bulgaria in the First Balkan War, and during the First World War they were used for both reconnaissance and fighting. The interwar period was a time of rapid technological advancement with planes being constructed of aluminium rather than wood and with engines being greatly improved. Awards were given for distance and speed records, spurring innovation.

In 1929, the first round-the-world flight was completed by the Graf Zeppelin airship and, in October of that year, the same aircraft commenced the first commercial transatlantic service. However, the age of the dirigible ended in 1937 with the infamous fire aboard the Zeppelin *Hindenburg*. It was on craft powered by jet engines (which were developed in the 1930s) that air transport would rely.

1.4.2 British Airlines in the 1920s and 1930s

During the 1920s Britain's external air services developed rapidly as the government granted Imperial Airways a monopoly of subsidised operations. In May 1928, the world's first purpose-built international air terminal was opened beside the Purley Way, south of London. In these early days of commercial passenger flights the passengers were weighed along with their luggage to ensure the aircraft would be balanced.

Domestic air services failed to develop during the 1920s for a number of reasons: ground organisation and navigational aids simply were not adequate; there was a shortage of pilots; Britain's weather conditions did not favour such services; the British public viewed flying with distrust and did not enjoy sufficient time off from work to take advantage of flights (until this time flights had been the sole reserve of the affluent); and air services failed to offer worthwhile advantages compared to the existing surface transport.

By the 1930s the first, second and fourth of these were beginning to be rectified, and so from 1931 many new companies were formed to establish internal air services. In 1935, there were nearly a score of companies operating some 76 services in all. The 1938 Holidays with Pay Act enabled a much larger proportion of the population to enjoy a week away from work than had ever been the case. However, the impact of this would only benefit the airlines in the future as the prices of flights in the 1930s and 1940s were still prohibitively high for the majority of the population. Even in 1952 there was only one class of seat: first class.

Domestic operations were never profitable during the 1930s. The bulk of the revenue came from passengers and so was highly seasonal. This, along with the adverse weather conditions and the lack of equipment for night-travel, meant that craft were under-utilised. The load factors were also very low, even in the peak periods, with few companies managing to exceed 50 per cent and none breaking even. The air services were simply more expensive than the other modes, and often failed to bring sufficient benefits. Only on long-haul services, particularly over water, did the airlines bring sufficient time savings. The airlines would probably have fared better had they transported more freight, but the craft were not designed for heavy loads and the competition was even fiercer in this market.

Once again there was too much competition and many of the operators were too small to be efficient. The industry naturally began to experience consolidation. In October 1935, a merger was announced between Hillman Airways, United Airways, Spartan Airways, and British and Continental Airways with the aim of creating an efficient domestic services organisation called British Airways. It became the government's second chosen operator for the development of continental routes, and so withdrew from domestic operations. The railways also initiated some consolidation by becoming the dominant interest in a large proportion of airlines as a way of defending themselves against the growing competition. Their involvement appears to have brought some improvements in efficiency but the services remained unprofitable and over capacity (see Section 1.1.3).

1.4.3 After the Second World War

At a conference in Chicago in 1944, 54 countries agreed on rules for international flights. Each country had the right to control its own airspace, and flights in and out of them would have to be agreed by the respective national governments. Bilateral treaties were to be agreed, normally through the International Air Transport Association (IATA), between countries to dictate the characteristics of services. Governments could protect their own airlines from competition.

The end of the Second World War ushered in the period of commercial flights. Initially, ex-military aircraft were converted into passenger and freight transporters. Within a few years numerous companies existed, with routes that criss-crossed Europe. By 1952 the British state airline BOAC had introduced the first jet airliner, the *DH Comet*; the first jet crossing of the Atlantic had been achieved; and the first charter airline had been established, in which entire aircraft were contracted out for a certain purpose, such as for package holidays and transporting army personnel. It was not long before the Boeing 707 ushered in the new age of commercial airlines. In 1969, Boeing unveiled the 747 (which is still one of the largest planes to have ever flown); and in 1976, the Concorde facilitated the first supersonic service across the Atlantic.

The last 30 years has witnessed not only a slowing of the technological advancement in commercial aircraft, but also incredible changes in the structure of the European airline market. There has been an increasing move towards liberalisation, with IATA now playing no role in fare setting and only a few fare agreements requiring government approval. However, the emergence of the low-cost airlines has perhaps been the most notable and the most wide-reaching change.

1.5 | Canals

Canals have proved to be an invaluable way of civilisations across the world connecting navigable rivers and seas throughout history. The first canal was probably constructed in Mesopotamia to control the waters of the Euphrates and the Tigris rivers. In 520–510 BC, Darius I built the *Great Canal*, linking the Nile to the Red Sea. The Chinese also have a history of great canal building. It was a Chinese engineer in the tenth century who invented the *pound lock* that allowed boats to easily pass both up and down a stretch of canal for the first time. The first of these used in Europe is believed to have been in the Netherlands at Vreeswijk in 1373.

The first European canal that was constructed purely for transport purposes was the Naviglio Grande. It was built between 1179 and 1209 in order to transport marble into the city of Milan for the construction of the cathedral. From that point on, European canals became increasingly ambitious and complicated. In 1391, the Stecknitz Canal rose 40 feet from Lubeck and then descended the same height to reach the Elba; all within 36 miles. In 1681, the Canal du Midi joined the Mediterranean Sea to the Atlantic. It consisted of 150 miles of man-made waterways, three aqueducts and a tunnel stretching for 180 yards. At one point it dropped 206 feet in 32 miles.

The first canals in Britain were Roman-made: often for irrigation, or were short stretches to connect navigable rivers. The real emergence of canals as a serious part of British transport came with the Industrial Revolution in the mid-eighteenth century. Between 1759 and 1761, James Brindley constructed the Bridgewater Canal for the Duke of Bridgewater who wanted a cheaper way to transport coal from his mines into the city of Manchester. On 17 July 1761, the first barge-load of coal was pulled along the canal and into the city by horses. It was the first canal in Britain to run its entire length independently of any river, and was a huge success. The price of the Duke's coal was halved and the investment in the canal was recouped within a few years. This canal captured the imagination of countless engineers across England and the wider world, and within a few years other canals were opened.

These early canals were built to a narrow width, causing the boats to be termed *narrow boats*. Due to the length of the locks they were restricted to a capacity of around 30 tonnes: ten times the amount that could be pulled in a cart, but not sufficient to compete with the railways in the nineteenth century.

Between 1770 and 1830, the canal system expanded to be nearly 4000 miles in length, and numerous companies competed fiercely with one another. The canals were used as toll roads, with customers paying a rate to use their own boats on them. The money collected was used to maintain the canals and to pay the lock-keepers that operated the system on a day-to-day basis.

From the 1830s the railways began to compete with the canals. Due to the limited capacity of the narrow boats, the railways were able to transport greater quantities and at greater speeds. The canal companies slashed their prices in an effort to compete, but their profits fell. The wages of the boatmen also fell, motivating them to take their families onboard the boats to live. In the mid-nineteenth century, there were some 10,000 boat people. It was at this time that the narrow boats were decorated. By the 1850s the cargo transported by the canals had fallen by nearly two-thirds. Many struggling canal companies were bought out by the local railway companies, often to simply close them down.

In many European countries (such as France, Germany and the Netherlands) the canals were modernised and widened to take much larger loads: often as much as 2000 tonnes. This made them more economical, allowing them to compete much more effectively with the railways. The canals of Germany and the Netherlands, in particular, are still viably transporting a significant amount of freight and over recent decades have even witnessed an increase in this. However, in the UK such modernisation never occurred, largely due to the powerful owners of the railways blocking any plans to do so. Consequently, the amount of freight transported by the canals in recent times has fallen to a mere 200 million tonne-kilometres. The one major exception to this is the Manchester Ship Canal, which was built in the 1890s to take ocean-going ships into the city.

During the early 1900s the British canal network began to be abandoned. It saw brief surges in usage during the wars, but these failed to help stop the long-term decline. Most of the remaining companies were nationalised in 1947 and were run by British Waterways. By the 1960s, now facing competition from road haulage as well as the railways, the network had contracted to less than 2000 miles. It was at this time that it was proposed that the system should take on more of a leisure function, and since then many hundreds of miles of the network have been restored. Due to the growing concerns about congestion and pollution there is now even emerging interest in the possibility of using the network for freight once more.

1.6 Lessons from History

A number of observations can be made from the preceding historical narrative, holding potentially important lessons for the European transport sector today and into the future.

1.6.1 The innate drive for transport innovation

An obvious first observation is that, since the beginning of human civilisation, there has been a drive for greater transport innovation in all cultures and societies. The ability to move goods and people from place to place has always been highly prized by the human race for social and economic reasons. Any possibilities to improve this in terms of speed, capacity, cost or comfort have been investigated and seized upon. This is evident from all the modes of transport discussed so far. Even in the airline industry, which has experienced a slowing in technological advancement over the last 30 years, there have been significant developments in the structure of the market, making air travel affordable to a much wider population than would have been anticipated 50 years ago. The drive for improved transportation is innate in human society and will continue into the future.

This drive emanates from both passengers and producers. There will always be a desire to visit new places, taste more exotic products and experience different cultures; and as such, there will always be a demand for cheaper, faster and more comfortable modes of passenger transport. Historically, developments in these areas have been profitable for transport operators, especially those that have reduced the durations of journeys. A similar account can be told of freight transport, as producers have always sought to transport greater volumes at quicker speeds and in more reliable fashion. For example, the desire to transport coal was the initial catalyst in the development of the British canal and railway networks.

Experience demonstrates that this drive for innovation can be shaped, but not halted. The *red flag law* in the UK, which insisted that every motorised vehicle should follow a pedestrian waving a red flag, effectively killed further motor-vehicle innovation in the nineteenth century. This failed to stop innovation in transport, though, as the attention of the engineers turned to the railways, which benefited from improvements in the steam engine and from increases in speed and reliability.

1.6.2 The myopia of policy-makers

The largest lesson from past government transport policy is that of the need to tread carefully, as legislation can have serious implications. Government control of transport networks during the First World War was largely successful. In the railways, for example, operating costs were cut to a minimum and efficiency was improved. It is likely that having such a pressing and immediate overall strategic purpose and aim for transport, namely to support the war effort, helped to discipline decision-makers. After the second global conflict, the long-term effect on the railways of government control was negative.

Devising transport policy requires an appreciation of the wider effects that it will have, which are likely to be significant due to the volume of demand in the sector and the size of the investments involved. An illustration of this is that of the introduction of charging regulations for the railway operators, which effectively meant they were obliged to transport cargoes offered to them at a previously and nationally agreed price. This was designed to stop the railway operators from exploiting the monopoly power that they enjoyed prior to the First World War but, in practice, it meant that they could not maintain a healthy profit as they had to raise their prices in other markets to cross-subsidise the loss-making freight markets. They simply could not compete, allowing the roads to expand at the railways' expense.

Devising transport policy also requires an appreciation of the long-term effects that it will have. The specific demands from a transport network do not remain constant; they evolve over time. The first railways were used for the transportation of coal from the mines to the markets in the growing industrial towns. However, it would not be long until the demands placed on the railways were to transport passengers from town to town as well. If policy-makers fail to appreciate the needs of the transport sector in the future, any current policy may be ineffective and wasteful. The clearest example of this is that of the railways modernisation plan in the UK in the 1950s. The government, investing large sums of money to keep the network the same as it had been in the past, failed to appreciate that much of the freight transport had already shifted to road haulage, making the investment largely ineffective and wasteful. Similar things can be said of the French maritime subsidies, which favoured sailing vessels and so hampered French competitiveness in the shipping market.

1.6.3 Political capture

Transport has always been a lucrative activity to be engaged in, and one that, at times, has brought with it tremendous social status. As a result of this, the politically powerful have sought to be involved, making the transport sector vulnerable to *capture* by these individuals and groups. The shape of the railway network in the UK was largely determined by powerful individuals blocking companies from creating the routes that would be optimal for the network. Very simply, bends were made necessary that would slow locomotives into the future and would stimulate the recent innovation of tilting trains. Another example of such political pressure is that of the canals in the UK, which were never modernised because of the influence of the railway magnates. This effectively consigned the canal network to abandonment. It is crucial that transport economists and policy-makers appreciate this tendency for transport developments to be captured when designing appropriate policy.

1.6.4 Competition, consolidation and collusion

A trend that has been common across all of the main modes of transport is that of consolidation. Shortly after its birth, the car industry comprised a highly competitive number of producers. The same is true also of the London bus market, the road-haulage market, the domestic airlines and (to a lesser extent) the railway and shipping markets. It is generally maintained by free-market economists that such competition is desirable, as it disciplines producers to become more economically efficient, benefiting society through improved quality and lower prices. In the transport sector, this conclusion needs to be tempered due to the innate dangers that accompany transport provision. This is demonstrated most clearly by considering the dangerous practices that motor-bus operators employed in the early twentieth century.

The periods of unrestrained competition in these markets all gradually gave way to consolidation, as the benefits that could be accrued from exploiting economies of scale, scope and density became apparent. This has also had the effect of causing freight transport to emerge as a separate business entity. The market for road hauliers transporting the cargoes of others has expanded dramatically, which has been mirrored in the shipping sector by the more recent decisions of the large oil and liner companies to reduce the size of their own fleets in preference for chartering the capacity they require.

This trend of consolidation has often created an incentive for transport providers to collude. By signing collusive agreements and creating cartels, producers have sought to maintain their independence rather than succumbing to the pressure that would see them swallowed by large entities. The London horse omnibus operators soon created associations after their appearance in the late 1820s, the conference system dominated the shipping industry in the twentieth century, and the German shipping lines sought to increase their international competitiveness by establishing their own shipping union.

1.6.5 The early start

A less practical, but interesting, historical observation is that of the disadvantages that come from economies having an early start in the development of their transport sector. Britain was the first industrialised economy and, as such, was the first to develop whole railway and canal networks (although individual canals had been constructed much earlier in other parts of Europe). This was beneficial, and even crucial, to the industrialisation of the economy, but would lead to unforeseen problems in the future. The canals were constructed in a narrow form and so the locks restricted the narrow boats to a capacity of only 30 tonnes. Initially this was far greater than the road-carts that had previously been used, but it was not long until the canals simply could not compete with the railways that were able to transport far greater volumes. However, in continental Europe, engineers were able to see and avoid these pitfalls by constructing wider canals that still compete economically with the railways.

A similar story can be told of the railways, but this time as a result of the Second World War. The war demolished huge amounts of the continental railway networks, meaning that they had to be rebuilt and could be significantly improved from the lessons learned from British experience. The British railways were spared the experience of such destruction, though, and so were never rebuilt or improved. The continental railways were able to benefit from Britain's early start, and the British system has suffered as a result.

The Importance of 2
Transport in the UK
and Europe

2.1 | Statistical importance

2.1.1 The overall importance of transport

Statistically, the transport sector is an important part of the UK and European economies, accounting for a substantial proportion of private spending, employment and government expenditure. Changes within the sector potentially have serious and widespread effects on welfare, and so it is important that the economic understanding of the sector is comprehensive. It is only with a sound base of understanding that policy-makers can most effectively develop the sector and pre-empt, and minimise, the effects of any adverse changes that (inevitably) occur. Establishing this understanding is the role of the transport economist.

Figure 2.1 illustrates that in 2005, UK households spent 159.08 billion euros on transport. The majority of this, 75 per cent, was directed towards the purchase and operation of personal transport equipment, the remaining 24.9 per cent towards transport services. Figure 2.2 illustrates that all of this accounted for 15 per cent of total UK household expenditure: the single largest proportion of all of their spending. A similar description can be made of the EU25. In 2005, private households spent 847.99 billion euros, or roughly 13.8 per cent of their total expenditure, on transport. Households in the UK devote a greater proportion of their spending to transport than do their European counterparts, but both are substantial.

In 2005, the first 15 member countries of the European Union collectively contributed 809.71 billion euros to the total household expenditure on transport of the EU25. This accounted for the vast majority of household transport expenditure in the European Union, and an average of 13.91 per cent of their national private expenditures.

The impact of these statistics goes further than at first it may appear. As households are devoting considerable proportions of their expenditure towards private

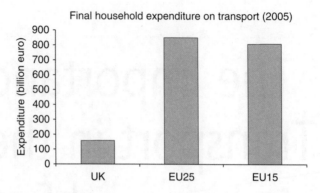

Figure 2.1 Household expenditure

Data Source: European Commission, Directorate-General for Energy and Transport in Co-operation with Eurostat, *Energy and Transport in Figures, 2006*

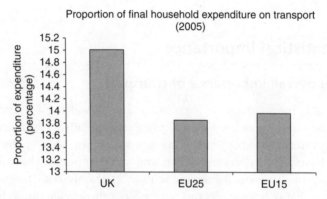

Figure 2.2 Transport's share of total household consumption

Data Source: European Commission, Directorate-General for Energy and Transport in Co-operation with Eurostat, *Energy and Transport in Figures, 2006*

transport, changes in the private transport sector can have significant effects on consumer confidence and, therefore, on wider spending. Consumers get locked into routines with their methods of transportation which are slow to change. One reason for this is ease of habit: it is easier to continue travelling the way that one is used to rather than trying something new. A second is the large initial capital investments involved in transport. As these capital outlays are significant, consumers are less likely to change their method of transportation quickly. For example, if we had recently purchased a relatively expensive new car, we are probably going to be reluctant to let it simply sit unused on our driveway. These two reasons mean that the demand for private transport is likely to be *price inelastic* (see Section 3.4); or in other words, unresponsive to a change in the price of it. If the price of private transport rises, consumers will continue to purchase it and so will reduce their expenditure in other areas of the economy. Similarly, if consumers expect that the price of private transport will rise in the near future, they are likely to increase their short-term saving and so cut back on consumption in order to

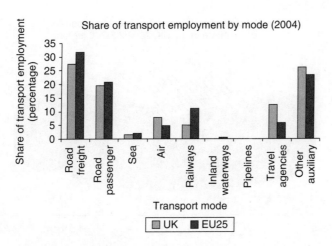

Figure 2.3 Employment in transport

Data Source: European Commission, Directorate-General for Energy and Transport in Co-operation with Eurostat, *Energy and Transport in Figures, 2005*

finance it. Changes in the transport sector, and especially private transport, clearly have wide-reaching effects across economies.

The transport sector also accounts for a substantial proportion of employment. In 2004, there were 1.1 and 8.2 million workers employed in the transport sectors of the UK and the EU25 respectively. The division of these is illustrated in Figure 2.3. Road transport accounted for 47 per cent of this in the UK and 53 per cent in the EU25; in both instances, road freight accounting for a greater proportion than road passenger transport. In the UK, the further categories of land transport had the following composition: 5 per cent in the railways, and effectively 0 per cent in both the inland waterway and the pipeline industries. After road transport, the second largest employing industry in the transport sectors of both the UK and the EU25, in 2004, was that of supporting and auxiliary transport, accounting for 26 and 23 per cent respectively. This category includes activities such as cargo handling, storage and warehousing. Travel agencies and tour operators accounted for 12 and 6 per cent of employment in transport in the UK and the EU25 respectively. The remainder was employed in the sea and air industries.

Not only does the transport sector have potentially wider implications because of the amount of household expenditure that it attracts, it also has the potential to affect consumer confidence and spending through its employment effects. If these workers fear that they are facing wage reductions or unemployment, their spending may again be contracted, causing effects to ripple throughout the economy.

A final indication of the statistical importance of the transport sector is the amount of government finance devoted to it. Figure 2.4 shows the central and local government expenditure on transport in the UK in the financial year 2002/2003. The total expenditure on transport in this year amounted to £13,241 million, which was an increase of £2217 million from the previous year, which in turn had been an increase of £2437 million from the year before. As Figure 2.4 illustrates,

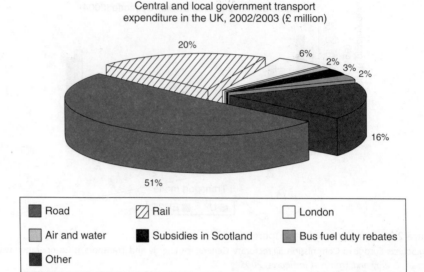

Figure 2.4
Government
expenditure on
transport
Data Source: Office of
National Statistics,
*Transport Statistics,
2004*

the largest proportion of this expenditure in 2002/2003, some 51 per cent, was directed towards road transport. The largest expenditure captured in the *other* category was non-specific spending on public transport and concessionary fares (which amounted to £2064 million).

2.1.2 The importance of the separate modes of transport

The historical narrative of the opening chapter is one of transport expanding greatly, but with the roads and the skies becoming increasingly important at the expense of the canals and the railways. These trends have continued in more recent years, as illustrated by Figures 2.5 and 2.6. Overall, freight transport within the EU25 increased by around 2.8 per cent per annum between 1995 and 2005; and passenger transport by around 1.8 per cent per annum between 1995 and 2004.

It is estimated that in 2004, some 3903 billion tonne-kilometres of freight were transported within the EU25. Of this total, 44.2 per cent was transported by road haulage, 39.1 per cent by sea, 10 per cent by rail, 3.3 per cent by the inland waterways, 3.4 per cent by pipeline, and the remaining 0.1 per cent by air.

As Figure 2.5 shows, road haulage has continued to increase in importance from 1250 billion tonne-kilometres (42.1 per cent of total freight transport) in 1995 to 1724 billion tonne-kilometres in 2005. Maritime transport has also expanded, from 1133 billion tonne-kilometres in 1995 to 1525 billion tonne-kilometres in 2005. This translates to an increase of 0.9 per cent in its proportion of the total cargo since 1995. Rail transport has experienced an absolute increase in usage, from 358 to 392 billion tonne-kilometres over the period, but has contracted in relative terms from 12.1 per cent. Similarly, the inland waterways have expanded in absolute terms, from 117 to 129 billion tonne-kilometres, but have also experienced a slight reduction in their proportion of the total cargo transported. The proportions transported by the pipelines and the air

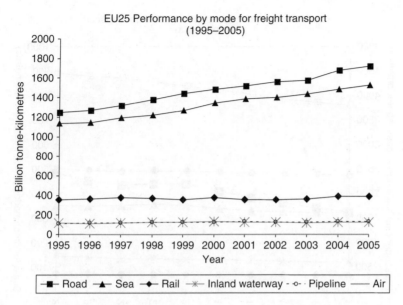

Figure 2.5 Modes of freight transport
Source: European Commission, Directorate-General for Energy and Transport in Co-operation with Eurostat, *Energy and Transport in Figures, 2006*

have remained fairly constant and so both have expanded in absolute terms: 112 to 131 billion tonne-kilometres and 1.9 to 2.5 billion tonne-kilometres respectively.

In terms of passenger transport, there were an estimated 5061 billion passenger-kilometres travelled within the EU25 in 2004. Cars and powered two-wheelers accounted for 75.9 per cent of this distance; buses and coaches 8.3 per cent; railways 5.8 per cent; and tram and metro services 1.2 per cent. Europeans each travelled an average of 10,225 kilometres in that year by these modes of land transport. Of the remaining 8.7 per cent of the total distance travelled, air and sea accounted for 7.9 per cent and 0.8 per cent respectively.

As Figure 2.6 illustrates, the most notable growth has been that of the use of cars and motorbikes, which has been a continuation of the trend stretching back to the middle of the twentieth century. The usage of these vehicles increased from 3907 billion passenger-kilometres in 1995 to 4601 billion passenger-kilometres in 2004. This represents an increase in the proportion of total passenger transport that these vehicles accounted for in the EU25 over this period of 0.4 per cent. Bus and coach usage expanded in absolute terms, from 474 to 502 billion passenger-kilometres over the period, but contracted in terms of their proportion of the total by 0.94 per cent. The railways, trams and metros experienced a similar trend, growing in absolute terms from 389 to 427 billion passenger-kilometres, but contracting proportionately by 0.50 per cent. Passenger transport by sea fell in both absolute and relative terms over the period; from 55 to 49 billion passenger-kilometres, a reduction of 0.26 per cent. That by the airlines increased from 324 to 482 billion passenger-kilometres, representing an increased proportion of the total of 1.66 per cent.

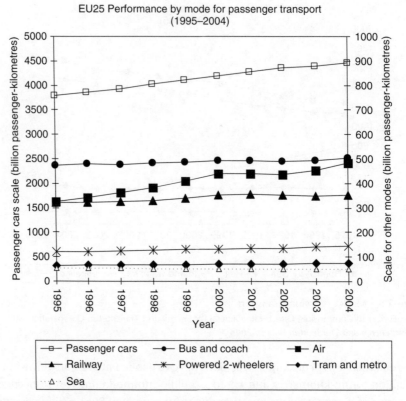

Figure 2.6 Modes of passenger transport
Source: European Commission, Directorate-General for Energy and Transport in Co-operation with Eurostat, *Energy and Transport in Figures, 2006*

2.1.2.1 Composite units

Throughout the section above, the volume of passenger transport has been measured in *passenger-kilometres* and that of freight transport in *tonne-kilometres*. These are known as *composite units* as they are composed of two separate units. It is important to use these when analysing transport because one is not simply interested in the volume of the cargo or the distance travelled. A huge number of passengers and a huge volume of freight may be transported but if it is only over a short distance the overall importance of the service may be minimal. Similarly, a huge distance may be covered but if it is only for a small amount of passengers or freight the overall importance may again be minimal. As such, it is crucial that *both* the volume and the distance are incorporated, which is the purpose of such composite units.

2.1.3 International comparisons

Transport has been important to human communities throughout history, but the particular modes of transport used have varied considerably across time and space.

The possible reasons for this variability are perhaps just as varied themselves: topography, natural resource endowments, wealth and anthropology, to name just a few.

Two useful comparisons with the EU25 today are those of the USA and Japan, as they are both at similar stages in their economic development. In Figures 2.7 and 2.8 it is clear that there is more overall transport, of both passengers and freight, in the USA than in either the EU25 or Japan. All three populations travel far more kilometres using the passenger car than any of the other modes of transport but this is most noticeable in the USA, where the railways are hardly used for

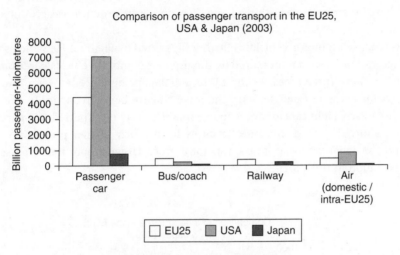

Figure 2.7 International comparisons of passenger transport
Data Source: European Commission, Directorate-General for Energy and Transport in Co-operation with Eurostat, *Energy and Transport in Figures, 2005*. *Note:* the data for Japan are for 2002

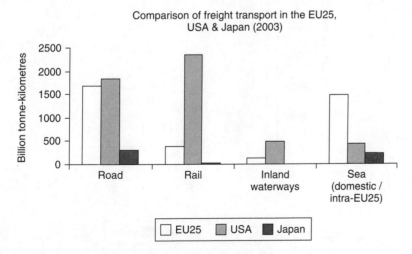

Figure 2.8 International comparisons of freight transport
Data Source: European Commission, Directorate-General for Energy and Transport in Co-operation with Eurostat, *Energy and Transport in Figures, 2005*. *Note:* the data for Japan are for 2002

passenger transportation at all. In Japan, on the other hand, the railways account for a much greater proportion of passenger transport. Figure 2.8 also illustrates that more freight is transported on the railways in the USA than by any of the other modes, whereas in the EU25 and Japan it is the roads that account for the largest proportions of freight transport.

One could assume from these statistics that the railway network in the USA would account for a much larger proportion of the transport infrastructure than in the EU25 or in Japan. However, Figure 2.9 demonstrates that the opposite is actually the case. Roads stretch for more kilometres in each of these three areas than do the railways or the navigable waterways, but it is in the USA that the largest proportion of the transport infrastructure is accounted for by roads.

This reliance on motor vehicles is further illustrated by Figure 2.10, which shows the degree of *motorisation*, measured by the number of motor vehicles per thousand people, in these three areas. In the EU25 and Japan there are between four and five cars for every ten people, with the lowest figure being in Japan. In the USA there are nearly eight cars for every ten people. This is to be expected as Figures 2.7 and 2.8 show that road transport accounts for a much smaller proportion of all transport in Japan and that it accounts for a much larger proportion of passenger transportation in the USA.

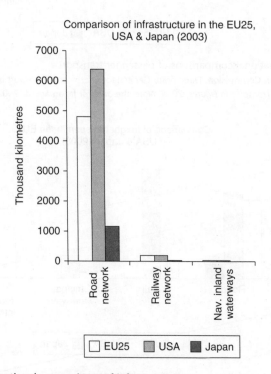

Figure 2.9 International comparisons of infrastructure

Data Source: European Commission, Directorate-General for Energy and Transport in Co-operation with Eurostat, *Energy and Transport in Figures, 2005*

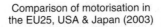

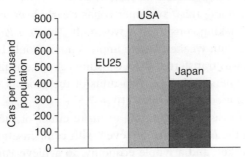

Figure 2.10 International comparisons of motorisation

Data Source: European Commission, Directorate-General for Energy and Transport in Co-operation with Eurostat, *Energy and Transport in Figures, 2005*

It is clear from these international comparisons that transport in the EU25 is not unique, although in the USA there is a much greater use of the railway network for freight and in Japan there is much less transport overall. What is noticeable is that there is a significant reliance on road transport for both passengers and freight in all three of these countries: an apparently inevitable consequence of economic development?

2.2 | Theoretical importance

2.2.1 Pareto efficiency

An outcome that economists desire of markets is that of *Pareto efficiency*. This is where the outcome of a market is such that it is not possible for someone to be made better off without making someone else worse off, even after any possible compensation has been made. In this way, total welfare or satisfaction in the market is maximised.

For example, let us assume very simply that there are two consumers in a particular market and that there are four units of a particular product that can be allocated between them. Each of these consumers enjoys 10 units of satisfaction (which shall be termed *utiles* for clarity) from receiving a single unit of the product; 7.5 utiles from a second unit of the product; 5 utiles from a third unit of the product; and 2.5 utiles from a fourth unit of the product. This incorporates the concept of *diminishing marginal utility*: the extra satisfaction (or *utility*) that a consumer derives from additional units of a product decreases as his or her consumption of that product increases.

Returning to the example, if all four units of the product are allocated to consumer A, the total satisfaction in the market is 25 utiles (10 + 7.5 + 5 + 2.5). If one of these units of the product is transferred to consumer B, the satisfaction of consumer A falls by 2.5 utiles but consumer B gains 10 utiles. Consequently, the total satisfaction in the market has increased to 32.5 utiles (10 + 7.5 + 5 + 10) and consumer B can compensate consumer A so that the satisfaction of the latter rises back to 25. By doing this, consumer B has clearly been made better off (by 7.5 utiles) without making consumer A worse off. This is a *Pareto improvement* in the market. A similar, but weaker, Pareto improvement would be made if a second unit of the product was transferred from consumer A to consumer B as well.

When both consumers each have two units of the product, the satisfaction in the market is maximised at 35 utiles (10 + 7.5 + 10 + 7.5). This is the *Pareto efficient* outcome because it is impossible to make either of the consumers better off without making the other worse off, even with compensation payments.

In order for a market, and a whole economy, to achieve Pareto efficiency it is necessary for it to have two characteristics. The first is that it needs to be *productively efficient*, meaning that the producers within it are producing their output without wasting any of their inputs. In other words, output is being maximised for a given amount of inputs. If it is possible to increase output in the example above to six units, both consumers could be made better off simultaneously and so the market could not possibly be at Pareto efficiency without so doing.

The second is that it needs to be *allocatively efficient*, meaning that resources in the market or the economy are being used to produce the products that generate the most satisfaction and that these products are then distributed to consumers in the way that will maximise that satisfaction. The latter of these aspects of allocative efficiency is demonstrated in the example above and the first is clear if the effect of there being a different type of product that would generate greater satisfaction for the consumers is considered. If there is such a product, then there would be a Pareto improvement by producing this alternative product and so the market could not be at Pareto efficiency without so doing.

The transport sector is necessary if both productive and allocative efficiency, and thus Pareto efficiency, are to be achieved. If by improving the transport system production costs could be reduced, the market could be made more productively efficient as average costs could be forced down and a greater output could be produced using the available resources. This would lead to a Pareto improvement.

If there are resources in the north of the country that would increase overall satisfaction if used in production in the south, they should be transported south to do so. Similarly, if there are products being allocated to consumers in the south that would lead to a Pareto improvement if allocated to others in the north, they should be transported north to do so. In both of these aspects of allocative efficiency, the transport system clearly plays a vital role.

An economy cannot be productive, allocative and overall Pareto efficient without an effective, well-functioning transport sector.

2.2.2 Agglomerations

Throughout history, humans have found it advantageous to gather into local communities of like-minded people, rather than being dispersed as individuals over wide areas. An *agglomeration* is a centre of economic activity; or in other words, a geographical location that is dense with production and trade. Since the onset of the industrial revolution in Europe, during the second half of the eighteenth century, there has been a pressure towards the development of such agglomerations. The earliest modern agglomerations were simply the first industrial towns, which generally developed around a particular industry. For example, Manchester and Liverpool were focused on cotton textile manufacturing. More recently developed agglomerations include the area of Eastern England known as *Silicon Fen*, which is dense with modern technology industries. The Italian textile and clothing industries, the largest of their kind in Europe, are also organised into agglomerations. The Varese Province has traditionally concentrated on cotton manufacturing, whilst the neighbouring province of Como on silk production. These are called *clusters* and are organised by entrepreneurs, known as *impannatori*, to include producers at every stage in the chain of production. The *external economies of scale* that these clusters afford the producers within them have contributed to them having lower average costs than their British counterparts, which in turn have helped them to keep the growing Chinese competition at bay, if only in the short term.

Agglomerations bring potentially significant benefits to the producers within them, and the larger they become, the larger the potential benefits are. The sources of these external economies of scale are as follows:

- *Reputation effects*. The first potential benefit is that of the area earning a positive reputation, which all of the individual producers within it can gain from. If a particular location becomes renowned for quality, consumers from an increasingly widespread area will be drawn to trade with the producers within it. The reputation effects associated with an agglomeration are likely to be larger than those with a single producer.
- *Suppliers*. Historically, agglomerations have often developed where supplies already exist, but there is a further dynamic effect: as particular types of producers gather in one location, their suppliers are likely to be drawn to locate in that area as well. The suppliers will want to do this to gain a competitive advantage over rivals through a reduction in transport costs and also through a greater ability to respond to the needs of their consumers, both of which can in turn significantly benefit the producers within the agglomeration.
- *Pooled labour*. For a similar reason as that above, workers with the skills demanded by the gathering producers are likely to seek residence in the area in order to gain employment. The best employees are attracted, improving the pool of labour available to the producers. In addition to this, if the producers face similar needs from employees, they are more likely to enter into joint training schemes, further improving the quality of labour available to all. Local educational institutions may also respond by tailoring their courses to meet the demands of the local producers through a desire to improve employment statistics and perhaps through mutually beneficial partnerships with the producers themselves. The effect of all three of these possibilities is an improvement in the pool of skilled labour available, reducing producers' individual training costs and increasing their productivity.

■ *Information transfer*. Producers within an agglomeration have a geographical proximity to one another that facilitates mutually beneficial information transfers that would be much less likely if they were geographically dispersed. By sharing information, all members of the community can experience greater technological advancement, helping them to become more competitive with rivals further afield.

■ *Infrastructure*. An agglomeration of similarly orientated producers encourages the development of a common infrastructure that benefits all. The mining communities of the North-East of England benefited from the development of a rail network that transported coal from the mines to the towns, something which would have been less economical and less likely if the industry was more geographically spread. Similar effects can be seen with communication networks as well, and they too lead to lower costs for all of the producers within the agglomeration.

Producers within an agglomeration benefit hugely from the transport networks that are more likely to be developed as a result of the agglomeration, but it goes further than this as the agglomeration is unlikely to develop in the first place without effective transport. The function of a producer can largely be seen as one of processing materials or information in order to add value to them and then selling them onto consumers for a satisfactory return. It has been noted that agglomerations often develop where supplies already exist and that one of the benefits of their development is that they attract further suppliers to locate within them, but it is unlikely that there will be a similar location of consumers. Before the industrial revolution, separate populations largely relied on their own local producers for the products and services that they required, although there was some trade. Agglomerations, on the other hand, often find themselves geographically separated from their consumers and so need an effective transport system for their survival. Without the capacity to move the final products to the consumers, agglomerations cannot possibly exist and so the potential benefits to the producers cannot be realised.

The Theory of Markets: An Overview

Saffron Walden is an historic market town in the north of Essex. Every Tuesday and Saturday the square (surrounded by Tudor-style, wooden-beamed buildings) is brimming with rickety stalls; sellers of fish, breads, cheeses and other fresh produce; and shoppers. The sellers are usually all wrapped-up, desperately trying to attract the punters as they wander by, and the shoppers are keenly looking for the latest bargain.

This scenario is typical of the initial image that people often have when they think of a *market*. However, in Economics the definition of a market is much broader than this traditional picture. It is a place where consumers and producers come together in order to exchange goods and services: to trade. Or alternatively, it is a place in which supply and demand interact. In fact, nowadays the word *place* needs to be used carefully as the development of the Internet and e-trading has meant that it is no longer necessary for it to be an actual physical place.

In this sense, the whole of the transport sector is made up of markets. There is the market for train and bus tickets; for cars, and the petrol that they consume; for freight distribution; and even the provision of street lighting can be seen as a market. As such, in order to develop a comprehensive understanding of the functioning of the transport sector, it is vital that economists first view the sector as being a collection of separate markets and then seek to understand how each individual market operates. This is to take a microeconomic approach to the study of the sector and is the purpose of Chapters 3 through 8.

Economists have broadly defined six distinct market structures, all of which are relevant to the transport sector. Collectively, these are known as the *theory of industry* because they are largely characterised by differences in the number, type and behaviour of the firms (the producers) within them. The consumers, assumed to be constant across them all, are left to one side, but their role is arguably the starting point of any economic activity and so it is with an analysis of the demand for transport that Part II begins.

As the models of these different market structures all focus directly on the producers, they all consider the same factors which are of utmost importance to production: that is, costs, revenue and profit. These three factors are the building blocks of the models and so they are introduced and explained in Chapter 4. Part II then moves on to draw these building blocks together to construct the actual models of the different market structures and to examine how they lead to the characteristics that can be observed in the real world. These models are supported by relevant and detailed case studies from the European transport sector, which also serve to bring the historical narrative of Part I completely up to date.

The Demand for Transport

In his book *A Treatise on Political Economy, or the Production, Distribution and Consumption of Wealth* (*1803*) Jean-Baptiste Say, a French businessman and economist, effectively said that there could be no demand without supply. This has become known as Say's Law and there are still influential supply-side economists who readily defend it and its consequential conclusions about economic management. The generally held belief in the world of Economics, however, is that the reverse is true, namely that it is demand that causes supply. In other words, an entrepreneur would not establish a business enterprise if there was no demand for the products or services that it would sell; and so the range of products and services supplied in the economy changes in response to changes in demand.

In fact, both of these assertions are correct. It is the simultaneous interaction between consumers expressing their demands and producers offering their supplies that creates a market.

It is vital that transport economists, seeking to understand the composition of the transport sector, first understand the nature of the demand for transport. This is the purpose of this chapter. For simplicity, in this chapter the term *product* is used to refer to both physical products and services within the transport sector.

3.1 Important definitions

As a society we have an infinite list of things that we would like. In fact, even our individual lists are of a considerable length. This is known as our *notional demand*. However, this concept is of limited use to economists. The vast majority of this demand will never actually influence the economy as we simply do not have the resources necessary to seriously consider satisfying it. Usually when economists talk about demand they are referring to *effective demand*, which is defined as the amount that consumers are willing and able to buy of a product at a given price. It is this definition of demand that is used throughout this book, unless it is otherwise stated.

A third and crucially important concept of demand in the transport sector is that of *derived demand*. This is where products are wanted, not because consumers value them in their own right, but because they allow consumers to satisfy other demands. For example, motorists do not buy petrol because they like petrol but because they know that it will allow them to travel in their vehicles from A to B. It is the travelling that the consumers really demand; the petrol is simply demanded to facilitate this. Other examples of derived demand include airlines demanding labour to pilot and crew their craft, and motorists demanding cars in the first place (although there are the cases of classic cars for collections). The majority of the demand for passenger transport is derived, as is all of the demand for freight transport.

3.2 | Determinants of demand

When analysing demand it is usual to focus on that for a particular product. The primary determinant of the demand is then simply the price of the product, and so it is against this price that the quantity demanded of the product is usually plotted as the basis of diagrammatical analysis. The *law of demand* states that as the price of a product increases, the quantity demanded of it will fall, and vice versa. This is illustrated by the inverse demand curve, which from this point on will be simply termed *the demand curve* (see the mathematical appendix for an explanation), in Figure 3.1:

At an initial price of P_1, consumers in the market demand a total quantity of the product of Q_1 units. As the price falls to P_2, consumers are willing and able to buy more of it and so the quantity demanded increases to Q_2 units. Such changes in the quantity demanded of a product that are caused solely by a change in its price are known as *movements* along the demand curve.

There are two parts to the explanation as to why the law of demand exists. First, there is the *income effect*. This is simply that as the price of a product increases, there is a reduction in the purchasing power of consumers as it is assumed that their incomes remain constant. Consumers simply cannot purchase as much of everything as they had done previously. As such, it is likely that there will be

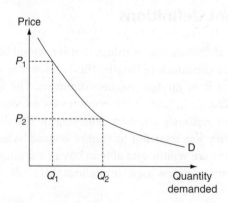

Figure 3.1 The demand curve

a change in the quantity demanded of the product which has become more expensive. This change can be positive or negative depending on the relationship between the incomes of consumers and the consumption of the different products that they consume (see the section on income elasticity of demand). Usually it will have a negative effect as consumers simply are not able to buy as many units as before. Secondly, there is the *substitution effect*. This refers to the phenomenon that as the price of a particular product increases, consumers will purchase more of *substitute* products instead, which are now relatively cheaper, in order to keep their overall level of satisfaction constant. In more formal terms, the substitution effect is the change in consumption of a product in response to a change in its price, holding the final satisfaction of the consumer constant (therefore abstracting from the income effect).

Indifference curve analysis, which is not elaborated upon here but is done so in other microeconomic texts, demonstrates that an increase in the price of a product will usually have a negative overall effect on the quantity demanded because the substitution effect is always negative and outweighs the income effect on the rare occasions when the income effect is positive.

The logic of both of these effects works the same in reverse as well and so as a product becomes less expensive, consumers are willing to increase their consumption of it (a positive substitution effect as they are substituting away from alternatives that are now relatively more expensive) and are able to buy more of everything (a positive income effect). This explanation ties in nicely with the definition of effective demand at the start of this chapter.

This explanation applies to the demand for passenger transport in particular. The same is also true of freight transport, which can be thought of as one of the inputs to the productive process, but there is one important difference in the terminology. The substitution effect is as before; defined in this case as being the change in the amount of an input used in production in response to a change in the price of that input, holding the overall output of the producer constant. The difference is that there is a scale or output effect rather than an income effect. This means that as the price of one of the inputs changes, there is a resulting change in the total volume of output that the producer would like to sell and so the employment of all of the inputs will also change. For example, if the price of road transport fell, the potential scale of an entire enterprise could be increased and so it is likely that the usage of all the inputs will increase, not just that of road transport, which has become more affordable.

There are two exceptions to the law of demand: *Giffen goods* and *goods of conspicuous consumption*. The first of these have not been recorded in the transport sector and so will not be elaborated upon here, but they are an intriguing microeconomic phenomenon. The second are those products that are demanded because they are expensive and so confer a certain degree of social status to the consumer. As the price of a good of conspicuous consumption falls from an exceptionally high level, it is conceivable that the wealthiest consumers could stop purchasing it because slightly less wealthy consumers are now able to do so, eroding the associated social status. For a certain price range, therefore, a reduction in the price of a good of conspicuous consumption could actually serve to reduce the overall sales of it, and so producers of these products have to be careful with their pricing strategies. Such products do potentially exist in the passenger transport sector, in the forms of the most luxury yachts and the most exclusive sports cars and jets. However, these can largely be ignored because they comprise a relatively small part of the upper-end of a few markets and because the phenomenon exists only for a relatively narrow price range. For any of these products, if the price continues to fall the consumer base available to them will inevitably increase again and so the quantity demanded of them will increase as well. As such, the law of demand can be assumed to hold for the vast majority of the transport sector, for the vast majority of the time.

Although the most important determinant of the quantity demanded of a product is the price that consumers are required to pay for it, there is a whole array of other factors that influence the quantity demanded of a product as well. Many of these determinants are common across all products but some are product- or sector-specific. Included in the array of determinants of the quantity demanded of products in the transport sector are factors, many of which arising from common sense, such as the following:

- *The price, availability and quality of substitute products.* A substitute product is one that can be purchased instead of another. Changes in the characteristics of substitute products can have a significant effect on the quantity demanded of the product for which they are substitutes. For example, if the fares of ferries crossing from England to France fell, the quantity demanded of Eurostar train tickets, substitutes to ferry tickets, is likely to fall as well, and vice versa. An historic example of these determinants in action is the decline of the inland waterways of the UK. The volume of traffic on the inland-waterway network fell drastically when the competing railways offered more frequent, less expensive and faster alternatives. In their turn, the railways lost traffic volume to the roads when relatively inexpensive and high quality road services became increasingly available across the country.
- *The price, availability and quality of complementary products.* A complementary product is one that is necessarily purchased to go with another. As with substitute products, changes in the characteristics of complementary products can also have a significant effect on the quantity demanded of the product which they complement. For example, if the price of petrol continues to increase, the quantity of cars demanded is likely to fall over time because consumers can no longer afford the required petrol. Similarly, if the frequency and reliability of local bus services to the local railway station improve, then the quantity of railway tickets demanded may also increase as it is more attractive to use public transport for longer journeys.
- *Income changes.* If the consumers' general disposable income increases, due to economic growth or a reduction in income tax for instance, the quantity demanded of most transport products will also increase, and vice versa. This is a particularly important effect because so much transport activity is closely

related to the volume of general economic activity: as the former increases, so will the latter. Incomes tend to rise by 2 or 3 per cent per annum above inflation. That implies they will double every 35 to 23 years and that the volume of transport is likely to expand rapidly.

- *Population changes.* If a particular population expands, the quantity of transport demanded in the area inhabited by that population is also likely to increase, and vice versa. Transport for London anticipates that between 2006 and 2025 the population of London will increase from 7.5 to 8.3 million. This will inevitably increase the demands on London's transport systems.

- *Popularity effects.* If a transport product becomes less popular, perhaps due to it becoming less fashionable or because of a health or safety scare, the quantity demanded of it is likely to fall. This determinant can be observed in the aftermath of the Hatfield railway accident in the UK: for a time, there was a contraction in the quantity of railway tickets demanded as a result of the accident. It can also be observed in the decline in the quantity of airline tickets purchased immediately after the terrorist attacks of 11 September 2001.

- *Speed.* This is an important determinant of the demand for both passenger and freight transport. Producers and their employees are likely to want to minimise transport time as it is often a source of reduced, or even wasted, productivity; and passengers travelling for social reasons will often view the journey time as cutting into their time of enjoyment at the destination.

For freight companies, time in transit incurs an *inventory cost*, which is the cost of the products being transported instead of being sold and the generated revenue then being invested. For example, if it takes six months to transport a cargo that is valued at £10,000, the inventory cost with a prevailing annual rate of interest of 5 per cent will be £250. The calculation of this is shown below, bearing in mind that 5 per cent = 0.05 = 1/20:

$$\frac{10,000}{20} = 500$$

$$\frac{500}{2} = 250$$

The inventory cost for a whole year is £500 and so that for half a year is £250. Consequently, a freight transport company would be willing to spend an extra £125 on cutting the transit time to three months.

- *Reliability.* Again, this is an important determinant of both passenger and freight demand. Passengers often have scheduled appointments to meet and freight companies are constrained by production deadlines, especially with the development of just-in-time production methods. As such, both are likely to be willing to spend more to ensure a greater reliability of service.

- *Bureaucracy.* Paperwork and administration causes time-costs and inconvenience and so if it was to become more restrictive and burdensome for a particular mode of transport it is likely that it will have a negative effect on the demand for that mode.

■ *Security*. Passengers are becoming increasingly aware of, and concerned about, the security of their transport, especially with the recent growth of terrorism. Freight companies can insure against loss and damage of products in transit, but it causes disruption to their production lines which can have wider business costs. Consequently, both consumer types will consider security levels seriously when deciding upon their chosen mode of transport.

These are but a few of the possible determinants of the demand for transport. The importance of each determinant is dependent upon the mode of transport under consideration. For example, a change in income may have less of an effect on the demand for bus transport than on that for rail; and a change in the price of complementary products in the car market is perhaps likely to be more significant than in the airline market. However, all of the determinants are likely to change the quantity demanded of a product in the transport sector even if the price of the product was to remain unchanged. Consequently, these are shown as *shifts* of the demand curve. An example is displayed in Figure 3.2.

The outward shift of the demand curve in Figure 3.2 shows that a positive change in one of the determinants of demand, for example an increase in the price of one of the main substitute services, has caused the quantity demanded of the particular product being considered to increase from Q_1 to Q_2 even though the price of it has remained constant. That is, the demand curve for the product has shifted outwards from D_1 to D_2, meaning that more units are demanded at any given price. The opposite can be shown by an inward shift of the demand curve: a negative change of one of the determinants of demand causes the demand curve to shift inwards, causing the quantity demanded of the product to fall.

A demand curve is a graphical representation of the relationship between the price of a product and the quantity demanded of that same product. In other words, a demand curve shows how quantity demanded responds to changes in the price that consumers have to pay. To construct a demand curve, it is assumed that the price of the product is the only factor that changes and that everything else remains the same: the *ceteris paribus* assumption. This is the explanation as to why changes in the price of the product can be shown by movements along the demand

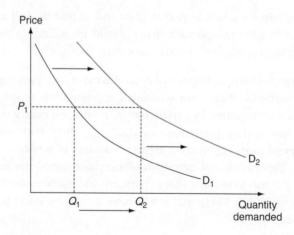

Figure 3.2 An outward shift of the demand curve

Table 3.1 The effects of changes in the determinants of demand upon the demand curve

Determinant	How the demand curve shifts if it	
	increases	decreases
Substitute availability	Inwards	Outwards
Substitute price	Outwards	Inwards
Complement availability	Outwards	Inwards
Complement price	Inwards	Outwards
Popularity	Outwards	Inwards
Disposable income	Outwards	Inwards
Population	Outwards	Inwards
Speed	Outwards	Inwards
Reliability	Outwards	Inwards
Bureaucracy	Inwards	Outwards
Security	Outwards	Inwards

curve. When there is a change in one of the determinants of demand other than the price of the product, this assumption is broken and so the whole curve has to shift to a new position. As such, all of the factors other than the actual price of the product determine the position of the demand curve and the price determines the position on the curve.

The effects on a demand curve of changes in the other determinants of demand outlined above are summarised in Table 3.1. An outward shift means that, *ceteris paribus*, the quantity demanded will have increased and an inward shift will have the opposing effect.

This form of the demand curve, which is the most commonly used form in economic analysis and which is used throughout this text, is actually known as the Marshallian demand curve (after Alfred Marshall, the Cambridge economist who developed standard microeconomic demand and supply analysis). It is based on the particular premise that income is fixed. As noted above, income is one of the factors that can cause this demand curve to shift. There are two other forms that the demand curve can take, but these are not used in this text. The first is the Hicksian demand curve, which shows the relationship between the price of a product and the quantity of it demanded, holding utility (welfare) constant. The second is the Slutsky demand curve, which shows the same relationship, but holding the purchasing power of consumers constant. These latter two forms of the demand curve are useful in more advanced analysis.

3.3 | The problem of the peak

Economic analysis is usually simplified by the removal of time as a factor that needs consideration. In practice this means that it is assumed, usually implicitly, that the number of units of a product demanded per unit of time is constant over the duration of the analysis. However, in transport economics this assumption cannot be made as demand does indeed vary by the time of the day, the day of the week and the month of the year. In each of these periods there will be *peaks* in demand: times when demand is particularly concentrated. These peaks are not random, but occur on a uniform basis.

This section focuses on the distribution of demand for road use in two different, but complimentary, ways. First, the volume of traffic on the roads: both passenger and freight. Secondly, the average speeds of the traffic on the road network. There will then be an appreciation of some of the other peaks in demand that occur in the transport sector and, finally, the implications of peaked demand for transport providers and policy-makers.

3.3.1 The peaks in the demand for road usage

The volume of traffic on the roads of Britain (by month of the year, day of the week and time of the day) clearly demonstrate the characteristic of peaked demand. The following data have been generated by automatic counts conducted at a number of fixed locations on major and minor roads across Britain (ONS and DfT, 2004). The data are recorded as index numbers, meaning that they have been converted into figures relative to a base-line figure of 100. In each case the base-line is simply the average traffic flow across the time period in hand. For example, Figure 3.3 shows the average daily traffic flows on British roads by the month of the year in the five years from 2000 to 2004. In this case the index numbers are relative to the overall average daily traffic flow per month during that particular five-year period. In January of those years the index number for the volume of cars and taxis was 91, meaning that the average traffic flow in January was 91 per cent of that in the overall average month in the period. The trends shown in the figures that follow are representative of the trends experienced every year.

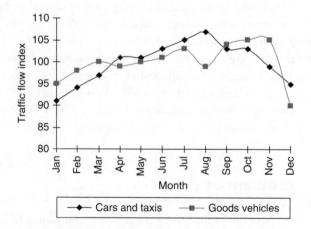

Figure 3.3 Average daily traffic flows by month, 2000–2004
Source: UK Office of National Statistics and the Department for Transport, *Transport Statistics Bulletin, Road Traffic Statistics*, 2004

Figure 3.3 clearly shows that, during the period 2000–2004, there was a peak in the demand for road use by cars and taxis in August, when the flow was 8 per cent higher than that in the average month of those years. Road use by cars and taxis was lowest in the month of January, rising to the peak in August before falling again to commence the subsequent year in the same way. There is a smaller peak in April that sheds some light on the most likely cause of the peaked demand: school holidays. It is likely that the roads were used most in August because families were travelling during their summer holidays, a characteristic that would be shared, but to a lesser degree, in April during the Easter school holidays. It is also likely that seasonal weather effects are a part of the explanation. People are less inclined to make journeys in the winter months when the days are shorter, colder and wetter, preferring to stay wrapped-up indoors; whereas during the summer months they are more likely to be out and about in the evenings.

The average daily traffic flow of goods vehicles by the month of the year in the UK in the period 2000–2004 was different. Once again the years started with a relatively low volume, in this case 95 per cent of that in the average month in the period. It then rose to a peak in November, after which it fell sharply. It is noticeable that there were two minor troughs in the demand for road use by goods vehicles, both of which coinciding with the peaks in demand for road use by cars and taxis: April and August. As such, it would appear that the two likely explanations are that of the demand for deliveries falling as the general populous take their holidays, and the supply of drivers to make such journeys falling as they also take their family holidays. As there were mini-peaks in the months immediately prior to these troughs, it would appear that the second of these explanations is the most important as businesses perhaps called for extra deliveries to tide them over the months when drivers were taking their annual leave. The overall peak in the demand for road use by goods vehicles was in November, coinciding with the deliveries of produce for Christmas and the New Year sales when consumption across the economy would be at its highest. This Christmas-effect is significant. Taking the average volume of UK retail sales in the year 2000 as the base-line (=100), the volume of UK retail sales in January 2006 was 127, rising steadily to 131.2 in August of that year and then falling to 130.5 in September, before rising once again to the annual peak of 133.5 in December (Retail Sales Index, ONS, 11/6/07). December peaks in retail sales are a regular feature of the British economy; inevitably having an effect on traffic volumes.

Figure 3.4 shows the average daily traffic flows of cars and taxis, and goods vehicles, on the British road network by the day of the week in the period 2000–2004. During the first four days of the representative week, the flow of cars and taxis remained fairly constant, around the average daily traffic volume of those vehicles in the five-year period. On Fridays this flow rose to 13 per cent above the average, after which it fell on Saturdays and Sundays to 8 and 9 per cent (respectively) below the average. This single peak on Fridays can be explained in two ways. First, it could imply an increase in circular journeys on Fridays rather than an increase in linear journeys (the latter would necessitate a peak on another day as travellers make the return journey). Secondly, it could be explained by

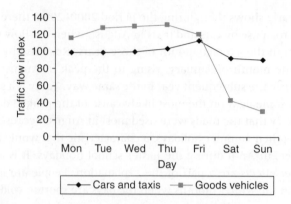

Figure 3.4 Average daily traffic flows by day of the week, 2000–2004
Source: UK Office of National Statistics and the Department for Transport, Transport Statistics Bulletin, Road Traffic Statistics, 2004

there being an increase in linear journeys, the return trips of which being obscured by the more-than-offsetting decline in typical journeys at the weekend. The true explanation probably lies with a combination of the two. It is likely that there are more circular journeys on Fridays as shopping and leisure trips are made at the end of the week, but that there are also people making journeys on Fridays, perhaps back home or on holiday for the weekend, to return on Saturdays and Sundays when the normal quietness of the roads masks these extra journeys.

Figure 3.4 also shows that the demand for road usage by freight vehicles remained fairly constant across the representative working week in this period of five years; hovering between 115 and 130 per cent of the average daily traffic flow of freight vehicles throughout the period. Unsurprisingly, the weekend flows were much lower: Saturdays and Sundays having flows that were 43 and 30 per cent (respectively) of the daily average in the five-year period. This pattern is to be expected due to the structure of the working week and the use of the weekend by employees for relaxation, recuperation and engagement in leisure and domestic activities.

Figure 3.5 shows the traffic flow of cars on the British road network by the time of the day, both during the working week and at weekends, for the year 2004. It clearly shows that there were two peaks in the demand for road usage by cars during a working day. The first of these occurred between 0700 and 0900 hours, when the average traffic flow was over 170 per cent that of the hourly average during 2004. The second was between 1600 and 1800 hours, when the flow was even higher at over 200 per cent of the hourly average in 2004. These occurred simply because of the structure of the working day. Between these daily peaks of demand, during the middle of the day, the flow hovered above 135 per cent of the average hourly flow; and during the night hours it fell to only 5 per cent between 0200 and 0400 hours.

At the weekends, the pattern of demand is different. On Saturdays the peak was at midday, when the traffic flow was 189 per cent that of the hourly average in 2004. The flow was sustained at a level in excess of 156 per cent of the hourly

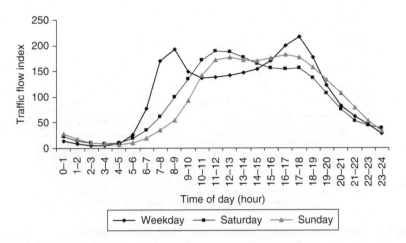

Figure 3.5   Distribution of traffic by time of the day, 2004: Cars
Source: UK Office of National Statistics and the Department for Transport, Transport Statistics Bulletin, Road Traffic Statistics, 2004

average between 1000 and 1800 hours, with the earlier hours in this period having the higher traffic flows. This pattern is perhaps unsurprising as people are likely to have a lie-in on a Saturday and so make their journeys later than they would during the working week. In addition, those going away for the weekend will set off during the earlier hours of this period so that they can make the most of their weekend.

On Sundays the pattern was the same as that on Saturdays, except that the peak occurred later (between 1600 and 1700 hours). People are also likely to have a lie-in on Sundays, but the explanation for why the peak occurs later in the afternoon is probably connected with that of the distribution of traffic flow across the days of the week, namely people travelling home, or back to where they live for work, on Sunday evenings in preparation for work the following day.

Figure 3.6 shows exactly the same information as Figure 3.5 but for freight vehicles rather than cars. The distributions are much different. During weekdays, the traffic flow remains beneath 50 per cent of the hourly average between the start of the day and 0400 hours, after which it rises to 190 per cent of the hourly average between 0700 and 0800 hours, just before the morning rush hour. It plateaus at around this level until 1600 hours when it then falls away so that it is under 50 per cent of the hourly average flow after 2300 hours. A greater proportion of freight journeys are made during the early hours of the day than of passenger journeys as road hauliers seek to avoid the traffic. In fact, there is a dip in freight traffic volume during the morning rush hour (0800–0900 hours) as drivers of freight vehicles actively avoid the congestion at that time.

During the weekends the traffic flow of freight vehicles never reaches the average hourly level. Similarly to cars, on Saturdays the flow is at its highest in the early part of the day; whereas on Sundays the peak occurs in the early evening. It is likely that this is due to the final weekly deliveries being made on Saturday

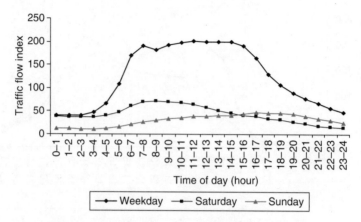

Figure 3.6 Distribution of traffic by time of day, 2004: Goods vehicles
Source: UK Office of National Statistics and the Department for Transport, Transport Statistics Bulletin, Road Traffic Statistics, 2004

mornings and drivers beginning their journeys, especially long-haul journeys, on Sunday evenings.

3.3.2 Traffic speeds in English urban areas

In 2004, the UK Department of Transport surveyed traffic speeds at different times of the day in the 18 largest urban areas in England, excluding the capital, by employing people to drive survey cars around the road network making records. The aim was to ensure a good coverage of all important roads in each area whilst keeping the size of the survey manageable. To ensure that the results were representative of actual traffic speeds the *floating car method* was employed, in which drivers tried to ensure that they overtook a similar number of vehicles to those overtaking them; and the results were calculated by weighting the average speeds on each link (a section of road between two control junctions, for example roundabouts and traffic lights) by the traffic flow on that link.

The average traffic speed across the major road network in 2004 was 21.0 miles per hour (mph) during the peak periods (0730–0930 hours and 1630–1830 hours) and 25.3 mph during the off-peak periods (1030–1230 hours and 1330–1530 hours). During peak periods, almost 30 per cent of time was spent at speeds below 5 mph and over 50 per cent at speeds below 20 mph. In the off-peak periods, around 20 per cent of time was spent at speeds below 5 mph and over 40 per cent at speeds below 20 mph.

The 2004 survey was the fifth of its kind by the Department of Transport. As such, it is possible to make comparisons of average speeds at different times of the day across recent years. The problem with this is that the survey network has changed and so the overall results of the five surveys are not consistent. This can be overcome by only including the results from the stretches of road that were unchanged across the surveys. Such comparisons show that average peak period traffic speeds fell by 0.3 mph between 1999/2000 and 2004 and average off-peak period speeds remained unchanged. Also, between these two years, the percentage of time spent at speeds less than 5 mph increased in the peak periods and to a lesser degree in the off-peak periods also, and the proportion of time spent at speeds around the speed limits decreased in both periods.

There are many factors that may affect average speeds:

- The type of roads used for the links and the distances between control junctions. Average traffic speeds are likely to be higher in areas with a higher density of dual carriageways and where the links are longer, as less time is required for slowing down and speeding up.
- Road factors, such as road-works, accidents and bad weather, are considered as being typical of normal journeying conditions and so are simply accepted in the survey. Atypical events, such as bomb warnings and serious flooding, may also affect average speeds but there were no such events in the 2004 survey.
- The behaviour of survey drivers can affect the results, but attempts were made to overcome these by employing the floating car method.

Therefore, the remaining factor that can explain the different average speeds in the peak and off-peak periods is the traffic density. These results are good evidence of the different levels of demand for road use in the two periods of the day and so of the problem of the peak.

3.3.3   Other cases of peaked demand in the transport sector

The phenomenon of peaked demand is not confined to the road network: it occurs across the sector.

- On railway and underground networks, commuter services experience far greater demand than services during the middle of the day or at night.
- Bus operators often experience a slightly different distribution in demand as they not only have the main business peaks but also have a smaller peak due to the school-run in the early afternoon.
- Airports and airlines are faced with similar peaks to those above during the day and during the week due to the structure of the business day. They also experience significant seasonal variations in demand as a result of the holidays: higher-than-usual demand for flights between June and September, with the peak occurring in August; and less significant peaks in March/April and December, coinciding with school holidays.
- Similar seasonal peaks to those for the airlines are experienced by ferry, coach and package holiday operators.

In addition to these regular peaks in demand, there are also one-off peaks. Vienna International Airport has been experiencing a growth in demand over recent years and so has implemented an expansion programme which should see the opening of a new terminal in the final quarter of 2008. During the first half of 2006 just fewer than 7.9 million travellers used the airport, an increase of 8.1 per cent over the same period in 2005. Part of this particular growth was due to the country's role in holding the presidency of the European Union. Vienna Aircraft Handling Gesellschaft m.b.H. registered nearly 250 extra flights and roughly 4600 more passengers during this time. Similar, but shorter, one-off peaks can be caused by sporting and business events at local and national levels, and often these cannot be fully confirmed in advance.

3.3.4   The implications

Peaked demand has a significant impact on the provision of transport infrastructure and services. In the provision of roads, for example, authorities cannot simply provide for the average monthly, daily and hourly traffic flows because that would fail to accommodate the peak periods when demand is significantly higher than this, thereby causing serious levels of congestion. On the other hand, if authorities were to provide enough capacity to accommodate the demand in the peak periods, the road network would be dramatically underused in the intervening periods, surely signifying an uneconomic use of resources. The distribution of demand for road use necessitates a certain degree of congestion in peak periods for the overall system to be efficient and economic.

A similar problem faces all transport service providers: companies providing bus, rail, ferry and air transport. If they were to provide enough capacity to accommodate the average demand across the months, days and hours they would be causing a shortage of supply in the peak periods. Passengers would have to wait for their services, and fares would rise at these times. On the other hand, if they were to provide enough capacity to satisfy the peaks in demand, they would be supplying too much and the services during the intervening periods would have low and uneconomic load factors. The fares on such services would have to be lowered and inefficient cross-subsidisation would be needed from the more profitable services.

Transport providers usually choose a compromising solution. They do put on more services during peak periods, but this means that surplus capital is lying idle during the intervening periods causing an inventory cost. Cole (2005) comments that rail providers operating services in large cities have up to 60 per cent of their rolling stock in sidings or garages during the middle of working days, nights and the weekends. Not only this, there are surplus employees during the intervening periods; and as the capital used in the peak periods is used much less than the capital that is employed throughout the day, it incurs higher average costs. It actually costs a provider more to operate an extra service in peak periods than it does to operate services throughout the day. As such, providers do not fully satisfy the peaked demand, meaning that there are waiting times, crowding and higher fares; the latter being necessary in order to cover the extra costs. As the demand for transport services is price inelastic at these times (see Section 3.4), this increase in fares actually serves to increase revenue for the providers and is combined with price discrimination. This is *peak pricing*. Providers can also store more aged pieces of capital for use during the peak periods so as to minimise the depreciation costs, or hire the needed extra capacity in these periods from third parties to eliminate the fixed costs involved in their purchase.

3.4 Elasticity of demand

It is likely that a change in the price of a product will cause the quantity demanded of that same product to change; as it is that changes in the prices of substitute and complementary products, or in the disposable incomes of consumers, will also cause the quantity demanded of the product to change. However, for the purpose of economic analysis it is necessary for economists to be more precise than this. Economists actually need a quantitative estimate of just how responsive the quantity demanded of a particular product is to a change in one of these determinants. This is where elasticity of demand is useful.

Elasticity is simply a means of representing how responsive the magnitude of one factor is to a change in the magnitude of another (both in percentage terms). The general formula defining elasticity is

$$\frac{\text{Percentage change in factor A}}{\text{Percentage change in factor B}}$$

This expresses the average percentage change in the magnitude of factor A for each percentage point change in the magnitude of factor B.

It is important to note that this concept is applicable to any pair of variables. One could, for instance, estimate the responsiveness of the number of holidays taken in France to a change in the volume of rainfall in Britain: the British rainfall elasticity of French holidays, in which the number of French holidays would be factor A and the volume of rainfall in Britain, factor B.

It is by calculating elasticity of demand that one can properly ascertain just how important a factor is in determining the quantity demanded of a particular product. If the resulting elasticity is close to zero then one can conclude that it is relatively unimportant; whereas the larger the coefficient is, the more influential the determining factor. The variable that is usually analysed as having an effect on demand is price and this will be the focus here, but in the transport sector the variables of quality and convenience are also highly important and the effects of changes in these could also be assessed using elasticities.

The real world is constantly changing in ways that cannot be observed. Consequently, it is important to note that an elasticity result does not simply relate to the historically observed relationship between two variables: there may have been unobserved changes that occurred that also affected the result. Economists overcome this by employing the *ceteris paribus* assumption: that everything else remains constant. In reality it is likely that there are changes in other variables and so it is vital to separate out the effects of the several influences. For instance, in recent years the price of fuel to motorists has gone up simultaneously as an increase in traffic flows. This does not imply that the elasticity of traffic flows with respect to the price of fuel is positive. At least two things have happened: fuel prices have gone up and household incomes have also gone up. We have observed the net effect of two or more separate phenomena.

3.4.1 Own-price elasticity of demand

This simply shows the responsiveness of the quantity demanded of a product, in percentage terms, to a percentage change in the price of that product. In other words, it is the percentage change in the quantity demanded in response to a 1 per cent change in its price. It is calculated using the following formula:

$$Ped = \frac{\text{Percentage change in quantity demanded}}{\text{Percentage change in price}}$$

As a result of the law of demand the resulting coefficient of this formula will always be negative; except in the rare cases when the law is broken. The law of demand states that there is an inverse relationship between a change in the price of a product and the effect it has on the quantity demanded of that same product; meaning that the formula will always comprise a positive figure and a negative figure. As such, more often than not, economists miss out the negative sign from the coefficient as it is assumed that readers will realise that it is such. However, for the purpose of clarity it is advised that the negative sign is inserted in brackets in front of the coefficient.

There are two different forms of price elasticity of demand. Firstly, there are *ordinary* price elasticities of demand. These measure the combined income and substitution effects of changes of price on the demand for passenger transport; or the combined scale and substitution effects of changes in input price on the demand for freight transport. These are the usual estimates that are used, and so will be the form used in the analysis that follows. They are more difficult to calculate for freight transport, as the calculations involve consideration of how the outputs of producers change with individual input prices. Secondly, there are *compensated* elasticities of demand which measure only the pure substitution effects of a change in price. These are used less frequently and so will not be included the analysis here.

There are also different aspects of the transport sector that one can focus on when estimating price elasticities of demand. One could look at the price elasticity of demand of the whole transport sector in relation to other sectors within the economy. Alternatively, one could look at that of the individual modes of transport, relative to the other modes within the sector. Lastly, one could focus on the price elasticity of demand of a particular producer within the market for a particular mode of transport. In this analysis, the focus is upon the elasticities of demand for the separate modes of transport within the transport sector.

If the resulting coefficient of price elasticity of demand for any of these different forms of price elasticity of demand is between 0 and −1, it means that the quantity demanded is not very responsive to a change in its price. Such products are said to be price *inelastic*. If the coefficient is less than −1 (for example, −1.5 or −2), the product is said to be price *elastic*: quantity demanded is responsive to a change in

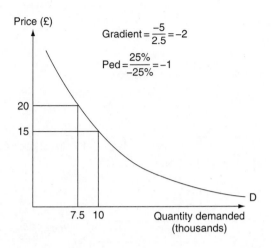

Figure 3.7 The difference between price elasticity of demand and the gradient of the demand curve

price. Finally, if the coefficient is equal to –1, the product is said to have a *unit* price elasticity of demand (or to be unitary price elastic): a change in its price causes an equal but opposite percentage change in the quantity demanded of it.

It is important to note that the price elasticity of demand for a product is not the same as the gradient of its demand curve. The two formulae are fundamentally different in that calculating the gradient of the curve involves absolute figures, whereas calculating the elasticity uses percentages. This is illustrated very simply in Figure 3.7.

In fact, the price elasticity of demand along a straight-line demand curve changes in a particular way; whereas the gradient will be constant throughout. The central point of a straight-line demand curve always has unit elasticity of demand. The upper section of the curve is price inelastic and the lower section is price elastic. This is an important rule and is illustrated in Figure 3.8, in which the percentage changes have been calculated assuming that the price is falling and the quantity demanded is increasing each time. It is possible to plot a demand curve with a constant price elasticity of demand, as outlined in the mathematical appendix to this section.

In many contexts, elasticity is more useful and meaningful than absolute gradient. For instance, suppose you are told by an economic analyst that if bus fares were to be increased by 5 pence per passenger journey, the number of passenger journeys would fall by 60 million per annum. That would imply an absolute gradient of –60/5 million journeys per pence. But should you be surprised: is that a big response or a small one? To assess that you need to know the absolute or *base* values of the two variables. Suppose these relate to bus journeys in London, of which there are about 1800 million a year at an average fare of about 50 pence per journey. Now you can work out that the price increase is about 10 per cent and the quantity reduction is 3.33 per cent, so the elasticity is –1/3.

This is a dimensionless number, independent of scale; found to be typical of urban bus operations around the world. It makes sense to apply this elasticity to a town, big or small, with high average fares or low ones. This is one of the advantages of the elasticity over the gradient.

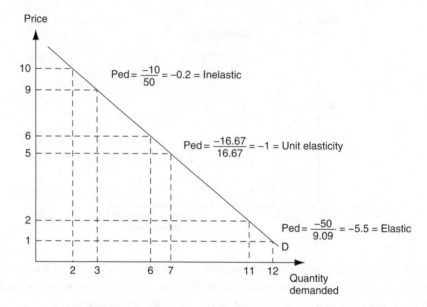

Figure 3.8 Price elasticity of demand along a straight-line demand curve

3.4.1.1 The uses of price elasticity of demand

Price elasticity of demand is useful in a number of ways, as it indicates the effect of changes in price:

- *For policy-makers*. The tool that a policy-maker should use to reduce the consumption of a particular product, for example petrol, is determined by the price elasticity of it. If it is price elastic, a relatively small increase in price (perhaps stimulated by an increase in taxation) would cause a much larger percentage reduction in consumption, and so the tool is likely to be effective; whereas if it is price inelastic, the consumption will be relatively unresponsive to an increase in price, and so taxation will be less effective. The same argument also works in reverse. If a policy-maker wants to increase the consumption of a product, for example public transport, the tool should be determined by the price elasticity of it. If it is price elastic, a small reduction in price (perhaps through a public subsidy) is likely to be effective; whereas if it is price inelastic, even a relatively large reduction in price is likely to be ineffective (and very costly).
- *For transport economists*. Price elasticity of demand is useful for transport economists forecasting the future trends of transport markets. For example, it is likely that as oil continues to be consumed, petrol will become increasingly expensive over time. It is only by studying the relevant price elasticities of demand that economists can forecast the likely effects of this increase in motor–vehicle costs on the trends of car and bus usage.
- *For transport producers*. It is generally assumed that producers aim to maximise their profits. As profit is the amount of revenue that is over and above the costs, producers need to maximise their revenue and minimise their costs to achieve this goal. This involves careful consideration when setting prices, and price

elasticity of demand facilitates this. If a product is price inelastic, the suppliers know that increasing the price will cause a smaller percentage reduction in the quantity demanded and so revenue will rise.

For example, if the price elasticity of demand is -0.5, an increase in price of 10 per cent will cause a 5 per cent reduction in the quantity demanded. If it is assumed that the initial price was £5 and the initial quantity demanded was 10,000 units, the initial revenue was £50,000 (£5 × 10,000 units). By raising the price to £5.50, the quantity demanded will be reduced to 9500 units but the total revenue will increase to £52,250. In this way, to increase the revenue of products that are price inelastic, it is advisable to increase the price.

If, on the other hand, the product is price elastic, the reverse is true. As quantity demanded will be changed by a larger percentage than the price, an increase in the price will lead to a reduction in revenue; whereas a reduction in the price will improve the revenue.

It is important to remember that it is likely that the price elasticity of demand of a product will vary along its demand curve. This means that, if the price elasticity of demand is calculated accurately, the analysis above is reasonable for minor alterations in price, but not necessarily so for larger changes. Larger changes would significantly change the position on the demand curve, and so include a wider range of price elasticities.

We can now see the vital importance of a unitary price elasticity of demand as a benchmark, dividing case. If demand is price inelastic (that is, the elasticity is between 0 and -1), raising price will increase revenue; but if it is price elastic (that is, the elasticity is less than -1), then raising price will reduce revenue. Whatever the objectives of a producer, whether its demand is price elastic or price inelastic is vital information.

3.4.1.2   The determinants of price elasticity of demand

There are five main factors determining how price elastic a product is. These apply to the demand for both passenger and freight transport demand, but the explanations focus upon consumers of passenger transport:

- *Proportion of consumer expenditure.* The smaller the proportion of total expenditure that a product accounts for, the more price inelastic it is likely to be. This is because any change in price will be less noticeable and so will be more easily absorbed.

  A simple illustration of this is to assume that a particular consumer takes a very short bus ride to the local village once a week. A return ticket costs £1.50. The consumer also uses the railways to travel to the nearest city once a week, a return ticket costing £50. The consumer spends £200 every week in total. If both the bus and train tickets increase in price by 50 per cent, the former will now cost £2.25 and the latter £75. As a consequence of the train ticket accounting for a much greater proportion of the total weekly expenditure, the consumer is more likely to decide to cut back on the number of trips to the city and to simply absorb the extra 75 pence spent on bus fares. The quantity demanded of train tickets is much more responsive to a change in price, and so is more price elastic. The same logic can be applied to a reduction in prices as well.

Similarly, the proportion of the overall cost represented by the trip in question will be a determinant of its price elasticity. A transport movement may be a small part of an overall activity, in which case a change in its price is less likely to change behaviour. A trip from home to Australia may involve a public transport trip to a nearby airport and then an expensive flight. Because the trip to the airport constitutes a small portion of the total trip cost, the propensity to take the whole trip will not be much influenced by a change in the cost of getting to the airport. Similarly the road haulage of goods low in value in relation to weight (such as coal) is likely to be more price sensitive than haulage of high value goods such as computer parts, because the transport cost is a much greater proportion of the overall production cost.

■ *Addictiveness*. The more addictive that a product is, the more price inelastic it will be, as consumers are more willing to pay any price increases in order to obtain it. Although one could think of relevant examples of this in the transport sector, such as the owner and pilot of a two-seater aeroplane who is addicted to the experience of flying over the countryside in which they live, in general this is not an important determinant of the price elasticity of products within the sector (although it is often asserted that people are addicted to their cars).

■ *Level of necessity*. The greater the necessity of a product, the more price inelastic it will be. Commuters who use the railways to get to work in London, for example, are likely to be much more willing to pay higher fares than travellers who use the railways simply for the occasional day trip. The former are compelled to accept the higher fares by the need to get to their office, whereas the latter are more flexible to find alternatives. This is a highly important determinant of the price elasticity of demand of products in the transport sector.

■ *The time scale*. The longer the time period involved the more price elastic the product is likely to be. For commuters, a week after an increase in fares the majority of travellers are still likely to be using the railways, and so the railway journeys are price inelastic. If after a year the fares are still relatively more expensive than the other modes of transport, more and more of the commuters are likely to have found alternatives. Consequently, the railway journeys have become more price elastic over time.

The reasons for this time delay are the time needed for the commuters to become dissatisfied with the price increase; the time needed for them to actually find out about and to organise using the alternatives; and the effect of any initial expenditure locking them into using the railways, for example the purchasing of a season ticket with the railways or with the local bus company to get them to and from the station. Eventually, commuters may decide to change the location of either their home or their work.

This last consideration is particularly important in the transport sector as all of the modes of transport potentially involve considerable initial expenditures for consumers. As well as the season tickets noted above, another example is that of the purchasing of a car. One of the reasons car use is so price inelastic is that if a consumer has recently purchased a vehicle, they are going to be reluctant to allow it to simply sit on the drive if the price of petrol increases. They will feel that they should still use it. However, as time goes by, this feeling will gradually diminish and the need to replace it will grow, so it will become more price elastic.

■ *The closeness of substitutes*. A substitute is a product that can be purchased as an alternative to something else. A close substitute is one that is very similar to the alternative: in terms of both price and functionality. A product cannot be said to be a close substitute if its price is significantly higher than the alternative, or if it only does a fraction of the functions that the other one does.

The greater the number and closeness of available substitutes that a product has, the more price elastic it will be. This is simply because consumers will be less willing and able to continue buying it if its price increases, as there are more satisfactory alternatives available. For example, a rural train service without any competing bus service and in a region with an exceptionally poor road infrastructure is likely to be much more price inelastic than a similar route with two competing bus providers and good roads for car users.

This is another important reason why car use is so price inelastic. The vast majority of journeys that car drivers make have a lack of close substitutes. There may be no bus services for the journey; or if there are such services, they may only run once every hour, taking twice as long as the car and so are not that close an alternative.

3.4.1.3 Actual price elasticities from the transport sector

There are many different methods that can be employed in the estimation of price elasticities. It is not the purpose of this text to outline these technical details, but rather to discuss the implications of the results. The estimates of price elasticity of demand for the different modes of transport in Europe are far from being fully comprehensive, but in an excellent working paper for the World Bank, Oum *et al.* (1990) surveyed 70 studies of demand elasticities across the transport sector in order to establish the most likely ranges that these elasticities take. The studies focus on many different countries, employ various methods and databases, and are best interpreted as ordinary demand elasticities. Some of their results are displayed in Tables 3.2 and 3.3. These results have been selected because of the confidence of the authors in establishing *most-likely* ranges.

The estimates in Table 3.2, which show the price-elasticity of demand for passenger transport, lead to four conclusions. First, they clearly show that the demand for passenger transport is more inelastic in peak periods than in others. This is a result that one would have expected, as there is likely to be a greater

Table 3.2 Price elasticity of demand estimates of passenger transport

	Elasticities	
	Peak	*Off Peak*
Car	0.10–0.70	0.20–1.10
Bus	0.10–0.70	0.10–1.10
Railway	0.20–0.40	≤ 1.00
	Leisure	*Non-leisure*
Airlines	1.10–2.70	0.40–1.20
Railway	1.40–1.60	0.60–0.70

Source: Oum, *et al.* (1990)
Note: All the figures are negative

Table 3.3 Price Elasticity of Demand estimates of freight transport

	Elasticities
Road Freight	0.70–1.10
Railway	0.40–1.20
Airlines	0.80–1.60

Source: Oum, *et al.* (1990)
Note: All the figures are negative

necessity amongst travellers to travel due to the need to get to work. Secondly, there is little difference between the price elasticities for the demand for car, bus and railway transport. In fact, that for the railways is possibly more inelastic. Thirdly, the demand for air and railway passenger transport is more inelastic when it has a non-leisure purpose than when it is for leisure. Again, this is to be expected as passengers travelling for business view their journeys as having greater necessity than leisure passengers, who are perhaps less concerned about their journeys. Finally, the demand for rail travel is more inelastic than that for air travel; perhaps suggesting that air travel is viewed as being less of a necessity.

Quinet and Vickerman (2004) note that a study of the impact of tolls on French motorway traffic generated estimates of the price elasticities of demand for road usage of −0.96 in the short-term and −1.28 in the long-term. This highlights another important conclusion: demand becomes more elastic over time, as alternatives can be developed.

The estimates of the price elasticity of demand for freight transport displayed in Table 3.3 lead to two further conclusions. First, they are all fairly inelastic as they have a median value that is greater than −1 (except for the airlines, which have a coefficient slightly above that figure). As such, the demand for freight transport is fairly insensitive to changes in its price. Secondly, the demand for transporting freight by the railways is likely to be the most inelastic and that by the airlines most elastic. This suggests that freight transportation by the railways is viewed as being the most necessary, perhaps due to a lack of alternatives, and that air freight is still not as important (which is confirmed by the figures in Chapter 2).

The overarching conclusion from these estimates is that the demand for transport is price inelastic. The best explanation for this is that it is a derived demand. Passengers do not demand transport for its own sake but because of what it facilitates: leisure and employment. Similarly, producers demand freight transport for its essential part in the production process. As such, it is viewed as a necessity by both categories of user.

3.4.2 Income elasticity of demand

This shows the responsiveness of quantity demanded to a change in the income of consumers. It is defined by the following formula:

$$Yed = \frac{\text{Percentage change in quantity demanded}}{\text{Percentage change in income}}$$

If the resulting coefficient of this is positive, it means that an increase in the incomes of consumers is associated with an increase in the quantity demanded of the product, or vice versa. This suggests that consumers demand more of it as their incomes rise. These are termed *normal products*, and include most products in the transport sector. If the coefficient is negative, it means that an increase in the income of consumers has coincided with a reduction in the quantity demanded of the product, or vice versa. This suggests that an increase in income causes consumers to switch to substitutes. These are known as *inferior products*. Examples may include the bicycle as consumers are likely to use their cars more and their bicycles less if their incomes rise.

3.4.2.1 The uses of income elasticity of demand

Income elasticity of demand is useful in two main ways:

1. *For policy-makers and transport economists.* Income elasticity of demand shows how increasing incomes are likely to affect the usage of the different modes of transport in the future. This allows economists and policy-makers to forecast and prepare for future problems, such as increased traffic congestion in particular areas or potential bottlenecks in the provision of passenger air flights.
2. *For transport producers.* It is vital that producers make investment decisions wisely and invest in projects that are likely to see an increase in demand and profitability. This can only be done if those demands are accurately forecasted. Income elasticity of demand estimates facilitate this.

3.4.2.2 Actual estimates of income elasticity of demand

Quinet and Vickerman (2004) have noted that Johansson and Schipper, in a work that was published in 1997, used data from 12 OECD countries over the preceding 20 years to calculate the elasticity of car ownership, average annual fuel consumption, annual distance driven, the demand for fuel and the volume of automobile traffic (all with respect to income); and that they found it to range from 0 to +1.2. They have also noted that Selvanathan and Selvanathan, in a work published in 1994, estimated that the income elasticity of demand for personal transport, public transport and communications ranged from +0.5 to +2.3 in the UK and Australia. Both of these studies show that passenger transportation is a normal good. This is especially true of private transport, as the second of the two works estimated that the income elasticity of demand for it in both of the studied countries was greater than +2. This is perhaps to be expected as private transport confers additional benefits, such as flexibility, which passengers will want to take advantage of if income permits.

Quinet and Vickerman (2004) have also noted that the French Ministry of Transport uses a range of figures, generally from +1.2 to +1.8, for its estimates of the income elasticity of demand for different modes and categories of transport. These estimate the relationship between gross domestic product (GDP) and the tonne-kilometres of freight traffic. Another study that Quinet and Vickerman (2004) comment upon is that of Van de Voorde and Meersman (1997). They have generated the estimates that are displayed in Table 3.4, which are based on data from Belgium.

In the short term, expansion in industrial production has a much greater impact upon freight transport on the railways than by road; but in the long term, this is more than reversed. This suggests that rail transport is more flexible, but that road transport is more desirable. As production initially increases, it is perhaps easier for producers to charter more capacity on the railways; but gradually they are able to obtain more road capacity which they then switch to. It is noticeable that transport by the inland waterways is an inferior good. Producers switch to other modes of freight transport when industrial production increases, explaining the decline that the inland waterways have experienced across Europe and especially in the UK.

3.4.3 Cross elasticity of demand

This shows the responsiveness of the quantity demanded of one product to a change in the price of another. It is defined by the following formula:

$$\text{Xed} = \frac{\text{Percentage change in the quantity demanded of product A}}{\text{Percentage change in the price of product B}}$$

Table 3.4 Income elasticity of demand estimates of freight transport in Belgium

	Short term	Long term
Road	0.89	2.38
Rail	1.45	0.45
Inland waterways		−0.34

Data source: Quinet and Vickerman (2004)

This is an important elasticity, as it shows the relationship between different products. If the resulting coefficient is positive, it means that an increase in the price of product B is associated with an increase in the quantity demanded of product A, or vice versa. Consequently, this suggests that the two products are substitutes, and so consumers have switched away from the first product. If, on the other hand, the coefficient is negative, it means that an increase in the price of product B has coincided with a reduction in the quantity demanded of product A, or vice versa. The implication, therefore, is that these are complementary products. If the coefficient is zero, the two products appear to be unrelated.

For instance, it is often argued that urban bus fares should be kept low in order to tempt people out of their cars. The effectiveness of this depends on the cross elasticity of car use with respect to bus fares.

3.4.3.1 Actual estimates of cross elasticity of demand

In the most comprehensive survey of transport demand elasticity estimates, which is explained in Section 3.4.1.3, Oum *et al.* (1990) have gathered a range of cross-elasticity estimates. Some of these are displayed in Table 3.5.

Table 3.5 shows that there are different relationships between the different modes of transport. In freight transport, rail and road are substitutes; whereas rail and the waterways are complements. This suggests that the railways and waterways are used for *transhipment*; or in other words, they are both used in the same journeys. As such, if the costs of one increases, there is a related contraction in the demand of the other. In passenger transport, bus and rail travel are substitutes, as are air and rail travel (although much more weakly so); whereas air and rail travel are complements. Again, this suggests that passengers combine both air and rail travel in the same journeys and so a change in the price of one causes an opposite change in the quantity demanded of the other.

Table 3.5 Estimates of cross-elasticities of demand of transport

Modes	Cross-elasticity
Rail-Truck (freight)	−0.18 to +0.50
Truck-Rail (freight)	−0.62 to +0.84
Rail-Waterway (freight)	+0.15 to +0.20
Waterway-Rail (freight)	+0.61 to +0.86
Air-Bus (passenger)	−0.02 to −0.01
Bus-Air (passenger)	−0.12 to −0.05
Air-Rail (passenger)	+0.01 to +0.04
Rail-Air (passenger)	+0.08 to +0.51
Bus-Rail (passenger)	−0.47 to −0.21
Rail-Bus (passenger)	−1.18 to −0.17

Data source: Oum, *et al.* (1990)

3.5 | Market price

The demand curve is one half of a model of price determination that lies at the heart of microeconomics, namely that of demand and supply. As noted in the introduction to this section, a market is a place where consumers and producers come together to trade. Therefore, to understand how the price in a market is determined, it is necessary to analyse this interaction between consumers and producers. This is what the simple demand-and-supply model does.

Effective supply is the quantity of a product that producers are willing and able to supply at every given price; and the law of supply states that as price increases this quantity will also increase. An alternative way of expressing this is that in order for producers to be encouraged to supply more to the market, it is necessary for them to receive a higher price. This leads to the conclusion that in price–quantity space, the supply curve will be upward-sloping (as shown in Figure 3.9). The reason for this is explained fully in Section 4.3.3.1, but for now it can be said that after a certain level of output, further increasing output will gradually cause costs to rise and so producers require a greater price to maintain profitability.

The demand curve shows the quantity demanded at every given price and so represents the wants of the consumers. If the price rises, consumers will be willing and able to purchase less of the product, and vice versa. In the same way, the supply curve represents the wants of the producers, as it shows the price required to induce them to produce a certain level of output. The market price is determined by the interaction of these two groups, which is illustrated by the point of equilibrium in Figure 3.9.

At any price higher than P_1, there would be excess supply and so producers would reduce their price in order to sell the excess stock. At any price lower than P_1, there would be excess demand and consumers would cause the price to rise as they compete with one another to obtain the products that are available. Both of these pressures would continue to have an effect until the equilibrium is reached. At this price, there are no excesses and so there is no pressure for the price to change. This price is also known as the

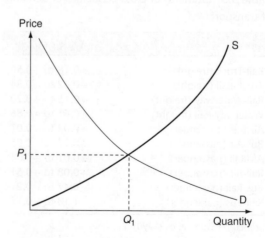

Figure 3.9 The market price

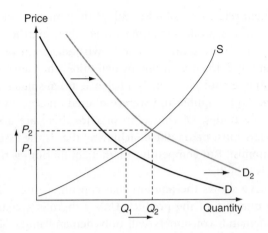

Figure 3.10 The effect of a shift of demand

market-clearing price, as it is the price at which all excesses in the market are cleared.

This now shows what the effect will be of any change in the determinants of demand (see Section 3.2). If there is an outward shift in the demand curve for air freight (perhaps caused by an improvement in its reliability or an increase in the earnings of importers), there will be excess demand at the initial equilibrium price (P_1) and so the price will be competed upwards to a new equilibrium of P_2, at which the market forces are balanced once again. As shown in Figure 3.10, this increase in demand has caused the amount of air freight to increase from Q_1 to Q_2, and the price of it to increase as well.

Similarly, if there was a change that caused the demand curve to shift inwards (perhaps due to a security scare in the airports or a significant reduction in the price of shipping), it would cause there to be an excess supply at the initial price. The providers of air freight would seek to fill up their spare capacity by reducing the price, and then reducing subsequent provision. This would cause both the price and the quantity of air freight to fall until the new equilibrium is attained.

3.6 | Market welfare

The concept of market welfare is difficult to quantify as it is measuring the degree of satisfaction of consumers and producers in a particular market. It may be thought impossible to do this accurately, as it involves a considerable amount of value judgement: opinions and feelings rather than facts. However, one of the most important contributions of the theory of markets is to offer an objective way of achieving this, which has formed the foundation of modern economic appraisal techniques.

This notion of welfare or value is founded on the notions of consumer and producer sovereignty. For consumers in market equilibrium, the price represents the price they are willing to pay for one extra unit. It is their own judgement about the value of the item relative to all other things they might have chosen to spend that same budget on. For producers in market equilibrium, the price matches the cost of producing one more unit. It is their own judgement of the value of the commodity in that sense. In equilibrium, by definition, the views of the two groups are consistent with one another: there is a balance, no mismatch and therefore no reason for change. So in equilibrium we are offered an objective, coherent view of how people value things. Of course, in practice there are all sorts of reasons that this simple view must be modified: achieving that is the essence of the art of the transport economist. But competitive market equilibrium is the foundation on which our analysis is built.

The demand curve shows the amount that consumers are willing and able to pay for a certain quantity of the product. Unless there is a change in the other determinants of demand, consumers will only demand more of a product if its price is reduced. Up until the market equilibrium, consumers do not have to fully pay what they are willing and able to, as the market price is lower than the value indicated by the demand curve for those units. For example, Figure 3.11 shows that consumers are willing to pay P_2 for the first unit, but they actually only have to pay the market price of P_1. The difference between the two prices is called *the consumer surplus* at that unit, and the whole area between the demand curve and the market price is the *consumer surplus* of the market as a whole. As consumers will only pay an amount that is at most equal to the satisfaction that it affords them, consumer surplus is a representation of their welfare: it shows the extra satisfaction that these products bring to them, that they do not have to pay for.

A similar representation of producer welfare can be found using the supply curve. This curve shows the price at which producers are willing and able to supply products to the market, but up until the market equilibrium the producers actually receive a higher price than the minimum that they would have supplied those units for. In Figure 3.11, for example, the producers would have been willing to supply the first unit for a price of P_3, but they actually receive the market price of P_1. This difference is known as the *producer surplus* at that unit and the whole area between the supply curve and the market price is the *producer surplus* in the whole market. This is a representation of producer welfare, as it shows the

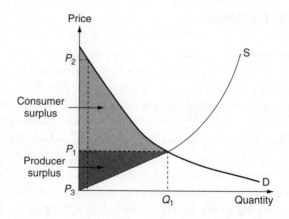

Figure 3.11
Market welfare

extra earnings that producers receive over and above their minimum requirements. Actually, a little reflection will show that producer surplus is the same thing as the excess of revenue above variable cost, or operating profit. Ultimately it will find its way into the pockets of the owners of the firm (often the shareholders), and that is why it is reasonable to reckon this as a benefit to somebody.

Total market welfare can be seen as being represented by consumer surplus plus producer surplus. This is a very useful tool as it indicates the different degrees of welfare at different market equilibria, and so it can be used to indicate the welfare effects, for the market as a whole as well as for the consumers and producers separately, of changes that cause the demand curve to shift.

3.7 | Markets in action: The effects of 11 September 2001 on the low-cost airlines

In his excellent book *No Frills: The Truth behind the Low-Cost Revolution in the Skies* (2006) Simon Calder explains how the terrorist attacks in the US on 11 September 2001 had a huge impact on the traditional airlines. For four days after the attacks, not a single flight was allowed to depart from the US and the airspace over London was also exceptionally quiet. On 14 September, Boeing announced 25,000 job cuts, which was followed over the next week by similar announcements from Virgin Atlantic (1200 jobs), Aer Lingus (1600 jobs) and British Airways (5000 jobs) among others. The Association of British Travel Agents (ABTA) soon announced that bookings for holidays the following summer were down by 50 per cent than that in the previous year.

The demand for the traditional carriers fell significantly. As such, the demand for kerosene (aviation fuel) also fell, causing its price to follow suit. Airports were prepared to negotiate airport charges in a way that had been unheard of before. Aer Rianta, the leading Irish airport authority, launched advertising saying that it would provide free facilities to new airlines for three years. With such reductions in costs, the low-cost airlines could provide seats more cheaply than before and so experienced an outward shift of their supply curve, as shown in Figure 3.12.

However, at the same time, passengers became more wary of travelling in the air. This compounded the usual seasonal decrease in passenger numbers following the summer peak, causing the demand curve of the low-cost airlines to shift inwards, also shown in Figure 3.12.

The low-cost airlines managed to achieve their goal of keeping load figures high in the aftermath of the disaster by slashing fares. In fact, Ryanair responded by hiring more people and within just over a month easyJet announced its intentions to raise share capital to purchase European airport slots that the traditional airlines had discarded. As Figure 3.12 illustrates, such expansion was the result of the supply curve shifting further than the demand curve. It is likely that fares were reduced to such an extent that the profit margins were

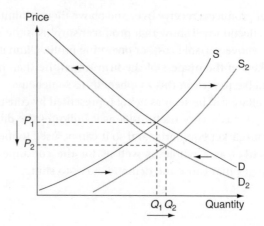

Figure 3.12 The Effect of 11 September on the Low-cost airlines

squeezed, which is shown in Figure 3.12 by the producer surplus, or operating profits, being reduced. However, the consumers, faced with lower fares and a larger range of routes, benefited as shown by the increased consumer surplus.

A longer-term effect of the atrocity was, and is, an increased demand for low-cost air travel from businesses which sought to cut expenses in fear of a global economic downturn. The low-cost airlines have gone from strength to strength, taking advantage of the necessary restructuring of the traditional airlines.

3.8 | The problem of rural demand

The provision of public transport services to satisfy the demand in rural areas has always been problematic. Such services have high costs, particularly the costs of infrastructure construction, but low revenues due to low load-factors. They are, in a word, *uneconomic*. However, the demand for these services is very real, as rural populations require them to get to work, to do their shopping, to access schools and health centres, and for social reasons.

This problem has worsened in recent times, for four main reasons. First, greater car usage has meant that the demand for public transport services has declined, but has not been eliminated. The result is that the load-factors of any services are now even less economical than before. This result has itself been worsened by the second reason, namely the growth of urban conurbations and the subsequent decline of rural populations. Thirdly, public services (such as libraries, cinemas and post offices) have increasingly been concentrated in urban centres, meaning that those residents of rural communities without their own means of transport increasingly require transport to get to them. Finally, an ageing population has meant that there are increasing numbers of elderly people who are more reliant on public transport rather than on walking or using bicycles. The last two of these reasons compound the problem caused by the first two: there are fewer people using public transport, but those that are using it are now more reliant upon it.

The provision of rural transport services is a real conundrum for policy-makers. Is it justifiable to provide such uneconomic services when the required public investment could be used to a greater welfare effect elsewhere? Are there any alternatives? Electoral support for such services has always been strong; perhaps because of a nostalgic desire to sustain traditional rural villages, or out of empathy for the populations that inhabit rural areas. The mobility of rural populations, and their ability to access other public services, is important; and without public transport services to rural areas, there is the potential that such areas would go to ruin, to the detriment of society as a whole. Perhaps these external benefits (see Section 9.1) do justify their provision. Either way, it is a problem that is not going away and so needs solutions. Nash (1982) has suggested the use of part-time and voluntary labour; and smaller vehicles, enabling greater flexibility, higher speeds, and services more specifically tailored to the needs of individual communities (smaller vehicles being able to access routes prohibitive to larger vehicles).

Markets, Costs and 4 Revenues

4.1 | Important definitions

There are four things that are absolutely necessary for any production to occur. These are called the *factors of production*.

■ *Land*. This refers to all the natural raw materials that are required for production, for example coal and water. It is not just physical land.
■ *Labour*. This denotes the workers that are required for production.
■ *Capital*. This includes all the man-made resources required for production, for example a robotic arm or a computer system. A sub-component of this factor is financial capital: the investment necessary for production to occur.
■ *Entrepreneurship*. This, or *enterprise* as it is also known, is the risk-taking involved in establishing a production process. It can be seen as the organisation of the other factors.

All production (whether it is of physical goods such as cars and motorbikes, or of services such as buses and trains) requires all four of these factors to be present in some form. Table 4.1 illustrates this with examples from the provision of bus services.

Two other important definitions at this stage are to do with the time horizon that is being analysed. The *short run* is defined as the period of time in which at least one of the factors of production is fixed. Usually it is the factor of land which is most likely to be fixed due to the element of the actual physical land involved, which is often much more difficult to expand than the other factors, such as the number of workers or equipment.

The *long run*, on the other hand, is the time period in which all of the factors of production are variable. If a producer wants to increase its floor space then it can do so freely in the long run, as it can with the other factors also.

Table 4.1 The factors of production in bus provision

Factor of production	Examples from bus provision
Land	Petrol, water and the physical land of the bus depot
Labour	Drivers, maintenance engineers and office staff
Capital	Buses, bus stops and office equipment
Entrepreneurship	Risk taking, investment and the organisation of the other factors

4.2 | Classification of costs according to their nature

A *cost* is something that a producer has to pay in order to remain in operation. There are three general types of costs.

4.2.1 Fixed costs

Fixed costs (FC) are costs that are the same irrespective of the level of output that is produced. A producer has to pay them even if zero units are produced. For example, a local road-haulage company will have to pay the same rent to lease the company head office, irrespective of whether it makes five or ten deliveries a day.

4.2.2 Variable costs

Variable costs (VC) are costs that change as the level of output changes. For example, that same road-haulage company will see an increase in fuel costs if the number of deliveries doubles. Also, it will need more land if it needs to operate more vehicles so, unlike for the head office, operational land costs will typically be variable.

4.2.3 Semi-variable costs

Semi-variable costs (SVC) are costs that are fixed over a certain range of output, but then change once the upper limit of that range is reached. They are then likely to be fixed again for another range of output, until another limit is reached. For example, the road-haulage company may be able to make up to ten deliveries a day using three drivers, but to then make an eleventh delivery it may need to employ another driver. In this way the labour cost was fixed up until ten deliveries a day and then *jumped* to a new rate for additional deliveries.

These different types of cost are illustrated in Figure 4.1:

The cost structures of the main modes of transport are shown in Table 4.2. It is assumed that the production from each is the passenger-distance travelled. A characteristic that is common across all of them is the large fixed costs involved.

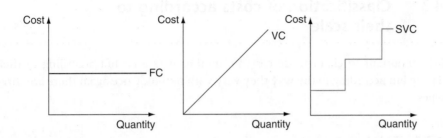

Figure 4.1 The type of costs

Table 4.2 The cost structures of the main modes of transport

	Fixed costs	*Variable costs*	*Semi-variable costs*
Car	▪ Capital outlay ▪ Insurance ▪ Road tax ▪ Depreciation	▪ Petrol ▪ Oil ▪ Wear and tear	▪ Component parts such as tyres and batteries
Train	▪ Capital outlay ▪ Track costs ▪ Insurance ▪ Basic administrative charges	▪ Fuel ▪ Wear and tear	▪ Components ▪ Labour costs
Aeroplane	▪ Capital outlay ▪ Insurance ▪ Basic administrative charges	▪ Fuel ▪ Wear and tear ▪ Landing fees ▪ In-flight provisions ▪ Air passenger duty (UK)	▪ Components ▪ Labour costs
Bus	▪ Capital outlay ▪ Insurance ▪ Basic administrative charges	▪ Fuel ▪ Wear and tear ▪ Licences	▪ Components ▪ Labour costs
Sea	▪ Capital outlay ▪ Insurance ▪ Basic administrative charges	▪ Fuel ▪ Wear and tear ▪ Harbour fees ▪ In-voyage provisions	▪ Components ▪ Labour costs

4.3 | Classification of costs according to their scale

It is important to characterise costs in another way also: not according to their nature but according to the way they vary with output. Once again there are three types.

4.3.1 Total cost

Total cost (TC) is the figure that is arrived at when all of the costs are added up.

$$TC = FC + VC + SVC$$

4.3.2 Average cost

Average cost (AC) is the cost for each unit of output produced. It is calculated, very simply, by dividing total cost by the quantity produced:

$$AC = \frac{TC}{Q}$$

As this is the average total cost, it comprises both the fixed costs and the variable costs. Identifying this is important in order to understand how average cost changes with output. It is also possible to calculate average fixed cost (AFC) and average variable cost (AVC) independently.

4.3.2.1 Average costs in the short run

In the short run, as output increases, average fixed cost falls. This is because the fixed costs are dispersed over a greater quantity of output. Figure 4.2 illustrates this phenomenon.

As can be seen, if the producer doubles its output to 200 units, total cost increases to £4000 but average cost falls to £20. This reduction in average cost occurs purely because the fixed cost has been spread out over double the output as before.

This effect is initially strong, but as output increases further there will be smaller reductions in average cost as the fixed costs cannot be significantly more dispersed. In the case above, the producer increasing output to 300 units would cause total

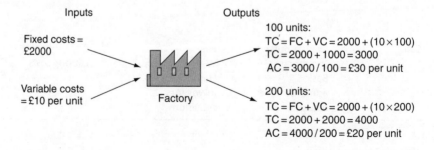

Figure 4.2 The reduction of the average fixed costs

Inputs

Fixed costs = £2000

Variable costs = £10 per unit

Factory

Outputs

100 units:
TC = FC + VC = 2000 + (10 × 100)
TC = 2000 + 1000 = 3000
AC = 3000 / 100 = £30 per unit

200 units:
TC = FC + VC = 2000 + (10 × 200)
TC = 2000 + 2000 = 4000
AC = 4000 / 200 = £20 per unit

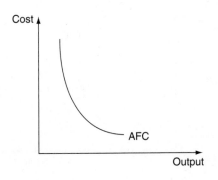

cost to increase to £5000, but average cost to fall to £16.67: a £3.33 reduction compared to the £10 reduction due to the previous increase of 100 units of output.

This leads to the conclusion that the average fixed costs will fall as output increases, but at a continually slowing rate. This is illustrated by the short run average fixed cost curve in Figure 4.3.

Variable costs respond differently to changes in output. When a producer is producing zero units of output, there will be zero variable costs. To produce one unit of output requires a certain amount to be spent on raw materials, labour and the like, and so variable costs will increase. To produce a second unit of output, the producer needs to incur a further increase in variable cost. This could be a doubling of variable cost, which would simply keep average variable cost constant; or, if the producer is able to become more efficient, it could be less than this and so average variable cost would decline.

Eventually, average variable cost is likely to rise as output increases further, because one of the factors of production is fixed in the short run. The other factors of production are increased in order to expand output, but the fixed factor increasingly reduces the productive effect they have. This can be illuminated by assuming that the producer in Figure 4.3 is able to increase its labour and capital freely, but its land is fixed in the short run (a reasonable assumption to make). Initially, the producer can increase its output by increasing the two variable factors; the land does not hinder it at all. However, once the factory floor is full, additional capital and labourers actually begin to get in the way of existing workers and their machines, causing overall efficiency to fall. The consequence of this is that additional units of capital and workers generate a diminishing increase in output. Or, conversely, in order for the producer to continue to increase its output by a constant amount, it will need to spend an increasing amount on additional capital and labour to do so, hence leading to increasing average costs.

The result of this effect is that short run average variable cost is likely to rise as output rises. This is illustrated by the short run average variable cost curve in Figure 4.4.

As output initially increases for a producer, the effect of decreasing average fixed cost dominates; but as output increases further, this effect continually weakens and that of increasing average variable cost becomes stronger. These two effects

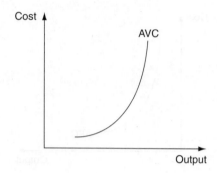

Figure 4.4 The short run average variable cost curve

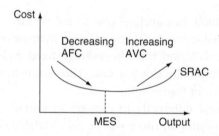

Figure 4.5 The short run average cost curve

combined cause the short run average cost (SRAC) curve to be of a U-shape, as shown in Figure 4.5. The bottom of the curve is where the producer is *productively efficient*: where it is producing at minimum average cost. In cases where there is actually a range of outputs at which the producer is productively efficient (the average cost curve has a flat base to it), the lowest output on the flat section of the curve is known as the *minimum efficient scale* (MES), as it is the minimum output of productive efficiency for the producer.

In the short run, a producer is anchored to its short run average cost curve by the fixed factor of production. The producer is only able to determine where upon the curve it operates. However, in the long run, a producer is able to change all of its factors of production, allowing it to switch onto a whole new short run average cost curve. The way in which the short run average cost curves lie forms the long run average cost curve: the long run average cost curve envelops the short run curves. This is known as the *envelope theorem*.

4.3.2.2 Average costs in the long run

The long run average cost (LRAC) curve is also likely to be U-shaped, with the short run curves lying inside it, as illustrated in Figure 4.6. The long run average cost curve has this shape not because of the effects of decreasing average fixed costs and then increasing average variable costs, but because of *economies and diseconomies of scale*. These are simply defined, respectively, as reducing and increasing long run average costs as a result of increasing output. They are long run effects because it is necessary that all the factors of production are variable for them to occur.

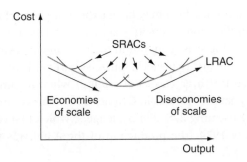

Figure 4.6 The long run average cost curve

4.3.2.3 Economies and diseconomies of scale

There are a number of possible causes of economies of scale.

■ *Technical economies of scale*. It is likely that a producer will be able to use larger, more efficient capital as its output increases, thereby reducing the average cost of each unit produced. This includes the capacity to use larger, more efficient transportation. A tanker containing 2000 gallons of liquid does not cost as much to produce as do two tankers each containing 1000 gallons, and so the cost per gallon falls as a result of using the larger tanker. Part of the reason for this is that it is not necessary to double the material used in the tanker in order to double the amount that it can contain. In effect, two ends of the tankers are not required to construct the larger one. This is illustrated in Figure 4.7, where the two shaded ends are not required when doubling the volume of the container, thereby saving material and expense. The volume of a container increases more rapidly than its surface area, whilst material costs and frictional losses are related directly to surface area. Furthermore, in this example, only

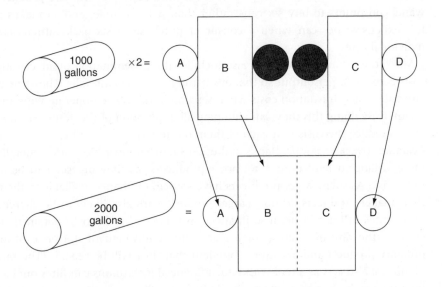

Figure 4.7 Technical economies of scale

one engine is required, which may have to be more powerful, but will be more economical than two smaller engines. Similar considerations have contributed to the ever-increasing size of aircraft in high-volume markets. The Airbus 380, for example, was the first twin-deck, four-aisle airliner (carrying 525 passengers when configured for three classes of seating) when it came into commercial operation for Singapore Airlines in October 2007. This compares to the A300, a twin-aisle aircraft seating 228–254 passengers, which first entered commercial operation in May 1974 (the production of the A300 was terminated in July 2007).

Another source of technical economies of scale for public utilities, including some transport services, is the properties of networks. Wherever services are delivered over a network of wires, pipes or transport routes the total costs of delivering a given standard of service (including reliability and variety) will often rise less rapidly than the number of customers served.

Technical economies of scale are purely technological, and are fundamental and unavoidable. The following additional forms of economies of scale are less fundamental and, in some cases, their existence is controversial.

- *Managerial economies of scale*. As a producer expands its output and reputation, it is likely to be more able to headhunt and employ the very best management and employees. These will demand higher individual remuneration, but if the increased efficiency they bring allows fewer workers to be employed, they can potentially lead to a reduction in average cost.

- *Marketing economies of scale*. Increasing output enables a producer to purchase its raw materials in bulk, giving it more bargaining power with its suppliers. As the suppliers will be keen to maintain dealings with a growing producer, they will be willing to enter negotiations to lower the price of their supplies, thereby causing average cost for the producer to fall. This is the same effect as that of buying a six-pack drink from a supermarket. The producer wants consumers to buy six cans rather than just a couple, and so makes it less expensive per can when a consumer purchases a six-pack rather than individual cans.

  Marketing economies of scale also includes the dissemination of advertising costs across a larger output so that advertising costs per unit falls. The same is also true of administration costs when separate producers co-operate with one another. By doing this they can eliminate all duplication of the administration and so reduce the costs that each of them has to pay.

- *Financial economies of scale*. Banks and other financial institutions are generally more willing to lend money to larger producers, as they are seen to be at lower risk. As such, larger producers have sources of finance available to them that smaller producers do not. Larger producers are also likely to be charged lower rates of interest because financial institutions are keen to obtain their custom (the rate of interest for a loan is the equivalent of the price of an ordinary product) and are more confident that they will be repaid. (The rate of interest also acts as a tool with which financial institutions can filter out bad investments: high risk producers would be less willing to accept higher rates of interest if they are aware that they may cause them repayment problems in the future.) Lower interest repayments mean that larger producers, with greater output, are likely to have lower average costs than smaller producers, which have to pay much more back to their creditors.

All of these effects cause long run average cost to fall as output increases, but gradually their strength will diminish and diseconomies of scale will begin to dominate, pulling long run average cost back up. Once again there are a number of possible causes of this.

- *Red-tape.* As a producer expands, the volume of paperwork and administration inevitably increases as it becomes more difficult to co-ordinate all of the different aspects of production. This increased red-tape makes the producer less efficient, as time is wasted completing forms and conducting checks, causing its average cost to rise.
- *Communication troubles.* The larger a producer becomes, the more difficult it is for the management to pass directions down the chain of command and to receive feedback from the workers beneath them. The first of these can lead to instructions not being carried out or being distorted; and the second can cause the management to become less responsive to the labour force, leading to the dissatisfaction and de-motivation of the workers. Both of these can again cause larger producers to see their average costs rise.

4.3.2.4   Economies of scope and density

Whereas economies of scale is the phenomenon of declining long run average cost as *output* increases, *economies of scope* is that of declining average cost as *network size* increases (it is not necessary for all of the factors of production to be fixed, and so it can be a short run phenomenon). As a producer organises its services over a greater number of routes and centres, it is likely to see, *ceteris paribus*, its long run average cost fall. This is because it is more able to engage in transhipment (also known as *consignment consolidation*), whereby it divides the journeys it makes into segments, merging as many of those segments as it can. For example, let us assume that a freight company is offering three transport services terminating in city A, but originating in cities B, C and D (the origin cities). It could simply arrange three completely separate vehicles to make three completely separate journeys, thereby fulfilling its obligations. Alternatively, it could organise three completely separate journeys from the origin cities to a fourth city (E) lying between the origin cities and city A. Once all three deliveries are made to city E, the cargo can be loaded onto a separate (larger) vehicle, which then makes a single journey to city A. The provider has to purchase a fourth (larger) vehicle to implement this strategy, thereby facing greater fixed costs. However, over time this investment will be more than recouped through lower variable costs generated by greater load-factors on its vehicles. The greater the proportion of the total distance travelled accounted for by the amalgamated service, the greater the variable cost savings.

Such a strategy can be used in both passenger and freight transport. Examples include the traditional organisation of the airlines, European shipping and the UK long-distance bus market (see Section 8.3.1). Britain's Royal Mail is another example, as it transports large consignments of post to single sorting offices in each area, from which the smaller final deliveries are then made.

The benefits of economies of scope are likely to diminish as the degree of transhipment increases. Greater transhipment necessarily requires more frequent loading and unloading of vehicles, increasingly offsetting the reductions in long run average cost. Greater transhipment also entails the use of increasingly circuitous routes, again offsetting the reductions in long run average cost. Finally, greater transhipment increases the time costs that consumers have to bear. There are less and less frequent services, as the products or passengers are increasingly required to remain at operation centres until the full load for the next stage of the journey has arrived and is loaded onto the vehicle. As time is such an important determinant of demand (see Sections 3.2 and 4.4), increasing time costs will gradually reduce demand, eroding the benefits of economies of scale.

It is also likely that there will be external limits to the degree of transhipment that is possible. These take two forms: legal and physical. There is often legislation stipulating the maximum loads allowed in vehicles, potentially constraining the degree of transhipment possible. There are also limits to the size of vehicles imposed by the available infrastructure: the width of roads, the height of bridges and the length of runways, to name a few.

Another phenomenon playing a part in the cost benefits enjoyed through transhipment is that of *economies of density*. This is where average costs are reduced as *existing capital is used more intensively*. In a similar manner to economies of scale, as the given capital is used more intensively, the fixed costs involved can be dispersed more across consumers. The subtle difference between economies of scale and economies of density is that the latter assumes that the capital is fixed; whereas in the former, increasing the capital stock is a way of reaping the economies. As capital is fixed in economies of density, it is a short run phenomenon.

4.3.3 Marginal cost

Marginal cost (MC) is the additional total cost incurred by producing one additional unit of output. For example, if the total cost of producing 1504 units of output is £2300 and if the total cost of producing 1505 units of output is £2320, then the marginal cost of producing the 1505th unit is £20.

Marginal cost has a definite relationship with average cost. If average cost is falling, marginal cost must be lower than average cost. This is because the only way to reduce an average is to add numbers that are less than it.

Figures 4.5 and 4.6 show that the average cost curve in both the short and the long run initially slope downwards, but that this slope gradually flattens out as the respective effects of reducing average fixed cost, and of economies of scale, weaken. Marginal cost must be lower than average cost in these ranges of output, but the difference between them must be declining (as the reduction in average cost slows down, marginal cost must be decreasingly less than the average).

The opposite is true if average cost is rising. In this case, marginal cost must be greater than average cost, because the way to increase an average is to add numbers which are greater than it. Figures 4.5 and 4.6 show that after the minimum point of the average cost curves, average cost begins to rise at an increasingly rapid rate. Marginal cost must be greater than average cost for this range of output, and it must be increasing to cause average cost to rise.

This analysis leads to the conclusion that at the minimum point of the short and long run average cost curves, marginal cost must be equal to average cost. This makes sense as the way to keep an average constant is to add numbers that are its equal.

Consequently, the marginal cost curve, in both the short and the long run, starts beneath the average cost curve and then increases at a quickening rate, passing through the minimum point of the average cost curve. A very simple example of this is displayed in Figure 4.8, where there is also a numerical example showing the relationship.

It is often assumed that marginal cost must be equal to average cost for the first unit of output produced, and so the curves should originate at the same point.

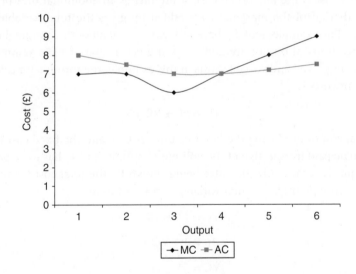

Output	TC	MC	AC
0	1	0	0
1	8	7	8
2	15	7	7.5
3	21	6	7
4	28	7	7
5	36	8	7.2
6	45	9	7.5

Figure 4.8
The MC/AC relationship

However, this is not the case because the fixed costs are paid to get the producer established, even if zero units of output are produced. Consequently, the fixed costs are theoretically shown on a cost diagram as being the marginal cost of producing zero units. The marginal cost of the first unit of output produced is simply the variable cost incurred as a result of producing this unit, which is likely to be lower than the average cost, as the latter also includes the fixed costs that have already been paid.

If one were to plot the average variable cost curve (instead of the average total cost curve which has been analysed above), it would originate at the same point as the marginal cost curve, because average variable cost must be equal to marginal cost for the first unit. This would complicate the analysis that follows and so is ignored for simplicity. Therefore, Figure 4.8 shows that the average cost curve is greater than the marginal cost curve for the first unit. There is also a gap left between the vertical axis and both cost curves in order to indicate that it is not appropriate to talk about the marginal cost of the 0th unit and that the average cost for this unit is 0 by definition.

4.3.3.1   Marginal cost and the supply curve

As marginal cost is the additional cost of producing an additional unit of output, it follows that all of the marginal costs added up gives the total variable cost of production. For example, looking back at Figure 4.8, if all of the marginal costs for the first five units of output are added up, it gives a total of £35. Assuming that there exist only fixed and variable costs in this example, the formula for calculating the different costs is

$$TC = FC + VC$$

The total cost of producing the first five units is £36, and the fixed cost (the cost that has to be paid irrespective of the volume of output, and so has to be paid even when output is zero) is £1, the latter being shown by the total cost for zero units being £1. Consequently, the total variable cost is as follows.

$$TC = FC + VC$$

$$36 = 1 + VC$$

$$VC = 35$$

This is the £35 given by totalling the marginal costs up to that level of output.

An alternative way of saying this is that the area underneath the marginal cost curve up until a certain level of output is the variable cost of producing those certain units of output. This is shown in Figure 4.9.

In the short run, a producer will be willing to produce a level of output at which the price covers at least the variable costs; or in other words, where price is at least equal to marginal cost. Consequently, the marginal cost curve is also the supply curve, showing the level of output that suppliers are willing to produce and supply to the market at every given price.

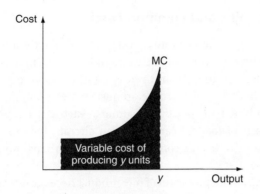

Figure 4.9 The MC curve showing variable costs

4.4 | Other types of cost important in transport economics

In addition to the categories of costs outlined above, there are five other types of cost that are important in the study of transport economics. These are outlined here.

4.4.1 Opportunity cost

Resources have multiple potential uses. For example, a corridor of physical land could be used, amongst a whole array of other alternatives, for a new railway line or a new motorway. Public financial capital could be used to fund the construction of a new airport terminal or further maintenance of the rail network. Time, an important but often-forsaken resource, could be used at work or to make a journey for leisure purposes.

Opportunity cost is simply the second-best alternative forgone as a result of making an economic decision. In the first example outlined above, if it is decided that the corridor of land should be used in the construction of a new motorway, the opportunity cost is the railway line that could have been located there (assuming that it was the second-best alternative). The opportunity to construct the railway line has been lost. Opportunity cost is an important concept in transport economics, and it is one to which we return at numerous stages throughout this text.

4.4.2 Time costs

Transport always takes time, a cost which is often at the forefront of users' minds when they make transport decisions. As noted in Section 3.2, passengers are concerned about the duration of journeys because it reduces their working or leisure time; and manufacturers are similarly concerned because the longer a journey takes, the greater the inventory cost. *Time costs*, simply the amounts of time involved, are such an important consideration that they often sway the mode of transport chosen by users, who are often willing to pay relatively significant sums to reduce the time burden.

4.4.3 Specific, joint and common costs

Across many sectors of the economy, costs can be directly attributed to specific consumers. In health care, the cost of treatment for sports injuries can be attributed to the sportspeople requiring them. In housing, the cost of decorating a property can be attributed to the owners. These are just two examples of *specific costs*: costs which can be attributed to specific consumers. Such costs exist in the transport sector also: the costs of loading cargo onto an aircraft, for example. However, in the transport sector, joint and common costs are perhaps more prolific than in other sectors.

Joint costs arise when the provision of one product necessarily causes the provision of a second product. A typical example is that of return trips. The provision of an outward journey necessarily creates the provision of a return journey as well. The cost of the round trip is the joint cost. As true joint costs (such as this) are generated in fixed proportions, there can be no variability in costs, making it impossible to specify the cost of one product when only the combined cost is known. Consequently, it is not possible to perfectly attribute joint costs to specific consumers, making pricing strategies more complicated.

Common costs are those shared amongst different consumers but in unknown proportions, arising when a product is provided for a range of consumers. For example, a road is used by the drivers of cars, buses and freight vehicles (among others). It is possible to attribute certain components of the overall cost of road provision, wear and tear of the road surface being largely related to axle-loading for instance, but not all. How should the costs of lighting, hedge-cutting and road-marking be allocated? Similarly to joint costs, common costs make pricing strategies more complicated. In fact, the existence of such costs contributes to the explanation as to why road networks are usually provided by national governments.

4.5 | Classification of revenue

A second important consideration of producers, and therefore a second part of the theories of the firm, is that of *revenue*. Revenue is simply the money that flows into a business from consumers purchasing its products and services. As with costs, revenue can be classified according to its magnitude; and also similar to costs, there are three different ways of looking at it.

4.5.1 Total revenue

Total revenue (TR) is the total amount of money that flows to a producer as a result of consumers purchasing its products or services. Assuming that a producer will sell its products or services to all consumers at an equal price (P), total revenue is simply this price multiplied by the number of units sold (or the quantity, Q). For example, if a taxi firm had 200 customers, each making separate journeys from a city centre to a railway station, and if the price charged for one of those journeys was £5, the total revenue received by the taxi firm would be £1000:

$$TR = P \times Q$$

$$TR = 5 \times 200$$

$$TR = £1\,000$$

It is important to note that this is not profit, because it has not taken any account of the costs that the producer has to pay. This is simply the revenue. Profit will be dealt with in Section 4.6.

The total revenue curve is illustrated in Figure 4.10. It takes on an inverted-U shape for the reasons explained below.

4.5.2 Average revenue

Average revenue (AR) is the revenue for every unit produced and is calculated by dividing the total revenue by the quantity produced:

$$AR = \frac{TR}{Q}$$

If a producer sells all of its products at a constant price, the average revenue will simply be equal to the price.

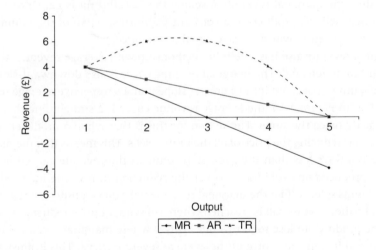

Output	MR	AR	TR
0	0	0	0
1	4	4	4
2	2	3	6
3	0	2	6
4	-2	1	4
5	-4	0	0

Figure 4.10 The TR/MR/AR relationship

The law of demand suggests that in order to increase the quantity demanded of a product without changing the product itself, or relying on or trying to influence any external factors, it is necessary to reduce its price and therefore its average revenue as well. This leads to the average revenue curve being downward-sloping in revenue–output space, as shown in Figure 4.10.

4.5.2.1 *Average revenue and the demand curve*

The average revenue curve shows the average revenue earned at each level of output. As a producer will usually charge the same price for each unit of output, the average revenue can be seen to be the price that the producer sets. Consequently, the average revenue curve shows the relationship between price and output, which is exactly the same as the demand curve. The difference is that the average revenue curve is looking at the relationship from the production side and the demand curve is looking at it from the consumption side.

4.5.3 Marginal revenue

Marginal revenue (MR) is the extra total revenue that is earned by producing and selling one extra unit of output. For example, if the total revenue of selling 3211 units of output is £6422 and if the total revenue of selling 3212 units of output is £6424, then the marginal revenue of selling the 3212th unit is £2. Once again, if the producer sells its products at a constant price irrespective of the volume sold the marginal revenue will simply be equal to the price.

Marginal revenue also has a definite relationship with average revenue, which is important to understand. The marginal revenue curve is also downward-sloping in revenue–output space, but it has a greater slope than its respective average revenue curve: if, as in Figure 4.10, the average revenue curve is a straight line then it will have exactly twice the slope. The reason for this is that when a producer reduces the price, it is reducing the price of all the units it sells. This means that the marginal revenue is always less than the average revenue as the revenue earned from the last unit produced and sold has to cover the reduction in revenue incurred on all previous units sold. At first the marginal revenue will still be positive, but as price is reduced further a point will be reached where subsequent price reductions actually cause the producer to lose total revenue. This is where marginal revenue becomes negative and it is in the centre of the average revenue curve. This is illustrated in Figure 4.10.

For simplicity the average revenue curve has been drawn as a straight-line curve, with a one-to-one proportional relationship between average revenue and output. The total revenue for each of the units has been calculated by multiplying the new output by the new price (all of the lower units will have been reduced as well) and these figures, along with the marginal revenue for each level of output, have been displayed in Table 4.10. The point at which the marginal revenue turns negative is at an output of 3, which is in the centre of the average revenue curve that starts at an output of 1. This causes the total revenue curve to have an inverted-U shape as it rises with output at first but at a decreasing rate until the marginal revenue turns negative at which point it starts falling but at an increasing rate thereafter.

There is a useful rule for calculating marginal revenue from the price elasticity of demand, which works out whether or not the demand curve is a straight line:

$$\text{Marginal revenue} = \text{price} \times (1 + 1/\text{elasticity})$$

Suppose you are selling flights from London to New York, the current fare is £200 and the elasticity is −2 (these tickets are elastic with respect to price − perhaps being for leisure travellers). Then the rule says that the extra revenue you would get by reducing the price just enough to sell one more ticket is 200 × (1 + (1/−2))=£100. You get nearly £200 from the extra ticket but lose £100 from having to reduce the price on all the tickets you would have sold anyway.

4.6 | Profit maximisation and alternative objectives

Now that the building blocks of the theories of the firm have been outlined, it is possible to analyse the theories themselves (which is done in the subsequent chapters). However, before proceeding to these it is necessary to consider the objectives of producers.

In neoclassical economics, it is assumed that producers aim to maximise their profits. In order to do this it is necessary for them to equate their marginal cost with their marginal revenue, which is known as the *profit-maximising condition*. Looking at Figures 4.8 and 4.10, it is possible to observe why. At lower quantities of output, the marginal revenue curve will be greater than the marginal cost curve and so producers should produce those units as they earn a profit. However, as the two curves are gradually converging, the difference between the two diminishes, meaning that marginal profit falls as output increases. Marginal profit remains positive until the two curves cross, though, and so producers should produce all of these units as they all contribute additional profit, even if the additional profit is less for each additional unit of output produced and sold. Producers should not produce more than the level of output at which marginal revenue is equal to marginal cost because that would be moving into the section of the diagram where marginal revenue is less than marginal cost, meaning that marginal profit is negative. If produced, these units of output would reduce total profit. Consequently, to maximise total profit producers should produce all the units of output up to, and including, the unit at which marginal revenue is equal to marginal cost, but no more.

It is generally assumed that this is the objective that producers have because it is the one that seems to most comprehensively resemble actual business practice. In the transport sector there are producers ranging from small private limited companies (such as taxi firms), through medium-sized public limited companies (such as road-haulage companies), to exceptionally large multinational companies (such as the largest airlines). Each of these business types are driven, at least partly, to achieve profit. The small private limited companies need to generate profit in order to maintain operations. The medium-sized, and multinational, public limited companies need to generate profit in order to return dividend payments to their shareholders, who discipline organisations with the threat of accepting takeover bids. In this way, profit maximisation can be taken to be a sound assumption for the theories that follow.

The assumption of profit maximisation is particularly strong in the case of *entrepreneurial capitalism*, which was the prevailing business environment during the time of the classical economists. In this paradigm, the owners of businesses are the ones to make the strategic decisions (they are the traditional *producers*). Griffiths and Wall (2000) explain that since the Second World War, there have been numerous significant changes to the organisation of producers which have undermined the strength of the profit-maximisation objective and which have made it difficult to identify who exactly the *producers* are. (As such, in the remainder of this section, the term *business* is used broadly to represent the productive unit, leaving the human decision-maker to one side.) First, the nature of *ownership* has changed with the emergence of large public limited companies, owned by numerous shareholders with limited liability. Secondly, the nature of *control* has changed as large numbers of shareholders cannot feasibly direct the activities of a business on a daily basis, and so have had to appoint boards of directors to fulfil this function. These first two changes mean that there is now a *divorce of ownership and control*, which did not exist in earlier times. This paradigm is that of *managerial capitalism*. Thirdly, organisational structures have become more complicated and hierarchical, causing co-ordination difficulties for top management. Fourthly, as businesses have grown in size, there is now much greater potential for conflict between functional areas and stakeholders (individuals or groups with an interest in how a business is run). Finally, in the modern business environment it is simply not possible for those in control of businesses to have access to all the information that they may require, even with the development of the Internet. Consequently, whereas the classical economists witnessed businesses that were owned and strongly directed by individuals (or small partnerships of entrepreneurs) with unlimited liability, there is now the potential for directors to pursue different objectives to the owners of their businesses; for directors to have their objectives constrained by the organisational structures of their businesses or the conflicts that exist between stakeholders within them; and for directors simply not to have access to the information that they require to pursue profit maximisation.

The last of these potentialities has been the particular focus of criticism of the neoclassical assumption of profit maximisation, especially from the Austrian school of economic thought. Anderson and Ross (2005) explain that managers of businesses simply cannot be certain of their marginal cost and marginal revenue curves. In fact, even if they could be correctly constructed, they cannot be plotted in the same cost–quantity space because they do not exist simultaneously. Generally, businesses pay their costs before they sell their produce, but there are cases where contracts of purchase are agreed before production occurs. Either way, businesses have to make their decisions based on their perceptions of the future, which are always going to be imperfect. As a result of the effects of time and uncertainty, it is simply not feasible for managers to equate marginal cost with marginal revenue. This has no real practical application.

It is because of these changes in the organisation of businesses, and the realisation that the neoclassical assumption simply is not adequate in the real world, that relatively new theories of business objectives have been developed. On the one hand, these new theories can be viewed as alternative end-objectives; but on the other, they can be viewed as being practical and realistic objectives that managers can focus on when striving for profit maximisation as the end result. This is still a lively debate in certain quarters of the economics profession, as illustrated by the very public split resulting from it in the economics department at Notre Dame University (Anderson and Ross, 2005).

4.6.1 Revenue maximisation

This theory was developed by William Baumol (1959). It is argued that managers will aim to maximise the sales revenue of their businesses. There are numerous potential motivating reasons for this.

- Consumers may view a business with falling revenue in a negative light, leading to further reductions in sales and the emergence of a vicious cycle effect.
- Financial institutions may be more reluctant to lend to a business experiencing a contraction in revenue because of concern about the potentiality of the business not being able to repay any loans that are granted. This will make it more difficult for managers to raise financial capital, potentially restricting opportunities for expansion; and it is likely to mean that any loans that are granted will involve higher rates of interest, increasing average cost.
- Related suppliers may be less willing to work, and develop contracts, with a business with falling revenue as it increases the uncertainty and risk involved in any agreements.
- Falling revenues may lead to a contraction in the number of staff employed by a business, which may include the number of managerial positions.
- Executive salaries and other non-pecuniary benefits may be related to the revenue of a business.

Whereas the profit-maximising condition is to equate marginal cost with marginal revenue, the sales revenue condition is to produce the level of output at which marginal revenue is equal to zero. Units of output below this have positive marginal revenues and so should be produced as they add to total revenue; whereas units in excess of this level have negative marginal revenues and so would detract from total revenue if they were produced (see Section 4.5.3).

In practice, revenue maximisation requires that a lower price is charged than if profit maximisation is the goal; or that sales and discounts are employed as a strategy for clearing stock. It also means that marketing is likely to be greater under sales revenue, as the aim is to sell more units of output even if it increases average cost to do so.

It is appreciated that, although the goal of managers may be to maximise revenue, it is likely that there would be a profit constraint to this. For example, to ensure the future growth of revenue it may be necessary for managers to secure a certain level of future investment. Such finance could be sourced internally, from retained profits, or externally, from financial institutions. Either way, a certain level of profit would be required; to attract external investment in the latter case.

4.6.2 Managerial utility maximisation

Williamson (1963) widened Baumol's model by introducing factors that managers would seek to optimise other than sales revenue. Williamson's model is based on the argument that managers seek to maximise their satisfaction (or utility) at work, which is determined by factors such as 'salary, security, power, status, prestige, [and] professional excellence' (Williamson, 1963); factors which are not necessarily of equal value or completely independent. Managers will prefer to spend money on these factors, which can be termed *managerial expenditure*, rather than trying to maximise profits. For example, managers may prefer to employ more subordinates as a wider personal span of control leads to greater prestige; or they may direct investment towards improved employee facilities over and above that necessary to optimise employee motivation as it too will lead to greater status within the workplace.

Williamson also appreciated that there would be a profit constraint involved. Future improvements in utility require finance which, as noted above, is dependent on a certain level of profit. As such, managerial utility will be maximised when the marginal utility achieved across all of the determinants is equal, given the profit constraint. In this case, utility could not be improved by further managerial expenditure because that would break the profit constraint, and it could not be improved by reallocating the existing managerial expenditure across the different determinants because the marginal utility from each is already equal.

Businesses in which this managerial utility maximisation is dominant will not be productively efficient as there is expenditure that is surplus to that necessary for production. They have a cushion of costs which can be trimmed should the market conditions turn unfavourable.

4.6.3 Growth maximisation

Robin Marris (1964) has taken more of a dynamic approach, claiming that managers focus on long-term considerations, namely the rate of growth of the business. In other words, it is not the current size of the business or department that matters, but rather the rate at which it is expanding. This is likely to be a key determinant of the power and status that a manager enjoys within the business. Owners also seek to judge how effective a manager is, so that their remuneration can be determined. Ideally, owners will want to evaluate such performance in terms of the contribution to overall profit levels. However, this is difficult to do and so the manager's contribution to the size of the activities of the business is often used as a proxy variable instead.

Managers are also concerned about the security of their positions, which can be jeopardised by the threat of hostile acquisitions. In order to protect themselves against such eventualities it is necessary for them to ensure that shareholders are content with their dividend payments. This establishes a trade-off between business growth and security. An increase in investment may be necessary to increase the rate of growth, but this is at the expense of the shareholders' dividends. At first, shareholders may be content with such sacrifices if they are convinced that they will lead to offsetting increases in the future stream of payments, but there will be a point at which they will disagree with similar decisions, leading to a reduction in the share value of the business and an increase in the likelihood of takeover. Managers will strive to maximise the growth rate subject to this share value constraint.

4.6.4 The behavioural theories

The classical theory of business objectives and the three alternatives outlined above are all based on the maximisation of a certain factor, albeit with a certain profit constraint. The behavioural theories have been developed using a different approach which seeks to explain business objectives by considering the organisational structure of businesses.

The first of these is that by Simon (1959), who appreciated that a business is actually a complex collection of different groups of stakeholders. Each of these groups will have different objectives. For example, the shareholders may simply want to see a good return on their investment and so will be looking for the business to maximise profit and so maximise dividend repayments. Employees, on the other hand, may want to maximise their salaries and improve the working conditions within the business. The overall objectives of a business are likely to be the result of interaction between these different groups, and so it is compromise rather than maximisation that is likely to dominate.

Simon claims that the overriding objective of a business is survival, and the specific practical objectives will be devised to satisfy each of the groups involved. This is known as *satisficing*. It is not to say that the resulting outcomes are necessarily different to those under the other theories, but rather that the process of achieving them will involve a repeating cycle of negotiation, objective-setting and satisfying, rather than the simple maximisation of a particular factor from the outset.

Cyert and March (1963) extended this analysis by suggesting that businesses are comprised of *coalitions*: groups of stakeholders that are in agreement about the objectives of the business. Such coalitions are not static, as individual stakeholders change their opinions based on the prevailing business environment. The coalitions within a business at one point of time engage in a process of bargaining which determines the objectives of the business. The dominance of the coalitions also changes over time, depending on the environment that the business finds itself in, and so business objectives are also continually changing. The role of managers is simply to set objectives that resolve the conflict between the different coalitions at a given moment in time, ensuring that no single coalition is wholly alienated as this would place the survival of the business in danger.

4.6.5 Wider, more altruistic objectives

The analysis up to this point has been focused on objectives that are solely for the benefit of those within businesses. However, there are cases of businesses that also exist for wider reasons. For example, some may seek to satisfy a public need, whereas others may hold environmental protection at the heart of their objectives, such as City Sprint (see below).

Many transport operators are not set up as for-profit organisations. They answer to a public authority such as local or central government, whose statutes require them to be operated *in the public interest*. They must do this subject to some constraints, most commonly some kind of restriction on their overall finances. Typically, this will include a maximum loss budgeted by the *parent* authority. Examples in the UK include some local authority bus and tram operators, the providers of the railway infrastructure (Network Rail) and all local and national roads. One of the interesting issues here is how to give an operational interpretation to the term *the public interest*, but it is clear that the determination of net revenue is as important to them as it is to a profit-maximising firm.

4.6.5.1 City Sprint

City Sprint is the UK's leading courier network, comprising 34 service centres that facilitate the provision of a local, national and international courier service to a customer base in excess of 13,000 diverse businesses. It was awarded the Best UK Courier Service of 2004 by the Institute for Transport Management, and had previously been given other awards including that of European Courier Company. City Sprint has a strong commitment to the environment as one of its stated objectives, in the pursuit of which it has achieved the following.

- It has made appropriate decisions regarding the composition of its 1200 strong fleet. In 2003, it introduced a number of Smart cars, one of which the Environmental Transport Association voted as its Car of the Year in 2002. Currently it has 15 such vehicles in operation; a number which it is seeking to expand. It also has the largest bicycle fleet in London, offering a *Mileage Savers Report* to customers, which outlines the number of litres of petrol saved by their use. Finally, in this respect, City Sprint has been testing a number of electric and petrol–electric hybrid vehicles with a view to introducing them to the fleet.
- It has developed a monthly emissions report, outlining the emissions of carbon dioxide that the organisation produces, with a commitment to identify processes to control and offset these.
- It has integrated recycling into its activities. City Sprint claims that the majority of its service centres currently recycle all office waste paper and printer cartridges, and the remaining centres are to be brought in line with this.

- It has adopted modes of communication to reduce the amount of waste paper and printer cartridges generated, namely the use of email and its website. In 2005, City Sprint launched a programme of contacting its customers in an effort to obtain email addresses that could then be used in the future. It is also looking to introduce a system of electronic invoicing.
- It has expressed a commitment to purchase and use paper that is either recycled or that is accredited as being from stock that adheres to environmental quality standards.
- It has employed a full-time environmental consultant to oversee and manage its environmental strategy. City Sprint has also expressed a commitment to developing and implementing a management system that is compliant with the ISO: 14001:2004 Environmental Management Systems standard.

4.6.6 Evidence and the importance of profit maximisation

Griffiths and Wall (2000) present the results of a comprehensive survey of studies into business objectives in practice. The overarching conclusion from this is that evidence exists for each of the different theories outlined above, which is perhaps to be expected considering the volume and diversity of business organisations.

The situation is perhaps made more complicated by the fact that, as explored in subsequent chapters, the transport sector is largely composed of relatively small businesses. Quince and Whittaker (2003) surveyed the directors of 153 small- to medium-sized businesses in the technology sector. The businesses surveyed had a median age of 18.5 years, turnover of £1.6 million, and workforce of 27. Three types of objectives were identified in the survey. First, the most strongly supported reason for establishing a business was that of autonomy and advancement, which includes income advancement and so supports the profit-maximisation objective. Secondly, the most strongly supported personal objective was to create a successful business, which again arguably supports the profit-maximisation objective. Objectives of personal satisfaction were less supported. Finally, the majority of respondents also supported the growth objective.

In reality, all businesses have a range of stated objectives and many will include those regarding wider ethical issues. They will all have a profit objective, though, in order to survive or to maintain the satisfaction of their stakeholders, which has been recognised in all of the theories above in some form. Consequently, although businesses do have other stated objectives it is the profit motive that lies at the heart of all entrepreneurship and so it is reasonable that economists take this as their assumed objective.

In fact, profit maximisation is growing in practical importance once again. Williamson (1975) traces the changes in organisational structure of businesses since the 1920s, claiming that there has been a shift from unitary to multidivisional structures. The first of these is the U-form structure, where a business has a single discreet structure, with long chains of command from top management which seeks to maintain control of the whole organisation. The second is the M-form structure, where a business is actually a composite of a number of smaller divisions, each controlled by a separate manager. In this latter form, top management does not attempt to exercise control over the whole organisation, instead focusing their efforts on simply monitoring divisional performance. Smaller divisions effectively reduce the pressures underpinning the behavioural theories and as those divisions achieving the most rapid growth in profit can be allocated additional resources, this structure also helps to overcome much of the non-profit-orientated behaviour of top management in traditionally structured businesses. This shift is relevant in the transport sector as it was General Motors that pioneered the innovation in the 1920s and it has since been copied by companies such as London Transport.

It is clear that the neoclassical formulation of managers equating marginal cost with marginal revenue is not realistic in the business world, but as a model it does usefully predict events. This is arguably the most important judgement regarding an economic model and has become known as the *Friedman (1953) thesis*. Also, although profit maximisation is not the sole important objective that exists among businesses, it is the one single objective that will optimise the effectiveness of the analysis to follow and focusing on this one objective will make that analysis as parsimonious as possible.

4.7 Market structures

The next five chapters are devoted to analysing the various market structures using the theoretical tools that have been outlined in this chapter, and then applying them to the transport sector of the European Union. There are four traditional structures that form a *spectrum of competition*. *Perfect competition* lies at the competitive extreme of this spectrum and *pure monopoly* lies at the non-competitive extreme. In between these there are the structures of *monopolistic competition* and *oligopoly* that appear on the spectrum as illustrated in Figure 4.11. There are then two more recently analysed structures, namely those of *natural monopolies* and *contestable markets*, which do not really fit in this spectrum but which are nevertheless crucial to a full understanding of the transport sector.

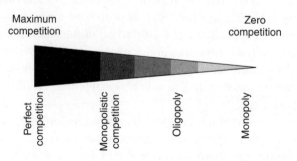

Figure 4.11 The Spectrum of competition

Competition and 5 Contestability

5.1 | The assumptions and the model

Perfect competition is the market structure that is represented by the simple demand and supply analysis in Section 3.5, and it forms the basis of free market economics. It is based on a number of strict assumptions (as in Chapter 3, the word *product* shall be used to represent both goods and services).

■ There are an uncountable number of small producers and consumers. As such, each accounts for such a small part of the market that they have absolutely no influence on the market price. They simply have to accept the price that is set. They are known as *price takers*.

■ All of the products supplied to the market are completely homogenous; that is, they are the same in all respects.

■ There is completely free entry to and exit from the market for the producers. In other words, there are no barriers to entry or exit.

■ There is perfect information within the market. This means that at all times, all of the consumers and producers are fully aware of what the others are doing within the market.

■ There is a free movement of products so their supply is responsive to market forces.

The market structure can be represented by the diagrams in Figure 5.1.

For perfect competition, as there are numerous producers and consumers, there are both a market diagram (Panel A) and then a diagram that represents an individual business (Panel B).

As noted above, the producers and consumers are so numerous that none of them has any market power. Consequently, the price is purely determined by the market: by the interaction of supply and demand. This means that the market price will be at the level that eliminates any excesses in the market (see Section 3.5), which is denoted by P_1 in Figure 5.1. This is then the price that all of the individual producers have to accept, as shown in Panel B.

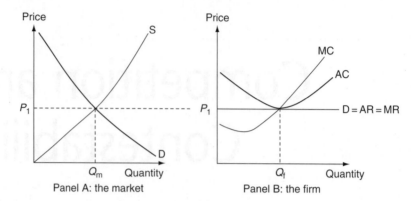

Figure 5.1
Perfect
competition

The reason that the demand curve for an individual business is horizontal is that it is perfectly price elastic. As all of the products in the market are homogenous, consumers are indifferent as to which producer supplies them with their products. As there is also perfect information and completely free movement of products within the market, consumers will always be able to make their purchases from the cheapest supplier: they always know the prices being offered by competitors and are able to purchase products from anywhere freely. This means that all of the producers have to sell their products at the lowest possible price, which is therefore the price determined by the market, P_1. If they charged higher than P_1, they would lose all of their custom to the competitors; and if they charged less than P_1, they would be failing to cover their costs and would close down.

As a consequence of this perfectly elastic demand curve every unit that a producer supplies will be done so at the given price, P_1. As every extra unit will always simply add P_1 to the total revenue of the producer, marginal revenue will be constantly equal to this price as well. Similarly, for any level of output, dividing the total revenue by the output will generate average revenue that is also equal to this price. The marginal and average revenue curves are, therefore, horizontal at the given price and so are the same as the demand curve, as shown in Figure 5.1.

To maximise profit, a producer has to equate its marginal cost with its marginal revenue. This means that the producer illustrated in Figure 5.1 will supply an output of Q_f to the market at the market price of P_1. To calculate the total market supply, as represented by Q_m in Figure 5.1, one needs to simply add up the amount supplied by each of the individual producers. This is called *horizontal summation*.

5.2 | Normal and abnormal profit

The accountancy definition of profit is simply the excess revenue over and above costs. However, in economics this is too simplistic. In Section 4.1 it was explained that there are four factors that are absolutely necessary for any production to occur. The employment of each of these earns a payment. Physical land earns rent and the other natural raw materials earn their price; capital also earns rent; labour earns remuneration; and entrepreneurship earns *normal profit*. This is the minimum amount of profit that is required for an entrepreneur to maintain a business in operation. If the level of profit falls beneath this, the organisation will be terminated as the entrepreneur will feel that it is not worth the effort. Consequently, this is viewed as being a cost to the producer. It is something that the producer has to pay, just like the rent that is due, the capital and the salaries that are demanded by the employees.

As it is a cost, normal profit is included within the marginal and average cost curves. In Figure 5.1, the producer is covering its costs by producing Q_f units at a price of P_1, meaning that it is earning normal profit but no more. This is the situation that the perfect competition model implies will exist when the market is in equilibrium.

Any revenue that is in excess of this amount is termed *abnormal profit*. If this exists, it will be possible to show this as an area on a producer's diagram. In perfect competition such abnormal profit can only be short-lived, which is explained in the next section.

The economic definition of profit is absolute: it is revenue net of all costs. Because accountants are addressing different questions to economists their definition of the word *profit* can be different. In particular they may define profit without deducting the servicing costs of financial capital employed by the producer.

5.3 The adjustment mechanism

As a result of the assumptions outlined above any divergence from the market equilibrium that is illustrated in Figure 5.1 will be short-lived. Figure 5.2 shows one case of disequilibrium in a perfectly competitive market. The market price, P_1, is higher than the average costs of the individual producers. Consequently, at the level of output at which they maximise profit, they will be making abnormal profit, which is illustrated by the shaded area in Figure 5.2. This will only be short-lived because entrepreneurs outside the market will see that the existing producers are making this abnormal profit and will take advantage of the completely free entry into the market in an attempt to enjoy this profitability as well. Total market supply

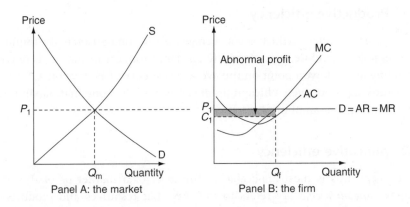

Figure 5.2 Short run disequilibrium

increases as a result of these additional producers, and so the market supply curve will shift outwards, causing the market price to fall. It will continue to fall until the market price is equal to average cost and all abnormal profit is eliminated, which is the situation shown in Figure 5.1. At this point the mechanism stops as further producers will no longer be attracted to enter the market, as further supply would cause the price to fall to a loss-making level.

The reverse mechanism occurs when the market price is too low and so is causing the individual producers to experience a loss. As there is free exit from the market, producers will begin to close operations and leave. As they do this, the market supply contracts and so the supply curve shifts inwards causing the price to rise. This continues until the price is equal to the average cost of producers, and so costs are being covered. Again, the adjustment mechanism swiftly moves the market back to the equilibrium shown in Figure 5.1.

5.4 | Efficiency

Efficiency is a term that economists use to refer to how closely a market structure satisfies a given optimal criterion, and so is a way of assessing the desirability of a particular structure. There are three main types of efficiency, which have been explained in Section 2.2.1 but which are further elaborated in this section.

Throughout, we assume away the possibility that producers are simply wasteful because they are incompetently run. That is, we assume that it is not possible to get the same outputs by using less of all the inputs. The cost curves we have drawn represent the cost of the cheapest possible way of producing the given levels of output. This is an important simplification: *x-inefficiency*, as it is called in the economics literature, is an important phenomenon. Much public policy has been directed towards alleged failures of this kind. For instance, it has been argued on occasion that public-sector transport operators, lacking the discipline imposed by commercial competition, become lazy and could produce a better result at lower cost.

5.4.1 Productive efficiency

Productive efficiency refers to the level of average costs in comparison to the minimum that is feasible. Therefore, a productively efficient producer or market is one that is operating at the lowest point on the average cost curve (see Section 4.3.2.1). In other words, a productively efficient producer or market is one that maximises its output from a given amount of resources.

5.4.2 Allocative efficiency

As a concept, this is most applicable to the level of a market or of the wider economy. *Allocative efficiency* refers to the way that resources and products are distributed, comparing a given distribution to that which would maximise the level of utility in the market. An allocatively efficient market is one that distributes and uses resources in the way that produces what consumers most value; and then distributes those products to those who will gain the most utility from them.

A more formal definition is that allocative efficiency is achieved when the price is equal to the marginal cost:

$$P = MC$$

As we noted above in the context of simple market equilibrium, the price that consumers are willing and able to pay for a product is an indication of the value that they place upon it; and the marginal cost is the cost of the extra factors of production necessary to produce the particular unit of the product. If the price is greater than the marginal cost, producers are extracting too much money from consumers and so the product is likely to be under-consumed; whereas if the price is lower than the marginal cost, producers are not receiving enough revenue to cover the cost of that extra unit and so there is too much consumption.

This offers a clue to one sensible interpretation of the *public interest* for a public enterprise: so far as their budgets will allow, they should seek to relate the prices they charge to marginal costs of supply.

5.4.3 Pareto efficiency

Again, this concept is most applicable to the wider market or economy level. It refers to the total amount of utility that is enjoyed within a market, comparing this to the maximum that could feasibly be obtained. A market with *Pareto efficiency* is a state in which no one can be made better off without making someone else worse off. This can be illustrated diagrammatically by maximising the total surplus in a market (see Section 3.6).

It is a state in which there is both productive and allocative efficiency. If the market was not productively efficient, overall welfare could be increased simply by using the resources available in a better way to increase the number of products produced for the consumers to enjoy. Similarly, if it was not allocatively efficient, the overall welfare could be improved simply by redistributing the resources and products in the way that would mean that more of the products that are most valued are produced and that these are distributed to those who gain the most utility from them.

5.4.4 Perfect competition and efficiency

The strongest argument that free-market economists use to support the liberalisation of markets, and the imposition of competition policy, is that such action will encourage markets to be more like that in the perfect competition model, thereby satisfying all three forms of efficiency above.

A perfectly competitive market is productively efficient, because the strong competition disciplines all producers to accept the market price that is at the level that simply covers their costs. This can be seen in Figure 5.1, where the price is at the lowest point on a producer's average cost curve.

Assuming that those consumers who most value a product are willing and able to pay the highest price for it, a perfectly competitive market is also allocatively efficient. These consumers are those towards the left-hand side of the market demand curve and so are the ones who actually receive the products. Those who do not receive a product are situated towards the right of the curve and do not purchase a product because it does not bring them enough utility for it to be rational for them to pay the market price for it. In this way, the market is distributing the products in the manner that will maximise overall utility. This is further shown by Figure 5.1, as price is equal to the marginal cost at the individual producer's chosen level of output, Q_f.

As there are productive and allocative efficiency within perfect competition, there is also Pareto efficiency. This can also be seen from Figure 3.11, in which the total surplus is maximised for that set of demand and supply conditions. There is no part of the potential area that is neither consumer nor producer surplus and so the market, for the given conditions, is maximising welfare. It is impossible to make the consumers better off without making the producers worse off, and vice versa, unless one of the curves is shifted, creating new conditions in the market which would be adapted to creating a new situation of Pareto efficiency.

This is why congestion and queues are undesirable in the sense that one can always improve on the situation. They come about because of under-pricing and the consequential excess demand. The people that are lucky enough to be served quickly may not be the ones that would be willing to pay most for the service. By making a higher charge, we can make sure the people with the highest value of that particular facility get to use it and the extra revenue extracted from them will be sufficient to more than compensate those that are *priced off* the facility. The net result is that, in principle, everyone can be made better off. Almost magically, the economic value of the facility is increased. We return to this proposition in Chapter 16.

5.5 | A fundamental model

There are few actual markets in the transport sector that are fully represented by the perfect competition model as the assumptions are too restrictive. In reality there are often significant barriers to entry in transport markets, particularly due to the high initial capital costs. There is an absence of perfect information as consumers and producers are not aware of exactly what decisions all the other producers in the market are making, although the expansion of the Internet is helping in this regard. There is also not a completely free movement of products and services in transport markets as the initial location of the capital is vitally important: a road-haulage company in France, for example, is unlikely to be a strong competition for a similar company in Holland. These, along with less substantial failures in regard to the other assumptions, cause the perfect competition model to work imperfectly, if at all. At best, the adjustment mechanism takes a substantially longer period of time to restore the market to the optimal equilibrium.

This does not negate the importance or the usefulness of the model, though. It can be viewed as being the ideal situation as it achieves Pareto optimality, and as such it can be used as a very effective benchmark against which all the other, perhaps more realistic, market structures can be compared. It also highlights important characteristics of a market structure that will lead to Pareto efficiency, and so can be converted into policy to encourage these to exist in actual transport markets. Moving a market towards this structure should result in improvements in efficiency that can be beneficial to all of society. These are the reasons why it is such a fundamental model.

5.6　A transport case study: Tramp shipping

Shipping is a vital part of the European transport sector, accounting for some 90 per cent of all products imported into the Union. The shipping market is made up of three parts. The first is the *liner market*. This involves the transportation of relatively small cargoes, although liner operators are increasingly transporting bulk cargoes, on a frequent and scheduled basis over predetermined routes. The second is the *bulk market*, which involves the transportation of large cargoes of homogenous products on a relatively infrequent basis (between six and twelve voyages a year per vessel). This market is dominated by the transportation of energy-related products such as coal and oil. The third is that of the *specialised market*, which involves the bulk transportation of products that can be transported more effectively by using specifically designed vessels, loading equipment, docks and other facilities. The last two of these comprise the *tramp shipping market* as the services within them have the common characteristic of being irregular.

5.6.1　Large numbers of small producers with homogenous products

As Figure 5.3 shows, there were 1451 ship-owning companies in the EU 15 in 2004, owning a total of 8323 vessels, including liner, bulk, specialised and deep sea ships. Over a third of those companies had only a single vessel; only one company had more than 200, in this case 261; and the overall average European fleet size was only of six vessels.

Although there are differences between the three shipping markets, many products can be transported by companies in all three, causing intense competition for these cargoes. Individually, the bulk market is particularly competitive as the service provided is homogenous, an individual vessel can be viewed as the competitive unit, and they are price takers. The specialised market is less so as there are fewer companies and many of their vessels have been specifically designed for certain uses, meaning that there is less homogeneity. Again, however, many of

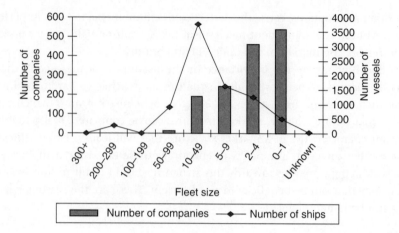

Figure 5.3 Fleet sizes of European ship owners, 2004

the products can also be transported by non-specialist vessels causing there to be a high degree of contestability within this market.

5.6.2 Free entry and exit

In order to enter the shipping industry, a company is required to have certain equity. There is also the cost of the vessel which can be extremely high as some gas ships cost in excess of US$100 million. This is a deterrent to entry but commercial shipping banks are willing to provide loans secured against a first mortgage on a vessel which eases this barrier.

There is then a whole array of support services that help new companies to enter the market. Ship management companies will manage vessels; chartering brokers will arrange the employment of vessels and the collection of revenues, and will deal with any claims; sale and purchase brokers will buy and sell vessels and the list continues. With such support and assistance it is relatively easy for new shipping companies to enter the market.

It is similarly easy for companies to exit the market as well. Any vessel which can have a life of up to 20 years can be sold in the second-hand market with assistance from the sale and purchase brokers.

5.6.3 Information

There is a high degree of knowledge within tramp shipping ensuring that there is strong transparency, allowing consumers and producers to know what their counterparts are doing and to make informed decisions based upon this. Information about revenues and asset prices is published daily by ship-broking businesses and this information is widely circulated throughout the industry. The costs of operating different types of vessel are also widely appreciated, making it easier for companies to estimate prevailing profit levels to again aid decision-making.

5.6.4 Movement of goods

The services provided by shipping companies are geographically mobile. Customers in one European country are able to freely purchase the services of providers in another, meaning that the market can be seen as a geographically extensive but single market. This is important to the perfect competition model as it enables supply to move in response to changes in demand. This flexibility in the tramp shipping market is helped by the wide range of ways in which shipping services can be purchased. These are displayed in Figure 5.4.

All of these different options have their advantages and disadvantages. There are three advantages to chartering for example. First, a shipper may not want to become an owner of a vessel. This may be because they do not have the technical capacity to own a vessel or because they simply cannot afford to. Secondly, it may be cheaper in the long run, especially if the owner has lower costs due to economies of scale. This is one of the reasons why the oil companies time-chartered much of their transport during the 1960s. Finally, it may bring speculative or arbitrage gains. A company may period-charter a vessel and then charter it out on the voyage-charter market to make a profit.

5.6.5 Market fluctuations

Investment decisions in the shipping industry come with time delays, especially in the purchasing of a new vessel as most are built to order. This characteristic means that there are continual fluctuations in the market and that it fails to settle at a

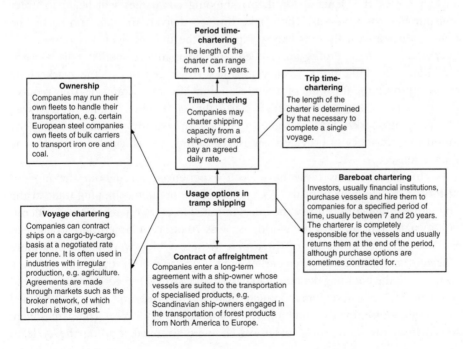

Figure 5.4 Usage options in the tramp shipping market

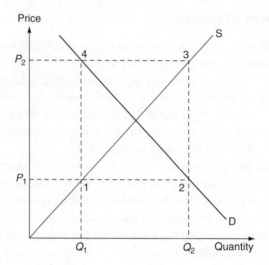

Figure 5.5 The
cobweb

steady equilibrium in the long run. This is illustrated in Figure 5.5, which is an
application of the cobweb model.

The starting point is that illustrated by points 1 and 4. They show a situation of profitability in the market as there is insufficient capacity to satisfy the
prevailing demand. In an attempt to respond to this shipping companies will
approach the second-hand ship market to purchase extra capacity. With consumers
bidding with one another for the available services and with providers spending
money on second-hand vessels the price in the market will rise towards the
short run equilibrium. As the price of second-hand vessels increases (due to
an increase in the demand for them) shipping companies will begin to order
and purchase new vessels. These take time to deliver, though, and so by the
time of their arrival there is excess supply in the market, which is represented
by points 2 and 3. Profits are eroded, the price in the market falls towards
the short run equilibrium, weak companies are forced out of the market and
ships approaching the end of their economic life are scrapped. This reduces
the capacity in the market which starts the cycle once again. In this way
the shipping market fails to settle at a long run steady equilibrium and the
productive efficiency of providers is ensured as only the efficient can survive the
fluctuations.

Fluctuations such as these have been experienced throughout the modern
history of the shipping industry. As a result of the booming shipping trade at the
end of the nineteenth century the liners invested in extra capacity. Derek Aldcroft
(1974) states that by 1914 the world fleet was 70 per cent larger than it had been
in 1900. By the time a lot of these new vessels, which were larger and more
efficient than those constructed earlier (which was to worsen the problem), were
constructed the booming demand had passed and had even deteriorated compared
to the norm. The market had too much capacity, and prices and profits plummeted
as a result, worsening the shipping depression at the time. Weak companies were
forced from the market and older vessels were scrapped, causing the cycle to

commence again. A similar story can be told of the excessive optimism in the industry in 1919–1920.

Figure 5.5 has been drawn such that the amplitude of the cycles neither increase nor decrease over time. But it is perfectly possible to draw it so the amplitude steadily increases over the years, in which case, although the market equilibrium exists it will never be attained because the dynamics of the market are unstable (a diverging cobweb model). Alternatively, the dynamics might be stable so that the oscillations reduce over the years and the market gets closer to its equilibrium (a converging cobweb model). Even so, world events will continually disturb the convergence so oscillations never stop.

5.7 | Contestable markets

In the late 1970s and early 1980s, William Baumol (1982a, 1982b, 1986) saw that there were markets that did not quite fit in with the traditional market structures. There were markets that were not perfectly competitive, but yet did not earn abnormal profits either. He developed the *theory of contestable markets* to try to explain markets such as these, applying them first to the American domestic airline industry.

The most important feature of a contestable market is that there are no barriers to entry and especially no sunk costs. This means that there is always a real threat that new producers will enter the industry to capture any abnormal profit that is being earned by charging a lower price. In fact, there is the threat of *hit-and-run competition*, which is where producers enter the market, set their price lower than the existing producers, capture the available abnormal profit and then exit the industry. This is why it is vital for the theory that there are no sunk costs, as the existence of these would prevent such competition. As a result of this threat, existing producers will be forced to behave in more of a perfectly competitive manner. They will have to be productively efficient so that they can compete with any potential entrants; and they will charge competitive prices and restrict earnings to normal profit in order to avoid attracting hit-and-run competition. Consequently, this market structure can be illustrated by the diagram for perfect competition (see Section 5.1.)

The difference between a contestable market and a perfectly competitive market is that it does not matter how many producers are actually there in a contestable market. It is the *threat* of entry by new producers that disciplines them all to behave in a competitive manner rather than the existence of actual competitors within the market.

There are three other factors that are necessary for a market to be contestable:

▪ Any entrants must have access to the same technology as existing producers.
▪ Existing producers do not have large reserves of finance that they can use to reduce their prices instantly to a level below that charged by entrants in a price war.

▪ There is a low degree of brand loyalty and so consumers respond instantly to any price difference by moving their purchases to the producer with the lowest price.

If any of these factors is broken, existing producers will have an advantage over new entrants and so hit-and-run competition may not be a real threat and so the market is less likely to be contestable.

5.7.1 The tramp shipping market

The tramp shipping market is composed of two parts: bulk and specialised shipping (see Section 5.6). However, it can also be divided into different sub-markets according to the cargoes transported; for example, energy-related products (which account for 70 per cent of all shipping volumes), forestry products, metals, chemicals and motor vehicles. The majority of products can be transported by ships in different sub-markets, though, and so even when there are relatively few companies within a particular sub-market they are forced to act competitively.

This is more difficult in some of the specialised shipping markets, such as that for liquefied gas, as the transportation of these products can be greatly improved by the employment of specifically designed equipment. However, many of these are still contestable as entry to them is relatively easy; for example, the market for liquefied gas shipping, in which there are only 43 providers owning 253 vessels. Tramp shipping markets, defined according to cargoes, are good examples of contestable markets.

Monopoly 6

6.1 | Definition and barriers to entry

This is the form of market structure at the opposite end of the competition spectrum from perfect competition. A *pure monopoly* is one in which there is only one producer within a market, although the British government considers any business with in excess of 25 per cent of the market share to be in a position to take advantage of monopoly power.

In order to maintain a monopoly position there inevitably has to be a strong *barrier to entry*. These can include the following.

6.1.1 Initial costs

This is a significant barrier to entry in the transport sector. Most transport markets require a certain initial expenditure on capital, be it the purchasing of a fleet of aircraft in order to enter the airline industry, or the purchasing of a licence to enter the taxicab industry. These are often high, and so act as an effective deterrent to a potential entrant, particularly if they are unable to raise the necessary funds, but also simply due to the effort that has to be exerted in order to raise it. Recognising this, public policy can seek to lower these barriers. When the British railways were privatised under the 1993 Act, the government wanted to encourage competition amongst train operators. So they set up three companies owning rolling stock (ROSCOs) from which any train operator could lease the equipment it would need to offer a service, without having to find the capital necessary to purchase its own vehicles. In the aviation industry, there has been the evolution of highly sophisticated specialisation of owning aircraft and engines, distinct from operating them under lease. Anybody who wants to operate a new air service will have no difficulty obtaining the use of one or more aircraft. But with both rail and air services there are barriers to entry to do with obtaining permissions to operate.

6.1.1.1 *Air Scotland*

Air Scotland was established in 2002 by Dhia Al-Ani in partnership with the Greek charter company Electra Airlines. It was Scotland's first-ever low-cost airline, initially flying from Glasgow and Edinburgh to six Spanish destinations. It was marketed as standing out from rival low-cost airlines flying out of English airports by flying directly from Scotland to main city airports rather than nearby destinations.

The creation of an airline involves tremendous costs. First, there is the leasing or purchasing of the craft, which in the case of Air Scotland initially comprised of two Boeings 757-200. This is followed by the securing of an operator's licence, which in the UK requires evidence of access to substantial amounts of finance by the Civil Aviation Authority. Then there are the airport, labour and marketing costs. Dhia Al-Ani invested £47 million in order to cover these costs and to commence the initial five-year project.

Since the two craft began scheduled flights in March 2003, the company has experienced a number of problems and as a result has changed ownership. It is currently operating under the licence of Greece Airways on routes from ten UK airports, particularly Glasgow and Manchester, to eight Mediterranean destinations and Athens.

6.1.2 Sunk costs

A sunk cost is an expenditure that a producer has to make in order to enter a market that is unrecoverable on exit from the market. A transport market that has considerable initial capital outlays does not necessarily have high sunk costs because the capital can be sold after closure. However, it is likely that transport producers will have significant sunk costs because of the licences and the marketing that are often necessary to establish themselves in their markets.

6.1.3 Brand loyalty

Many transport markets have well-established producers within them. Eddie Stobart, for example, is the UK's largest independent logistics company with a fleet of 800 trucks and a turnover in excess of £140 million. In 2005, it obtained its first Tesco Distribution Centre contract. A new entrant to the road-haulage market may find such existing competition a deterrent to entering the market. The importance of brand loyalty and image is further illustrated by the re-branding exercise adopted by British Airways (BA).

6.1.3.1 British Airways image revitalisation

British Airways, in 1997, attempted to revitalise its image in order to increase the number of passengers by 70 per cent to some 51 million by 2005. It was concerned that it was lacking real brand loyalty because it was viewed by customers as being aloof due to its British origins. It sought to change this image into one of being a vibrant, friendly and global airline and so it invited more than 50 artists to submit designs that would replace the traditional Union Jack motif. It also set about replacing the *speedwing* arrow logo with an abstract design, replacing the dark blue livery with bright colours and making staff uniforms brighter and softer. It finally considered dropping *British* from its name but decided against this.

There were concerns at the time that if it went too far it could alienate existing British customers that were loyal to the airline. This is possibly why it decided to maintain its name and keep the red, white and blue colours somewhere within the designs.

It was expected that this would cost the airline around £60 million, an amount which it thought worthwhile if it would transform the airline's image and secure brand loyalty.

6.1.4   Anti-competitive behaviour

This refers to any action that is intended to drive competition from the market. It can take many forms; for example, a few are listed as follows.

6.1.4.1   *Predatory pricing through cross-subsidisation*

This is where producers in a number of markets use abnormal profits earned in one market to fund losses in another so that the price can be maintained at such a low level that competitors are forced out. Producers can also use their financial reserves to fund such predatory pricing. Once the competitors have been driven out of the market the dominant producer is then able to enjoy the market power it has gained by charging higher prices that consumers have no alternative but to pay. However, as a strategy, this can only be sensible if there is good reason to think that there will not be immediate re-entry from some competitor seeking a share of the created excess profits.

6.1.4.2   *Vertical restraints*

This is where a producer gains control of either suppliers or outlets so that competitors simply cannot function within the market. Such control can be obtained through *exclusive dealing contracts* or, in other words, contracting so that it will only deal with suppliers or outlets if they agree not to deal with any competitors. It can also take the form of the imposition of supplementary terms in contracts that restrict competition, such as only selling a dealership one type of product if it also purchases another in the range, or prohibiting a dealer in one geographical market from trading in another in order to maximise prices in both.

6.1.4.3   *Negative branding*

Producers can use the media to establish a negative view of competitors amongst consumers. This could be through false allegations of consumer exploitation or unethical practices.

6.1.4.4 Collusion

This refers to agreements amongst existing producers to co-operate with one another and so to form a *cartel*. This can be used to keep prices at a level that potential competitors cannot enter the market successfully, to limit production and so maintain prices at an artificially high level (in effect this would shift the supply curve inwards, see Section 3.5) or to divide the market between them so that each of them has local monopoly power and so can exploit consumers.

Such behaviour is illegal according to the competition policy of the European Commission (EC) which shall be outlined in Section 6.4. Example allegations of each of these forms have been made in the rivalry between BA and Virgin Atlantic (Virgin).

6.1.4.5 A case study of anti-competitive behaviour: The British Airways and Virgin Atlantic feud

Ever since the launch of Virgin in an attempt to disturb the transatlantic monopoly enjoyed by BA there has been a bitter rivalry between the two airlines, which has led to serious allegations of anti-competitive behaviour.

In the early 1990s, Virgin accused BA of *dirty tricks* in its attempt to prevent the fledgling airline from developing into a serious competitor. These allegations included the following.

- The poaching of Virgin's passengers by using ticket touts to offer cheaper fares at airports and by obtaining Virgin passenger lists to target passengers for special deals.
- Pressuring travel agents into promoting BA instead of Virgin. The European Commission would later find BA guilty of paying anti-competitive bonuses to such agents.
- Making Virgin flights less attractive to consumers by delaying onward flights for Virgin travellers.
- Feeding damaging stories and information about Virgin to the media.
- Applying for routes that would secure it an unfair advantage. Cases of this included the application for a new Gatwick–Denver route and the purchasing of CityFlyer, BA's franchisee airline that operated flights from Gatwick to airports in the UK and Northern Europe, which would give it further dominance at Gatwick (in 1997 BA and CityFlyer were the two largest operators at the London airport with 28.6 and 12.8 per cent of the flights respectively).

Each airline sued the other for libel, resulting in BA apologising and paying £610,000 for damages along with legal fees totalling some £3 million.

In June 2006, BA was accused of engaging in price fixing in a transatlantic competition investigation by the UK Office of Fair Trading and the US Department of Justice after allegations were made by Virgin. The investigation was particularly focused on the possibility that there had been collusion between the transatlantic airlines on fuel surcharges.

Fuel surcharges have been increasingly used by airlines since 2004 to compensate them for the rising costs of aviation fuel. They apply to every *sector* of a journey meaning that passengers making single journeys but having to change en route have to pay them twice. It is alleged that BA has been working in collusion with other airlines to raise these, which they did seven times between May 2004 and April 2006, from £2.50 to £35 for a long-haul flight.

Virgin's fuel surcharges have been rising in line with these but it has been alleged that it was prompted into informing the Office of Fair Trading in order to take advantage of the European Commissions' leniency policy (see Section 6.4) and gain immunity from sanctions and prosecutions following the start of an earlier investigation into airline collusion over fuel surcharges in Europe's cargo market.

The possible sanctions for BA if it is found to be guilty include a financial penalty of up to 10 per cent of turnover, or £850 million if the wrongdoing is found to apply to its worldwide operations; costly lawsuits from passengers; the loss of its dominant position at Heathrow, Europe's busiest airport; and criminal prosecution of individual protagonists under the UK's Enterprise Act.

6.1.5 Economies of scale

If a producer is able to grow to such a size that it is operating on a significantly lower average cost curve than its competitors it will be able to sustain a lower price whereas its competitors will fail to compete. This makes it difficult for new entrants into a market and prior knowledge of the potential for this can effectively deter them from entering in the first place. See Section 4.3.2.3 for a technical explanation of economies of scale.

6.1.6 Patents and licences

A patent offers fixed-term legal protection for a business from competition, allowing it to enjoy abnormal profits for the lifetime of the patent. They are usually awarded for producers using new technology in order to act as an incentive for technological advancements. Licences work in effectively the same way but are intended to reduce harmful or unnecessary competition and to encourage investment into the particular service.

6.2 The model

For the purpose of this section it shall be assumed that the market is one of pure monopoly. This will allow the analysis to be clearer and it will also enable stark comparisons to be made with the perfect competition model as they are the two extreme market structures. The analysis can be applied to less extreme cases of monopoly but this simply weakens the conclusions.

As there is a complete absence of competition, a pure monopoly is able to determine the price that it charges. In other words, it is a *price maker*. Alternatively,

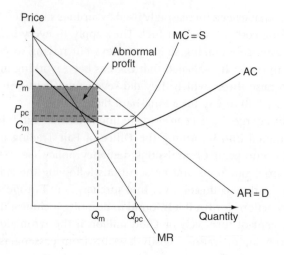

Figure 6.1
Monopoly

it is able to determine the quantity that it sells but it is not able to do both as it has to operate with the existing demand conditions.

As it is a pure monopoly there is only one diagram for the market and the individual producer as the former accounts totally for the latter. The producer maximises its profit by producing Q_m units at a price of P_m. This has to be at least sufficient to make normal profit otherwise the producer would choose to cease operations but it is likely that there will be abnormal profit to be made. This is the situation in Figure 6.1, where the abnormal profit is shown by the shaded area.

Assuming that the cost schedules and so the cost curves are the same irrespective of whether the market has a monopoly or a perfect competition structure, it is possible to make direct comparisons between the outcomes of the two structures. This is also shown in Figure 6.1. As the marginal cost curve is equal to the supply curve and as the average revenue curve is equal to the demand curve, the resulting equilibrium in perfect competition would be a quantity of Q_{pc} and a price P_{pc}. It is clearly the case, therefore, that the price under monopoly conditions will be higher and the quantity lower than that under perfect competition.

As a monopoly producer faces little or no competition for its products there is a lack of an incentive for it to innovate and to release new and improved competing products to the market. Consequently, not only are the prices likely to be higher under a monopoly, the quality of the products is likely to be lower and to fall over time. In this way, a monopoly structure can have long-term dynamic negative effects on consumers.

Figure 6.2 shows the level of efficiency of a market under monopoly conditions. First, the producer is not operating at the lowest point on its average cost curve and so the market is not productively efficient. Secondly, the price is higher than the marginal cost at that level of output and so the market is failing to achieve allocative efficiency as well. This means that the producer is overcharging and so too little is being supplied and consumed from an efficiency perspective.

The reason that the monopoly is doing this is that it increases its producer surplus and therefore its welfare. Compared to perfect competition producer surplus has

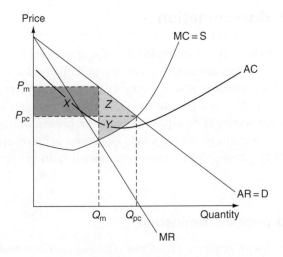

Figure 6.2 Efficiency under monopoly

been increased by area X but reduced by area Y. As the former is by far the larger of the two there is a significant net increase in producer surplus as a result of this pricing strategy. This comes at a cost, though, and that cost is borne by the consumers who see a reduction in their welfare of areas X and Z. Overall, this means that area X has simply been transferred from the consumers to the producers, but areas Y and Z have been completely lost, which is known as the *deadweight welfare loss of monopoly*. Therefore, the market is not Pareto efficient because it is possible to make one of the parties better off without it being at the expense of the other simply by eliminating this welfare loss. A profit-maximising monopoly is likely to lead to inefficient market outcomes.

Another way of expressing these results is to note that since

$$\text{profit} = \text{revenue} - \text{cost}$$

profit can only be maximised when the revenue from selling one more unit is balanced by the cost of producing it, otherwise the firm could do better. In other words,

$$\text{marginal revenue} = \text{marginal cost}$$

Another way of saying the same thing is

$$P \times \left(1 + \frac{1}{\varepsilon}\right) = \text{MC}$$

where P is the price, ε is the elasticity and MC is the marginal cost. So if the elasticity is −2 this reads as follows:

$$\text{price} = 2 \times \text{marginal cost}$$

Notice that this rule only makes sense if the elasticity is less than −1. If the demand was inelastic then the firm could not be maximising profit because raising price would give more revenue *and* reduce costs because fewer units would have to be supplied.

6.3 | Price discrimination

As a monopoly producer is a price-maker it is not only likely to set a price that is higher than that in perfect competition, but also potentially able to engage in *price discrimination*, which is where it sets a different price for different customers for the same product. There are three forms of price discrimination and all are used within the transport sector. The purpose of using this pricing strategy is to increase profit beyond the maximum that a single price can achieve and to maximise producer welfare by transferring as much consumer surplus to producer surplus as possible.

6.3.1 Perfect price discrimination

The first type is that of *perfect or first-degree price discrimination* and it shows most clearly the benefits to the producer of engaging in this strategy. It is illustrated in Figure 6.3.

Perfect price discrimination is the strategy of selling each individual unit to the consumer who values it the most and so is willing to pay the most for it. In Figure 6.3, for instance, the first unit has been sold to a consumer for P_1 whereas the third unit has been sold for the lower price of P_3. In this way the producer is theoretically able to convert all the consumer surplus to producer surplus as each consumer is paying exactly the amount that is equal to the value that they place upon the product. In Figure 6.3 this is illustrated by the fact that the shaded rectangles are now the producer surplus earned from the first three units, leaving only the small triangles as consumer surplus.

An example of this from the transport sector is the private market for second-hand cars. The sellers of the cars negotiate with the buyers on an individual basis and will sell them to those who place the highest bid.

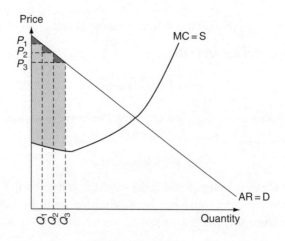

Figure 6.3
Perfect price discrimination

6.3.2   Second-degree price discrimination

This is also called *excess capacity pricing*. It is the strategy of charging late consumers a lower price in order to sell any remaining spare capacity and so earn some revenue from it. Figure 6.4 illustrates how this works.

It is assumed that the marginal cost is constant up until a certain level of output, denoted Q_{fc}, at which it then *jumps* to a new level. The explanation for this lies with the definitions of costs. The fixed costs are paid in order to establish the business even if there is no output supplied to the market. The marginal cost of the first unit, therefore, is simply the variable cost associated with that unit. Each subsequent unit of output may then cost a constant amount until full capacity is reached, at Q_{fc}. To supply further output requires further expenditure causing the marginal cost of that unit to *jump* to a much higher level, but falling again thereafter to the earlier constant variable costs. The pattern then repeats itself, but gradually the marginal cost curve will turn upwards due to the reasons outlined in Section 4.3.3.

The producer will maximise profits by selling Q_1 units at a price of P_1, leaving a level of excess capacity that is equal to $Q_{fc}-Q_1$, which will incur minimal extra costs to supply. If the producer sells these units for a higher price than their marginal cost it will be adding to its profits even if that price is less than P_1. Consequently, it will sell these for P_2, which is the maximum that consumers are willing to purchase them for, as shown by the demand curve. In this way it is selling exactly the same product for different prices to different consumers and so is engaging in price discrimination.

This is the reason why there are last-minute ticket deals for many airline and bus services. There are the initial costs of hiring or purchasing a coach; purchasing the necessary insurance, route licences and fuel; and employing a driver and administration staff. These comprise the cost of establishing the business in the first place and so can be seen as being the cost of producing zero units or in this

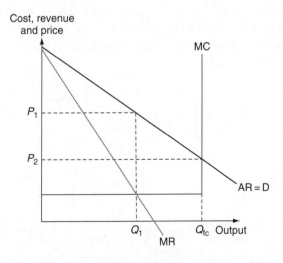

Figure 6.4
Second-degree price discrimination

case of transporting zero passengers. The marginal cost of transporting the first passenger is then simply the variable costs incurred by doing that, namely the cost of processing the necessary administration of selling the relevant ticket. The marginal cost of transporting the second passenger will be the same as this and so will the third and the fourth and so on until the coach is full. At this level, one more passenger will generate the additional cost of hiring or purchasing a second coach; purchasing additional insurance, route licences and fuel; and employing further staff and so the marginal cost *jumps* to a higher level. Further passengers will simply generate the variable costs again, though, as that expenditure has already been made and so the marginal cost falls back again and the pattern is repeated.

If the first coach can seat 50 people the bus company could employ the profit-maximising rule, selling (for instance) the first 35 tickets for a price of £30. At the last minute, though, it will seek to fill the coach by selling the remaining tickets at a discount rather than operating the coach service with 15 spare seats that could be earning some profit.

6.3.3 Third-degree price discrimination

In *third-degree price discrimination* the producer is able to separate the market into different *segments* based upon the demand characteristics of the consumers in each and then to set an optimal price in each segment. This is illustrated in Figure 6.5. The consumers in segment B have a very price-elastic demand for the product, whereas those in segment C are much more price inelastic. The producer will view each segment as being a separate market and so will aim to maximise profits in each. This leads to it setting a higher price in segment C, as the consumers are relatively unresponsive to a change in price, and a lower price in segment B, where the consumers are much more responsive to a change in price. The consumers in segment A are in between both of these and so will be charged a price that is in between as well.

As can also be seen from Figure 6.5, the quantity sold to segment C is less than that to segment B. This is also to be expected as the price-inelastic consumers in segment C are likely to be fewer in number than those in segment B and are likely to form more of a niche market.

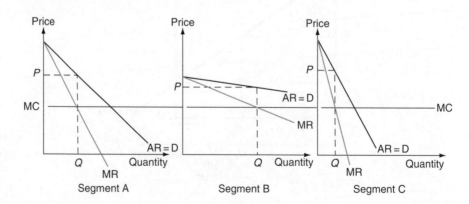

Figure 6.5
Third-degree price discrimination

There are two ways that a producer can divide the market into segments. First, it can do so by dividing the market into clear groups that then have to prove their identity. An example of this is the way that local bus companies divide their markets into segments that include children and old age pensioners, who have to prove their identity in cases of uncertainty. Both of these segments benefit from lower prices because the companies understand that they are likely to have a more price-elastic demand than adults of working age.

The second way that companies can do so is to employ a self-selection strategy. This is where the company simply creates a set of conditions that are likely to cause the different segments to reveal themselves and then allow the consumers to select which segment they belong to. An example of this is that of the airlines operating within Europe. To fly on Fridays and Mondays is considerably more expensive than to fly mid-week because the consumers who are more likely to do so are those in employment and so need to be at work during the week. On the other hand, those who are able to fly mid-week are likely to be those who are not employed and so have a more price-elastic demand as they are more sensitive to changes in price.

This second way is also the explanation as to why the fare for a seat of a transport provider differs depending on the date of purchase. Passengers who book in advance are usually able to benefit from discounts which are sometimes significant, whereas those who book late are usually penalised for doing so. Leisure travellers are more likely to be able to book in advance as they will have to book their time off work in advance as well; whereas business travellers are more likely to need to make bookings with short notice in response to the changing business environment. The demand of leisure travellers is likely to be more price elastic than that of business travelers, which providers are able to exploit by changing fares over time.

The rule outlined for maximising profit by setting marginal revenue equal to marginal cost shows how this behaviour can enhance profits. Suppose the producer can separate the market in two segments. Then the rule for profit maximising that marginal revenue should equal marginal cost applies in *each market:*

$$\text{price}_1 \times \left(1 + \frac{1}{\text{elasticity}_1} \right) = \text{marginal cost}_1$$

$$\text{price}_2 \times \left(1 + \frac{1}{\text{elasticity}_2} \right) = \text{marginal cost}_2$$

Therefore, even if the marginal costs do not vary significantly the prices *will* vary to exploit the different demand elasticities. Relatively inelastic markets will suffer relatively high prices even though there is no cost justification.

Another way to write the same rules is as follows:

$$\frac{\text{price}_1 - \text{marginal cost}_1}{\text{price}_1} = -\frac{1}{\text{elasticity}_1}$$

$$\frac{\text{price}_2 - \text{marginal cost}_2}{\text{price}_2} = -\frac{1}{\text{elasticity}_2}$$

This is a famous *inverse elasticity rule*: the proportionate deviation of price above respective marginal cost is inversely proportional to the respective elasticity. So in a highly elastic market price will be close to marginal cost. But if the elasticity is close to unity (e.g. −1.1: remember, these rules only make sense if the market is not inelastic) then the firm will exploit its market power in that market by raising price far above marginal cost. For this reason the inverse of the price elasticity (with a sign change) is sometimes used as a measure of monopoly power. As we will see below, under competition legislation a firm with a degree of market power is said to have a dominant position. It is not illegal to have a dominant position, but it can be illegal to *abuse a dominant position*. This is essentially because the abuse causes inefficiency by raising price above the marginal cost.

6.3.3.1 Third-degree price discrimination by Eurostar

A very simple example of third-degree price discrimination is that by Eurostar, which has a monopoly in rail travel between England and mainland Europe. Figure 6.6 displays the price of tickets purchased on 27 June 2006 for a journey from Brussels to Lille the following day, returning the day after that.

There is a marked difference in price between the two classes of tickets. For the extra £19 one gets extra features such as a fast-track check-in at Brussels, power sockets at the seats, business lounge access in Brussels, choice of full service *at seat* dining, and drinks, newspapers and magazines on board. These fail to change the essence of the product, though, as the ticket is still primarily purchased in order to transport the passenger between the two cities. Consequently, the operator is selling what is effectively the same product to different groups of consumers at different prices and is able to do so because of the different demand elasticities that exist in each segment. The business segment are much more price inelastic than the standard segment and so are less responsive to the increase in price than their standard-class counterparts would be.

The operator is using a self-selection strategy here and is trusting that the fast-track check-in process and the provision of power sockets and newspapers

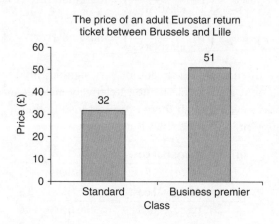

Figure 6.6
Eurostar tickets

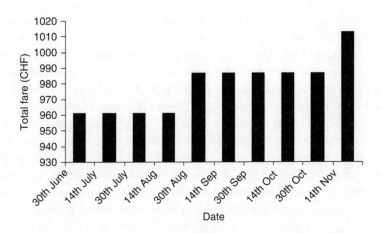

Figure 6.7 The price of a ticket (CHF) on a KLM flight over time

will encourage those who will be working to reveal themselves. It is also trusting that those who are having their journeys paid for by their companies will be attracted to the additional extras in this package, whereas those who are paying themselves and so are more sensitive to the price will decide that they do not justify the extra £19 charge.

6.3.3.2 Third-degree price discrimination by the airlines

As will be explained in Section 8.3, the European airline industry is a composite of numerous smaller markets based on geographical routes, for example the market for air travel between England and Southern France or that connecting Southern Ireland and Scotland. These individual markets are becoming increasingly oligopolistic as new airlines enter them. The wider market for air travel, in which passengers are indifferent between destinations, is certainly an oligopoly with a handful of airlines providing a range of different options. Price discrimination is used within oligopolies as the producers have certain degrees of market power. The more market power they have, the more able they are to exploit price discrimination.

Figure 6.7 shows the way in which the fare of a standard-class seat on a KLM flight between Geneva and Rome on 15 November 2006 varied over time. The fare is priced in Swiss francs (CHF) and includes a constant 96 Swiss franc surcharge for fuel, airport duty and service fee. As the date of departure drew closer the fare was raised in order to exploit the likelihood that those booking later were business travellers or leisure travellers in more desperate need of the seat and so willing to pay more to obtain it.

6.4 | Yield management

Yield management is often confused with third-degree price discrimination because the *yield* is the amount that consumers actually pay. There is, however, a subtle difference between them. Third-degree price discrimination is based upon the different elasticities of demand that consumers have, whereas yield management is based upon the differences in the amount of demand that exists for different products. Transport providers – including the airlines, railway and bus operators, and ferry companies – often employ analysts to monitor the sales of their seats. Those that are selling well obviously have a high demand and so the fares will be increased accordingly to ensure that the providers are maximising their revenue. It is simply a case of the providers utilising supply and demand – as demand increases, or shifts outwards, the price will rise. Similarly, those seats that are selling poorly obviously have a low demand and so prices will be reduced in an attempt to stimulate further demand. In this way, consumers that had purchased tickets before the price change will have paid a different amount than those who delay their purchases, but this is not the same as third-degree price discrimination because they do not necessarily have a different elasticity of demand for the seat.

In reality, transport providers utilise both third-degree price discrimination and yield management. They know that traveller demand is likely to become more price inelastic as the departure date approaches and so they plan to increase the *base price* accordingly. The analysts that are employed monitor and change those base prices in response to the actual levels of demand – upwards if the demand is higher than expected and downwards if the opposite is true. By using both strategies transport providers are able to increase the revenue that they earn.

6.5　European competition policy

Competition policy is designed to ensure that markets function as closely to the perfect competition model as possible and so to minimise the negative outcomes of monopoly, namely higher prices and lower quality for consumers and overall market inefficiency. That of the European Commission is based upon five supporting strands, which are illustrated in Figure 6.8. As shown, these strands are based upon the concept of *subsidiarity*. This simply means that they will be enforced in the individual member countries wherever possible and the Commission will only actively intervene in situations that affect more than one member country.

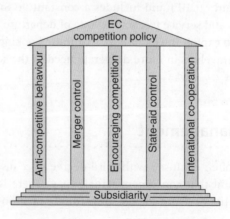

Figure 6.8 EC competition policy

The third and fourth strands, those of encouraging competition and state-aid control, are analysed in detail in Chapter 12 and so it is the remaining three that are outlined here.

6.5.1 Anti-competitive behaviour

In Section 6.1 the different forms that anti-competitive behaviour can take and the way they can be used to create a situation of monopoly dominance were explained. The first strand of the competition policy of the European Commission is aimed at minimising such behaviour and it in turn has two parts to it.

First, Article 81 of the European Commission Treaty makes harmful collusion illegal. Agreements such as those of price fixing, limiting production and the division of markets are prohibited as they are deemed to work against the interest of the market. In order to aid the detection of such cartels the European Commission has introduced a *leniency policy* which grants immunity to the first cartel member that informs the Commission of its existence. A case study of this policy in action is that of the rivalry between BA and Virgin in the opening section of this chapter.

There are restrictive agreements that may actually be positive, though, and so the Commission has established detailed *block exemption regulations* that outline the conditions to be fulfilled by certain categories of agreements if they are to be allowed. Current block exemption agreements include those for research and development, specialisation, technological transfers and distribution. They have been specifically applied to the car industry.

Secondly, Article 82 of the Treaty prohibits the abuse of market power, which includes predatory pricing and vertical restraints. Examples of the enforcement of this law include those of Volkswagen AG and Michelin.

This strand of the policy is firmly based on the principle of subsidiarity. Each member country has a competition commission that has the authority to investigate and enforce the Treaty. They can require businesses to provide necessary information and can carry out surprise inspections. If the businesses involved are based across the European Union, however, the Commission will intervene with the same investigative and enforcement powers. Any producer that is found guilty of any breach of these policies can be fined up to 10 per cent of their annual turnover, be required to pay legal costs, and have illegal agreements terminated. The revenues raised by these means go towards the Commission's budget and to help finance the European Union. The competition commissions of the individual countries and the European Commission co-operate with one another through the European Competition Network to ensure that the law is applied consistently across the Union and to ensure that there is no duplication of investigations.

6.5.1.1 *Volkswagen AG and Michelin*

There is a wide difference in the prices of cars across the European Union although this is contracting as the Single European Market strengthens. In 1998, Volkswagen

AG was found guilty of prohibiting its Italian dealers from selling its cars to German and Austrian consumers whose domestic markets were characterised by higher prices. This was seen as contravening Article 82 of the European Commission Treaty as it was a form of vertical restraint and so the manufacturer was fined EUR 90 million.

In 2001, the French tyre-manufacturer Michelin was found guilty of using a package of rebates and bonuses to make dealers dependent on its tyres and so preventing them from doing business with its competitors. This was seen as an abuse of its dominant position, particularly in the market for the tyres for heavy vehicles where it had a market share in excess of 50 per cent. The Commission fined the company EUR 20 million.

6.5.2 Merger control

A *merger* is the legal integration of two or more business entities. Mergers can be mutually agreed by the participant businesses or they can take the form of hostile takeovers. They can also be horizontal mergers, which are integration of businesses that are at the same stage of production; or vertical mergers, where the businesses are not at the same stage of production, for example a manufacturer integrating with a dealer.

Mergers can be positive in that they can bring improvements in productive efficiency as the combined producer can exploit economies of scale more effectively. The danger, though, is that some mergers can actually damage competition by creating a producer with a dominant market position that can then abuse its market power. It is to protect against this potentiality that mergers of a certain size are scrutinised and controlled by Regulation (EC) No 139/2004.

If the two businesses are solely within one member country of the European Union, it is left to the competition authority of that country to ensure that the merger does not damage the level of competition within the market. If they extend beyond the national borders of any one country, though, and if they have combined annual turnovers exceeding EUR 5000 million worldwide and EUR 250 million within the European Community, they will be examined by the European Commission. Smaller cases can also be referred to the Commission by the competition authority of an individual member country. If it is deemed that the proposed merger will significantly impede competition within the European Union it will be prohibited. These rules apply to all mergers of businesses that affect the European Union, even if their registered offices are outside of the Union.

Over 90 per cent of cases that are notified to the European Commission are approved after the initial 25-working-day period of scrutiny. Most of those that go through to the further period of investigation (between 90 and 125 working days) are granted conditional authorisation. This means that the merger is permitted but that the combined producer has to take certain actions to reduce any damage to the market, such as selling a part of the combined company or licensing certain technology to competitors enabling them to compete more effectively.

6.5.2.1 The merger of TotalFina and Elf Aquitaine

These two businesses were the main players in the French market for petroleum products and so when they proposed a merger it was taken seriously. The combined business would have operated around 60 per cent of the service stations on French motorways and would have been the leading supplier of liquid petroleum gas. It was felt that it would have been able to use its market power to push up the prices for independent petrol distributors and so the European Commission gave it conditional clearance based on it agreeing to sell a large proportion of its operations, including 70 French motorway service stations.

6.5.3 International co-operation

As illustrated in the section above, any producer whose actions affect the European Union is subject to the Commission's competition policy, even if it is registered in a non-Union country. This, along with the fact that businesses registered within the Union but which affect non-Union countries and so are subject to their competition laws as well, makes it necessary for the Commission to co-operate on an international level.

There are over 100 countries and regions with competition laws and almost all of them actively participate in forums such as the International Competition Network (ICN). The first way, therefore, that the Commission seeks to co-operate with these countries is by playing a role in these forums. The Commission also works with non-Union countries on an individual basis, especially when they are investigating the same situations and so want to avoid contradictory investigations.

6.6 | Public service vehicle operations in Britain

The public service vehicle (PSV, or bus and coach) industry remains by far the most dominant form of public transport in Great Britain. The Commission for Integrated Transport (June 2004) asserts that in 2002/2003 some 4.4 billion passenger journeys were made by bus compared to 2 billion journeys on all rail modes in the same year.

Defining the market for it, though, is problematic. In terms of the product it is debatable as to whether there is a separate market for PSV transport or whether it is simply a part of the wider market for road transport and so should be seen as one of numerous substitutes. In terms of geography, it is unclear where the market boundaries end. In this section let us assume that there is a separate PSV market, according to the convention by the British Competition Commission. Given this definition and the resulting absence of close substitutes, the market demand for bus travel is likely to be relatively price inelastic. There are also two geographical definitions: local markets, which exist within a local authority's jurisdiction, and the national market, comprised of the former. In this latter distinction the emphasis

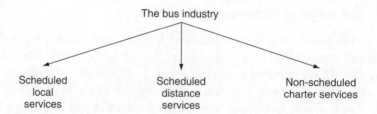

Figure 6.9 The structure of the bus industry

shall be firmly on local markets because operators are only in direct competition with one another if they are operating the same routes in the same locality.

The industry comprises three separate sub-markets, as illustrated in Figure 6.9. The scheduled services are simply the vehicles that stop at set places along predetermined routes at predetermined times. Local services are those within city or county boundaries, and account for 45 per cent of the total distance travelled by passenger transport services in 2002/2003 (The Commission for Integrated Transport, June 2004), whereas distance services are those that traverse such boundaries. The non-scheduled charter services are those that are privately hired for particular journeys.

In 2002/2003, there were 1800 private-sector bus operators and 17 local authority–owned companies in Great Britain. The national industry was, and is, dominated by five large companies: First, Arriva, Stage Coach, Go-Ahead and National Express, which together account for approximately 80 per cent of employment and 70 per cent of the market turnover. This oligopoly situation is worsened when one considers local PSV markets. As these five businesses dominate the national market but do not all have a large share in each of the individual local markets, it suggests that they are each concentrated in different local markets. This means that local markets are highly monopolised, which is a conclusion that was supported by the case studies looked at by National Economic Research Associates in its report to the Office of Fair Trading (December 1997).

This monopolisation of local services is sustained by barriers to entry, and as such small-scale entry into the market may only be successful in exceptional circumstances. A large-scale entrance is likely to be more successful, but this is less common. There are five particular barriers to entry.

1. *Supply-side economies of scale*. Large operators are able to purchase new vehicles significantly more cheaply than small operators and by virtue of having younger fleets subsequently enjoy lower maintenance costs. National Economic Research Associates on behalf of the Office of Fair Trading (December 1997) has estimated the initial capital cost savings as being up to 20 per cent for the larger companies. The five dominating operators have a considerable advantage in each of their local markets because of their national size.

2. *Demand-side economies of scale*. Large operators within a local market are able to tie in passengers through the employment of discounted return journeys and network tickets that can be used on any of its vehicles within an area. Small entrants, therefore, are likely to secure a less than proportionate share of the market in relation to the number of services that they offer.

3. *Competitive responsiveness*. One can view each route as a separate market, which means that incumbents are able to use their multiple markets to respond effectively to small scale entrants. To aid this, price and service characteristics can be adjusted rapidly.
4. *Lack of service differentiation*. New entrants have only a limited potential to differentiate their service or to reduce their operating costs through technical innovation.
5. *Reputation*. The reputation of an incumbent for responding aggressively and effectively to entry acts as a not-insignificant barrier to entry.

Within the non-scheduled, chartered sub-market, of the five dominant companies only National Express holds any real significance and there are a large number of small enterprises. This is supported by the fact that more than 70 per cent of the companies in this sub-market have less than 50 employees. As such, this sub-market can be viewed as a monopolistically competitive market.

In addition to the specific barriers to entry outlined above, in order to establish a PSV operating company in any of the three sub-markets it is necessary to obtain an operator's licence; to purchase or hire a fleet of vehicles and organise the required insurance; to employ the necessary drivers and administration staff; and to conduct the necessary marketing. Such licences used to be granted by local authorities under an act of Parliament dated from the mid-1800s. Motorised vehicles with more than eight seats were then handed over to the Traffic Commissioners when they were established in 1930 and they have been regulated by them ever since. Vehicles with eight or less seats remain under the regulation of the local authority, except in London, where they were under the control of the Metropolitan Police until recently when their licensing was handed over to the Mayor of London and merged with Transport for London.

Between 1930 and 1985 the Traffic Commissioners enforced a severe form of *quantity licensing* in which it was difficult or impossible to obtain licences to operate extra services in competition with existing bus or rail services. Fares were also regulated. After the 1986 deregulation outside London, the number of licences issued could not be restricted and the remaining licensing system was aimed at safety rather than fare or service levels.

The process of applying for a PSV operator's licence is made to the local Traffic Commissioner in the same way as that for a road-haulage operator's licence (see Section 7.3 for full details). It is necessary to be of good repute and to be professionally competent; and to have the same adequate finance, off-street parking and maintenance facilities as those for road-haulage vehicles. There is no need to advertise the location of the proposed operating centre in the press, though, and the PSV discs, which must be displayed in the windscreen (green for international operations, blue for national operations only, and orange for small vehicle restricted operations), are not vehicle specific and can be moved between vehicles. The one stricter condition is that it is an absolute offence to use a vehicle on the road without a disc displayed, whereas a road-haulage vehicle can be used for 28 days before a disc is required.

Similar legal costs are required and the Traffic Commissioners have the same avenues of decisions open to them. If the application process has been successful the new licensee will need to obtain the required vehicles. This can again be expensive as new 53/55-seat coaches range from about £280,000 up to £400,000, although a new 75-seat, double-deck, good quality tour coach costs slightly more than this upper figure, but are becoming unpopular. A new double-deck bus for routine local bus work costs about £180,000 and a short single-deck bus between £90,000 and £120,000. A new entrant is likely to purchase used vehicles, such as a ten-year-old good quality tour coach, which still costs in excess of £60,000, or a 20-year-old one from £10,000 upwards. Considering these considerable capital costs, leasing vehicles is common and even some of the dominant companies employ this strategy: Arriva, First Group and Stagecoach, for example.

National Express do not own any of the coaches used on its services but contract out the routes to independent operators. It normally requires that vehicles used must be less than five years old, which has caused many operators to use personalised number plates or vehicles registered in Northern Ireland in order to disguise the age of the vehicle. This rule has also been adopted by a number of holiday companies as only WA Sheerings and a couple of smaller companies have their own vehicles. The actual operator of a route must have its name and address painted on the nearside (usually low down) in letters of 25 mm (1 inch) height. This is called the *legal lettering*. This is a convenient strategy for established operators but is not practical for new entrants. However, it does afford entrants a potentially easier foothold in the market.

As with the road-haulage market, this leads to the conclusion that entry into the PSV market is expensive and that this, combined with the fact that financial institutions can be unhelpful to potential entrants, makes entry into the market difficult. This, along with the bureaucracy, licences and legal costs, means that the non-scheduled, chartered services sub-market is monopolistically competitive (see Chapter 7 for a full exploration of this market structure). More importantly for this section, though, the additional barriers to entry into local PSV markets mean that they are effectively monopolies.

6.7 Natural monopolies

Natural monopolies are markets which can only sustain one producer. Generally they are markets in which the capital costs are so high that the producer needs to receive all of the market revenue just to stay in operation. Any competition within such a market would cause all producers to fail to make normal profit and so would lead to all producers being forced out of the market and there being a complete absence of supply. In fact, some natural monopolies go even further than this and actually need government subsidisation to keep even one producer in production.

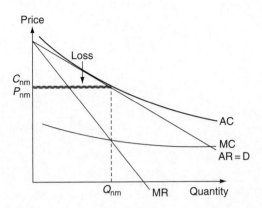

Figure 6.10 Natural monopoly

A simple example is that of a railway. The initial capital costs are considerable as they include the need to purchase and lay down the tracks and to purchase or hire the necessary locomotives and carriages. If two rival businesses did this, creating the situation in which there were two sets of tracks and two services going to and from the same places, both would soon be forced out of production because splitting the demand and revenue between the two would not be sufficient to sustain either. In this situation, for any rail service to be provided, it is vital that there is only one producer that receives all of the revenue.

This is shown graphically in Figure 6.10 by having the marginal cost curve still falling at the profit-maximising level of output.

What this diagram shows is that at the profit-maximising output, where $MC = MR$, the producer is actually making a loss, and so would leave the market. This is a natural monopoly because it clearly illustrates that there is only room for one producer (if we shared the average revenue between two, the situation would be even worse) and that in this case, the single producer can only continue to operate if it is subsidised by the government.

In the transport sector, with the huge initial capital costs in many markets, this is a crucial market structure. It has also been used as a justification for nationalisation or regulation of such markets and for government intervention and subsidisation.

If, as in natural monopoly, average costs are always falling then it will be in the public interest to have one provider rather than two or more: one can always do it cheaper. But then the one supplier will have a dominant position and if left to its own devices it would exploit that dominance to the detriment of the public interest. This conundrum is the motivation for the evolution of the system of independently regulated, privately owned monopolies that now provide network services over pipes, wires and rails.

Monopolistic Competition 7

7.1 | The model and outcomes

The market structure of monopolistic competition can be viewed as the middle structure between monopoly and perfect competition. It is one in which there are many firms that are all supplying similar, but not identical, products to the market. There are barriers to entry and exit but they are not completely prohibitive and so there is a constant fluidity to the market as firms do enter and exit.

In perfect competition there are no barriers to entry and so potential new producers are able to enter the market as soon as there is any abnormal profit, immediately competing that profit away. In monopolistic competition, though, there are barriers to entry, meaning that potential new producers are not able to enter the market as quickly. This means that it is possible for producers to earn abnormal profit in the short run and so the short run diagram of monopolistic competition is the same as the monopoly diagram (Section 6.2). The barriers to entry are not completely prohibitive, though, and so gradually new producers will respond to the market signal of abnormal profit and will enter the market. The share of consumers that each business within the market has will fall as a result of this causing the average revenue curve for each producer to shift inwards and the price that it is able to charge to fall, until it is tangential to their average cost curves at the profit-maximising output. Figures 7.1 illustrates this and shows that the market will settle at a long run output at which only normal profit is being made by each producer – a price of P_{mc} and an output of each producer equal to Q_{mc}. No more producers will enter when this point is reached because that would cause them to make a loss.

Assuming that the cost curves are the same under monopolistic competition as they are under perfect competition, which is an unrealistic assumption because the cost curves could be significantly different due to the scale of the producers, it is possible to compare the outcomes of each market structure. Figure 7.1 does this and shows that the price under monopolistic competition will be higher and the output lower than under the more competitive structure.

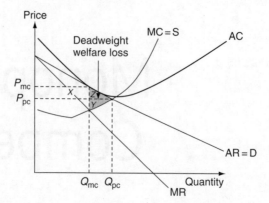

Figure 7.1 A monopolistically competitive producer in the long run

A monopolistically competitive producer is unlikely to be productively efficient because there is not the same degree of competitive pressure as in perfect competition. Figure 7.1 shows this by the fact that the producer is not operating at the lowest point on its average cost curve. It is producing an output that is lower than that necessary for productive efficiency so that it is able to charge a higher price for it. This higher price means that there is also a failure to be allocatively efficient as the price charged, P_{mc}, is greater than the marginal cost at that output, meaning that consumers are being charged too much.

The producer does this because it increases the size of its producer surplus. Compared to the producer surplus under perfect competition it loses area Y but gains area X, causing a significant net gain. This gain is at the expense of the consumers, though, who experience a reduction in surplus of areas X and Z. Consequently, there is a reduction in total market welfare of areas Y and Z – the deadweight welfare loss. This market structure is clearly not Pareto efficient because it is possible to make one of the parties better off without making the other worse off simply by eliminating the welfare loss, but this efficiency loss is not as large as that under monopoly because it is closer to the perfectly competitive structure.

7.2   Competition

In perfect competition the products are homogenous and so the only form the competition can take is that of price competition. In monopolistic competition there will be price competition and in the long run producers are unable to charge a price higher than that leading to normal profit. If they did so, new entrants would come into the market to compete the abnormal profit away.

The products are not homogenous in monopolistic competition, though, and so there will also be *brand competition*. Producers will attempt to differentiate their product from those of their competitors. If consumers view it as being different in some way the producer will effectively have a niche market monopoly within the wider market. It will be able to use this market power to charge a price that will earn it abnormal profit in the short run until its competitors respond to compete it away.

There are a number of ways that a producer can achieve this and all are to be expected within a monopolistically competitive market:

- *Advertising*. The most obvious way is to engage in marketing to create an image that sets it apart from the competition.
- *Product development*. The second is to invest in research and development so that the product has characteristics that the others in the market simply do not have.
- *Patent protection*. Once a product has been developed that is set apart it is to be expected that the producer will attempt to obtain legal protection for it for a time.

7.2.1 The Reliant Robin

The Reliant Robin is a good example of such product differentiation. The three-wheeled vehicle was one in a range of cars manufactured and licensed by Reliant Motors Ltd since 1935. It was launched in 1973 and was vastly different from the other products in the motor-vehicle market as it could be driven by people holding only a motorcycle licence. The advertising focused on this advantage and that the vehicle would be good value for money and cheap to run. The Robin Reliant targeted consumers that no other car could do and so it earned Reliant Motors Ltd monopoly power within its niche market – that of the less wealthy consumers. Even within its particular market Reliant Motors produced a variety of Robin models including the Standard Robin, the Super Robin and the Robin Van to add further differentiation to its image.

Unfortunately, the project failed to be the success that was hoped for. As the incomes of consumers continued to rise and as it became the norm for people to hold full driving licences the demand for the powered three-wheeler declined. The manufacturer changed hands a number of times until it was announced that there would be no more Robins produced after February 2001. This was not the end, though, as in April 2001 B&N Plastics started to remake the Robin under licence from Reliant but has in turn encountered production difficulties. Today the vehicles are more collectors' items rather than being popular with road users.

7.3 | The road-haulage market in the European Union and Great Britain

The road-haulage market in the European Union is a good example of a mono-polistically competitive market and it is one of vital importance. In terms of value added, it accounts for the largest proportion of that of all road, and other land, transport in the EU25, with 64.4 per cent. This sector in turn accounts for half of the value added from the whole of the transport sector.

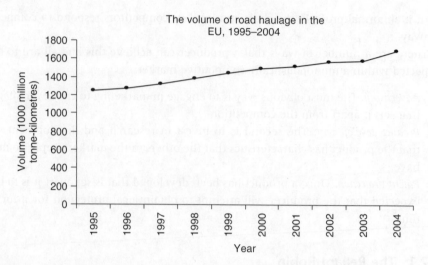

Figure 7.2   The growth in the volume of freight transported by road in the EU
Source: European Commission, Directorate-General for Energy and Transport in co-operation with Eurostat, Energy and Transport in Figures, 2005

Figure 7.2 shows that the road-haulage market has experienced strong and consistent growth in terms of the volume of freight that it transports, rising from 1.248 billion tonne-kilometres in 1995 to over 1.6 billion tonne-kilometres in 2004. This has caused its share of the total freight transported by all the modes of transport to increase from 42.1 per cent in 1995 to 44.3 per cent in 2004 (see Section 2.1.2).

Not only has the volume of freight that it accounts for increased, road-haulage companies have also diversified considerably. No longer do they simply transport goods, they also compete in their provision of logistics services and warehousing. There are third-party logistics companies that offer the service of organising a manufacturer's supply and delivery chains to ensure that the correct resources and final products are in the correct place at the correct time. Such diversification and competition to differentiate their products is exactly what the monopolistic competition model would predict as businesses attempt to establish market power.

In order to establish a road-haulage company it is necessary to obtain an operator's licence; to purchase or hire a fleet of vehicles and organise the required insurance; to employ the necessary drivers and administration staff; and to conduct the necessary marketing. These costs can be significant indeed and so there are clearly barriers to entry in the road-haulage market, but these are by no means entirely prohibitive. This is evidenced by the 485,220 road-haulage companies that existed within the European Union (excluding Greece and Poland) in 2003 (except for Luxembourg and Malta, whose figures were for 2002, and Belgium, whose figures were for 2001). This is such a large number that the barriers to entry cannot be insurmountable, which is another characteristic of monopolistic competition.

This can be seen in more detail by further analysing the road-haulage market in Great Britain. Entry to the British road freight market is strictly controlled and has been since the Road Traffic Act of 1930. This act established a number of Traffic

Commissioners whose principal duties were to licence road freight and passenger operators and to licence and regulate the fares of bus companies. There are now seven Commissioners across the country that still grant licences and hold their own disciplinary courts, called Public Inquiries (known as PI's in the industry). Operators view them with a sense of fear as they act as judge, jury and executioner.

In order to obtain an operator's licence, applicants must satisfy the following conditions:

- They must be of *good repute*, in effect, meaning that they hold no serious criminal conviction, including a series of speeding convictions.
- They must be *professionally competent*. Practically, this means that someone in the organisation holds a Certificate of Professional Competence in Road Haulage. This qualification is obtained by passing one of two sets of examinations that the Oxford, Cambridge and Royal Society of Arts Examination Board (OCR) have been contracted by the UK Department of Transport to set. One of these is for a national certificate and the other for an international certificate. The contents and style of these examinations are strictly stipulated by the Council Directive 98/76/EC of the European Commission, which ensures that assessment is comparable across European Union member states.

To achieve the National Certificate candidates must pass all three modules: the Legal and Business Context (or Core) examination; the National Road Haulage examination and the National Road Haulage case study. To be awarded the International Certificate candidates must additionally pass the International Road Haulage examination. There are four examination sittings each year and 600 centres across the country at which applicants can sit them. Transport companies offer courses to help applicants in passing them, such as Professional Transport Services that charge £550 for a five-day teaching course to achieve the National Certificate. The examination itself costs a further £175. The examinations are at a level that is equivalent to an A-level. The average pass rates for the three modules for the National Certificate over recent sittings are displayed in Figure 7.3. They range from almost 66 per cent at the beginning of the period to a low of 55.18 per cent in March 2006. The pass rate of the additional module for the International Certificate ranges from 41.2 to 58.9 per cent over this same period. Clearly, many candidates fail the course and so are required to enter the examinations again, re-incurring the entrance costs and any additional tuition that may be deemed necessary.

- They must have *adequate finance*. Applicants are required to show that after they have acquired their vehicles they have access to sufficient finance for them. In practice, this currently means £6200 for the first vehicle and a further £3400 for each additional vehicle.
- They must have a centre from which to operate that has sufficient off-street parking for all vehicles allowed on the licence.
- They must have maintenance facilities, which can take the form of a legally binding agreement with a commercial repair garage or agent.

■ They must advertise their intention to use the proposed premises as an operating centre in a local newspaper, asking for objections from the local populous on environmental grounds. The cost of such advertising varies hugely according to the area. The wording is strictly set out by law and even the omission of a full stop can result in a re-advertisement being insisted upon by the Traffic Commissioner.

The application form is then completed and submitted with £215 to start the application process. The details are then published in the Traffic Commissioners' publication *Applications and Decisions* to be read by statutory objectors, such as the Police, local authorities, employers organisations and a number of trade unions connected with the industry. They all have a right to object and if they do so the Traffic Commissioner has three courses of action available. First, the objection can be overruled, which almost never happens, or a public inquiry can be called to make the decision. Applicants may want to be represented in such enquiries but this can be costly as transport solicitors charge from £280 per hour, although there are some cheaper options. Secondly, the Commissioner can call for a meeting with the applicant in Chambers, at which the applicant may also wish to be represented. Finally, the Commissioner can simply refuse to grant the licence, in response to which the applicant can call for a public inquiry. If there are no problems with an application an offer of a licence will normally arrive within nine weeks when a further £336 will be required. It is then necessary to purchase a licence disc for each vehicle with the choice to pay for a year at £44 or for five years at £180. Applicants often hire the services of a consultant, such as Professional Transport Services, to guide them through the applications process. This costs

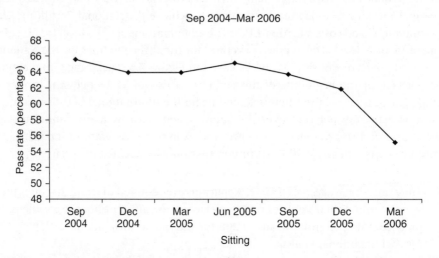

Figure 7.3 The recent average pass rates across the three modules of the OCR Certificate of Professional Competence in National Road Haulage.
Source: The Oxford, Cambridge and Royal Society of Arts Examination Board (OCR)

around £400, in addition to the other costs and fees, to set up a reasonably simple licence.

Once the application process has been successfully navigated the new licensee will need to obtain the needed vehicles. Trucks can cost anything from £60,000 to £120,000 each to purchase new, but most operators choose to buy second hand, which range in price from less than £10,000 and up to £60,000. In the second-hand truck market it is the age and condition of the vehicle that determines the price. Some companies choose a third option, which is to lease their vehicles, but this rarely happens at the start of a company's trading life as its creditworthiness will be as yet unproven.

All of this leads to the conclusion that entry into the road-haulage market is expensive. This is not necessarily a formidable barrier to entry, though; if there is access to the necessary sums of finance it can be overcome, as in the tramp shipping market. Unfortunately, banks and other financial institutions are not very often likely to support proposed road-haulage ventures as there is a high failure rate in the market. If a vehicle is stopped at the roadside and found to be defective, for example, it will be issued with a prohibition notice which prevents the vehicle being moved even by towing. A serious one of these or a number of minor ones will lead to the operator being called to a public inquiry where his or her operator's licence can be curtailed, suspended or revoked. If any one of these happens the enterprise is likely to fail. No operator can avoid these potentialities. In February 2005 Eddie Stobart, Britain's largest hauler, had his licence revoked in the Eastern Traffic Area. He managed to convince the Traffic Commissioner of the area to grant a new licence after about six months but during that time all Eastern area vehicles were stopped and all work had to be covered by vehicles from other areas returning to their registered bases on regular intervals. For the same reason, overdraft facilities are difficult to come by without adequate security.

As such, there are barriers to entry into the road-haulage market: bureaucracy, licences, capital costs with scarce sources of finance and sunk costs. Membership of the Road Haulage Association or the Freight Transport Association is helpful, though, as is employing the services of a transport consultant, such as those from Professional Transport Services, and so the barriers are far from completely prohibitive. This is demonstrated by the number and sizes of operators that exist in the market. Figure 7.4 shows that in 2004/2005 the number of licences that had been issued to engage in commercial road freight was 101,900. This had fallen by 23,200 since 1993/1994 but remained a substantial amount. The average size of a road-haulage fleet in 2004/2005 was 3.9 vehicles, which was an increase from 3.2 in 1993/1994 but which was still a relatively small number. Figure 7.5 shows the composition of the market in terms of the fleet sizes of each of the licensed operators. By far the largest number of operators, some 48,200, had only one vehicle and the next largest, with 15,800 operators, had two. There were only 300 companies with between 101 and 500 vehicles and hardly any with more than 501.

With such barriers to entry, a significant, but not vast, number of small providers; non-homogenous services, product differentiation and brand marketing; and the

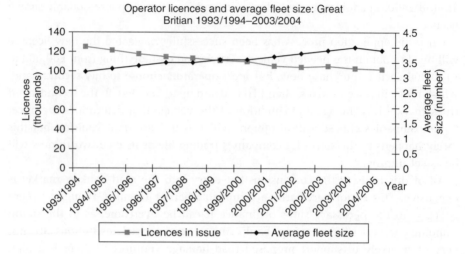

Figure 7.4 The composition of the road-haulage market in Great Britain
Source: UK Department for Transport 2006

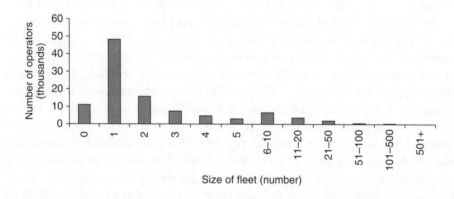

Figure 7.5 Operator fleet sizes in Great Britain, 2003/2004
Source: UK Department for Transport 2006

potential for abnormal profits in the short run, the British road-haulage market, and that in the wider EU, is clearly one of monopolistic competition.

7.4 | The taxi market in the City of Leicester

Taxi markets are location specific and so it is not appropriate to look at them at a national level. In each locality it is likely that the market will comprise of two distinct operations: hackney carriages and private hires. This section shall examine the sub-market for each in turn, focusing in particular on the City of Leicester. Not all of the specific details are necessarily applicable across the country or across the European Union.

Hackney carriages can ply for hire, usually operating from taxi ranks. One does not need to obtain an operator's licence to establish a hackney carriage business but it is necessary to be a licensed hackney carriage driver to use vehicles that have been registered by the local authority for such use. Leicester Council does, however, only licence a limited number of cabs which are then required to have fare metres

Table 7.1 Hackney carriage fares within the boundaries of the City of Leicester, 2006

	Tariffs (£)		
	Switch-on	Each 115 metres or part thereof	Each 25 seconds waiting time
Day times: Monday to Saturday (0600 to 2200)	2.20	0.10	0.10
Night-time (2200 to 0600)	2.70	0.10	0.10
Sundays	2.70	0.10	0.10
Bank-holidays	2.70	0.10	0.10
24 and 31 December from 0600 to 2100	5.20	0	0
25 and 26 December and 1 January from 0600 to 2100	5.20	0	0
24, 25 and 31 December and 1 and 2 January from 2100 to 0600 and 26 December from 2100 to 0000	5.70	0	0
Soiling charge		50.00	

Source: Leicester City Council

fitted and calibrated to the current pricing schedule, which is shown in Table 7.1. These schedules are usually reviewed every 18 months or if representation is made from the hackney carriage trade.

For journeys outside of the city boundary fares are negotiable between the driver and the hirer before the hiring commences. Where no fare is agreed in advance of the journey the maximum charge is limited to the amount which would be payable if calculated on the above scale.

Scheduled rates such as these ensure that the operators do not raise the fares above that which the Council deems appropriate. Figure 7.6 illustrates how price ceilings such as these work. The free market would establish a rate of P_1 at which Q_1 journeys would be purchased. The Council, however, would view this as being too high a rate and so enforces a price ceiling at P_c by requiring all operators to use metres that are calibrated appropriately. As this price is lower than that which the market would have stabilised, it actually causes an excess demand as there are more passengers wanting to hire vehicles at that rate than there are vehicles in operation. In this situation, passengers have to wait longer at the ranks than they would like to. In terms of welfare, area A in Figure 7.6 is transferred from being producer surplus to being consumer surplus. Areas B and C are lost, though, and so account for the deadweight welfare loss of the price intervention. Area B is lost from the consumers, but as area A is greater than this the consumers are net beneficiaries, which is the objective of the intervention. Area C is lost from the producers, which means that the producers are worse off to the extent of areas A

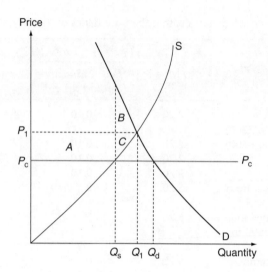

Figure 7.6 Price ceilings

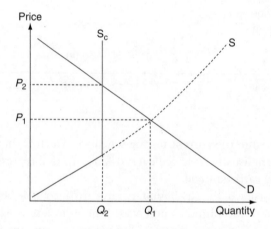

Figure 7.7 The imposition of a supply constraint

and C. Overall, as there is a deadweight welfare loss, society is also worse off and is no longer Pareto efficient. Councils are willing to accept this result to provide passengers with the increase in consumer surplus.

As the Council is only willing to licence a set number of vehicles the hackney carriage market is also subject to a supply constraint, which is shown by the vertical section of the supply curve (S_c) in Figure 7.7. For this to have any effect on the market supply the constraint must be at a quantity of supply less than that which would prevail in a free market. This is shown in Figure 7.7 by the supply constraint being at a quantity of Q_2 instead of the free market equilibrium of Q_1.

Figure 7.7 clearly shows that as a result of restricting supply the price in the market is driven upwards, from P_1 to P_2. This would reduce the welfare of consumers to a level below that in the free market, which strengthens the reason for the Council imposing a price ceiling as well.

It appears at first sight that having both of these interventions is superfluous. If the price ceiling is set correctly, the quantity supplied will automatically fall to the desired level of Q_2. The problem, however, is that it is not practically feasible for policy-makers to perfectly estimate how quantity supplied will respond to an enforced change in price. In other words, they cannot perfectly construct the supply curve in the market. As such, simply relying on a price ceiling would leave the resulting quantity supplied in the market to an element of chance and so it is necessary to impose both forms of intervention in order to be certain of the outcomes. This is important to ensure that the burden of inspections and licensing is not too onerous and expensive.

Private hire operators, on the other hand, can only accept bookings to carry passengers or goods by prior arrangement. It is necessary to obtain a number of licences before establishing a private hire operation. All of these licences are reviewed annually.

- Premises must be licensed as a Private Hire Operators base.
- All vehicles to run from the business must be licensed as private hire vehicles.
- All drivers must be licensed as hackney carriage and private hire vehicle drivers. Leicester has a dual licence for drivers as opposed to either private hire drivers or hackney carriage drivers.

The cost of establishing such an operation is dependant on the number of vehicles operating from the premises. For one vehicle it is £340; for two to twenty vehicles it is £405 and for operations greater than this it is £478.

Private hire operators do not have to abide by a set maximum fare tariff, as hackney carriages do, and so are free to charge whatever fares they can negotiate with their customers. They are also inspected annually or whenever the Council receives a complaint.

In 2006/2007 there were 166 private hire operating companies advertising in the City of Leicester, offering a wide array of slightly differentiated services including cars that are specialised for the disabled; executive and luxury operations, using more expensive vehicles; larger vehicles for transporting six or more passengers; services that specialise in transporting passengers to schools or to the local airports; and services guaranteeing female drivers. The fares that these companies charge are also far from uniform.

With such a volume of operators in the market – offering slightly differentiated services, investing in advertising and charging different prices – and with the existence of non-prohibitive barriers to entry in the form of licences and fees, the market is clearly one of monopolistic competition.

Oligopoly 8

8.1 Definition and model

An *oligopoly* is a market structure that is dominated by a few large producers and as such it lies towards the uncompetitive extreme of the spectrum of competition (Section 4.7). The goods that they sell can be highly differentiated and there are significant barriers to entry preventing many businesses from entering the market. In the other market structures each of the producers can be viewed in isolation but this is not the case in an oligopoly. As there are only a few producers they each have to consider how the others will respond to any decisions that they make. In this way they are in fact interdependent decision-makers.

This means that if one of the producers reduces its price the others are likely to follow suit sparking a price war as each producer strains to gain a market advantage. If one of the producers decides to increase its price, though, its competitors are likely to look upon this in delight and to keep their prices constant in an attempt to attract more consumers with their relatively lower prices. As a result of this the producers are likely to be reluctant to change their prices. In other words, it is likely that there will be a high degree of *price stickiness*. There can be significant changes in the costs that the producers have to pay but these are unlikely to be transmitted through to changes in the final price of the products that they supply.

This unique characteristic means that whereas the three other market structures have been modelled in effectively the same way using the same diagram as the base, this structure calls for a slight adaptation. This is shown in Figure 8.1. The average revenue curve is *kinked*, which causes there to be a vertical section in the marginal revenue curve. If it is assumed that the marginal cost curve intersects the marginal revenue curve along this vertical section then the marginal cost curve is able to shift without it leading to a change in price – the profit-maximising producer will maintain a price of P as that corresponds to the level of output at which marginal cost is equal to marginal revenue.

This shows the price stickiness that exists within an oligopoly but it does not facilitate any further analysis. For this it is necessary to assume that there is a single marginal cost curve and to then add the corresponding average cost curve. This is done in Figures 8.2 and 8.3. As there are only a few producers, and as they sell products that can be significantly differentiated, they are able to exert a degree of

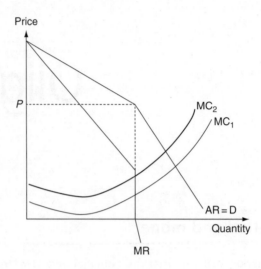

Figure 8.1 The oligopolistic kinked demand curve diagram

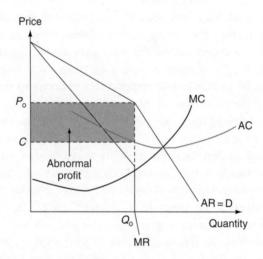

Figure 8.2 Abnormal profit under oligopoly

market power. As such the price in an oligopoly, denoted by P_o, is likely to be higher than the average costs that the producers have to pay, C, and so they earn abnormal profit which is then protected in the long run by the barriers to entry that exist.

Figure 8.3 shows the lack of efficiency within an oligopoly. The oligopoly is failing to produce the level of output at which its average costs are minimised and so it is failing to be productively efficient. The oligopoly price is also significantly higher than the marginal cost at its level of output, Q_o. As such it is not allocatively efficient either. These two characteristics lead to the conclusion that an oligopoly fails to be Pareto efficient.

An oligopolistic producer uses its market power to raise its price, P_o, above that of the price under perfect competition, P_{pc}. It does this in order to increase its welfare, as shown by its producer surplus which is increased by area X. It loses area Y, but there is clearly a net increase in its welfare as a result. Area X has, however,

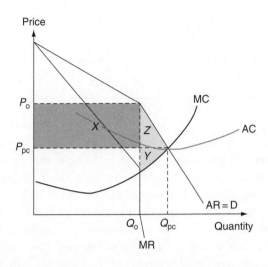

Figure 8.3 The efficiency under oligopoly

been transformed from being consumer surplus and so the producer has used its market power to benefit at the expense of the consumers. The consumers also lose area Z from their surplus, which along with area Y form the *deadweight welfare loss*, meaning that the overall welfare under oligopoly is less than that under perfect competition. It is possible to make one of the parties better off without making the other worse off simply by eliminating this welfare loss.

8.2 | Location decisions

As there are only a few producers in an oligopoly, each of them will seek to obtain a degree of market power by differentiating their products from those of their competitors, which is the same as in monopolistic competition (see Section 7.2). A model by Hotelling shows, however, that there will be a tendency over time for the degree of differentiation to fall. In other words, there is likely to be a convergence in terms of the characteristics of the products that are supplied to the market. This convergence can also be seen in terms of the geographical location of the producers.

During the 2006 Football World Cup there was a large screen erected in a park in the centre of Cambridge. Thousands of fans gathered in the sweltering heat to watch as England took on Paraguay and then Sweden, and beer vendors set up stalls to sell their produce. Let us assume that the fans were uniformly spread out across the park in front of the screen and that they had no preference for the beer that they drank other than wanting to walk the shortest distance to get to the vendor.

Let us further assume that there are two vendors A and B, and that they locate themselves in the way shown in Figure 8.4. As the consumers are indifferent between the beer that the vendors are selling and so will make their purchases from the nearest stall, vendor A will receive all of the custom from the people to

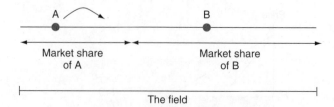

Figure 8.4
Hotelling's location model

the left of its position and half of that from those to its right. Vendor B, on the other hand, will receive all of the custom from its right and the remaining half of the custom from its left. Vendor B is clearly in the better location.

Vendor A will seek to rectify this situation by moving its location to the right, increasing its custom as it does so. Vendor B will respond by moving its location more towards the left in order to increase its custom as well and so the two will converge in the centre. At this point they have an equal share of the market; they are unable to improve on this and so will settle into those locations.

If another vendor was to enter the market, one of the vendors will always have to be in between the others. This is a disadvantageous position to be in and so the central vendor will *jump* over one of the others to seize the share of the market to that side. As a result there will always be movement and the market will not settle down into an equilibrium state. This situation is unique to a market with three vendors, though, and adding further vendors once again leads to a steady state – that for four producers is illustrated in Figure 8.5.

This model can be applied to an oligopoly in two ways. First, it implies that there will be a convergence in the actual geographical location of the producers. It is to be expected that businesses within an oligopoly are likely to position themselves close to one another.

Secondly, though, it has a deeper implication in terms of the product differentiation that is likely within an oligopoly, or indeed within a monopolistically competitive market. If the field represented in Figures 8.4 and 8.5 is taken to be the spectrum of tastes that consumers have then over time it is likely that the degree to which the products differ will decline as producers seek to capture the custom of the more moderate consumers. This implication is strengthened by the fact that, in reality, consumers' tastes are not uniformly distributed and are actually likely to have a more normal distribution with the greatest concentration in the more

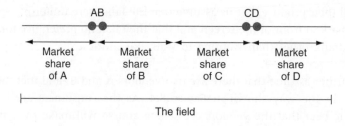

Figure 8.5
Hotelling's location model with four producers

moderate region of the spectrum, which is where the producers will seek to locate themselves.

This conclusion does not contradict Section 7.2 because it is complicated by considering the effect of the spectrum of tastes being extremely wide. In this situation producers are likely to be perfectly happy locating at the extremes in order to avoid direct competition. It is with this aim that producers in monopolistic competition and oligopoly often invest considerable amounts in order to differentiate their products to such a degree that they are effectively a separate market – a niche market. This is especially the case in monopolistic competition, where there are so many producers. The potential gains from converging with the others are minimal due to the sheer number of competitors, whereas the potential gains from locating oneself at an extreme of the spectrum and so creating a niche market are greater. In this way it is to be expected that there will be more product differentiation under monopolistic competition than under oligopoly, in which this location model is much more relevant.

This simple model has many applications; for instance, the *positioning* of rival political parties seeking support from a left-to-right spectrum of electors or the behaviour of commercial television channels in designing their programming to appeal to the greatest audience.

8.3   The European air industry

8.3.1 The structure of the market

The airlines are difficult to classify in terms of their market structure because of the nature of the industry. There are two main types of flight – *scheduled* flights, which run to a regular timetable; and *chartered* flights, which are purchased on an individual basis. There have also been different types of operating companies that specialise in each.

Traditionally, each of the main European nations have had their own scheduled airlines, such as British Airways, Air France and Lufthansa, and these have been viewed as comprising an important part of the national identity. As such, governments have been willing to protect, both financially and through legislation, their *flag carriers*, creating monopolies on all domestic flights. *Cabotage*, the practice of flying a domestic route in a foreign country, has also been traditionally disallowed in times of war, when governments would not want foreign fleets within their airspace.

On international routes the airlines, knowing that they are all protected from being forced out of the market by their respective governments, have traditionally sought to establish colluding duopolies rather than engaging in wasteful and pointless competition. British Airways worked with Aer Lingus on all flights between Britain and Ireland, pooling all revenue and then sharing it according to the number of seats that each airline sold. Similar agreements were established between British

Airways and Lufthansa between Britain and Germany, and British Airways and Air France between Britain and France.

The physical structure of the industry was developed around the idea of hubs and spokes. There are a number of hub airports around the world, such as London Heathrow, connected by the main international routes, which have traditionally been characterised by colluding duopolies. There are then numerous smaller domestic routes, the spokes, which have traditionally been monopolised. This structure was intended to reduce the number of low-loaded flights travelling long distances, as smaller craft transport passengers to the hubs, at which they fill fewer large craft to make the long journeys. A similar structure is also employed in other parts of the transport sector. In shipping, freight is transported into a small number of large European ports by large ships, from where it is transferred to other ports by smaller vessels. In the British bus market, Victoria Coach Station acts as the major hub for long-distance services.

This lack of competition within the European air industry ensured that prices were maintained at such an inflated level that air travel was the exclusive reserve of the affluent. It also discouraged the airlines working to improve the quality of the services in terms of frequency, reliability and comfort.

These conditions continued in Europe until the late 1970s when British Midland, now BMI, started to push the British government for permission to begin flying between London and Scotland. Despite the efforts of British Airways the government agreed to creating competition on these routes. Since then there has been an increasing movement towards liberalisation of the European air industry, culminating in April 1997 with stage three of the European Union's *Open Skies* legislation, which theoretically allows any European airline to operate on any route within the Union – theoretically because *slots* at airports, especially the busiest, are still limited and fiercely contended, meaning that certain routes are effectively closed to new entrants. For instance, London Heathrow, the world's busiest airport, simply has no extra capacity to grant to new operators. This situation is worsened by the *grandfather rights*, which allow airlines that have traditionally operated certain slots at certain times of the year to continue using them.

In some parts of Europe, governments still protect their own flag carriers. Switzerland is not a part of the Open Skies initiative. In March 1998 easyJet purchased 40 per cent of TEA Basel AG, a Swiss charter airline, later renaming it *easyJet Switzerland* and moving it to Geneva. Following opposition from Swissair, the Swiss government allowed easyJet to fly from Switzerland to Spain but on the condition that cheap flights were part of a package. EasyJet's response demonstrated the company's view of the legislation, pitching a tent on a remote Spanish hillside and informing passengers that they were welcome to use it if they wanted to. The Swiss government eventually relented, allowing easyJet Switzerland to freely determine its routes and fares. The French government and the French air traffic controllers in organising departures and landings have also been accused of unfairly favouring the national airline.

Establishing an airline is also a costly business. Calder (2006) outlines these costs. A new Boeing 737-700, the aircraft of choice among the low-cost airlines, has a listed price of $30 million but this could be negotiated down to $25 million. It would be necessary to have three of them in order to operate at a reasonable frequency and to cover maintenance time. For those who fail to have $75 million at hand, it is possible to lease them for around $100,000 each a month or to purchase them second-hand for around $15 million a piece. On top of this, in order to utilise airtime fully it is necessary to have five crews for each craft – that is, five pilots, five second officers and five sets of cabin staff – and that a cheap pilot will demand a minimum salary of £80,000. These are just the airborne staff. It is also necessary to hire an experienced pilot as the chief operating officer, engineers, a sales team and so on. Calder states that each craft requires a minimum of 90 workers. Finally, before being able to depart, it is necessary to obtain the necessary licences from the authorities and to have done enough marketing to ensure that the craft will be full. A significant proportion of this initial investment represents a sunk cost to the entrepreneur, creating a considerable barrier to entry.

Despite these obstructions, and the European law that limited non-European Union holdings in the airlines of member states, the European air industry has opened up considerably. It is now characterised by a high degree of fluidity as new airlines emerge and others exit the market at a remarkable rate. This is especially true of the low-cost airlines. Ryanair was the first low-cost airline within Europe, commencing operations in 1985. It was to be followed by many others, including easyJet (1995), Debonair (1996), Go (1998), Buzz (2000), Germanwings (2002), SkyEurope (2002) and Duo (2003). With the lack of spare capacity, the high costs and the threat of fierce competition from existing airlines at the busiest airports these new entrants have largely focused their operations around smaller airports outside the major urban conurbations, many of which are former military airfields. As a result, as well as the traditional hub-and-spoke structure, the European air market now comprises of a whole network of shorter point-to-point routes across the continent. Instead of routes being dominated by monopolies and duopolies, there is now widespread competition between operators offering routes between the same countries which are of varying degrees of closeness. There is also a high level of competition for travellers who are less concerned about the precise foreign destination. As such the European market should be viewed as being a series of oligopolistic markets with operators offering similar services, with longer external flights still being dominated by the traditional carriers.

Currently there are few actual routes, using the same airports, on which airlines are in direct competition with one another. There are still a considerable number of smaller airports in Europe that are still to be used, especially in the accession countries, and it is likely that these will be the target of further expansion for a while. Gradually, though, the head-to-head competition will become more prevalent.

8.3.2 The economics of the low-cost airlines

The low-cost airlines have revolutionised the European air industry. The first low-cost airline in the world was that of Southwest Airlines (initially incorporated as Air Southwest), which commenced operations in Texas in 1971. Rollin King and

Herb Kelleher had the new idea to establish a passenger service that was affordable to the masses by eliminating all unnecessary costs. This stood in stark contrast to the existing operators that were safe to be inefficient through governmental support and that maintained air travel for the affluent. In 2005 Southwest was the world's third largest carrier in terms of passenger numbers, behind Delta Air Lines and American Airlines, and today it is held to be the ultimate model of how to run a low-cost airline successfully.

The idea was pioneered in Europe by Richard Branson's Virgin Atlantic. Travellers in Europe had little access to cheap flights across the Atlantic and so Virgin Atlantic established a route between Gatwick and Maastricht at the cheap flat rate of £19 each way, enabling travellers to then board transatlantic flights from the English capital. Due to poor performance it was dropped after five years, leaving it up to Ryanair to be Europe's first truly low-cost and successful airline. The Irish operator took up the gauntlet, commencing operations in 1985. It is now one of the largest airlines in Europe.

The strategy of the low-cost airlines is simply to reduce its fares by reducing costs as much as possible. The most important aspect in doing this is to maximise the utilisation of the aircraft; or in other words, keeping the aircraft in the air as much as possible by reducing the turnaround time at airports. This has been achieved in three main ways. The first is by dispensing with pre-assigned seats. Instead travellers are given a number or letter when they check in which determines when they are called to board the flight, allowing boarding to be completed much more smoothly. Secondly, using the smaller airports has also helped in this as at these there can be quicker boarding, less chance of air traffic delays and quicker taxiing. The smaller airports bring direct financial benefits as well as they charge less for using their facilities (and they can be negotiated downwards) and they often grant subsidies to airlines for using them. In 1998 Ryanair commenced operations to Rimini. The local airport authority, Aerodria, gave a package of subsidies worth a total of £400,000 to the airline for doing so. Finally, by linking as many of its airports as possible to each other the craft can be operated on different routes facilitating greater utilisation. This also allows the exploitation of economies of scale in advertising as it costs the same amount to advertise five different flights on an advertising board in a terminal as it does to advertise a single one. As well as this, costs have been lowered by the following ways.

- *Maximising the efficient employment of resources.* The cabin crews also clean the craft to save on hiring others to do so and the craft are used as advertising boards to raise extra revenue. Ryanair have advertised companies such as Jaguar cars and *The Sun* newspaper on the sides of their planes.
- *Reducing the frills.* Low-cost airlines usually do not provide free hot meals or refreshments. Customers are expected to purchase such items separately, earning the airlines further revenue which can be significant. Debonair has veered from this strategy by providing refreshments and by increasing *seat pitch*, the distance between the front of a seat and the front of the seat behind, to make the travellers more comfortable.

▧ *Using the Internet.* Traditionally, airlines sell their tickets through travel agents in return for a 9 per cent commission. Ryanair was the first to tackle this convention by reducing the commission by one and a half percentage points. EasyJet was then the first airline to dispense with the travel agents completely, a move which has subsequently been followed across the industry. Using the Internet to sell seats has significantly reduced *distribution* costs as well as providing the airlines with useful marketing material – 'cutting out the middleman to save you money'.

▧ *Aggressive marketing strategies.* Stelios Haji-Ioannou, the founder of easyJet, spent in excess of a million pounds on advertising to establish the business. Since then much more has followed. The airlines have even ventured into TV documentary series that follow their daily operations.

▧ *Adopting the policy of no refunds.*

8.3.3 Competition in the European air industry

Since liberalisation and the emergence of the low-cost airlines there has been fierce competition within the industry. This has taken many forms: fare reductions, use of legal authorities, marketing, acquisitions and expansion. Two examples of the first of these are outlined here but it is easy to find others throughout the industry.

The year 1995 was the year that saw easyJet commence operations between Luton and Scotland (Glasgow and Edinburgh). British Airways already had to share the London–Scotland route with British Midland due to the latter's penetration into the market in the early 1980s. Both of these carriers vehemently fought easyJet by offering flights for £58, the fare offered by the new entrant but with the additional frills and departures from the world's busiest airport. Competition even came from the railways as Virgin trains, GNER and Scotrail all cut their fares.

In 2001, Go announced flights from Scotland (Edinburgh and Glasgow again) to Dublin. The Scotland–Ireland routes were the domain of Ryanair and Aer Lingus, and the first of these viewed Dublin as its territory. Both of the existing carriers slashed their prices and Ryanair, which had been flying from Prestwick, commenced new flights from Edinburgh. All three lost money in the price war and the entrant was forced to abandon its plans in the area in 2002.

The airlines have also used existing legislation to hamper rivals. Examples are again easy to find across the continent. Ryanair has been taken to court on numerous occasions for different reasons. Virgin Express lodged a complaint about the subsidies the Irish carrier was receiving at Charleroi, and Air France did similarly regarding the subsidies at Strasbourg. In the first case Ryanair stayed but reduced its planned operations and in the second it relocated to Baden-Baden.

As noted above, the airlines have engaged in aggressive marketing techniques in attempts to outdo their rivals. Stelios Haji-Ioannou, before stepping down as chief executive of easyJet, was often at the leading edge of this. When Barbara Cassani established Go under the British Airways umbrella, Stelios and six colleagues purchased tickets on the inaugural flight and turned up in bright orange suits to take the media attention away from the entrant. Ryanair has also engaged in such marketing, causing the intervention of the advertising watchdog on more than one occasion about the labelling of destinations (it has been known to use the names of major cities that are in fact 60 miles away for airports), the announcement of fares (it has announced fares that bear little resemblance to the actual amounts passengers have to pay) and the comparison of fares with those of other airlines.

Airlines, especially the low-cost airlines, have been eager to expand in order to capture a greater market share. They have done this not only by establishing new routes of their own but also by acquiring failing airlines: British Airways bought Dan-Air in 1992 in order to obtain an established European network; the Dutch airline KLM bought Air UK to form KLM UK; Ryanair purchased Buzz; easyJet bought into TEA Basel AG in 1998 and then bought Go in 2003. These are just a few of numerous examples.

8.3.4 The pricing and booking strategies of the airlines

The airlines have demonstrated a number of different pricing strategies. The first is that of *penetration pricing*, which is where a business, trying to establish itself in a new market, sets its price beneath those of the incumbents in order to attract and capture customers. Often this necessitates setting a price that is lower than that required to cover costs, thereby generating a loss, until the entrant is established and can then raise its price again. Ryanair used such a strategy when launching its Dublin–London route in competition with British Airways and Aer Lingus; and easyJet did similarly when commencing its London–Scotland route.

The second is that of *loss-leader pricing*. This is subtly different to penetration pricing as it is where a business, which has interests in multiple markets, sets a price in one market purposefully beneath that necessary to cover costs in order to attract customers, not just in the loss-making market, but in more profitable markets as well. The intention is that the extra customers in the profitable markets will generate revenues that will more than offset the loss in the loss-making market. The important part of the strategy is to make a loss in a market that has such a weight with customers that it will encourage them to use the business in other markets as well. Ryanair, for example, by publicising its extremely low fares on London–Ireland routes may actually attract many more passengers on its other European routes which outweigh any losses incurred. Germanwings, Ryanair and SkyEurope have all adopted such strategies.

The third is that of *predatory* or *destructive pricing*, which is where a business reduces its prices in order to capture the customers of its competitors. In practice this is the same as penetration pricing; the distinction is that of the intention behind the strategy. The section above has numerous examples of predatory pricing. The intention is that by doing so the rivals can be forced out of the market and the prices increased once again. If successful, the business will have increased its market power and so can raise prices to beyond those that existed previously, generating more producer surplus than before. As with the other strategies, this often involves reducing prices to below those necessary to cover costs. It often becomes a battle of attrition with competitors reducing their prices in retaliation. For this strategy to be successful, therefore, the initiating business needs to either have access to reserve capital to accommodate any losses or be able to use *cross-subsidisation* to cover any losses with the revenue from more profitable markets. Competition law generally regards the second of these options as being illegal as it is a way in which large enterprises can force smaller competitors out of the market to the detriment of consumer welfare. In 1998, easyJet lodged a legal complaint that British Airways was unfairly cross-subsidising Go but it failed to amount to anything.

In terms of bookings, the airlines have been engaged in *flight amalgamation* and *overbooking*. The first of these is the practice of combining two or more flights, each of which is only partly loaded. For example, a particular airline may have two flights on exactly the same route scheduled on the same day. If both of these are only half-booked it is logical for the airline to cancel the first departure and transfer the passengers onto the later one. The drawback is the customer dissatisfaction caused; a drawback that has caused airlines such as Ryanair to publicly announce that they will no longer use it as a cost-saving strategy.

Overbooking is based on the premise that some passengers will fail to actually use their booking and so by booking more than the capacity of the aircraft the airline can ensure higher loading. This is, of course, a gamble as too many passengers may arrive at the departure gates for a flight. In these situations the airlines simply offer passengers monetary compensation. As situations where compensation is required are rarer than situations in which not all passengers turn up, the airlines are net winners in this game.

A recent development is that of *callable* flights, which is where passengers are offered the option of surrendering their seats for a refund plus an additional payment. This is helpful in situations of overbooking as it allows last-minute travellers who are willing to pay more to obtain seats to do so, whilst at the same time generating increased revenue for the airlines which can be split with those passengers that had booked for a lower fare at an earlier date. For example, an easyJet flight between Newcastle and Barcelona may be fully booked far in advance with each passenger having paid a flat fare of £30 when Newcastle United makes it through to the Champions League semi-final against Barcelona. Thousands of *Geordies* now want to take that flight and are willing to pay much more to do so. With a callable flight, the airline could charge the football fans £150 per seat and then offer those who booked earlier a refund plus an additional £50 to surrender their seats. In this way, all can benefit.

8.4 | The global car industry

The car industry is a crucial part of the global economy. Sixty million cars and trucks are manufactured each year, millions find their employment in the industry and it accounts for approximately 10 per cent of GDP in the developed countries. The products are responsible for almost half of the world's annual oil consumption and use nearly half of the world's annual output of rubber and a quarter of its glass. The industry has often been ahead of its time, being the first to use planned obsolescence, a leading industry in unionisation and one of the first to come under scrutiny for safety and environmental concerns.

The modern car industry first emerged in France and the USA in the early 1900s with the development of mass production techniques (see Section 1.2 for an account of the early development of the industry). Toyota made considerable refinements to the production process with the introduction of its just-in-time technique in the 1960s which saved producers from locking up capital in excess stocks and enabling them to be more responsive to consumer demands. Honda and Nissan have taken this further. The former was the first manufacturer to make every one of its factories capable of producing every model of its cars and the latter has introduced a full build-to-order process which, it estimates, saves it $3600 per vehicle. The challenge with this, though, is how to combine this technique with the capacity required to reap economies of scale, which in the case of the car industry is significant – some 250,000 units per annum for assembly plants and between 1 and 2 million units for body panels.

The industry has been continually consolidating and as such has moved from a state of monopolistic competition to one of oligopoly. In the 1920s there were some 270 manufacturers, mostly within the US. Over time there have been numerous mergers and takeovers, for example that of BMW purchasing Rover in 1994, and so today the market is dominated by just seven large groups and three smaller ones. In terms of volume the six largest groups account for 70 per cent of global car sales.

Huge amounts of money are invested in advertising and other marketing by car manufacturers each year; and there is continual research and development as producers strive to obtain market power. This has been driven further by the fragmentation of consumer demands within the market. In the early 1990s Ford could rely on selling 750,000 of its F-150 pickup trucks each year but now it is required to have many variations in order to achieve such sales levels. The producers are continually launching new models and upgrading their current models with additional features in order to compete with one another. As the analysis in Section 8.2 suggests, there are companies such as Lamborghini and Mercedes-Smart that target the extremes of consumer tastes, but within the main part of the market there is product differentiation between the producers but not as much as there used to be under monopolistic competition.

Market Failure in the Transport Sector: An Overview

Chapter 5 explained how perfect competition in the free market leads to the optimum social outcomes of productive efficiency, allocative efficiency and ultimately Pareto efficiency. *Market failure* is simply the term given to situations in which the free market, that is a market without government interference, fails to achieve these desired outcomes.

Chapters 6 through 8 outlined how real markets rarely exhibit the competitive characteristics necessary for the desired outcomes to be perfectly achieved and what the more realistic market structures were. They also examined the results of the first form of market failure, namely that of *market power*.

The purpose of Part III is to examine the other forms of market failure that exist in the transport sector. The first of these is that of externalities, a widespread failure in the transport sector including congestion, accidents, infrastructure damage and all forms of pollution: atmospheric, noise, visual and light. The second is that of public goods, which, as Chapter 10 outlines, are products that will not be provided by the free market. There are numerous examples of such products that are essential to the effective functioning of the transport sector, causing this to be a market failure with significant implications as well. The third is that of demerit goods, such as motor vehicles, the effects of which are subtly different to those of negative externalities but nevertheless generate substantial costs within the transport sector. The final is that of inequality, which is exacerbated by the transport sector, and the effects of which are worsened by the problem of asymmetric information in certain key markets.

These are all problems that affect the daily lives of the vast majority of people, often in significant ways. As such, they have much transport policy directed towards them. An analysis of these policies and their effectiveness is the subject of Part IV.

Externalities 9

9.1 | Definitions and the model

An *externality* is an unconsidered cost or benefit experienced by a third party due to an economic decision made by others. The word *unconsidered* is used to highlight the point that the decision-makers do not consider the effects on the third party. There are two types of externality. An *external benefit* is an effect that is positive for the third party and an *external cost* is one that is negative.

Every decision incurs a cost and a benefit. For example, the decision to provide one more bus service will cost the bus company more for vehicle hire and for petrol, but it will also raise the company a certain amount of revenue. These costs and benefits can be sub-divided into private and social costs and benefits. A *private cost or benefit* is one that is experienced solely by the decision-maker, whereas the *social cost or benefit* is the total experienced by the whole community:

social cost (or benefit) = private cost (or benefit) + external cost (or benefit)

The examples above are all private in nature but relevant external costs include the extra pollution emitted and the extra congestion caused and relevant external benefits include the creation of an additional employment position.

The marginal cost or benefit for any of these is simply the extra cost incurred or benefit enjoyed from producing one additional unit of the product. The marginal cost curves can be assumed to be upward-sloping because of decreasing returns to scale, and the marginal benefit curves can be assumed to be downward-sloping due to diminishing marginal utility. In reality, there is likely to be a range over which these are constant, but for simplicity they can be modelled as increasing or decreasing from the start.

It can be assumed that a producer will ignore the external costs or benefits. This may be a conscious decision on the part of the producer but often it is simply a failure to appreciate the existence or extent of the third-party effects. Consequently, producers will supply the level of output at which the marginal private cost is equal to the marginal private benefit, which is shown by Q_1 in the figures that follow. Intuitively, at any output less than this the marginal benefit (revenue in this case) is likely to be higher than the marginal cost and so the producer would increase its total benefit (revenue), or producer surplus, by producing more.

At any output greater than this, though, the marginal cost is likely to be greater than the marginal benefit and so the reverse is true – producing these extra units serves only to reduce the producer surplus.

The same reasoning can be applied to explain why total social benefit, or social welfare, is maximised at the level of output at which marginal social benefit is equal to marginal social cost. At any output less than this the marginal social benefit is likely to be greater than the marginal social cost and so social welfare can be increased by producing more. Similarly, at any output greater than this the marginal social cost is likely to be greater than the marginal social benefit and so producing these units serves to reduce social welfare.

In the previous chapters it has been assumed that the private costs and benefits have been equal to those for society as a whole. As such the producers equate the marginal cost with marginal revenue and social welfare is maximised. In reality, however, the transport sector is full of cases in which this is not the case and in which significant external costs and benefits exist, causing the market to fail in maximising social welfare. This is shown diagrammatically in Figure 9.1.

In Panel A it is assumed for simplicity that the marginal social benefit is equal to the marginal private benefit. The marginal social cost (MSC) curve diverges from the marginal private cost (MPC) curve, the gap in between them being the external cost of production. Social welfare is maximised at output of Q^* but the quantity actually produced by the producers in the market is Q_1. This means that every unit between Q^* and Q_1 is causing an extra cost to society that is not being paid for by the producers. Unit Q, for instance, is causing an external cost denoted by x. Adding up the external costs for all of these units generates the total external cost to society from this production. This is equal to the shaded area and is termed the *externality*. In this case it is a negative externality caused because there are external costs that producers or consumers do not pay and so too much is produced or consumed compared to the social optimum.

In Panel B it has been assumed, again for simplicity, that the marginal social cost is equal to the marginal private cost. This time it is the marginal social benefit (MSB) curve that diverges from the marginal private benefit (MPB) curve. Social welfare is again maximised at Q^* but the market will result in an output of Q_1. Each unit in between these causes an extra benefit to society

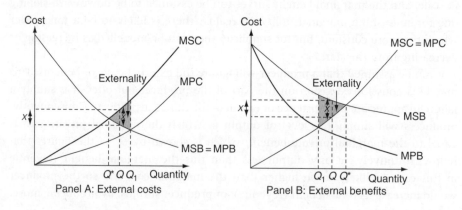

Figure 9.1
Externalities

Panel A: External costs

Panel B: External benefits

to be lost; for example, for unit Q the extra benefit lost is denoted by x. The sum of all these extra benefits forgone is the total social welfare that is lost in this production, is represented by the shaded area and is again termed the *externality*. In this case it is a positive externality because there are extra benefits to others that producers or consumers do not take into consideration, causing there to be too little production or consumption compared to the social optimum.

It is often asserted that Panel A shows production externalities and Panel B consumption externalities. This assertion is too simplistic, though, as both diagrams can be used to show either production or consumption externalities. The difference is that Panel A illustrates negative externalities, of both forms, whereas Panel B illustrates positive externalities.

The marginal private cost curve in Panel A can be seen to show the costs to a consumer of purchasing a product, which could be making a journey in the car. It is likely to be upward-sloping as more journeys mean an increased rate of wear and tear to the vehicle and increasing opportunity cost of making a journey. It diverges from the marginal social cost curve because the consumer does not consider the costs of pollution, of congestion and of an increased risk of accidents that the extra journeys cause. The marginal private benefit curve is simply the benefit gained from making the journeys. As such, Panel A can be used to show negative consumption externalities, such as those caused by over-usage of cars.

Similarly, Panel B can be viewed, not just as showing a positive consumption externality as well, but as a production externality as well. The marginal benefit curve can be interpreted as showing the benefit accruing to the producer from producing units of a product, and so in this case is comprised mainly of marginal revenue. It diverges from the marginal social benefit curve because the production of the product creates benefits to others that are not appreciated by the producer. These do not necessarily have to be to other producers, they could be to consumers. Consequently, as producers decide how much to produce they equate the marginal private cost to the marginal private benefit, meaning that too little is produced from a social efficiency standpoint.

9.2 | Missing markets

As well as being the existence of costs or benefits to third parties, externalities can also be viewed as the absence of markets. Chapter 5 shows how a free market leads to Pareto efficiency and there is no reason why this should not be the same in a market for an externality. The problem is that these markets do not exist; for example, there is no market for the air pollution caused by motor vehicles, the sea pollution from shipping or the wider health benefits from cycling. As such there is no price for these *products* leading to an inefficient level of production or consumption. If there were such markets, prices would be established and the free market would achieve Pareto efficiency.

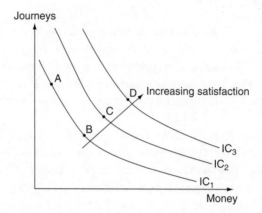

Figure 9.2
Indifference curves

This can be illustrated by a simple example. Let us take the negative externality caused by motor-vehicle air pollution and assume there are two different groups of car users. They both have money and a desire to use their cars and so their welfare is increased either by having more money or by making more journeys. These desires are shown in Figure 9.2.

Each indifference curve shows combinations of money and journeys between which the consumers are indifferent. As such, consumers are indifferent between combinations A and B as they are on the same indifference curve. Satisfaction is increased with greater amounts of money and journeys, which are shown by indifference curves that lie further away from the origin. In this way, combination C is preferable to A and B, and D is more preferable still.

It can be assumed that there is a limited capacity for journeys on the road network, which if exceeded causes congestion above the optimal amount. Each group of users, therefore, does not want the other group to make many journeys because it damages their satisfaction. This can be illustrated by an Edgeworth box, as displayed in Figure 9.3.

The satisfaction of group A is increased by moving diagonally up and to the right from the bottom left-hand corner as in Figure 9.2. The diagram for road users B has been pivoted and so their satisfaction increases by moving diagonally downwards

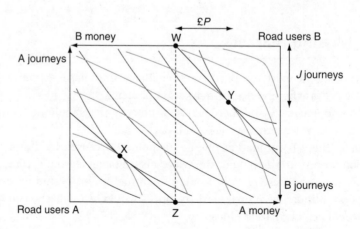

Figure 9.3 An Edgeworth box for road use

and to the left from the top right-hand corner. The vertical axis represents the optimal amount of road use and the horizontal axis represents the total amount of money within the market.

Let us further assume that there is an equal allocation of money between the two groups. This allocation is shown by the vertical dotted line in the figure. The outcome of the market depends upon the initial legal rights of the groups. If group A has the legal right to be the only road users on the road, the starting point of the market is at point W, where there is an equal distribution of money and group A is having the right to dominate the roads. In order for group B users to make journeys they have to pay group A for the right to do so. As there is a market they will negotiate a price and will share the journeys. It will end up that group B will pay £P to make J journeys. If, on the other hand, it was the legal right of group B to control journeys the starting point would be at Z and the final outcome would be at point X.

In both of these cases the market has distributed the optimal number of journeys between the two groups in a Pareto-efficient manner. It is Pareto efficient because the marginal rate of substitution (the slope of the indifference curve) of the indifference curve of group A is equal to that of group B; or in other words, they are tangential. This means that it is not possible to make one group better off without making the other worse off. In this way the free market for road use has obtained an efficient distribution of road journeys between consumers which does not cause too much congestion.

However, in reality, there is no such market for road journeys and so consumers decide how many journeys to make based purely upon their own marginal costs and benefits. This leads to an inefficient amount of congestion in which the whole of society is worse off.

9.2.1 The Coase Theorem

Edgeworth box analysis can be used to show that a special situation potentially exists. If each set of indifference curves are actually horizontal translates of one another, the resulting set of Pareto-efficient allocations will be a horizontal line. This means that the volume of the externality will always be the same, irrespective of the assignment of property rights. The demands for the product causing the externality do not depend on the distribution of income. Therefore, a reallocation of income affects the distribution of income, but it does not affect the efficient amount of the externality. This special case is known as the *Coase Theorem*.

The analysis above implies that if a fully functioning market for an externality is created, the amount of that externality can be theoretically determined by controlling the legal rights and distribution of income accordingly. However, the Coase Theorem shows that this may not always be possible, even if a fully functioning market is established, because the amount of the externality may be independent of these variables.

In reality, the conditions necessary for the Coase Theorem to exist are exceptionally special, and so such an outcome is highly unlikely. Also, the primary problem with externalities is that markets simply do not exist, never mind ones that are fully functioning.

9.3 | A lack of ownership

A third way of looking at externalities, which is hinted at in the above section, is that there is a lack of ownership of the affected resource. This is really only applicable to negative externalities, such as in road use there being no ownership of the number of journeys that can be made, and in the case of pollution there being no ownership of the atmosphere or of rivers or seas. These resources are termed *commons* as they resemble the traditional British common, which was a piece of land that had no owner and so was available for every villager to keep their cattle (it can be pictured next to the village green on which cricket is being played in front of the village church). As they are not owned there is no one to ensure that they are used optimally.

The *tragedy of the commons* is a theory that was first expounded by Hardin (1968) for the example of the traditional British common. It is assumed that there is a constant marginal cost (MC) to keeping a cow on the field, which can be zero. The benefit that comes from doing so, though, depends on the number of cows that there are on the common. The more cows there are the less benefit each cow receives due to the competition for the grass. This can be modelled very simply by saying that the benefit to each cow is the average benefit (AB). The marginal benefit (MB) is, as usual, the extra benefit that each additional cow generates. The curve for this will clearly be negatively sloped as each additional cow causes there to be more competition for the available grass, thereby reducing the average benefit to all. This situation is shown in Figure 9.4.

If the common is publicly available for everyone to use, each individual cattle owner will simply continue placing cows on the common until the benefit that is received (the AB) is equal to the marginal cost of doing so (MC). As such, a total

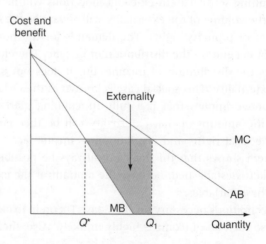

Figure 9.4 The tragedy of the commons

of Q_1 cows will be kept on the common. This is overuse of the common, though, because the socially optimum number of cows to keep on it is Q^*, where the marginal cost is equal to the marginal benefit. As there are more cows than this on the common each additional cow actually reduces social welfare by causing a marginal cost that is greater than its marginal benefit. This causes a negative externality that is illustrated by the shaded area.

The problem here is that there is no ownership of the common. If there was a single person or organisation that could control the number of cows kept on the common, they would be able to ensure that only Q^* cows were there. It is because there is no such control that the externality arises.

There are some cases in the transport sector that mirror this traditional example perfectly. The cases of too many boats on a river, too many planes in the sky and too many cars on a road are all examples; air, noise and water pollution can be similarly modelled.

9.4 The transport sector and global warming

9.4.1 Global warming

The sun's radiation reaches the Earth in short wavelengths but these are then transformed into infrared, long-wave bands when reflected back from the Earth's surface. The *greenhouse gases* in the Earth's atmosphere, namely carbon dioxide, chlorofluorocarbons, methane, nitrous oxide and ozone, along with water vapour, allow the short wavelength rays to enter the atmosphere but not the longer wavelengths to exit from it. They trap these latter waves within the atmosphere, thereby warming the Earth's surface temperature. This is a natural process that raises the Earth's average surface temperature from an uninhabitable $-18°C$ to $15°C$, in which life can exist.

Since the industrial revolution, circa 1750, the human race has been continually increasing the concentrations of these gases in the atmosphere in various ways; particularly the burning of fossil fuels and deforestation. Excluding the other greenhouse gases, the concentration of carbon dioxide alone has risen from 280 ppm in 1750 to 380 ppm today (Stern, 2007). This has been accompanied by rising concentrations of other greenhouse gases such as methane and nitrous oxide.

Over this period, the world's global mean surface temperature (the average temperature across the surface of the Earth: up to 1.5 metres above the ground and 1 metre in depth in the seas) has increased: by $0.7°C$ since 1990. In fact, the ten warmest years on record have all been since 1990 (Stern, 2007). Some meteorologists and climatologists argue that this has been caused purely by natural forces, such as increasing solar intensity and the regularity of *sunspots*. However, chemistry and physics do suggest that increasing greenhouse gas concentrations would also lead to warming due to the effect outlined above. In fact, while natural factors can explain much of the trend in global temperatures in the early nineteenth century, the rising concentrations of greenhouse gases provide the only plausible explanation for the observed trend in the last 50 years (Stern, 2007).

9.4.2 The contribution of the transport sector

Table 9.1 displays the emission of three greenhouse gases from the transport sector in the EU25. This includes transport by road, rail, air and water within the EU25, but excludes international transport. As it shows, the transport sector accounted for over a fifth of total EU25 carbon dioxide emissions in 2002 and this had increased by over 4 per cent compared to 1990. The vast majority, some 80 per cent, of the carbon dioxide emissions from the transport sector emanate from the roads, with the airlines being the next largest contributor. The production of electricity consumed by electric vehicles also releases carbon dioxide, especially if it is derived from burning coal, oil or gas. Nuclear industry, hydro, wind and tide may produce less, but constructing and maintaining the necessary facilities and transmission networks do have significant carbon dioxide outputs of themselves. The proportion of the other two gases accounted for by transport in the EU25 was much less in both 1990 and 2002, but that for nitrous oxide had increased by over 250 per cent.

Overall, the transport sector emits a significant amount of the greenhouse gases into the atmosphere and an amount that is set to continue to increase in the future. A report by the European Union Road Federation (2006) provides statistics of the emissions of all six of the greenhouse gases identified in the Kyoto agreement. These show that the transport sector is the third largest emitter with 19 per cent share of total emissions behind the energy sector (30 per cent) and the manufacturing and industrial sector (20 per cent). This conclusion is strengthened when it is considered that carbon dioxide is the most concerning of the greenhouse gases because it has an atmospheric life of up to a century and so causes costs for longer than the others.

These figures are underestimates of the true situation as the transport sector contributes to global warming in two additional ways. First, there are the non-carbon dioxide effects of aviation, which are outlined below. Secondly, there are unidentified carbon dioxide emissions further upstream in the production chain of transport. The refineries that produce transport fuel release carbon dioxide themselves. Similarly, the production of the electricity consumed by electric trains and road vehicles necessarily releases carbon dioxide as well.

Table 9.1 Greenhouse gas emissions from EU25 transport

	Tonnes (thousands)		Share of all emissions (%)	
	1990	2002	1990	2002
Carbon dioxide	762,416	911,336	18.5	22.9
Methane	246	142	0.9	0.7
Nitrous oxide	40	87	2.8	7.1

Source: Eurostat (2005).

In 2050, transport emissions are expected to be double that of current levels, but its overall contribution to global warming greater than this because of the increased reliance on synthetic fuel, commonly known as *synfuel* (Stern, 2007). Synfuel is oil produced from coal and gas; a production process that is twice as damaging as that to refine conventional oil. As the cost of conventional oil rises, producers will increasingly substitute it for synfuel.

9.4.3 The contribution of aviation

Aviation is different to other forms of transport in terms of its effects on global warming because it has more significant contributing effects other than the emission of carbon dioxide through the burning of fossil fuels. In fact, the impact of aviation is two to four times higher than the impact of its carbon dioxide emissions alone (Stern, 2007). As such, it is necessary to assess the overall contribution of aviation to global warming by focusing on its *radiative forcing*. A comprehensive report by the Intergovernmental Panel on Climate Change (IPCC, 1999) outlines just this.

Total aviation emissions have increased as the demand for air transport has outpaced the reductions in unit emissions from technological and operational improvements. The report looks at seven influences which aviation has on global warming, all of which have positive radiative forcing and so as they increase they tend to warm the Earth's surface. The results of this are displayed in Table 9.2.

Table 9.2 The contribution of aviation to radiative forcing

	Results
Carbon dioxide	▪ Emissions of carbon dioxide in 1992 accounted for 2 per cent of total anthropogenic carbon dioxide emissions.
Ozone	▪ Emissions of nitrous oxide in 1992 increased ozone concentrations at cruise altitudes in northern mid-latitudes by up to 6 per cent compared to an atmosphere without aircraft emissions. ▪ Emissions of sulphur and water in the stratosphere deplete ozone but the degree of this effect is not yet quantified.
Methane	▪ The methane concentration in 1992 is estimated to be about 2 per cent less than that in an atmosphere without aircraft.
Water vapour	▪ A fraction of water vapour emissions is released in the lower stratosphere where it can build up to larger concentrations.
Contrails	▪ In 1992, aircraft contrails are estimated to have covered 0.1 per cent of the Earth's surface, with larger regional values.
Cirrus clouds	▪ Extensive cirrus clouds have been observed to develop after the formation of persistent contrails. It is estimated that in the late 1990s between 0 per cent and 0.2 per cent of the Earth's surface area was covered by aircraft-induced cirrus clouds.
Sulfate and soot aerosols	▪ Sulfate and soot aerosol mass concentrations in 1992 resulting from aircraft were small relative to those from surface sources.

Source: IPCC (1999)

The best estimate of the radiative forcing caused by the aviation industry in 1992 is about 3.5 per cent of the total of that by all anthropogenic activities. From the range of simulations conducted in the report this figure could be about two times larger or five times smaller than the best estimate. It is likely that the contribution of aviation to overall global warming is approximately equal to this.

9.4.4 Global warming as a negative externality

Global warming is an example of a negative externality but it is, by nature, different to others. First, it is global in its causes and its consequences. The effect of greenhouse gas emission is geographically non-specific; an emission of one unit in the UK has the same impact globally as one unit in Italy. Secondly, the effects it has are long-term and persistent. Some greenhouse gases, such as carbon dioxide, exist in the atmosphere for hundreds of years and so the effects are cumulative. The world is already committed to a certain degree of future warming because of its greenhouse gas emissions in the past. Thirdly, the uncertainties and risks in the economic effects it has are pervasive. Finally, there is the serious risk of *threshold effects*. It is usual in economics for trends to be measured as having linear effects. However, it is uncertain, and perhaps unlikely, that nature can continue to respond to rising temperatures in the way that it has been. It is possible that temperatures will reach a certain level at which nature simply cannot cope, leading to sudden dramatic and irreversible damage.

Currently, the concentration of greenhouse gases in the atmosphere, as measured by carbon dioxide equivalent, is 430 ppm and is rising at 2 ppm each year. If these trends are maintained, this concentration could reach double its pre-industrial level as early as 2035, which would virtually commit the world to a global average temperature rise of over $2°C$. In the longer term, there would be more than a 50 per cent chance that the temperature rise would exceed $5°C$; a rise outside the experience of human civilisation. The Stern Review (2007) estimates that the overall costs of this will be equivalent to losing at least 5 per cent of global GDP each year from now on.

Table 9.3 displays both the past observed effects and some of the estimated future effects of global warming. All of the predicted effects have been given a degree of certainty of over 66 per cent by the IPCC (2001), and those for precipitation, sea level and agriculture have been given over 90 per cent.

Table 9.3 clearly shows that the effects of global warming are already being felt. In addition to the observed effects shown, there are the following effects.

■ There have already been significant ecosystem changes. Many species have been moving pole-wards by an average of 6 kilometres each decade for the past 30–40 years. Flowering and egg-laying have been occurring two to three days earlier each decade in many Northern Hemisphere temperate regions.

■ The diurnal land surface temperature range has decreased. The average night-time minimum temperature has increased at twice the rate of the daytime maximum.

Table 9.3 The past and future effects of global warming

	Observed	Predicted
Precipitation	Varies across regions, but in the Northern Hemisphere increased by 5–10% over the 20th century.	Global average annual precipitation is estimated to rise during the 21st century, although it will continue to vary regionally.
Sea level	Global mean sea level increased at an average annual rate of 1 to 2 mm during the 20th century.	Global mean sea level is estimated to rise by 0.09–0.88 m between 1900 and 2100; causing tens to hundreds of millions more people to be flooded each year.
Ice and snow cover	The duration of ice cover of rivers and lakes decreased by approximately 2 weeks over the 20th century in parts of the Northern Hemisphere. Arctic sea-ice has decreased in extent by 10–15% since the 1950s in spring and summer.	Glaciers and the Arctic ice-sheet are estimated to continue their widespread retreat. The Antarctic ice-sheet is likely to increase in mass during the 21st century, but to then contract significantly thereafter with further temperature increases.
Agricultural	The growing season has lengthened by about 1–4 days per decade during the last 40 years in the Northern Hemisphere.	It is estimated that agricultural productivity may increase with small temperature increases, but then decrease with further rises. This is likely to be particularly harmful in Africa, where hundreds of millions may be left without the ability to produce or purchase sufficient food.

Source: IPCC (2001)

- The costs of extreme weather events have increased dramatically. The IPCC has estimated the global costs of extreme weather events between 1950 and 2000. These are displayed in Figure 9.5 and they clearly show how both the number and the cost of events have increased dramatically.

  Global warming is also likely to cause the following.

- Increased flood risk during the wet season and reduced dry-season water supplies to one-sixth of the world's population, predominantly in the Indian sub-continent, parts of China and parts of South America.
- Ocean acidification. It is likely that this will have major effects on marine ecosystems; possibly harming vital fish stocks irreversibly. Increased ocean acidity makes it harder for many ocean creatures to form shells and skeletons.

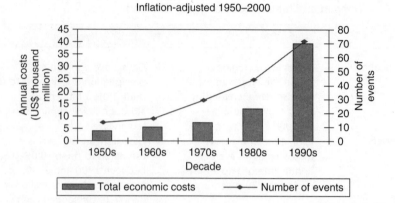

Figure 9.5 Global costs of extreme weather events
Source: IPCC(2001)

Such effects would damage creatures at the bottom of the marine food chain, thereby causing widespread damage to stocks of fish that are directly important to human civilisation.

- Increased deaths from malnutrition and heat stress, although in higher latitudes cold-related deaths will decrease.
- Serious ecosystem changes. One study estimates that around 15–40 per cent of species will face extinction with a temperature rise of 2°C.

These costs are likely to be felt most heavily by the poorest populations in the world. The IPCC tentatively asserts that GDP is likely to fall for many developing countries for all magnitudes of warming and the effects on GDP are likely to be mixed for developed countries for up to a few degrees of warming and negative for further increases. The costs are also likely to bear on populations living in low-lying lands and on small islands, which are vulnerable to displacement due to the sea level rises, and the poorer people across the world, which will be most vulnerable to health threats from heat stress, water-borne pathogens, flooding and the availability of food.

The Stern Review (2007) concludes that the worst of these impacts can be avoided if governments take action against it now. It estimates that for this to be realised the concentrations of greenhouse gases would have to be stabilised at between 450 and 550 ppm. This would require emissions to be at least 25 per cent below current levels by 2050. It states that the costs of such action can be limited to around 1 per cent of global GDP each year. Action is certainly economical. However, there is a real danger in current policy thinking in assuming that all sectors of an economy should cut emissions by the same amount. An economically efficient outcome will require different sectors to cut emissions by different amounts (see Chapter 15 for more on this).

9.5 | Congestion as an externality

Congestion can be defined as a situation in which users of a transport system are delayed because the system is approaching its capacity limit. Congestion is most notable on the roads but it also exists in European airports and along certain stretches of the European rail network. It is made worse in the European Union by the systems of the different member states not integrating fully, causing delays as vehicles move from the jurisdiction of one to that of another, for example the crossings of the Alpines or through the Pyrenees.

Congestion is a concern because of four effects that it may have. First, it causes time to be wasted for both passengers and producers, which can be seen as a reduction in GDP and in the competitiveness of European businesses. Secondly, it may add to pollution as vehicles are running for a longer period of time, and as the section above has outlined this can be costly. Thirdly, it causes safety concerns. Finally, it causes a deterioration of the transport infrastructure.

These are all external costs as the user of the transport does not consider them when making consumption decisions. For example, when one decides to make a journey in a car there is no consideration of the delays that it may cause to other road users, which generate monetary costs for businesses and opportunity costs for leisure passengers, and which may add to environmental damage and reductions in safety. Transport users do not have to fully pay for these costs and so there is over-usage of certain modes of transport, as shown by Panel A in Figure 9.1, causing a cost burden for the wider society.

9.5.1 Road congestion

The European Commission (June 2003) has estimated that 7500 kilometres of the European Union's major roads are blocked by traffic jams every day. There have been various estimates of the monetary costs that this causes, some 2 per cent of annual European Union GDP. These usually take as the benchmark a situation of freely flowing traffic and as such may be an overestimate of the costs. This is because in that situation the road infrastructure is being underused to an extent that investment in it is actually inefficient. If capacity is to be used fully it is necessary to have a certain degree of congestion. In the Netherlands it has been estimated that it is efficient for 2–3 per cent of drivers to encounter congestion daily (European Conference of Ministers of Transport, 1998). Using this as the benchmark, the European Conference of Ministers of Transport concluded that the congestion on Europe's roads is not a widespread problem, but it is a regional problem and in some regions it is a real problem. On a daily basis in the UK, for example, a quarter of the main roads are jammed for an hour and there are between 200 and 300 incidents of major congestion.

The environmental damages are also difficult to quantify. Congestion causes vehicles to be running for longer, which serves to increase emissions; but also more slowly, which has the effect of reducing the rate of emissions. Overall, it is likely that the former effect outweighs the latter. It is certain, however, that with certain weather conditions congestion in urban areas can cause local concentrations of pollution to rise to harmful levels and that the vehicle users are in the most damaging position when this occurs.

With regard to safety, it is a concern that congested roads are more prone to accidents. Psychological effects worsen this as studies have shown that people perceive that they have waited in traffic longer than they actually have. As stress levels mount as a result of this perception it becomes increasingly likely that drivers will make mistakes both in the congestion and once it has cleared. There are no estimates of the number of accidents that are directly caused by congestion, but 40,000 people die on European roads every year: 112 each day. This costs the European Union 2 per cent of its annual GDP, excluding many of the wider effects of accidents that are more problematic to enumerate in monetary terms.

9.5.2 Other congestion

The European Commission (June 2003) has estimated that at the European Union's main airports some 35 per cent of flights are delayed by at least 15 minutes. This congestion has been caused by the dramatic growth in the use of the airlines, but it is worsened by airlines having to use certain corridors to avoid military space, causing them to queue whilst waiting for specified slots. This especially affects the area covering the South of England, the Benelux countries and France, where two-thirds of all air traffic delays in the EU occur. The Commission has estimated that such delays cost European airlines between 1.3 and 1.9 billion euros each year.

The use of the rail network has fallen over time and so, overall, has spare capacity. There are still bottlenecks, though, especially where passenger and freight services use the same stretches of line. In fact the European Commission (June 2003) has estimated that approximately 20 per cent of Europe's main lines (16,000 kilometres of track) are classified as bottlenecks.

9.6 | The positive externalities of cycling

A positive externality is not simply the reduction of a negative externality. A reduction in road congestion or a reduction in the amount of pollution emitted into the atmosphere should not be seen as positive externalities of cycling. As well as this, benefits of cycling to the cyclist, for example increased fitness and mood, should not be seen as positive externalities either as they are being enjoyed by the user. With these aside, though, cycling does bring two main positive externalities: effects that benefit people other than the cyclist himself.

First, it is likely that cycling increases an economy's productive capacity. It is generally accepted that cycling improves one's fitness, strength and psychological well-being and as such is likely to lead to an increase in a worker's, and therefore the workforce's, productivity. In addition, if these health benefits lead to a reduction in the time that workers have off work the economy will be more productive through a reduction in *wasted* time. If these are true then cycling will generate, perhaps in only a small way, further economic growth which will benefit all and not just the cyclists themselves.

Secondly, it is likely that cycling reduces the health cost burden of an economy. The personal health benefits of cycling that were noted above will lead to a reduction in the amount of funding that is necessary for health provision. One study suggests that new cyclists covering short distances can reduce their risk of death, mainly through a reduction in heart disease, of up to 22 per cent (Rutter, 2000), which in turn will have wider benefits for society through a reduction in the cost of health care. This capital can be invested in more productivity-enhancing ways.

These positive externalities are still to be fully numerated in monetary terms but they can be illustrated by Panel B in Figure 9.1, where cycling generates an external benefit that is not enjoyed by the cyclist. As such, the free market leads to too little cycling compared to the socially efficient level.

9.7 Sustainable development and ethics

The term *sustainable development* has been defined as 'development that meets the needs for the present without compromising the ability of future generations to meet their own needs' (World Commission on Environment and Development, 1987). It is a concept of intergenerational equality: any expansion or growth that the present generation implements should not harm the welfare of the generations that follow.

This concept can be simply modelled by making an initial assumption that it is through production that a generation satisfies its needs (greater output affords a generation the ability to satisfy more of its needs, although it may not choose to use it in this way). Chapter 4 explains that four factors are absolutely necessary for any production to occur: land, labour, capital and entrepreneurship. If we make a further assumption that the quantity of labour and entrepreneurship is fixed, it becomes the case that the level of output is dependent on the quantity of land (*natural capital*) and capital (*physical capital*) used in production, and the efficiency with which those resources are used.

Two further concepts of sustainable development can now be drawn: strict and relative sustainable development. *Strict sustainable development* requires that the natural capital stock is perfectly maintained from generation to generation. In other words, natural resources are not damaged or used at all by development; and if they are, the damage is repaired so that nature returns to as it was. *Relative sustainable development* requires that the productiveness of the total capital stock (natural plus physical) is maintained across generations. In other words, any reduction in the natural capital stock is offset by an increase in physical capital, so that the overall productive potential of society is at least as great as it was before (allowing future generations to satisfy their needs). As development is absolutely necessary to correct the shortcomings in the human world (such as starvation, poverty, disease, illness and the like) the latter concept is perhaps the more useful of the two concepts.

Historically, the physical capital stock expands over time (societies today have much more extensive infrastructure networks and access to far greater man-made resources than ever before), but at the expense of natural capital (stocks of natural commodities, such as oil and gas, are continually being consumed, but, perhaps more importantly, whole ecosystems are being diminished). The question that needs to be addressed is whether the condition for relative sustainable development is being satisfied? This is difficult to answer because it necessitates that the productive potential of both the physical and the natural capital stocks are valued; a calculation which is particularly problematic in the latter case, where our understanding of the role that the environment fulfils is still so limited. Chapter 13 takes up such valuation problems in more detail.

The concept of relative sustainable development is applicable to the transport sector, as well as to overall economic development. Has the current transport sector been developed in a way that is relatively sustainable? Is the consumption of natural capital in the transport sector, which is significant when one considers the fossil fuels that are burned within it (which is a direct consumption of those stocks, but which also *consumes* the purity of the atmosphere), more than offset by increases in the productiveness of the physical capital stock? These are considerations that must be taken into account when future transport projects are planned.

Every journey made by road, rail, sea or air consumes natural capital in some way, thereby diminishing the natural capital stock and degrading the environment for future generations. It has only been relatively recently that industrialised populations have engaged in transport in the volume that they are now enjoying, but those involved still account for a small proportion of the global population. Amongst industrialised populations, it has become an unquestioned belief that it is a human right to travel (increasingly taking holidays abroad), and to transport products (where does our food originate from?), across the world. There is very little consideration as to the effects of these decisions on sustainability. Perhaps it is time that this perceived right is questioned, because it implies a right to enjoy the Earth's resources at the expense of future generations, which may struggle to satisfy their needs with the less productive total capital stock that results.

It becomes apparent that the situation may actually be worse than this when one considers that there is a complimentary effect of consuming natural capital. Not only does such consumption mean that the natural capital stock available to future generations is reduced, it also creates additional costs that future generations have to pay. Global warming is an effective illustration of this. As noted above, the consumption of fossil fuels is reducing the natural capital stock available in the future in terms of both the actual stocks of those fuels and the purity of the atmosphere. However, the anthropogenic emissions of greenhouse gases, caused by the consumption of fossil fuels, are also causing the Earth to warm, in turn leading to continually increasing costs of severe natural events (see Figure 9.5). Future generations not only have a reduced natural capital stock to use, but are also faced with greater costs. In this sense, relative sustainable development actually requires the *net* productiveness of the total capital stock to be maintained: the productiveness of the available resources minus the costs associated with that capital stock.

Public and Demerit Goods

10.1 | Public goods: The theory

So far, it has been assumed that products are *private goods*: products which have two specific characteristics. The first characteristic is that they are *excludable*, meaning that once they have been produced for the benefit of one consumer, others cannot benefit from them. The second is that they are *rival*, meaning that as more people consume them, the benefits to those already consuming it are reduced. Motorbikes and railway tickets are good examples of private goods. Once a consumer has purchased them, it is possible to prevent other consumers from using them; and if others did somehow manage to use them, the benefit to the original consumers would be diminished. However, in reality there are some crucial products in the transport sector that are *public goods*, which means that they do not have these characteristics; or in other words, they are *non-excludable* (it is not possible to prevent other consumers, who have not paid for them, from benefiting from them) and *non-rival* (as additional consumers benefit from them, the benefits accruing to those already consuming them are not reduced).

As a public good is non-excludable and non-rival, rational producers will not provide it in a free market. This is for three reasons. First, producers know that if they wait for someone else to provide it, they can benefit from it for free. This is called the principle of the *free rider*. Secondly, there is no profit to be made from providing it because consumers will not pay for it if they too can just free-ride. Finally, there are monetary valuation problems, as consumers will not honestly reveal how much they would be willing and able to pay for it. This non-provision of public goods is a real problem in the transport sector as such products are vital to the effective functioning of the sector. Some of these are analysed in the case studies below.

In addition, there are also *quasi-public goods*. These are products that are not always fully non-excludable and non-rival. These products will also not be fully provided by private producers in the free market.

10.2 | Galileo

Satellite navigation systems are important examples of public goods. There are currently two systems in operation: the Global Positioning System (GPS), which is dominant; and the Global Navigation Satellite System (GLONASS). These are both military controlled, the first by the US and the second by Russia, and were both funded completely by public finance.

The European Union has been dependent on the GPS system for its navigation for many years, causing it problems in terms of the availability and accuracy of the service. This is because the GPS system is military controlled, and so its signals can be degraded or switched off; but more importantly, because the available technology causes its availability to vary due to geographical factors and its accuracy to drift by up to 10 metres.

Galileo (Amos, 2005) is being developed as the solution to this problem. It is to be a civilian-controlled satellite radio navigation system comprising 30 satellites (27 of which are to be operational and 3 spare), and 26 sensor stations positioned across the globe, feeding information back to two central control stations in Europe. The satellites are to have atomic clocks installed in them, which tag the signals that the satellites emit with the precise time at which they were sent; and users of the system will have receivers, which have an accurate record of the orbits of the satellites. These receivers could be installed into vehicles, mobile phones or other devices. By reading the satellite signals the receivers will be able to determine how long the signals took to get from where the satellites are positioned at any time. When a receiver is able to read the signals from at least four satellites simultaneously, it will be able to calculate its global position with an accuracy of 1 metre. The commercial services that Galileo will provide, in which the signals are encrypted, will increase this accuracy to a matter of centimetres. It is hoped that Galileo will be fully operational in 2008.

Galileo is to be complementary to the existing systems. It is hoped to be operable in all but the most extreme circumstances; and it will have an integrity mechanism built in which will inform users within seconds of a failure of a satellite. This increased accuracy and availability makes it ideal for use in the transport sector, where safety is crucial. The system will also provide a global search and rescue function. Each satellite will be able to transfer distress signals to rescue co-ordinating centres and will feed back to the user that the distress signal has been received and is being dealt with.

Galileo will allow transport operators to control their services much more closely and to optimise service timetables, fuel costs and safety. This is likely to be particularly important in the airline industry, in which Galileo will also form a vital part of the central control system. Due to the European Union's Open Skies Initiative, operators will be able to use more than just the specified air corridors that are currently allowed. This is to be controlled and monitored by a new air-traffic control system, which will rely heavily on the Galileo system for its successful operation. Galileo will also become increasingly important in the road sector, not just for road users scheduling and monitoring their journeys but also for authorities, as it will provide the tools necessary for widespread road-user charging.

The Galileo project was launched in Paris, in May 2003, by the European Union, the European Space Agency and a consortium of ten European companies. It is proposed to be a public–private partnership, but the commercial revenue that could be made is uncertain and so is the private investment that will follow. As users will have to purchase the necessary receivers, Galileo will be excludable; but the commercial possibilities are uncertain and there is a high possibility of free-riding by other producers wanting to avoid contributing to the initial capital costs. The quality of the provision will be independent of the number of users and so it will be non-rival. As a result, it is an example of a quasi-public good and so the cost of 3.4 billion euros is largely being funded by the public sector, which will remain the major player in the provision until the possibility of private financial gain becomes known. Galileo would not have been launched without public funding.

10.3 | Street lighting

Street lights are important for three reasons. The first is that, by illuminating roads, they improve the vision of drivers and so reduce the likelihood of road accidents. The second is that, by illuminating pavements, they improve safety for pedestrians. The third is that they help to reduce property crime, by improving the visibility of passers-by. The first two of these shall be looked at in turn.

Selected results from a report by the UK Department for Transport (2004), which show the number of accidents by road type and the presence of street lighting, are displayed in Figure 10.1. In built-up areas, where the speed limit is below 40 mph, there were over 33,000 more accidents on roads with street lights than without. The likely explanation for this peculiar result is that the vast majority of built-up

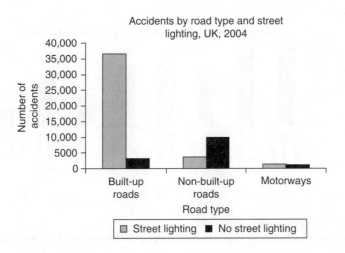

Figure 10.1 The effect of street lighting on accidents
Source: Department for Transport (2004)

roads are now lit, and only those roads that are lightly used are not. With the vast majority of traffic flowing down lit roads, one would expect there to be far more accidents along these. Similarly, there were slightly more accidents on lit sections of the motorway network than on unlit sections, but again this can be explained by observing that the lit sections are usually at roundabouts or junctions, where one would expect a greater number of accidents. More illustrative statistics are those for roads in non-built-up areas, as there is a less biased divide between roads that are lit and those that are not. As Figure 10.1 shows, there were more than double the number of accidents on unlit roads than on roads that had lighting, suggesting that street lighting does help to prevent traffic accidents and the economic costs that these incur.

A report first published in 1999 by Crime Concern and the Social Research Associates of the UK Department for Transport (1999) surveyed over 900 house-holds from across seven different areas of the UK regarding personal security. As part of this, the respondents had to identify (from a list of eight options) which factors made them feel unsafe when walking along pavements. The averages of the percentage of respondents from each area identifying each of the options are displayed in Figure 10.2.

Poor lighting was identified as the second greatest factor causing a feeling of being unsafe amongst pedestrians, behind that of loitering people. Poor lighting was more of a detriment to pedestrian safety than places being lonely, drunks being present and there being places in which strangers could hide. The typical area that had the greatest proportion of respondents identifying poor lighting as such was that of an Inner London middle-class residential area, with an adjoining area of a lower reputation. The age group with the largest proportion of respondents identifying poor lighting was that of the under 25-year-olds, 65 per cent of whom identified it. The report suggested that an explanation for this latter statistic could be found in how more than a third of older respondents stated that they did not go out alone, or at all, after dark; and so they may not view street lighting as a factor that they are concerned with.

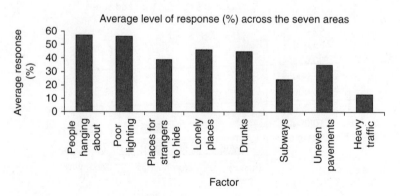

Figure 10.2 Pedestrian safety responses
Source: Crime Concern and the Social Research Associates of the Department for Transport (1999)

This impact on safety alone makes the installation and maintenance of street lighting important, but it is likely to generate wider economic benefits as well. Studies show that if people feel unsafe to make pedestrian journeys, less public transport will be used and non-essential journeys may be deterred due to the extra effort necessary to make them by car (the extra effort coming from problems with congestion, parking and not being able to drink when at the destination due to motoring laws). Therefore, such avoidance of the feeling of being unsafe can lead to a reduction in spending. Oc and Trench (1992) estimate that such a cost amounted to a reduced business turnover of £24 million per year in the city centre of Nottingham and 600 fewer jobs.

Street lights in the UK each cost between £30 and £50 a year to operate and maintain. When it is considered that there are approximately 113,000 such lights in the county of Kent alone, the huge monetary costs become apparent. The vast majority of street lights are owned and maintained by local government, with a few by private developments and on private land. Street lights are a good example of public goods, as they are both non-excludable and non-rival. It is not possible to exclude a pedestrian walking along a pavement, or a driver passing along a road, from benefiting from a street light unless it is positioned so that it only shines on private land. Similarly, the hundredth pedestrian or driver that regularly passes through the light will not diminish the benefits enjoyed by the other 99 regular consumers of the light. As a result, private producers will not be willing to supply such lights because they cannot make a full financial return from doing so.

Street lights are vital to the effective and safe functioning of the transport sector. As such, it is a significant failure of the free market that they would not be provided, and one that has wide-reaching costs. This is why they have to be provided by public authorities.

10.4 | Provision of roads

The majority of the road networks across the European Union are provided by the public sector. This is to be expected in the case of public goods and in the case of quasi-public goods which almost satisfy the conditions of non-excludability and non-rivalry. However, roads cannot be said to be in either of these categories. First, roads do not satisfy the condition of non-excludability, as it is possible to prevent people from using roads of all sizes. Large toll roads require payment for access, excluding those unwilling or unable to pay; and roads on small private estates have barriers that can only be operated by those with the necessary code. Secondly, roads do not always satisfy the condition of non-rivalry either. For the majority of the time, and on the majority of roads, an additional vehicle on the road does not reduce the benefit gained by users already on it. However, during peak times this is certainly not the case; additional vehicles inevitably increase congestion, thereby eroding the benefits to those already using the road. Consequently, roads are not public goods, and can only be deemed weak quasi-public goods at best.

The free market should theoretically be able to provide the roads demanded by an economy, as private producers should be able to earn a profit from doing so. As the demand for roads in an area increases, private producers should be attracted to provide them in response to the profit signal; charging drivers to use the new facilities and ensuring that those who would free-ride are not able to do so. During the 1800s, this is exactly how roads in Britain were provided; in the form of the turnpikes (see Section 1.2.2). These were largely very effective, responding to the demands of an expanding industrial economy. In fact, if the free market was to function effectively, it should provide roads in a more economically efficient manner than the public sector: providing those roads that are most demanded by the economy, rather than those favoured by politicians and bureaucrats.

So why is it that, across Europe, the majority of roads are provided by the public sector? There are a number of potential explanations, all of which probably contributing to the answer:

- *The existence of common costs* (see Section 4.4.3). Roads serve a diverse range of needs, and are used by a diverse range of vehicles: bicycles, cars, buses, vans and the largest freight vehicles, to name but a few. Many of the costs involved in the provision of roads can be attributed to the different users. The wear and tear caused to a road by a given vehicle is largely related to the axle-loading of that vehicle, for example. However, there are some costs which cannot be apportioned; those for the provision of road markings, signs and hedge-cutting are good examples. These common costs make the pricing of roads to individual users difficult, and so it is perhaps easier if roads are provided by the government, which can then cover the costs with public funds.

- *The fulfilling of other governmental needs*. In the past, governments have needed road networks for military and communication reasons, and so have found it beneficial to ensure adequate provision themselves. Governments also find it beneficial to provide roads publicly, as it helps them to work towards wider planning goals; the encouragement of businesses to locate to certain deprived areas, for example. However, this reason cannot be sufficient for the public provision of roads, as these goals could be achieved through public regulation of private provision.

- *Issues with privately provided roads*. It has been argued that the administration costs of the provision of private roads would be substantial and wasteful. It has also been argued that it would be impossible to comprehensively exclude those unwilling and unable to pay for the right to use the infrastructure. However, recent technological advances have served to weaken these two arguments. National road-pricing schemes, which would allow excludability to be enforced across a nation, have been technically feasible for a number of decades now; and the associated administration costs have been reduced (although two-thirds of the revenue generated by the London Congestion Charge is used simply in its administration).

- *The nature of road investment*. Investment in road provision is not immediately recouped. In fact, investors may have to wait a considerable time before they see an increased return. It has been argued that this would act as a deterrent to such investment, thereby minimising any involvement that the private sector would be willing to offer. Some European countries (such as France, Italy and Spain) have overcome this by securing private investment in road networks with government guarantees. Such guarantees have been effective in offsetting any deterrent to private investment (these countries now have the greatest coverage of toll roads in Europe), but they can inadvertently support economically inefficient producers, and can lead to sudden burdens on public finances if the guarantees are ever called upon.

■ *The existence of external benefits* (see Section 9.1). It is true that the free market should be able to provide a more economically efficient road network than the public sector could, as every road would be profitable. However, this is only when the private costs and benefits to the producers are considered, ignoring the positive externalities that could arise from the provision of other, less profitable, roads. Roads to rural areas may not be profitable, and so would not be provided; but they do serve a number of functions; for example, ensuring mobility for rural populations, promoting the maintenance of rural areas and facilitating tourism. These functions, and others like them, generate external benefits which would not be considered by private producers. As the model in Section 9.1 predicts, the free market would under-provide roads compared to the socially optimal provision.

It is likely that all of these reasons play a part in explaining why European roads are largely provided by the public sector. However, Button and Pitfield (1991) explain how, in practice, public provision of the roads in Britain arose inadvertently in the mid-1800s and has never ceased. The British government was concerned about the rapidly expanding monopoly power of the railways at this time, and so took control of road provision from the turnpike trusts in an effort to ensure that there would always be an integrated road network available. Another factor that inevitably played a part in this decision was that, although they had largely been effective and had responded to the needs of industrialisation, the turnpike trusts were actually wasteful and corrupt, and had failed to provide an integrated national network (see Section 1.2.2).

With congestion on the roads of Europe increasing all the time, and with the current political reluctance to introduce national road-pricing schemes, it seems inevitable that road capacity will have to be expanded. This is likely to involve significant costs, and so the issue of private investment in road networks is likely to resurface; potentially leading to increasingly widespread coverage of toll roads.

10.5 ▌ The theory of demerit goods

Demerit goods are products that are less beneficial, or more harmful, to consumers than they actually appreciate. There is information failure because the consumer is not perfectly informed about the effects of the products. The result is that

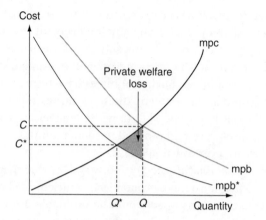

Figure 10.3
Demerit goods

consumers are more willing to purchase the product at a given price than they would be if they were fully informed, causing over-consumption compared to the socially optimal level (in which all costs and benefits are fully considered). Consumers benefit less than they had thought and so social welfare could be increased by having them substitute other available products for these goods.

Diagrammatically, this can be shown as in Figure 10.3.

Consumers believe that a demerit good is better for them than it actually is. They believe that it brings a marginal benefit as shown by the curve mpb, when in actual fact it only brings them that shown by mpb*. Consequently, they decide to purchase Q units of the good at a cost of C; whereas if they were to fully appreciate the true benefits it brings, they would purchase the lower quantity of Q^* units at the lower cost of C^*. The units up to Q^* are consumed, generating consumer welfare as illustrated by the area beneath the mpb* curve and above the mpc curve. However, the units between Q^* and Q incur an increasingly larger marginal cost than the marginal benefit they bring, thereby actually reducing overall consumer welfare. This *private welfare loss* caused by the demerit good is shown by the shaded area.

It is often commented that a demerit good is just the same as a negative externality, but this is not the case. The subtle difference is that a negative externality causes a reduction in the welfare of third parties, which have been given no consideration by the decision-makers; whereas a demerit good causes a reduction in the welfare of the decision-makers themselves, in this case the consumer. This is highlighted in Figure 10.3, as all the curves are private so it does not incorporate other parties.

There are examples of demerit goods within the transport sector. It has been claimed that the concentration of gases emitted by a motor vehicle are greater within the vehicle than outside it. Drivers rarely consider this possibility, and so are potentially harmed more than they realise by using their vehicles. If this is the case, there will be over-consumption of private road transport compared to the socially optimal quantity.

Similarly, using air transport often leads to minor viruses being contracted by the passengers (due to the air-conditioning systems employed in aircraft). As passengers fail to consider this when purchasing their tickets, it is likely that there will again be over-consumption compared to the socially optimal amount. Although this effect is usually only a minor cost to individual passengers, the social effects are likely to be more substantial.

Inequality, Poverty and Asymmetric Information

11.1 Inequality and poverty

Inequality can be defined as the unequal distribution of wealth in an economy; and *poverty* as a state in which a person is unable to meet their basic needs because of a lack of resources. These can be seen as inadequacies of markets on two levels. The first is on an ethical level and so is purely based on value judgements, or opinions; and the second is on an economic level by assessing their impact upon efficiency.

In a modern economy, where everyone should be viewed as being equal and should be presented with equal opportunities, wide-reaching inequality and deep levels of poverty are not acceptable. This is not to say that everyone should receive the same outcome from the economy as that would remove the incentives that are necessary for an economy to function effectively and so would actually be counterproductive.

It has been implicitly assumed up until now that those who have demanded products the most, and so receive the greatest welfare from them, have been willing and able to pay the most for them. This leads to the free market maximising overall social welfare. In reality, however, this is not the case if inequality and poverty exist. There are products that are being produced and allocated to people on the basis of an ability to pay when in fact greater welfare would be generated by producing products that are most needed by poorer consumers and allocating them according to the needs instead. When poverty exists the free market cannot possibly lead to the optimal social welfare due to the inequality in purchasing power and so it is Pareto inefficient.

This inefficiency is made worse when the production side of the economy is examined. An employee requires a certain standard of living in order to work efficiently. Malnutrition, dehydration, anxiety, stress and tiredness are all consequences of poverty and they all reduce the productivity of a worker; and

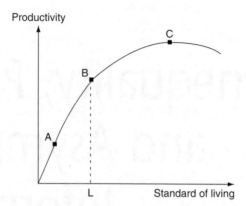

Figure 11.1
The productivity effects of standard-of-living curve

in the case of children, their ability to learn and develop fully at school, which inhibits the productivity of the future workforce. Improving a person's standard of living is likely to have diminishing returns to the workforce, meaning that the productivity of a worker is likely to increase dramatically as the standard of living approaches that required but this slows down thereafter. In fact, it is likely that after a certain standard of living has been obtained the productivity of a worker actually decreases as they are increasingly content with their situation and focus increasingly on leisure. This relationship is illustrated in Figure 11.1.

Figure 11.1 shows that total productivity would be higher if all workers obtained the minimum standard of living for them to be productive, denoted by B with a standard of living of L, than if some were at point C and others at point A. This is from a purely physical standpoint and misses the likelihood that if everyone was at point B there would be a likely psychological loss of incentives to work productively, but it illustrates the important and realistic point that large degrees of poverty consign those negatively affected to conditions in which they cannot be physically productive, causing the overall productive capacity of an economy to fall. If an economy fails to use its productive resources effectively, it cannot be productively efficient and so cannot be Pareto efficient either.

11.2 | Inequality in Europe

Europe is continually getting richer. The European Union's statistical body, Eurostat, has stated that in 1995 purchasing power parity (PPP) GDP per capita was 15,200 in the EU25. By 2003 this had increased to 21,400, placing it favourably with Japan's 24,400 but a little way behind the USA's 32,900. This masks considerable inequality and poverty, though, both between member countries and within them.

The highest GDP per capita (PPP) in the EU25 in 2003 was that of Luxembourg with 45,900 and the lowest was 8800 in Latvia. The UK was one of the richest with

25,300. As these statistics take account of what money can buy, such inequality is striking.

The European Union measures inequality as the ratio of total income received by the top quintile of the population to that of the lowest quintile of the population in terms of PPP disposable income received. According to this measure, Eurostat estimates that inequality in the EU25 was 4.8 in 2004. This means that the fifth of the population with the highest incomes are, on average, receiving almost five times as much as the average of that of the fifth of the population with the lowest incomes. Again, although it is difficult to get comparative figures from across all member countries, this does vary between countries. In the Czech Republic, for example, it was 3.4 whereas in Greece it was 6.0.

The European Union takes a relative measure of poverty so as to include the social implications of poverty. It measures it as the percentage of a country's population with a disposable income (PPP after social transfers) less than 60 per cent of the national median. The Eurostat estimate of this in 2004 for the EU25 is 16 per cent, meaning that 16 per cent of the European population has a disposable PPP income that is less than 60 per cent of the median in their respective countries. Once again this varies considerably, as in 2004 in Ireland it was 21 per cent whereas that in Luxembourg and Norway was 11 per cent.

Europe as a whole is becoming wealthier but these gains are not being experienced equally across the population. There remains a significant proportion of the population whose incomes are not rising in line with the average and so who are experiencing worsening social conditions, and there is a significant proportion of the population that is being left in poverty.

11.3 The exacerbation caused by the transport sector

Figure 11.2 is a very simplistic layout of a typical city that has been drawn in order to help illustrate the way in which transport can exacerbate inequality. It is assumed that the city centre is the location of most jobs, including those that are paid most highly: solicitors, accountants and the like. The suburbs contain some jobs, the inner suburbs more so than the outer suburbs, but these are generally less well remunerated, for example shop assistants and café owners. Finally, there are the technology parks, in which the technology companies are situated and so in which the moderately to high paid technology jobs are based. These are very basic assumptions but ones that do resemble reality.

It is further assumed that there are three ways of getting to a place of employment. One can live nearby and so can walk to work; own and run a private vehicle, which is illustrated by the main road; or use public transport, which is illustrated by the railway line. All of these options are significantly determined by a person's wealth. Housing varies in price, with those having access to the highest paid jobs being the most expensive. This is shown in Figure 11.2, with the housing in the city centre and along the closest stretches of the commuter belts (along the main road

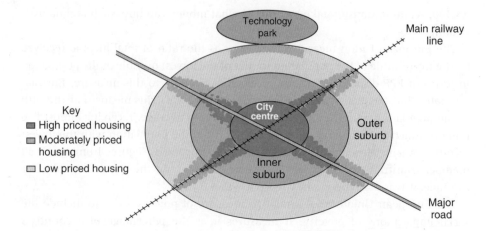

Figure 11.2
The layout of a typical city

and the railway line) being the most expensive; followed by the inner suburbs, along the moderately close stretches of the commuter belts and the housing closest to the technology park; and the cheapest housing being that furthest away from the city centre and the means of commuting.

Assuming that transport, whether private or public, becomes more expensive the further one has to travel and that people are afforded employment opportunities purely on their ability to travel to work, it can be seen that transport clearly exacerbates inequality. Those who are able to obtain the highest paid jobs are likely to be those who are already wealthy as they need to be able to afford the highest priced housing in order to walk to work; or the highest and moderately priced housing in the inner and outer suburbs so that they can travel to work. Similarly, those who are already poor are unlikely to be able to obtain the highest or even the moderately paid jobs as they are only able to afford the cheapest housing in the outer suburbs and do not have the means to travel to a place of high paid employment. In this way inequality is likely to worsen over time, especially if the wealthy begin to migrate out of the city centre in order to enjoy the countryside, forcing the prices of those houses upwards, which is a realistic trend.

This is a very simple model as it does not include factors such as the qualifications required to satisfy certain employers. It does, however, show the important role that transport plays in inequality. Along with the prices of housing, transport restricts the employment opportunities available to the poor, further confining them in poverty; whereas the wealthy are able to thrive.

This model can be extended to deal with other issues to do with inequality and poverty as well. If employment opportunities are replaced by educational opportunities it can be used to show how transport has a significant influence on the qualifications that people obtain, which in turn have much longer-term impacts on their earning potential. If these opportunities are replaced by health care facilities the model can be used to show how transport is a determinant of the quality of health care that people are afforded and so the likely standard of their health. This also has longer-term earning effects. In both of these cases transport can exacerbate inequality. It quickly becomes apparent how crucial the transport sector is to the standard of living that people enjoy across the economy.

11.4 Asymmetric information – The market for lemons

In 2000, George Akerlof was awarded the Nobel Prize for economics for developing the market-for-lemons model. Amongst others, this model can be used to describe the market for second-hand cars. The model assumes that there are buyers and sellers of second-hand cars. It also assumes that there are two types of car: those that are of good quality and those that are not, and that the market comprises 50 per cent of each type. The sellers know which cars are good and which are bad, but the buyers (usually) do not. All the buyers know is that there is an equal chance of obtaining each type of vehicle. There is an asymmetric distribution of information in the market, with the sellers knowing more than the buyers.

The sellers have a reservation price, the lowest price they are willing to sell for, of £3000 for a good car and £1000 for a bad car. The buyers, knowing the probability of obtaining a good or bad car, are only willing to pay £2000 for a second-hand car; as they cannot be sure of getting a good car so they will only be willing to pay an amount between the two reservation prices (consumers will be willing to pay the average price for a car in this case, as there is an equal chance of purchasing a good or bad vehicle). At this average price, the sellers are unwilling to part with their good cars and so remove them from the market. In this way, there is *adverse selection* in the second-hand car market, with buyers only being offered bad quality cars. Buyers will then be unprepared to pay £2000 for a car, because they know that all of the good cars have been removed from the market. The price in the market will fall to the lowest reservation price and the market will settle at an equilibrium in which bad quality cars are sold for £1000.

This outcome is clearly second best for society, as there is now a missing market. Instead of selling good cars in the second-hand market, owners may run them into the ground or sell them to private contacts. Even if buyers would be happy to pay more for known good cars than the owners want for them, there is no trade in them. This outcome potentially hits middle-income people hardest, as they are likely to be unable to afford a brand new car but could have afforded to purchase a second-hand one that was of a decent quality. However, the good second-hand vehicles are now unavailable and so the middle-income people have to run their vehicles into the ground or purchase those of lesser quality. Either way, these options are likely to generate a stream of further costs, restricting their potential for wealth advancement.

As those who can afford to buy new cars are able to avoid these costs, they are able to progress. In this way, such asymmetric information within the second-hand car market is likely to further exacerbate inequality. However, the poorer members of society may actually benefit from the situation in that they are more likely to be able to afford a vehicle now that the lowest reservation price is available. Combining this with the model in the previous section leads to the conclusion that the poorest may be afforded better employment opportunities as a result, but these may be restricted again by the stream of maintenance costs that subsequently arise.

The model is simplistic and overlooks a number of factors in the market. First, there is likely to be a whole spectrum of vehicle quality. Secondly, buyers are not going to know the reservation prices and so, in negotiating prices, may still offer above that of good quality cars enabling them to obtain quality vehicles. Thirdly, a way in which the market attempts to solve this problem is by using reputation to signal quality. Buyers of second-hand cars often know of a dealer from whom they can be confident of obtaining quality vehicles and so to whom they are willing to pay higher prices. Alternatively, buyers can purchase inspections from trusted independent experts. Fourthly, buyers may be able to score a bargain from sellers who fail to appreciate the value of their vehicles or who are altruistically motivated. Despite these complications, the model holds important conclusions as to the functioning and impacts of a market that is so significant in the transport sector.

Policy: An Overview IV

Part III expounded the potential failures that arise in the transport sector. All these cause the sector to be either productively or allocatively inefficient, thereby preventing the sector from maximising overall welfare. It is the role of government policy to correct these failures. This is the focus of this penultimate part.

Chapter 12 outlines the policies of deregulation and privatisation. These policies, which are most effective when combined, are aimed at reducing market power and at promoting competition within the transport sector. They have been the source of much controversy and debate, particularly regarding the deregulation and privatisation of British Rail, but they are at the heart of competition policy within the European Union. Extensive studies are explored of the policies as applied to British Rail and British buses, drawing out crucial lessons that are applicable in all countries. The privatisation and deregulation of British ports and European bus markets are also explored, as are those in the German and Irish transport markets as a whole.

Chapter 13 outlines the mechanism by which large-scale, public investment decisions can be made, namely cost–benefit analysis. The computer model used by the Department for Transport in the UK to do this for trunk road investment, COBA, is assessed in detail in order to illuminate the mechanism in practice. Chapter 14 develops the investment theme and explores what form transport investment takes across the European Union. It takes the Channel Tunnel as a case study of this. Investment is a solution to the market failures of public and merit goods.

Chapter 15 takes up economic theory again, expounding the theory behind the three general policy solutions to negative externalities, namely command and control solutions, taxation and tradable permits. Each of these is applied extensively to examples within the European Union, and the potentially significant problem of bureaucratic rent-seeking is considered.

Chapter 16 explores the market failure of road traffic congestion and the different road-pricing schemes that could be introduced to correct the problem. This particularly draws upon work conducted by Glaister and Graham (2004) on road-pricing schemes within the UK. In this chapter, readers are able to engage with the actual design of such schemes and the issues that surround their implementation.

Privatisation and 12
Deregulation

Cessation of hostilities at the end of the Second World War brought with it the decision by governments, across Europe, that their national transport systems were no longer economically viable. As such, there was widespread *nationalisation* and *regulation* of the sector across the continent, as governments sought to restore its effective functioning after the preceding destruction and disruption. Government ownership and control of these industries continued in Europe until 1979 when Margaret Thatcher's Conservative government in the UK pioneered the implementation of *privatisation – the transfer of all or part of the ownership of business organisations from the public sector to the private sector –* and *deregulation: the loosening of government controls of an industry, enabling it to be increasingly directed by the free market.* Since then, these two policies (especially the former) have been sources of great debate and controversy amongst economists and wider commentators.

The theoretical underpinnings behind this industrial transformation came largely from the work of Friedrich von Hayek, who resurrected and reinforced the importance that Adam Smith and other classical economists had placed on the free market. In the opinions of Hayek and Smith, markets function effectively without unnecessary intervention by governments. The argument that governments should reduce their involvement in economies, and return industries back to private owners, was once again thrust to the forefront of economic discourse.

Privatisation is simply the transfer of ownership from the public sector to the private sector. It does not, by itself, affect the degree of competition within an industry. The privatisation of a public-sector monopoly will result in a private-sector monopoly, unless it is accompanied by deregulation as well. Consequently, in practice, the two policies have often been inextricably linked, which is why they are both dealt with in this chapter, rather than being separated as is often the practice.

Privatisation and deregulation are key strands in European Competition Policy (see Section 6.5). The European Commission has laid down strict criteria against which any public-sector expenditure is judged; prohibiting state aid which gives domestic producers an unfair competitive advantage over those in other countries. Privatisation is encouraged in order for member states to meet these criteria. The European Commission also encourages member states to open up their markets to increased competition, both of a domestic and of an inter-European nature, namely to introduce deregulation.

12.1 | Arguments in favour of privatisation and deregulation

Deregulation is intended to promote the influence of competition and the free market in an industry. The underlining motive is to increase productive, allocative and Pareto efficiency by subjecting decision-makers to increased competition and the market signal of profit, rather than the other more subjective and inefficient objectives of central planners. With entrepreneurs competing with one another to maximise profits, resources will be used in the most efficient manner and market welfare will be maximised. This is the fundamental argument for deregulation, although it also reduces the administrative burden on the authorities.

There are numerous additional arguments underpinning the implementation of privatisation.

- *Promotion of the entrepreneurial spirit.* By transferring the ownership of a business to private individuals, the business can fail. The new owners can no longer rely on public finances to ensure its survival, and so there is a new impetus impelling the owners to be successful. In addition, it was noted in Section 4.6.6 that a survey of relatively small technology companies by Quince and Whittaker (2003) had showed that the single largest personal objective of entrepreneurs is to create a successful business. This desire may be weakened in larger businesses, as the lifestyles of entrepreneurs are perhaps less likely to be as dependent on the success of the business; but it is still the case that having private ownership is likely to result in a stronger entrepreneurial drive towards success than under public ownership.

- *Subjection to competition within capital markets.* Although privatisation does not imply an increase in competition within the product markets, it does inevitably result in greater competition in the capital markets. Private owners cannot rely on public finances, and so will inevitably have to seek necessary funds from financial institutions and other private sources. These will only lend capital if they are satisfied with the organisation and operation of the business and if there is a promising future ahead of it. This acts as a disciplining pressure, rewarding economic efficiency and good strategy and punishing poor enterprise. Similarly, public limited companies are liable to be taken over in the share market if they do not satisfy their current shareholders. As shareholders are likely to focus on the return to their investment, and as takeovers jeopardise the jobs of directors, this threat will spur directors towards entrepreneurial success: a spur that would not exist under public ownership.

- *Elimination of political misuse.* A danger of public ownership is that the business can be used to achieve political ends, instead of being solely focused on being operated in the most economically efficient manner. For example, a public-sector business can be used to safeguard employment which is actually uneconomical, because it would be politically unpopular with the electorate to announce significant job reductions.

This possibility can be developed further. In Section 15.6, the work of Svendsen (2003) is outlined, which suggests that bureaucracies are inclined to strive for budget maximisation rather than cost minimisation. Public-sector businesses are managed by largely unelected bureaucrats who transcend elected governments. Consequently, the application of Svendsen's work to this situation would suggest that the managers of public-sector businesses may actually seek to increase the administrative burden and associated costs, leading directly to less economically efficient enterprises. Removing ownership from government, and management from bureaucrats, should result in efficiency gains.

■ *Erosion of crowding-out.* Crowding-out is the notion that as the public sector expands, it inevitably causes the private sector to contract. There is only a certain amount of investment that is feasible within an economy. If the public sector accounts for a larger proportion of this, the opportunity cost (the cost in terms of the next best alternative forgone) is that the private sector receives less. This is illustrated by the production possibility frontier in Figure 12.1. A production possibility frontier shows the trade-off between the production of two products, in this case that between public and private investment. Usually a production possibility frontier is convex due to the effect of diminishing returns to scale. However, with investment there is no reason why there should not be a continually proportionate trade-off. At point A, the economy is maximising its investment as it is situated on the frontier, and is devoting Y_1 investment to the public sector and X_1 to the private. If the government were to expand public investment, to Y_2, it would inevitably incur an opportunity cost of lower private investment, to the extent of $X_1 - X_2$. The exception to this is the case when economic growth causes the investment possibilities to increase, as shown by a new production possibility frontier such as PPF$_2$, which potentially allows greater investment in both sectors, such as point C.

The actual mechanism by which this occurs can be understood by considering the capital markets. In order for the government to increase public investment,

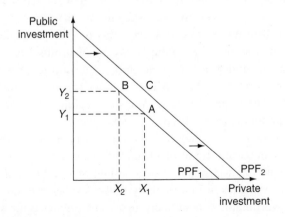

Figure 12.1
Investment crowding-out

it has to raise the necessary finances by borrowing; which in turn requires an increase in the interest rate that it offers on its bonds. This increased interest rate filters through the capital markets, discouraging private borrowing and investment.

An argument for privatisation is that it results in a smaller public sector, lower public investment and so less crowding-out. The encouragement of private investment and enterprise is a cornerstone of the promotion of a thriving enterprise economy, and so privatisation can play a pivotal role in this.

- *Widening of shareholdings and economic interest*. As privatisation involves the purchasing of shares by members of the public, it serves to widen the population's interest in the economy. This, in turn, should encourage other members of the population to become shareholders in other businesses, leading to a greater degree of accountability within the economy and more efficient operations. There is also political motivation here, as the government facilitating greater shareholdings will pursue policies that will allow them to be successful and lucrative. New shareholders will appreciate this, and so will look favourably upon the administration that facilitated their shareholdings in the first place.

  This is perhaps most important in employee buyouts, which are designed to align employee rewards with the performance of the business in which they work. By aligning the two, the intention is for employee productivity and their interest in managerial decisions to be increased, as they strive for their own financial gain through the success of their business. This was a significant factor in the privatisation of British ports, which is explored below.

- *Fiscal improvement*. Privatisation leads to a fiscal improvement for the government in two respects. First, it removes one recipient of public expenditure. After the Cold War, Western governments sought to reap a *peace dividend* by reducing the size of their armed forces, saving themselves a certain amount of military expenditure.

  Secondly, it generates immediate revenue for the government, which will improve the public balance sheet and can be used for spending. This is particularly attractive in the run-up to elections, when additional spending can improve the public perception of the government; a temptation that John Major's Conservative government appears to have succumbed to in the privatisation of the British railways. However, this revenue does need to be offset against the elimination of a potential stream of profits from the business if it was to remain under public ownership in the future. It is important that businesses are correctly valued when they are privatised; otherwise it could eventually be a detriment to public finances: 'selling off the family silver' too cheaply as opponents of privatisation have argued.

- *Tackling of unionisation*. Public-sector enterprises have often been the focus of much unionisation, and the results from this sector have then been a signal of the government's stance in labour negotiations across the economy. Unions in public-sector industries are particularly powerful, because the leaders appreciate that governments are unlikely to accept public-sector strikes and the disruption they can cause, and that they have public funds that can be accessed to finance union claims.

A key part of Thatcher's drive for free-market efficiency was the elimination of union power, so that labour markets could be allocatively efficient. Privatisation is a facilitating factor in this, as it removes the government from the effects of strikes, and removes the businesses from having access to public funds, meaning that they can fail if union action is too severe. Both of these weaken the bargaining power of the unions with the new owners and employers. By weakening union power in the public sector, the government is making its stance on unionisation across the economy absolutely clear: a key part of any policy to tackle unionisation.

12.2 Arguments in favour of nationalisation and against deregulation

- *Effective organisation of natural monopolies.* Privatisation and deregulation only have a beneficial effect if the market can sustain competition or is truly contestable. A deregulated natural monopoly, or a market with irremovable and extremely high barriers to entry, is likely to be harmful to the social interest, because competition cannot be promoted and so it would afford a producer with market power free reign to maximise producer surplus at any cost. In the case of a natural monopoly market, in which not even one producer is profitable, privatisation and deregulation would simply cause the production to cease, which may also be against the interests of society. In both of these cases, an authority should maintain ownership and take on the responsibility of regulation to safeguard the wider interests of consumers and society.

- *Markets with safety concerns.* As noted in Section 1.2.4, one of the reasons why the British bus industry was initially regulated in 1930 was in response to unrestrained competition, resulting in dangerous driving. The nature of the transport sector is a potentially dangerous one, and so it is necessary to have certain regulations imposed upon operators within it. Consequently, there must be limits to any deregulation that is introduced.

- *Effective control of externalities.* The transport sector is permeated with externalities: atmospheric pollution, noise pollution, congestion, blight and accidents, to name but a few. Deregulated private operators have a high propensity to ignore such considerations in their pursuit for profit and private gain. As such, there is an argument in favour of public ownership and regulation so that the social optimal output and operation of these industries can be promoted. See Chapter 9 for an exposition of such externalities.

- *Redistribution of income and wealth.* The widespread nationalisation that occurred in Europe after the Second World War was a strand in the development of welfare states. Governments began to take an active role in the promotion of a good standard of living for their populations, with the provision of benefits and national health and education systems. Publicly owned transport industries can play a role in the redistribution of wealth from the affluent to the poorer sections of the population, through the subsidisation of services for the poor.

■ *Promotion of marginal cost pricing.* Allocative efficiency, as noted in Section 5.4.2, is achieved when the price is equal to the marginal cost of production. This is achieved in perfect competition, which maximises market welfare, but not in less competitive situations in which operators pursue profit maximisation at the expense of consumers. A publicly owned, or regulated, operator is perhaps more likely to implement marginal cost pricing than a private and deregulated operator.

■ *Job protection.* Competition in a product market often leads to a consolidation in the labour market, through job losses and wage reductions. A publicly owned enterprise can be used to safeguard employment. The proposed closure of the British car-manufacturer Rover highlighted this, as it stimulated a popular pressure for the British government to intervene to protect against job losses. Prime Minister Tony Blair intervened in the negotiations between owners and unions but was unwilling to safeguard the jobs that were at stake.

The economy and the demands within it are continually changing, and so there have to be changes in the use of the resources available to it in order to ensure that Pareto efficiency is achieved. It is economically efficient for labour to be lost in some areas of production and reabsorbed in others. The problem is that this process is inevitably painful and, because labour is not fully mobile (both occupationally and geographically), long-lasting, making it politically damaging.

■ *Share-ownership consolidation.* The share market is not perfectly competitive. There exist monopoly buyers, who have the market power to influence the price of the shares. As such, there is often share consolidation which serves to ensure that recently privatised and profitable enterprises are owned by large holdings, minimising any wider interest in the health of the economy and working against an equitable distribution of wealth. It has been argued that public ownership is a more effective tool for achieving these aims.

12.3 | Political risk and the need for governmental commitment in privatisation

The success of privatisation is dependent upon the degree of commitment to the free market expounded by the government. Privatised businesses are likely to be large employers, and so governments are likely to be inclined to protect them to safeguard against the political consequences of business failure. If the government fails to make its commitment to the free market undeniably clear, there is the danger that the newly privatised business, appreciating the political desires of the government, will choose to pursue an objective that is somewhat weaker than that of full economic efficiency. This is called *political risk*. The drive for efficiency will be rationally reduced if the business feels that it will be supported by the government should it drift into difficulties. If the government does not make its commitment to the free market undeniably clear from the outset, it is actually promoting the scenario in which the privatised business fails and receives governmental support.

This can be illustrated using *game theory*, which is the fascinating *analysis of strategic interaction between economic agents*. There are two forms that game theory can take. The first is the analysis of *simultaneous games*, in which the economic agents make their decisions at the same time. These games are analysed using *pay-off matrices*, which show the different pay-offs that the different combinations of decisions would result in, thus enabling the analyst to predict which is most likely. The second is the analysis of sequential games, in which one agent makes a decision before the other, allowing the *follower* to base its decision upon what has already occurred. These games are analysed using *extensive form diagrams*. It is this latter form that the privatisation analysis takes in Figure 12.2.

Privatisation is the first step in the analysis, after which the newly privatised business has to decide whether it is going to strive to be successful (*high effort*), or take a more relaxed approach which is more likely to fail (*low effort*). The first of these options is costly to the entrepreneur in terms of time and stress, and so there is a tendency for the entrepreneur to choose to pursue the second, less costly course of action. However, a large factor in this decision is that of the likely course of action of the government. If the government allows the business to fail if it gets into trouble, the result will be outcome D, which is where the business fails causing job losses. However, this comes at a cost to the government, as the resulting job losses will be politically unpopular. Consequently, there is a tendency for the government to choose to rescue the business in times of trouble (*rescue*). The entrepreneur is likely to appreciate that the government's dominant strategy is to come to the rescue, reinforcing the entrepreneur's dominant strategy to take the more relaxed approach. Overall, the *dominant equilibrium* of this game is outcome C, which is where the business fails and the government comes to the rescue. There is a natural pressure for privatisation to fail, which it would do in cases where the government intervenes to help.

It is the responsibility of the government to avert such a result, by making its commitment to the free market undeniably clear. If the entrepreneur is certain

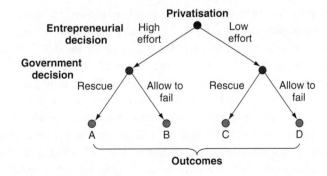

Figure 12.2
Privatisation and governmental commitment

that the government will not come to its rescue in times of trouble, then the result if it chooses the *low effort* strategy would be outcome D. The entrepreneur will want to avoid this, and so will choose the *high effort* strategy, resulting in outcome B (the government will not be required to come to the rescue if it is successful). The newly privatised business, and privatisation as a whole, will be successful. As this is the objective of privatisation, it is vital that the government makes this commitment absolutely clear from the outset. The fact that governments fail to do this is the explanation for why many privatisations fail. The case of British Rail, outlined below, is a good example of this.

This logic is the same as that behind the commitment of governments not to pay ransom fees to release members of their populations that are taken hostage. If guerrilla groups know that they will not receive a penny in ransom, it is counterproductive for them to take hostages in the first place; but if the government undermines this resolve by paying such a fee, it is likely to open up the doors for numerous other hostage situations. The problem is that in order to make such a resolve clear, it is often necessary to ignore the calls to pay a ransom which can be politically damaging. Similarly, it may be necessary to allow a privatised business to fail, shedding workers, in order to promote efficiency from future privatisations.

12.4 | The methodology of privatisation

There are two main forms that privatisation can take. First, whole enterprises can be transferred from public to private ownership through the selling of shares. This can be done to private investors in general, or it can be directed purely at the current directors and workforce. The National Freight Company of the UK, which was privatised in 1982, was sold exclusively to employees: an *employee buyout*.

Secondly, markets can be broken down in constituent parts, each of which is then put up for competitive tender. This is where already-existing private businesses compete with one another to secure the right to operate that part of the market by submitting proposals regarding how they would operate it. Often, the proposal which involves the lowest government subsidy (or the largest payment to government) will be accepted, although competitions can be altered to include certain minimum service characteristics.

In the transport sector, whole-enterprise privatisations are most suitable for businesses that will provide infrastructure, actually manufacture products or have the structure of a natural monopoly. For example, in the UK, British Airports and Rolls-Royce were privatised in this way in 1987; Rover Group a year later; and Railtrack, the railway network provider, by 1997. Competitive tendering is most suitable in service industries, where the market can be effectively broken down into smaller parts and where local monopolies are likely to result. For example, bus industries across Europe as well as the British train services have been privatised through competitive tendering, both of which shall be explored below. The resulting operators are often termed *franchised monopolies*.

A practical problem is calculating the price at which public enterprises should be sold. Experience in the UK tends to support the claim that public enterprises are sold too cheaply, thereby adding weight to the 'selling-off the family silver' argument against privatisation. Begg *et al.* (1991) display the results by Yarrow (1985), which show that British Aerospace and Jaguar were sold for £21 and £25 million less, respectively, than their stock-market valuation immediately after privatisation.

12.5 The privatisation and deregulation of British rail

12.5.1 The privatised structure

The privatisation of the railways was discussed by Margaret Thatcher's Conservative government, but it could not reach an agreement as to the details and so the issue was put to one side. The discussion was reopened when the subsequent Conservative administration, under John Major, was drawing up its manifesto for the 1992 general election.

The original intention was to privatise Railtrack by selling shares to the general public at some ill-defined point in 'the medium term', certainly after the next general election. A decision to accelerate the process came for two reasons. First, the government was advised to do so by the financial markets following unexpected difficulties in other privatisations. Secondly, the government wanted to get everything done in advance of the election, so that the Exchequer would have access to the generated revenue and because it was becoming clear that there would likely be a change of government, and Labour would certainly not have completed privatisation unless they received it as a done deal. Confusion and poor decision-making was caused by the resulting scramble, leading to an outcome that was much less satisfactory than it could have been.

The prospectus for the sale of shares was issued in 1996, and the privatisation was duly completed before the 1997 general election, in which, as widely expected, the Conservatives were defeated by Labour.

The privatised structure was complex, as illustrated by Figure 12.3.

12.5.1.1 Train Operating Companies

The Train Operating Companies (TOCs) competed for 25 franchises, each of 7 years' duration (sometimes 15 due to an appreciation of the need for long-term structural work), which were designed by the *Office of Passenger Rail Franchising (OPRAF)*. The franchise contracts comprised stipulated minimum services to be provided by the operator and flexibility above this standard, affording the operator room to develop and improve services, something which OPRAF hoped would happen. The competition was primarily over who would be able to satisfy the specifications

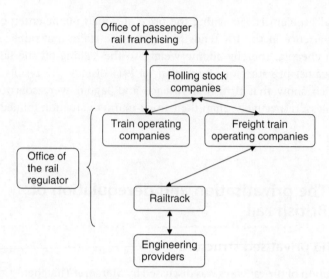

Figure 12.3 The privatised rail structure

for the smallest cost, or largest payment, to the government. The attractiveness of service improvements on offer was certainly a secondary consideration.

The TOCs were to keep their revenues, meaning that they were also to bear the revenue risks. Some passenger fares were to be regulated, though not all; for example, commuter markets would be regulated (the inelastic nature of demand in these markets would tempt operators to exploit consumers in terms of the fares charged), but many of the other markets were already highly competitive with road and air alternatives and so fare regulation was less necessary. The TOCs would bear their own operating costs, but charges for access to track and stations for the basic service patterns were to pass straight through for payment by OPRAF and therefore by the taxpayer.

12.5.1.2 Railtrack

Railtrack would remain as the infrastructure owner. It would be an independently regulated monopoly, as it is a natural monopoly, with private shareholders. It would be primarily disciplined by competition for corporate control. Crucially, it was deliberately put beyond the direct control of the government.

Railtrack was to do the following:

■ Own the fixed infrastructure, including stations, land, buildings, signals and maintenance depots, many of which were leased to the TOCs.
■ Directly control 14 large mainline stations.
■ Be responsible for central timetabling and the co-ordination of all services; signalling, which would lead to potential liability for the accidents that were to occur; planning and implementing investment in infrastructure; and the safe operation of the network under the supervision of the Health and Safety Executive.

Railtrack would be financed by the TOCs paying to use the infrastructure, but the Secretary of State retained the power to give direct grants for freight facilities if justified on public interest grounds. It was to procure most of the services it needed on the open market, in particular the necessary engineering services.

New senior managers, including the first chairman, Robert Horton, were drafted in from other industries. It has been alleged that many of the best senior rail engineers were alienated and left, perhaps contributing to a tendency to underestimate the extreme complexity of a large railway system. Many of the new managers had previous experience of unregulated industries and so found difficulty with the public accountability of their new industry. In particular, an uneasy and even confrontational relationship between the infrastructure company and the Rail Regulator was to develop, to the detriment of the whole industry.

12.5.1.3   Engineering providers

Existing rail-engineering services were broken into 13 companies and sold to the private sector. The idea was that these would then compete with one another to secure railway contracts from Railtrack. However, the problem was that they were sold with the benefit of negotiated procurement contracts already put in place by the government. There was not an open competition to determine the terms on which Railtrack would procure what they needed. Two explanations for this decision have been put forward: first, the outgoing Tory government was determined to complete the privatisation quickly; and secondly, the pre-arranged contracts had been struck on generous terms in order to inflate the sale price of the engineering companies at a time the Exchequer was in particular need of funds. Whatever the reason, the consequence was that the benefits of fully competitive procurement contracts were denied to Railtrack at the start of the new regime.

12.5.1.4   The office of the Rail Regulator

The Rail Regulator, appointed by the Secretary of State, was to be independent. It was to have four statutory functions.

- The granting, monitoring and enforcement of Railtrack's network licence and the operator's licences of the TOCs. This meant that it was responsible for the protection of the interests of providers and users of rail services; ensuring through-ticketing for the benefit of passengers; and guaranteeing the proper operations of Railtrack and the TOCs.
- The approval of access agreements between Railtrack and passenger and freight operators, including the regulation of the charges for use of the infrastructure, the allocation of train paths and the settling of timetable disputes.
- The enforcement of domestic competition law.
- The approval of railway line closures.

The Rail Regulator was to have considerable powers, but there were contracts that it was not to regulate; for example, the terms of leases for rolling stock and for stations, and the contracts between Railtrack and providers of engineering services, which actually accounted for the greatest part of Railtrack's expenditure. It was also given no power to regulate passenger fares.

12.5.1.5 The Office of Passenger Rail Franchising

The OPRAF, headed by the Franchising Director and directly accountable to the government, was to regulate passenger fares through the contracts offered for passenger franchises. This was necessary because, unlike the other utilities, the railway could not be expected to become self-financing. Public subsidy was inevitable and it was the Franchising Director's job to administer it, except for certain freight grants and any capital grants. The Director's function was to design rail passenger franchises and sell them to TOCs using a competitive tendering procedure.

The OPRAF had other responsibilities too, including the encouragement of investment, improving services and developing arrangements to ensure the continuation of some former facilities (such as concessionary travel for staff, through-ticketing and certain travel cards and railcards). Although a part of government, and answerable to ministers, it had a separate budget and considerable discretion about how that budget was to be allocated. To that extent, its actions were transparent to the general public, helping to facilitate proper public debate about taxation and spending policies that were unavailable before privatisation.

12.5.1.6 Freight companies

Freight services were always to be entirely provided by open-access, competitive companies – that is, there was no attempt to create any analogous arrangement to the subsidised passenger rail franchises. The first intention had been to offer the existing freight business for sale as a number of companies. However, having tested the market, only two companies were created, but there has since been significant competitive entry by other carriers. Freight access charges were set to cover rather modest estimates of variable cost alone, in order to maximise the chances of viable rail freight developing and on the argument that much rail infrastructure is maintained primarily for the benefit of passenger services. This strategy proved to have two failings. First, as the volume of heavy freight usage increased, it was to become apparent that the cost of track wear and tear from freight was significantly higher than had been assumed. Secondly, as track became congested, these low prices were to mean that rationing had to be enforced and that the price signals were not capable of bringing about efficient use of the network.

12.5.1.7 Rolling Stock Companies (ROSCOs)

There would be three ROSCOs, which would own existing rolling stock, acquire new stock and lease it out on a commercial basis. These were established to eliminate the sunk costs from the TOCs. They were, and remain, unregulated.

It is unclear to what extent these companies competed amongst themselves, as there are important technical restrictions on the transfer of rolling stock between different lines. It was always open to TOCs to procure rolling stock in other ways, and several (including Virgin) have purchased their own, putting additional competitive pressure on the ROSCOs. There have been criticisms regarding the earnings of the ROSCOs and the low prices at which they were sold, but on the whole they have been a successful part of the privatisation.

12.5.2 The story of the privatisation

It had always been intended that fierce competition would be promoted amongst the TOCs, although it is doubtful whether this could actually be facilitated because of capacity constraints and the tension between competition and effective franchising. However, this doubt became irrelevant, as the government fundamentally changed this policy immediately after the passing of the Railways Act in 1993. Under the old regime there had been important cross-subsidisation between profitable and unprofitable routes. Open competition for operator franchises would have brought this to an end and so, since the government had committed itself to not allowing any service reductions, it would be necessary to replace it with substantially increased direct subsidies from the Exchequer. The Treasury was not willing to allow this to happen and so a new policy, *Moderation of Competition*, was issued, which the Rail Regulator had to accommodate by developing a horribly complicated set of rules regarding competition amongst the TOCs. There has been competition, but on nothing like the scale that the original design had envisioned.

South West Trains was the first company to secure a contract, in February 1996. The last was Scotrail in April 1997. Despite the change in government policy, competition for the new contracts was strong and seemed to become more aggressive over time as bidders gained confidence. Some of the bids were highly ambitious, but OPRAF took them at face value rather than investigating them further. Overall, 13 separate companies won contracts. Fifteen of the contracts went to bus operators, and the Virgin Group won the large West Coast Main Line and Cross Country contracts.

Had the contracts been honoured, government subsidies would have fallen from £1.8 billion to £0.9 billion each year; but after a promising start, with falling subsidies and unprecedented rise in passenger numbers, two problems began to emerge. First, some of the TOCs discovered that they had been over-ambitious in reducing employee numbers and that they could not run services with the numbers they had planned, causing quality to deteriorate. Secondly, the expanded number of trains, which had been encouraged by the terms of the contracts, began to impede one another, causing reliability to deteriorate also.

In May 1997, there was a change in government which brought to power the party that had made its distaste for rail privatisation very clear from the outset. Immediately, the new government began to draw attention to the failings of the industry and to promise government *action*, rather than standing back and allowing the privatised industry to rectify itself. It was apparent that the government wanted to re-establish control of the industry.

Railtrack came under increasing pressure, which took three strands.

- It made a number of imprudent investment decisions, including that of committing itself to Virgin's proposal for the development of the West Coast Main Line. It is hard to believe that it would have made such a large commitment on the basis of improperly quantified risks, had it not implicitly been assuming that should things go wrong, the government would come to the rescue.
- Poor reliability was attributed to performance failures by both Railtrack and the TOCs, which was perhaps unfair for Railtrack as it was successful in reducing delays up to 1999/2000. In fact, in this year it achieved a 10 per cent reduction in delays, the best ever performance on the network, but was fined for failing to meet the Regulator's target that was almost 3 per cent higher. Consequently, Railtrack had its network licence modified by the Regulator to encapsulate higher targets.
- There were two major accidents, both in West London: one in 1997 at Southall in which seven people were killed; the other in 1999 at Ladbroke Grove in which 31 people were killed. Both accidents involved trains failing to stop at red signals. The general public was joined by government ministers in immediately laying the blame at the door of privatisation and Railtrack.

This mounting criticism was a pivotal point in the history of rail privatisation in the UK. The government could have taken the stance that the industry was now privately owned, run and regulated, and that it would be inappropriate and damaging for it to intervene. Instead, it chose to make a very public intervention which heightened the perception that privatisation had been a failure, and that the government would seek to regain control of the industry. The evidence is clear that safety was improving before privatisation and it continued to improve at much the same rate afterwards.

In October 2000, arguably the last blow was dealt to Railtrack. Following a third accident, this time at Hatfield which was caused by a cracked rail, Railtrack's management effectively closed the network by imposing restrictive speed limits and many cancellations, allowing it to implement a precautionary programme of engineering works in case similar cracks existed elsewhere. The disruption was compounded by one of the wettest autumns in recent years, which led to embankment slips and flooding. It was later established that there were no problems comparable to that responsible for the Hatfield crash, but the response of Railtrack served to destroy train services and the businesses of the TOCs. There was a catastrophic decline in passenger numbers, and Railtrack suffered financial penalties under the performance regime.

With this programme of engineering works and its commitment to the imprudent West Coast Main Line developments, Railtrack was facing a major financial problem. The government had already made substantial special grants available to rescue it and a further deal between them was agreed, which seemed to stabilise the situation for a while. In October 2001, without warning, the Secretary of State for Transport Stephen Byers invoked the special provisions of the Railways Act to put Railtrack into administration. The government could have encouraged a conventional takeover of Railtrack, but it appears that Byers was determined to take the opportunity to destroy the privatised shareholder ownership structure that the Labour government had inherited in 1997.

Eventually, a new entity (Network Rail) was allowed to take over Railtrack's assets, without any active competition to do so. Network Rail is a company limited by guarantee, run by an executive accountable to around 120 *members*, each chosen to represent one of the interests in the railways. There are no conventional shareholders, but profit on operations must be earned in order to repay the debt holders. It was further intended that Network Rail would earn additional profits in order to build up a *buffer fund*.

The government also replaced OPRAF with the Strategic Rail Authority (SRA), which obtained its legal powers in early 2001. The government had hoped that it would negotiate changes to the operating licences of the TOCs but these proved slow. In late 2001, it began to transpire that several TOCs were in serious financial difficulty, largely due to rising labour costs, and so in 2001/2002 (for the first time) government subsidies were significantly above what had been specified in the previously agreed contracts. By July 2003, nine of the franchises had failed financially, but it was decided that bankruptcy was not going to be enforced. The operators were allowed to continue.

The SRA further weakened competition in the industry in two ways. First, it granted short-term extensions to franchises without going through any competitive process. Secondly, it came under pressure because of the poor performance of commuter services operated by Connex from the south-east suburbs of London and so, rather than allowing another privately owned TOC to take over the routes, it took over the operation itself. Thus South East Trains became directly owned and operated in the public sector: the first step towards actual re-nationalisation.

Little has been narrated about the freight side of the industry. It seems that competition for these services has worked reasonably well. There has been significant investment and innovation in both the nature of the services offered and the methods used to deliver them. For instance, the freight operators were able to purchase a quantity of cheap and reliable locomotives from General Motors of America, something that had not happened previously. There has also been growth in the rail freight industry, which has been coupled with improved services and facilities.

It has not all been a success story, though. In 2004, a rail freight operator lost the contract to run special mail trains due to concerns over service reliability. Also, the growth that there has been has largely been in traditional sectors; for example, moving coal to power stations over longer distances. There has been less success in winning new markets.

12.5.3 The reason for failure

The fundamental principle driving the railways policy of the 1990s was not privatisation but deregulation: to establish competition throughout the industry. The initial policy was designed to do this, but at the same time to cater for the natural monopoly that existed in the infrastructure and for the need to preserve the scale of the industry through subsidisation. Despite the government policy change in favour of moderating the competition, the policy was successfully implemented and it started to produce some remarkably good results until two phenomena ultimately caused it to fail: *policy risk* and *political risk*.

12.5.3.1 Policy risk

Policy risk is the risk of the government not implementing the necessary policies. Glaister (2004) identifies three strands of this in the narrative above:

- *Decision-making.* Ministers were slow to make up their minds about exactly what they wanted, and execution of policy was unduly rushed because of the late decision to privatise Railtrack in advance of an impending general election.
- *Funding.* The Treasury proved to be unwilling to provide the public funds necessary to allow competition for passengers to operate as originally envisaged, and so competition had to be *moderated*.
- *Competition for engineering services.* A proper competition was not held for the right to provide by far the most important services to Railtrack: engineering. This was allegedly because such competition may have reduced the privatisation revenues for the Treasury.

12.5.3.2 Political risk

Political risk is the result of action to avoid political damage that could be caused to the government. The railways have always enjoyed an important position in the eyes of the British electorate. They have traditionally been a source of pride for the populous and have almost come to symbolise the vitality of the country. Knowing this, governments proved to be short-sighted in their approach to the industry. They have been unwilling to tolerate the potential criticism that they feared would be aroused if they had allowed the company failures which are essential to the development of an effective competitive process. When TOCs failed, the government bailed them out. When Railtrack made a fatally bad investment and mismanaged its information systems, the government again came to the rescue for a while, before bringing it back under governmental control. As the game theory analysis predicts, the result of this action was an industry that could continue to be dependent on the government and so did not need to become economically efficient and self-sustaining.

This may have been particularly marked in the rail industry. An incentive for over-ambitious bidding for initial contacts would have been created if the TOCs had anticipated that the government would not be able to stomach bankruptcy of a public passenger rail service should things go badly. This appears to have been the case, as it was not long after the franchises had been secured that some of the TOCs experienced difficulties because their plans had been too ambitious. However, it is also possible that they may have been victims of the *winner's curse*, which can occur in auctions where there is uncertainty about the future value of the item being bid for. The bids of some will be too high by chance, and some will be too low. The bidder who has the misfortune to have the highest estimate of the value will be the one that wins the auction, thereby paying too much.

Political risk has been particularly evident in the governmental action with respect to the labour market. Competition in the labour market had accounted largely for the success of previous privatisations and deregulations, such as that of the bus industry, which is examined below. However, in the railway industry, unit labour costs have run well ahead of average earnings, as governments have been unwilling to introduce the necessary competition because of the fear of politically damaging job losses.

12.6 The privatisation of British ports

The ports of Britain have also been the subject of privatisation and deregulation. In 1983, Britain had approximately 70 commercially significant port authorities. Associated British Ports (ABP) was by far the largest, controlling 19 ports and accounting for approximately a quarter of total port revenue. ABP, along with the other nine largest authorities, accounted for approximately 80 per cent of the total port revenue, illustrating clearly that the industry had an oligopoly structure with one dominant operator within it.

British ports were also firmly in the public sector. Only three of the larger ports (Felixstowe, Liverpool and Manchester) were privately owned. The others were all in the public sector, although the nature of this varied. Some were public trusts (Trust Ports); others were owned by local authorities; and others were run by public-sector companies, such as Sealink (a subsidiary of British Rail).

In February 1983, approximately 51.5 per cent of the shares of ABP were offered for sale. The sale was heavily oversubscribed, with 45,300 successful applicants. In addition to the public offer, 1 million shares, accounting for approximately 2.5 per cent of the total shares of the company, were offered free of charge to port employees, all of which were taken up. In April of the following year, the government sold its remaining shares, with incentives aimed at encouraging employees to further invest. In total, the privatisation of the ports raised approximately £80 million for the Treasury.

The employees were encouraged to invest in an attempt to strengthen the link between the privatised businesses' performance and their rewards. By aligning these it was hoped that it would promote employee productivity and interest in the successful management and direction of the business. By 1993, two-thirds of ABP employees owned shares that had appreciated considerably in value.

In 1991, the government made the decision to allow the Trust Ports to become private companies with shares in their own right. Tees and Hartlepool, and Bristol, self-privatised in 1989 and 1990 respectively, becoming financially successful ports. In 1992, the ports of Tilbury, Medway and Clyde were sold as employee buyouts.

The privatisation was accompanied by significant deregulation. After the Second World War, the National Dock Labour Scheme (NDLS) was introduced, effectively giving the registered dock workers of the Transport and General Workers' Union monopoly control of all dock work. By restricting competition for dock work, the Scheme led to inefficient labour practices, chronic over-manning and higher operating costs for the ports. The government abolished the Scheme in August 1989, enabling the ports to function much more efficiently. The ABP cut its labour force by approximately 65 per cent, increasingly labour productivity and leading to higher profitability than had been enjoyed previously.

Haarmeyer and Yorke (1993) note that in 1981 the ABP made a profit of £1 million with 9300 employees, whereas by 1990 the figures were £60.2 million and 3633 employees.

Privatisation has also encouraged innovation and diversification. Ports have been upgraded, such as the reopening of Alexandra Dock at Hull in 1991; some have been used for other commercial purposes. Ports in Southampton, Liverpool, Hull and Central London have developed thriving retail and residential areas. Privatisation has stimulated levels of investment far greater than that under public ownership, leading to greater profitability.

12.7 | The privatisation and deregulation of British buses

Section 6.6 outlines the nature of the British bus industry today, but this is very different to how it was before 1986. Prior to 1986, the industry was composed of four sectors. First, there were the large publicly owned corporations: the *National Bus Company* in England and Wales and the *Scottish Bus Group* north of the English border. These companies provided more than half of the local bus miles outside London. Secondly, there were seven *Public Transport Companies* that operated in each of the seven largest metropolitan areas. Each of these was owned by a *Public Transport Executive*, which in turn was controlled by the local County Council. The executive was responsible for the provision of bus services within its jurisdiction, which it organised largely through its transport company directly. These accounted for a quarter of the local bus miles outside London. Thirdly, in 44 of the larger cities in the shire counties there was a municipal bus company which collectively accounted for about 12 per cent of the local bus miles. Finally, the remaining bus miles were accounted for by small private companies that operated commercial routes in rural areas, or subsidised services in metropolitan areas. The industry prior to 1986 was heavily regulated and under public control.

The Transport Acts had been initiated by a White Paper published in June 1984, which drew attention to the shortcomings of the industry; particularly wide differences in costs and efficiency between operators, and extensive cross-subsidisation. The White Paper proposed privatisation and deregulation, believing the industry to be highly contestable and ripe for efficiency gains through an increased threat of competition.

Gómez-Ibáñez and Meyer (1993) have called the British Transport Act of 1985 'one of the most dramatic and ambitious efforts ever undertaken to privatize local public services'. The act, officially implemented on 26 October 1986, brought in the privatisation and deregulation of the bus industry in England and Wales, except in London. It introduced three main changes.

- First, governmental controls on the entry into the bus industry were greatly relaxed so that companies could operate virtually any service, at fares of their own choosing, by simply giving the local authorities 42 days' notice.
- Secondly, the publicly owned bus companies were reorganised as separate companies. There were 72 National Bus Company subsidiaries sold off in England and Wales between 1986 and 1988, generating more than £325 million for the government. No single buyer could purchase more than three of them, or acquire companies operating in contiguous areas. In the metropolitan areas, the Public Transport Executives had to separate themselves from their Public Transport Companies. In other words, the companies were established as independent, for-profit companies that could no longer rely on public subsidies. They did not have to be sold off to the private sector, although by 1991 two of them had been. The same was also true of the municipal companies in the shire cities.
- Thirdly, the act divided the bus market into two sectors: the *commercial sector*, which comprised services that were profitable for private operators to provide; and the *tender sector*, comprising unprofitable but socially beneficial services. This latter sector would involve private operators bidding for services put up for tender by local authorities in return for financial support. The intention was that competition in the tendering process would minimise public expenditure in the industry.

The regime was extended to Scotland by the Transport (Scotland) Act, 1989. In Northern Ireland, bus services remain publicly owned and operated in a regulatory environment.

12.7.1 The results

Gómez-Ibáñez and Meyer (1993) comment that on deregulation day 80 per cent of the pre-reform bus mileage was registered for commercial service: a proportion that would grow over time.

It is difficult to isolate the precise effects of the Transport Act because there were exogenous factors that would have affected the industry without the reforms. Such factors included the government cutting subsidies simultaneously to deregulation and privatisation, continued economic growth and the trend of the private car becoming relatively cheaper. However, despite these, tentative lessons can be drawn from a cursory analysis of the data.

12.7.1.1 Bus usage and services

In 1985/1986, the industry had been experiencing long-term decline for many years. The Commission for Integrated Transport (2004) states that the number of local bus passenger journeys fell from over 16 billion in 1950 to 5.6 billion in 1985/1986. In a world in which the private car was becoming relatively cheaper all the time, the local bus was increasingly viewed as a poor substitute. Deregulation did not turn this decline around, but it has helped to slow the rate, which has levelled off in recent years. In England as a whole, there was an 18.9 per cent reduction in local passenger journeys between deregulation and 2002/2003, although there has been growth in bus use in London, Brighton, Edinburgh, York, Nottingham, Oxford and Cambridge. London bus usage rose by an astonishing 32.7 per cent between 1984 and 2002/2003.

Relatively few unprofitable services were registered on a commercial basis, although local authorities restored most of them through competitive tendering. However, virtually all areas saw a reduction in services at certain times, and on certain routes, inevitably, leading to the conclusion that not all passengers benefited.

12.7.1.2 Competition

Gómez-Ibáñez and Meyer (1993) assert that, within a year of deregulation, only 3 per cent of all the local bus mileage outside London was served by more than one operator. As such, from the point of view of passengers, the reforms failed to bring more choice. However, almost every British county has seen new entry on at least part of their bus network and there has been fierce competition in certain areas. An example of this is that in the Portsmouth area between Transit Holdings Portsmouth and People's Provincial, involving fare wars and aggressive on-the-road conduct over a period of several years until they reached some degree of mutual accommodation. Most companies have also taken defensive measures to become more efficient, even in areas where there has not been new entry, supporting the argument that the market is contestable.

The period since 1985 has seen a remarkable concentration in the bus industry in Great Britain, as large holdings have made acquisitions across the country. So much so, by 2005 the industry was dominated by five operators, together accounting for approximately 80 per cent of employment. The remaining 20 per cent was largely employed by companies with fewer than ten workers. The concentration is even greater than this when one considers that the industry comprises local bus markets collected into 11 regions and that none of the Big Four has a significant presence in all of the regions. The non-scheduled service sector is less concentrated, with less than 30 per cent of employees working for companies with more than 50 workers.

12.7.1.3 Innovation

Deregulation has stimulated considerable innovation in the British bus industry. In England outside London, vehicle-kilometres increased by 17.5 per cent between 1984 and 2002/2003 as operators sought to develop new routes and higher frequencies of service. There has been a clear positive correlation between competition levels and service mileage increases.

Arguably the greatest innovation, which contributed largely to the increasing vehicle-kilometres, was that of the minibus. In 1985, there were 6500 vehicles with between 9 and 16 seats; whereas by 2003, that number was 11,700. The number of double-decker vehicles in operation has fallen since deregulation. Minibuses have a number of advantages. First, they have lower operating costs as drivers are usually paid less than their colleagues operating larger vehicles, they can be more cheaply maintained and they operate at higher speeds. Secondly, minibuses also enable operating companies to develop routes that are more convenient for passengers, accessing roads that double-decker vehicles cannot; and ensuring that a route can have several branches to serve different neighbourhoods at its outer end, and still maintain reasonable load factors on both the trunk and each branch of the route. Finally, this last point has also led to a greater sense of safety, as passengers are travelling with people from the same neighbourhood, and are also closer to the driver.

Another effect of this innovation is that the average age of the fleet has fallen, from 9.9 years at the end of 1994 to 8.4 years at the end of 2001. This increased competition can certainly be attributed to deregulation, and is certainly a positive result.

12.7.1.4   Fares

The National Economic Research Associates (1997) have commented that, nationally, bus fares have continued to rise significantly in real terms throughout the post-deregulation period. For example, between December 1988 and January 1996, fares increased by 54 per cent compared to an increase in the retail prices index of 36 per cent. However, this increase has varied across the country, with fares increasing most rapidly in metropolitan areas and only gradually in the shire counties. They have also increased more rapidly in areas with low competition: for example, in the Isle of Wight, where Southern Vectis enjoys an especially strong market position; in Hastings, following a merger; and in Bognor, following the exit of a competitor.

An increase in fares was likely to occur for two reasons that are exogenous to the reforms. The first is the reduction in public subsidies that occurred at the same time as the reforms. This would have affected the metropolitan areas the most; areas in which fares have most significantly increased. Secondly, the downward trend in passenger numbers would have placed an upward pressure on fares, as companies seek to maintain profits in the face of reduced load factors. As such, it is necessary to look at the operating costs and profitability of the companies to gain a clearer picture of the effects of reform.

12.7.1.5   Efficiency and profitability

It is important to assess the unit cost of the services rather than the total cost, as the latter of these measures will be greatly affected by changes in subsidy and in the total mileage covered. The Commission for Integrated Transport (June 2004) claims that the average operating cost, per mile, was reduced by 44 per cent in real terms between 1986 and 1996, particularly in the capital. As competition (and the threat of competition) has increased, companies have needed to become more efficient; something which they have done by increasing the use of smaller vehicles, reducing the real wages of its drivers and focusing on the profitable commercial routes, sometimes at the expense of unprofitable but socially beneficial routes.

On the revenue side, between 1984 and 2002/2003, passenger receipts across Great Britain increased by 1.21 per cent, although this can be explained by the substantially increased receipts in London masking a slight fall, 0.7 per cent between 1985/1986 and 2002/2003, in the other regions of Britain. Overall, the industry has become more profitable due to deregulation, which is perhaps to be expected with companies focusing on the profitable commercial routes. Industry profitability increased particularly strongly in the mid-1990s.

Increasing efficiency and profitability is another directly beneficial effect of the reforms, although it can be partly explained by the market concentration that has occurred since deregulation, allowing the big five operators to exert their purchasing power in the capital markets. Out of the Big Four, Stagecoach has enjoyed the greatest increase in profit margins, possibly due to the reduction in its operating costs with the renewal of its vehicle fleet on increasingly advantageous terms. This and the reduction in certain unprofitable routes lead to the conclusion that deregulation may not have been completely positive in terms of efficiency and profitability.

12.7.1.6   Public subsidies and the costs of tendered services

Initially there were relatively few bids for subsidised routes, but local authorities generally responded with policies to stimulate greater competition and to attract smaller bus operators, such as the offering of cost-of-service contracts in East Sussex (which served to eliminate any risk for the operator). This has indeed stimulated greater competition, and so the level of revenue support required to maintain non-commercial services has fallen rapidly in real terms since deregulation, successfully achieving an important objective. Public transport support for local buses in England outside London has fallen by 60.6 per cent between deregulation and 2002/2003. The largest reduction in subsidisation has occurred, perhaps unsurprisingly, in metropolitan areas. However, in the first years of the twenty-first century it has risen but is still lower than in most European Union countries. Much of the increase is accounted for by the provision of services for populations in rural communities.

12.7.1.7   Overall results

Gómez-Ibáñez and Meyer (1993) claim that the deregulation and privatisation of the bus industry helped to offset the negative effects of subsidy cuts and the adverse external trends. This was especially the case in areas of resulting high competition.

12.7.2 A further act: Deregulation weakened?

In 2000, another Transport Act for England and Wales was passed, aimed at improving the quality of bus transport. The act required local authorities to prepare *Local Transport Plans* and bus strategies to address the needs of their areas. They can also introduce two schemes to improve local provisions: *Quality Bus Partnerships* and *Quality Contracts*. Both of these, and especially the latter of the two, can be viewed as being a move towards *regulatory contracting* again, as the authorities seek to adopt a more actively controlling responsibility. Such recent trends towards re-regulation have been common across Europe.

Quality Bus Partnerships involve action from both parties: the authority can upgrade bus stops, shelters and lanes; and in return the operators can agree to meet certain quality standards. These can be voluntary, in which case there is no obligation on either party; or statutory, in which case operators are not permitted to run services in the partnership area unless they meet the required standards, and the authorities are obliged to implement their agreed improvements. There were 380 partnerships in operation in 2004, an increase of 17.6 per cent since 2000. It has been suggested that the improvements to services that these bring have led to substantial increases in passengers, although they have focused on the more profitable areas, meaning that certain bus users have lost further commercial services.

Quality Contracts afford local authorities greater control over timetabling and fares. They revoke the deregulation and give local authorities powers to contract local bus services, in which they specify bus routes, frequencies and fares. Operators bid for exclusive rights to operate within the area. As the government considers such radical action to be a last resort, local authorities have to submit a case of evidence in application for the permission to implement a Quality Contract, and one may only come into force after 21 months have elapsed from the date of initially establishing the scheme. However, it is not a requirement that a Quality Bus Partnership should have failed before an application is made.

Local authorities are not compelled to use any of these powers.

12.7.3 The lessons from London

London has not been deregulated as the other areas of England, Wales and Scotland have been, but the operators there were subject to new competitive pressures by a requirement that they compete for contracts to operate the services. Routes, timetables and fares continue to be planned centrally, but yet it has experienced the greatest increase in bus usage. Commentators have suggested that perhaps it would be beneficial to the whole industry if regulation was re-introduced, along the lines of London, across Great Britain. However, this ignores the uniqueness of the London experience, which can be outlined through comparisons with Belfast, where services are also still regulated, with the difference that operations are provided directly in Belfast instead of being secured under contract as in London.

Belfast has not enjoyed the growth of bus usage as London has done. In fact, bus passenger journeys have continued to decline, and frequency and reliability being increasingly affected by congestion. The causes of London's beneficial experience cannot solely be the regulatory framework there. The explanation lies in the unique characteristics of the British capital. First, it has coupled bus service improvements with private vehicle demand restraints, such as a reduction in the availability and an increase in the cost of parking spaces, and the introduction of the congestion charge. Secondly, the population of the city has expanded, along with a higher level of economic growth and high levels of tourism. Thirdly, there is a limited ability to expand rail travel. In contrast to these, Belfast has failed to invest in bus priority and car restraint measures and has substantially increased parking spaces since 1980, which are relatively cheap compared to other metropolitan areas. Finally, there has been a rapid increase in the level of public subsidy granted to buses in London.

The overriding lesson must be that a scheme to encourage bus usage must include measures to restrain the use of alternatives, notably the car. This is perhaps the explanation as to why Cambridge has also enjoyed increased bus usage: parking spaces have been limited and made considerably more expensive, and effective park and ride schemes have been developed and expanded. Regulation on its own is not sufficient.

12.8 | Competitive tendering in bus markets across Europe

Hensher and Wallis (2005) have studied a range of privatisations and deregulations in bus industries across the world. The Scandinavian countries have invested particularly heavily in policies to reform their bus industries. In Sweden and Denmark, competitive tendering for local bus services was introduced in 1989 and 1990 respectively. In both countries, the bus industry was predominately publicly owned but is now predominately in the private sector. Finland saw the introduction of competitive tendering later, in 1995, and now has an industry that is a mix of public and private ownership. Norway has followed a similar path to Britain, with competitive tendering being introduced but then replaced by negotiated performance-based contracts akin to the quality contracts in Britain. From January 2001 onwards, Norwegian contracts are more long-term and give operators responsibility for a specific service on which they must focus on user demand and need.

There has been a tendency across Europe to weaken the impact of initial competitive tendering through authorities stipulating stricter conditions on the services being tendered for. Hensher and Wallis (2005) explain how experience shows that there are usually significant cost savings in the first rounds of competitive tendering, but that subsequent rounds see costs rise once again. They claim that a contributing factor in this is the higher service characteristics demanded of operators by authorities in subsequent rounds which have often been introduced.

12.9 | A summary of the experiences in Germany and Ireland

12.9.1 German experiences

Germany has had a strong history of public sector involvement in the economy. During the 1970s, the size of the public sector in industry was expanded sharply, in response to the threat of increasing foreign competition; and until relatively recently the government in Germany has been reluctant to implement widespread deregulation and privatisation. The German Constitution protected the state monopoly of the railways and inland waterways until 1996. However, privatisation and deregulation have been implemented gradually.

A wave of privatisation and deregulation was implemented in 1994. It was in this year that Lufthansa (the national airline) was completely privatised; shipping was deregulated; and the railways were reformed. The railways were transferred from being a public enterprise to being one under private law in the form of a joint-stock business. The state is still the owner of the railways, but the separate branches for infrastructure, freight transport and passenger transport (the latter being separated further into local and distance services) have been established as entities in their own right. A competitive tendering procedure was introduced during the railway reforms to promote economic efficiency within these separate branches. Road haulage was also deregulated in 1994, but it was only after 1998 that entry restrictions and cabotage prohibitions were completely removed.

The airline market was deregulated in 1998 in accordance with legislation at the European Union level. However, across the European Union, this deregulation has not been coupled with the removal of discriminatory access rules to airports. Grandfather rights, for example, still apply. This is true of the reforms to the German airline market as well.

Privatisation and deregulation in the German transport sector have had a positive impact on the performance of these markets. In the road-haulage market, for example, prices have fallen (in fact, during the first year after deregulation, prices in the long-distance market fell on average by 2.4 per cent below the lowest prices when regulated tariff schedules were in use); the quality of services have risen; and there has been an increase in economic efficiency. There has been the entry of new producers into transport markets, for example Aero Loyd and Germanwings in the airline industry; and product differentiation and development has increased.

12.9.2 Irish experiences

The Irish transport sector was heavily under the control of the public sector. The Air Navigation Order of 1935, for example, gave the Minister for Industry commercial control over air services; control which was actively used to protect the national airline, Aer Lingus, from competition both at home and from abroad. However, during the 1970s and early 1980s, there was a growing disillusionment with the effectiveness of such state ownership. The National Prices Commission (1972) found that bus and railway fares in the public sector were substantially greater than those of small independent operators. In 1984, Aer Lingus was shown to enjoy labour productivity of only 53 per cent of that of the average across 17 major European airlines (Barrett, 1987). The political conditions were becoming ripe for privatisation and deregulation.

The Irish also took great interest in British privatisations, particularly the transformation of British Airways from being a loss-making airline with 54,000 employees in the early 1980s to one making almost £200 million profits with 36,000 employees in the mid-1980s. Being suitably impressed, the Irish airline market was deregulated in 1986, although Aer Lingus remained in state control (in fact, in 1992 it became insolvent but the government rescued it with an injection of capital worth £175 million).

The deregulation led to an immediate reduction in fares of 54 per cent on the Dublin–London route and an increase of 92 per cent in passenger numbers in August 1987 compared to the levels two years earlier. The number of tourists increased from a pre-deregulation level of 2 million per annum to three times that level within a few years (Barrett, 2006). Aer Lingus was restructured in 2001, reducing the workforce by a third, to 4000 workers; and it was announced in May 2005 that it would be privatised.

In 1992, the Britain–Ireland shipping line (which had been nationalised in 1965 in order to increase its participation in Britain–Ireland shipping routes) was completely privatised. Initially, the losses that Britain and Ireland had been suffering prior to privatisation outweighed the profits of the purchasing company; but within three years the fleet had been increased and profits were in excess of £11 million.

A final deregulation to mention is that of the road-haulage market, which was introduced in 1988. Under regulation, 83 per cent of road freight in Ireland was transported by businesses in their own fleets. There was relatively little purchasing of specific road-haulage services. However, following the deregulation of the market, the share of the freight transported by specific haulage providers had increased to 63 per cent by 1993 (Barrett, 1998).

Project Appraisal: 13
Cost–Benefit
Analysis

The basic economic problem is that society has unlimited wants and needs, but only a finite amount of resources available to meet them. Consequently, it is vitally important that resources are used in the most productive and beneficial way. There are two general forms of project appraisal. The first is that of *financial appraisal*, which simply evaluates a project according to the net financial gain that it brings. In the comparison of two projects, the one which brings the greatest profit to the investor will be the one selected. The second is that of *economic appraisal*, or *cost–benefit analysis*, which includes all costs and benefits to society: not just financial. In this case, the project which is the most beneficial to society as a whole will be the one selected.

Financial appraisal has been used ever since entrepreneurs began contemplating where to make their investments. Cost–benefit analysis is a more recent development in project appraisal, having been pioneered in the US in the 1930s when the Federal government had to decide whether to invest in large, publicly funded irrigation, hydroelectricity and water supply projects. Cost–benefit analysis is also a tool that is continually being improved. It is by no means perfect, as shall be explored in this chapter, but it is certainly being developed.

13.1 | The need for, and types of, cost–benefit analysis

Private-sector decision-makers are likely to base their decisions upon the results from financial appraisals because they are pursuing the objective of profit maximisation or the maximisation of shareholder return. However, for a public-sector authority this is not always appropriate because simple financial costs and benefits fail to include external costs and benefits, as explored in Chapter 9, and because they are distorted in the market and so do not reflect the true costs and benefits for a project. Public authorities also usually have other objectives than profit maximisation; for instance, to ensure that all of the local population has access to appropriate transport services, or the minimisation of environmental damage. The closure of a rural railway line and the construction of a new runway at the local airport may be profitable, but it may certainly contradict these additional objectives. There is a need for authorities to use cost–benefit analysis. This need is strengthened by the political pressure on authorities to be seen spending the tax revenue taken from their population in the way that is most beneficial to the whole of society.

Importantly, some facilities are provided with no, or subsidised, charges to users. This can be because the costs of collecting charges are prohibitive or because marginal costs of supply are low. In these circumstances there will be little, or no, revenue and this facility will not be financially viable. Therefore, cost–benefit analysis is necessary to judge whether the facility offers good value for public money.

There are three types of cost–benefit analysis. The first, and most common, is *ex ante cost–benefit analysis*. This is analysis conducted during the decision-making process regarding the value of projects and so is based on predicted values. The second is *ex post cost–benefit analysis*, which is conducted after a decision has been made and a project completed and so involves actual values. The purpose of this second analysis is an evaluative one. It is intended to assess whether the investment is worthwhile, thereby informing future similar decisions. The final type is *in media res cost–benefit analysis*, which is conducted during the lifetime of a project. This last type is useful in decisions regarding whether a project should be extended or whether investment should be redirected towards other projects. It would rarely be used to terminate a capital investment before completion because of the investment that has already been sunk into it and so which would be lost, but it is used to terminate the provision of services where they are not socially efficient. *Ex post* analysis is likely to be more accurate than *in media res* analysis, which in turn is likely to be more accurate than *ex ante* analysis because of the movement from using estimates to using actual values.

It can be useful for governments and analysts to compare the *ex ante* analysis of a project with the *ex post* analysis of the same project as this highlights the accuracy of the *ex ante* procedures. This, then, can help to improve the accuracy of cost–benefit analysis of future projects.

13.2 | The methodology of cost–benefit analysis

Cost–benefit analysis can be viewed as comprising seven steps, each of which is explored below through application to the construction of a transport link between two towns either side of a mountain.

13.2.1 Step 1: Specify the options

The first step is to identify all of the potential alternatives. For the construction of a mountain-range transport link this would appear to be straightforward. One potential option could be to construct a road-tunnel; another could be to construct a railway-tunnel; and a third could be to construct a road that would follow the perimeter of the mountain. However, it becomes more complicated than this when one considers that there may be numerous forms a tunnel could take and there are numerous facets to a road or a railway that could be altered, for example the materials used to build it or the size of it. Consequently, an analyst needs to be careful to select a manageable number of the most feasible options.

In cases of policy implementation there may not be an obvious alternative, for example the introduction of stricter environmental standards on automobiles. In these cases it is important to analyse the option against a counter-factual *business-as-usual* policy in which the status quo is maintained.

13.2.2 Step 2: Identify the impacts

It is then necessary to list all of the potential costs and benefits surrounding the project. For our example the costs for each option would include the initial capital cost of construction, the ongoing maintenance costs, the loss of tourists visiting the mountain and the damage to the mountain environment. The benefits are likely to include journey-time savings, increased trade between the two towns and regions, a reduction in accidents on the mountain passes and reduced congestion.

Again, however, it is not as simple as this would imply. First, a decision has to be made regarding where the line is drawn. Should only local factors be considered or should the analysis be extended to include national and global considerations? For example, new road infrastructure is likely to increase the volume of vehicles on the road network, thereby leading to increased emissions and environmental damage overall; or, the level of tourism throughout the country may increase as tourists can travel with greater ease. Should these be considered as well? Secondly, there may be conflicts regarding how an impact is viewed. The local towns, for instance, may view a reduction in tourists to visit the mountain as a cost, whereas landowners on the mountain may welcome such an impact. Which view should be adopted by the analyst?

13.2.3 Step 3: Predict the total impacts over the lifetime of the project

Usually, projects do not only create immediate costs and benefits. Infrastructure projects especially, for example our transport link, have lifespans stretching for many years and costs and benefits will be generated throughout them. A tunnel through the mountain will be used by vehicles, be it trains or automobiles, in ten years' time and so will be generating a benefit to the users, but it will also need to be maintained in that period, thereby creating a cost. All of the impacts identified in step 2 need to be totalled for the entire lifespan of the project in order for a true evaluation to be made.

This involves effective forecasting, which is also problematic. If trends remain the same across time, forecasting would be simple as the trends could simply be extrapolated. The problem is that they do not. The usage of the transport link, for example, is likely to change over time as the population of the connected towns, or the level of economic activity within them, change. There are numerous other factors affecting the use of the link which need to be considered as well, some of which are unknown to the analyst. This makes accurate forecasting problematic and is worsened by the unintended effects of the project itself. There may be *offsetting* or *compensating effects* which negate a potentially beneficial effect of the project. There may also be *spillover effects*, which can be both positive and negative. For example, because the transport link makes it easier to travel between the towns, consumers may be drawn away from one and to the other, thereby causing an offsetting effect that negates the predicted increase in tourism to the first town and also a spillover effect as the total number of journeys made along the link increases unexpectedly.

The relationship between variables is extremely complicated and so accurate forecasting of the impacts over time is fraught with difficulties.

13.2.4   Step 4: Monetise the impacts

Steps 2 and 3 generate a list of all of the impacts but they are all in different units. Journey-time savings will be in hours, whereas the effects of greater tourism could be in currency terms or increased employment. This means that it is impossible to compare the impacts and so all of them need to be measured in a single unit: money.

This can be difficult, and controversial, to do. In cost–benefit analysis it is usually done through a *willingness-to-pay approach*, in which the value is simply the amount that people are willing to pay to avoid a cost or to generate a benefit. For impacts in which there are markets that function effectively this can be straightforward as the value can be read from the demand curve. For impacts in which there are no markets, or for which the markets are imperfect, it is more difficult. There is no obvious market for life, for instance, so how does one value a life? In these situations it is necessary to impute shadow values that should reflect the true economic value of the impacts.

In many cases it is possible to find an implicit or proxy market. For instance, a project will not save the life of any specific individual – it will reduce the risk of death for all those who would have used the alternative facilities. People do pay money to reduce the risk of death in several ways, and so these can be used to estimate the total willingness to pay for the reduction in risk offered by this proposal.

13.2.5 Step 5: Discount the impacts to obtain present values

For projects with costs and benefits that stretch over many years, it is important that the values be discounted so that they reflect the true value of the costs and benefits today. This need arises because people would rather consume now than in the future. Or, in other words, a sum of money today is worth more than the promise today of the same sum of money in ten years' time. Inflation is a part of this, but the major factor is that of peoples' preferences.

Such discounting is done by dividing the value of a cost or benefit in year t in the future by $(1+s)^t$, where s is the social discount rate. If a project has a lifespan of n years and C_t and B_t are the costs and benefits in year t respectively, then the present value of the costs and benefits are as follows:

$$PV(C) = \sum_{t=0}^{n} \frac{C_t}{(1+s)^t}$$

$$PV(B) = \sum_{t=0}^{n} \frac{B_t}{(1+s)^t}$$

These formulae simply add up the value today of all the future costs and benefits, each discounted by its appropriate factor. The difficulty here is in establishing the value for the social discount rate.

13.2.6 Step 6: Conduct sensitivity analysis

Throughout all of the steps so far there have been elements of uncertainty which can hugely affect the results of the analysis. So it is important that the analyst weighs each element in the analysis according to how certain it is: those elements that are certain should be given a stronger weighting than those which are less so. This will help the final decision to more accurately reflect the true values of the impacts.

13.2.7 Step 7: Compare the net present value of each alternative

The net present value is simply the present value of the benefits minus the present value of the costs. For a project that is being assessed in isolation, the authority should proceed if the net present value is positive. As all of the social costs and benefits have been included in the analysis, this rule would ensure that social welfare would be improved as a result of implementing the project. If there is more than one option being assessed, such as the different transport links between the two towns, then the project with the greatest net present value should be selected as that would lead to the greatest overall welfare improvement given the costs incurred.

This last decision rule does not necessarily mean that the resources will have been used in the most efficient manner, though. The analyst can only compare the options that were specified in step 1, and so this rule would ensure that the resources are used in the most efficient way given the options. There may be another option, however, that was not specified at the start of the procedure which would have generated an even greater net present value and so would have been a more efficient use of the available resources.

13.3 | Valuing non-marketed products

A range of methods have been developed to establish monetary values for products that are not marketed, and so do not have prices already established for them. The most accepted of these valuation methods are briefly outlined here, using the taxonomy of Markandya *et al.* (2002). It should be borne in mind that each of these techniques suit different situations and products and that there are advantages and limitations to each. However, it is not the purpose of this section to elaborate on these complications (for a more thorough analysis of these valuation methods and their application to environmental issues, see Markandya *et al.*, 2002).

13.3.1 Revealed preference direct proxy methods

Revealed preference direct proxy methods establish monetary values for non-marketed products by identifying the value of an equivalent marketed product (a proxy). If the products are truly equivalent, the market price of one will reveal the value that consumers place on the other. Amongst such methods of establishing a monetary value for a non-marketed product are the following.

- The *productivity change method*. This method is applicable in situations in which the non-marketed product is an input in the production of a product with an established market value. *Ceteris paribus*, the value of a change in the non-marketed product can simply be estimated as the resulting change in the market value of the marketed output. For example, the value of a clean river can be estimated if it is possible to view it as an input in the production of marketed products (fish or leisure activities). If altering the river changes the value of those products, it is possible to infer the value of the river itself.
- The *opportunity cost method*. In this method, the value of a non-marketed product is estimated by obtaining the value of it in its second-best employment (assuming that the second-best employment of it has a market value). For example, the value of an area of historic forest could be estimated by the value it would generate if it was used as the location for a new airport terminal (assuming the airport terminal is the second-best use of that land). This method implies that the value of a non-marketed product is at least equal to its opportunity cost.
- The *defensive expenditure method*. This method is applicable to the valuation of non-marketed negative effects. Such values are estimated by analysing how much people are willing to spend to avoid them. For example, to value the cost of increased noise along a truck road, one could look at the amount the local populous is willing to spend on double-glazing. Estimates derived from

this method should be viewed as being minimum values as consumers may be willing to spend more, but are not required to do so.

- The *cost of illness* and *human capital methods*. These methods estimate the value of non-marketed products through its impact on health. The human capital approach measures the value of a product simply by assessing the value of the lost output as a result of it. The cost of illness approach is more comprehensive, including other expenses associated with the product, lost wages, and values for any suffering caused and the possibility of increasing the risk of mortality. For example, in establishing a monetary value for a certain reduction in road accidents, the human capital approach would simply assess the resulting increase in GDP; whereas the cost of illness approach would include estimates of the reduction in the costs of the emergency services and the reduction in suffering.

- The *shadow project method*. An estimate of the value of a non-marketed product is established in this method by obtaining the cost of providing an alternative to the product elsewhere; in other words, the cost of replacing the product. For example, the building of a new harbour may destroy a coastal habitat. The value of this habitat is required if a full cost–benefit analysis of the project is to be conducted, and it could be estimated by calculating the cost of recreating the habitat on another part of the coast.

- The *substitute cost method*. This takes a similar approach to the shadow project method, except that it does not look at replacing the product elsewhere, but at substitutes that are already in existence. There are three necessary conditions for this method: first, the substitute chosen should provide an identical function to the product being valued; secondly, the substitute should be the least-cost alternative; and thirdly, there should be a demand for the substitute. For example, the blocking of a certain tributary into a reservoir, in order to facilitate the construction of a rail line, could reduce the concentration of a needed mineral in the water supply (the tributary provided that mineral as it passed over specific geological deposits en route to the reservoir). The value of the tributary could be estimated as the cost of adding the minerals artificially.

13.3.2 Revealed preference indirect proxy methods

This second group of methods does not look directly at the market prices of products considered to be proxies for the non-marketed product in question. Instead, they identify the relationship between changes in a non-marketed product and the price of other, marketed, products. Revealed preference indirect proxy methods are applicable to situations in which a non-marketed product affects the preferences of consumers about marketed products. By establishing a value for the changes to consumer preferences caused by a change in a non-marketed product, one is able to indirectly establish a value for that same non-marketed product. There are three such methods which are accepted.

- The *travel cost method*. In this method, a non-marketed product is valued by calculating the expenditures incurred by consumers in getting to it. Observing the number of trips made by consumers to get to the product at different levels of travelling costs (including any entrance fees) allows the demand curve for the product to be constructed. The constructed consumer surplus, the area beneath the demand curve, is the willingness of consumers to pay for the product, and so is its monetary value. It is generally accepted that this method is one of the most effective approaches in the valuation of recreation services, and so could be applied to the valuation of areas of natural beauty.

- The *hedonic pricing method*. In this method, a non-marketed product is valued by calculating the differential premium on property as a result of its proximity to the product. As there are numerous variables that contribute to the determination of property prices, this method is not as straightforward as it first may appear. In fact, it is necessary to hold all of these other variables constant, so that the effect of the non-marketed product can be isolated. It is also necessary for the housing market to be competitive. If these conditions are satisfied, hedonic pricing views, for example, the difference in price *between* a three-bedroom house close to a coastal bay of outstanding natural beauty *and* an identical house in a similar area but without such natural beauty nearby as the value of the bay.

- The *wage differential method*. This is similar to the hedonic pricing method, but focuses on wages instead of house prices. It can be assumed that wage rates reflect a whole range of factors, including safety. If all of these factors are held constant, employees should demand higher wages for jobs involving greater risk. Therefore, the value of safety (also known as the *hedonic wage*) is reflected by the difference in wage rates between two jobs that are identical in every way, apart from the degree of risk involved. In order for this method to work, a number of conditions need to be satisfied: first, the labour market functions freely (it is competitive and workers are fully mobile); secondly, it is possible to isolate and measure degrees of risk; thirdly, there is perfect comparability between different risks; and fourthly, there is perfect information about the risks involved. If these conditions are satisfied, this method is useful in the estimation of how much people value safety and is important in the appraisal of many transport projects.

13.3.3 Stated preference contingent valuation methods

Stated preference contingent valuation methods involve the employment of questionnaires or experimental techniques in establishing how much consumers value a non-marketed product. The questionnaires or experiments simulate a hypothetical (contingent) market for a non-marketed product, in which respondents are required to reveal their willingness to pay for changes in the products provision.

These methods have numerous limitations, many of which are obvious, but they are continually being refined and developed, leading to improvements in their findings.

13.4 Decision-making in practice

Cost–benefit analysis is concerned with helping decision-makers to consider all of the impacts of a project and the true extent of these different impacts so that they allocate resources in a socially efficient way. However, in practice, decision-makers are not solely economic analysts. Instead, they are bureaucrats and politicians that have other interests as well. For example, in Section 15.6 the possibility that bureaucrats actually seek to maximise their allocated budgets through cost maximisation is explored. In this situation, the results from cost–benefit analysis may not lead directly to a decision as there may be bureaucratic pressure in favour of a different option. Similarly, politicians have to consider the pressures from their electorate. As some members of the electorate hold greater sway than others, the decision-making process can be driven by politicians seeking to maximise the benefit (or minimise the cost) to a certain part of the population rather than to the whole of society.

13.5 The limitations of cost–benefit analysis

There are two general criticisms of cost–benefit analysis. The first is a criticism of the utilitarian and Hicks–Kaldor assertion that if total social welfare is increased that is desirable even if it involves a reduction in the welfare of an individual or a group of individuals. This assertion lies underneath the methodology of cost–benefit analysis.

The second is a criticism regarding the practicalities of the analysis, which can take numerous forms, including the following.

- The ease with which important costs and benefits can be omitted from the analysis, thereby biasing the results. This is worsened as the lifetime of a project is extended, as future events that may influence the costs and benefits of a project are unknown and often unpredictable.
- The difficulty of placing a monetary value on the costs and benefits that have been identified. This often involves value judgements, which may be inadvertently biased.
- The difficulty of conducting effective sensitivity analysis. The actual degrees of risk and uncertainty involved in the necessary estimations are in themselves uncertain, making sensitivity analysis imprecise as well.

Cost–benefit analysis is continually being refined and improved. More sophisticated techniques, and computer simulations, are constantly being developed which are contributing to more accurate estimations. However, it is still far from being precise and so further developments are necessary.

13.6 | The COBA model

Since 1998, the UK Department for Transport has been using a computer-based cost–benefit analysis model as part of a wider appraisal process to assess the worthiness of new trunk road developments. The cost–benefit analysis part of the appraisal is known as the COBA model. It serves as an effective example of cost–benefit analysis in practice as it clearly follows the seven steps as outlined above.

The COBA model is a particularly specific analysis. It focuses on each link of a proposed trunk road development separately, but it only identifies and assesses two groups of costs and three groups of benefits. The costs included are the *capital costs* and the *maintenance costs*. The benefits included are those of *journey-time savings*, *vehicle operating cost savings* and *reduced accidents*. The methodology behind the value estimation for each of these is outlined in turn.

13.6.1 Capital costs

Capital costs are the initial construction costs of the development, including land purchase and design expenses. Estimates are also included for the costs of delays imposed on traffic flows as a result of the construction work being conducted.

13.6.2 Maintenance costs

The maintenance costs are the annual costs of maintaining the new infrastructure so that it can be fully used. The COBA model divides these into two categories: *non-traffic-related costs* and *traffic-related costs*. Examples of the possible elements of each of these costs are displayed in Table 13.1.

As well as these, the costs of any delays imposed on the traffic as a result of maintenance work are also incorporated into the analysis. Also, a new road development is likely to shift traffic away from existing roads and onto the new one. As such, the costs to maintain the existing roads are likely to decrease, which is a factor that is considered by the COBA model.

Table 13.1 Examples of the possible elements of maintenance costs considered in the COBA model

Non-traffic related costs	*Traffic-related costs*
Drainage; lighting; safety barriers; bridges and subways; remedial earthworks; verge maintenance; sweeping; and road markings	Reconstruction; overlay; resurfacing; and surface dressing and patching

Source: The COBA Manual, the Department for Transport, May 2004.

13.6.3   Journey-time savings

A new development should reduce the time that drivers spend on the road, by reducing congestion. As such, it should generate more time for production or leisure, the benefits of which are quantified, valued and included in the analysis.

The COBA model categorises time savings in three ways. First, there is *working time*. In an efficiently functioning free labour market the price of labour – in other words, the wage rate – will be equal to the value of the output that a worker produces during an hour. As such, increases in working time can be valued simply by considering the average hourly wage rate. COBA then also adds employment charges onto this value. Secondly, there is *commuting time*, or the time spent travelling to and from a place of work; and thirdly, there is *other time* (non-work, or leisure time). It is more difficult to estimate the value of this as there are no directly relevant market prices. In order to do so, therefore, a willingness-to-pay approach is adopted, in which estimates are drawn from empirical studies of the willingness-to-pay of commuters to increase the speed for particular types of trip.

The COBA model also categorises vehicles in three ways: cars and light goods vehicles (LGVs); other goods vehicles (OGVs); and PSVs. This allows it to estimate the value of time savings according to the type of vehicle and the purpose for which it is being driven.

Finally, the COBA model estimates the occupancy of the vehicles so that the value of the time savings can be estimated per person rather than simply per vehicle.

The estimates that have been developed for use in the COBA model are displayed in Table 13.2.

The COBA model estimates the hourly flow of traffic for each link of a proposed trunk road development, categorised according to Table 13.2. It then converts this to the hourly flow of people by multiplying each of the different categories of vehicle by the relevant occupancy rates, also shown in Table 13.2. These occupancies vary throughout the week, which is a factor that is taken into consideration during the analysis. It then calculates the value of the time savings by multiplying these flows of people by the actual time savings generated and then by the value of their time (Table 13.2). Finally, the COBA model converts these resource savings to actual market prices by multiplying them by $(1 + t)$ where t is the average rate of indirect taxation.

13.6.4   Vehicle-operating cost savings

The vehicle-operating cost savings follow from those above. If traffic congestion is reduced and vehicles are able to flow more smoothly, there will be less wear and tear to vehicles from stop–start driving. There will also be an improvement in fuel efficiency. The monetary savings from these are included in the analysis, and

Table 13.2 The value of time estimates used in the COBA model

Type of vehicle	Purpose	Weekly average occupancy	Value (pence/hour)	
			Per occupant	Per vehicle
Car	Working	1.00 driver	2186	
		0.20 passengers	1566	2499
	Commuting	1.00 driver	417	
		0.14 passengers	417	475
	Other	1.00 driver	368	
		0.85 passengers	368	681
LGVs	Working	1.00 driver	842	
		0.20 passengers	842	1010
	Commuting	1.00 driver	417	
		0.59 passengers	417	663
	Other	1.00 driver	368	
		0.59 passengers	368	585
OGVs	Working	1.00 driver	842	842
PSVs	Working	1.00 driver	842	
		12.2 passengers:		
		– working (2.9%)	1672	
		– commuting (20.5%)	417	
		– other (76.6%)	368	5916
Average vehicle				930

Source: The COBA Manual, the Department for Transport, May 2004.

are then converted to market prices in a similar way to those for time savings by consideration of the indirect tax rates.

13.6.5 Reduced accidents

New infrastructure should be safer and so should reduce the likelihood of accidents. This is particularly the case for roads that bypass highly populated areas and so divert traffic away from pedestrians. The value of lives saved and the non-fatal accidents avoided are included in the analysis.

The casualty costs used in the COBA model are displayed in Table 13.3.

As well as the casualty costs, the COBA model also incorporates estimates of the costs in terms of the damage to property, insurance administration and police time. It also makes an allowance for damage-only accidents. The estimates used

Table 13.3 The casualty costs used in the COBA model

Cost per casualty (£)	
Degree of accident	Cost (£)
Fatal	1,249,890
Serious	140,430
Slight	10,830

Source: The COBA Manual, the Department for Transport, May 2004.

Table 13.4 Accident costs used in the COBA model

	Cost per accident (£)						
		Damage to property			Police time		
	Insurance	Urban	Rural	Motorway	Urban	Rural	Motorway
Fatal	230	5,977	10,136	12,894	1,463	1,387	2,030
Serious	143	3,203	4,620	11,002	122	341	320
Slight	87	1,890	3,063	8,566	44	44	44
Damage-only	42	1,352	2,019	1,941	3	3	3

Source: The COBA Manual, the Department for Transport, May 2004.

are displayed in Table 13.4, in which urban roads are those with speed limits of 40 miles per hour or below and rural roads are those with speed limits above 40 miles per hour.

The COBA model combines these estimates with those of the likely reduction in accidents of the road development and those of the proportions of the different degrees of accident they are likely to be. From these, estimates of the total value of the accident savings can be calculated.

13.6.6 Criticisms of the COBA model

In addition to the general criticisms of cost–benefit analysis, the COBA model has come under criticism because of its narrow focus on user-costs and benefits. There is no attempt made to estimate and incorporate the wider external costs and benefits of any trunk road developments, such as the environmental damage or the improved social integration a new road may bring.

It was in response to these criticisms that the British government set out a new approach to road appraisal in 1998. Up until 1998 the COBA model had been the sole method of trunk road project appraisal in the UK. Under the new approach, however, it became simply a part of it. The impacts on the environment, on social accessibility and on the effects on transport integration were also brought into the analysis. This was certainly a step in the right direction, but these additional considerations are simply judged against a seven-point scale and so it cannot be said that they are rigorously assessed. As with all cost–benefit analysis models, further development and refinement is necessary.

Transport 14
Investment

During the initial period of transport expansion in Europe, private investors led the way in the construction, seizing the opportunities for financial improvement that were emerging as a result of the industrial revolution. The period that has become known as the Railway Mania in Britain was a time of unprecedented railway development as entrepreneurs sought to establish themselves in the market. It was as a consequence of this that the British capital witnessed the construction of numerous stations spread across the city. However, gradually, local authorities saw the need for a more centralised approach in the confusion and so transport investment was brought inside the fence of public finances, which is where it has largely remained until relatively recently.

In Europe today there are three sources of transport investment, which are displayed in Figure 14.1. Over recent decades there has been a general movement away from source one, through source two, to an encouragement of source three from both of the other sources.

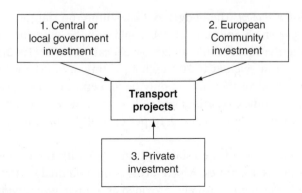

Figure 14.1 Sources of European transport investment

14.1 | Central or local government investment

Farrell (1999) explains that although it is difficult to generalise about how European countries organise their planning and investment decisions, there are four basic models: the Scandinavian, German, Mediterranean and Anglo-Saxon. The first of these entails strong local authorities empowered to make their own decisions, financed by their own tax base. The second, which also includes Austria, Switzerland and Belgium, is a federal structure in which decisions that affect the whole country are made centrally, but domestic policy being determined by the regions with co-operation in both decision-making and investment where appropriate. The third is one of centralised decision-making based on competition between different interest groups, with weak local authorities. France and Spain have moved away from this model towards the German one. The final model, adopted in the UK, Ireland and the Netherlands, is one of executive government by the party in power, with financially weak local authorities dependent on central funding and the use of boards and trusts.

As such, it can be seen that transport planning and investment becomes more centralised as one moves through the models in the order in which they are outlined. However, there are general changes to these structures occurring, with local authorities being strengthened through amalgamation with one another, given more responsibility to make transport decisions, and given greater discretion in the spending of their funds from central government.

14.2 | European Community investment

The Treaty of Rome (1958) gave the European Commission responsibility for developing common policies in respect of land transport. However, it was slow to respond; faced with resistance from national governments and transport operators and related manufacturers. It was not until 1985 that a serious attempt at developing a common policy framework was begun. The Commission is now a vitally important source of transport investment, which it provides through six channels.

- *The Commission Budget.* The budgetary expenditure on transport infrastructure has been very small and, until 1994, could only be used for land transport. In the first ten years of such a budgetary allocation (1982–1992), expenditure amounted to just over ECU 700 million: a tiny sum. These funds are also restricted in terms of their usage, only being permitted for feasibility studies, interest rate subsidies, contributions to loan guarantee fees and direct investment grants which cannot exceed 10 per cent of the total required to launch the project.

- *Structural Funds.* These were established in 1975 with the express purpose of reducing regional disparities, which includes the potential for transport investment. Such investment is usually provided as a direct grant, with the amount going to each country being established in advance for a five-year period, independent of the quantity of projects. In the second half of the 1990s, almost two-thirds of such expenditure on transport was located in Greece and Spain, although the accession countries of the early 2000s are likely to cause this to be redirected. There is a strong bias towards road investment as that generates the greatest economic benefits for the local area and because rail infrastructure in the recipient countries is poorly developed.

- *The Cohesion Fund.* This fund was created in 1993 and is solely targeted at transport and environmental projects in poorer member countries. This investment is allocated annually on a project-by-project basis and cannot be used to subsidise transport services. In the second half of the 1990s the majority of this investment was allocated to Spain. Projects are usually co-financed with national governments, but funding can be allocated to public–private partnerships, such as in the case of the Tagus Bridge in Portugal.

- *European Investment Fund.* This was established in 1992 to stimulate investment in the Trans-European Networks and small and medium enterprises (SMEs) through commercial operations. Its primary role is to bear investment risks in projects that private investors are unwilling or unable to bear and, as such, to encourage private involvement. The Fund is relatively small with capital provided by the European Investment Bank, the European Union and financial institutions. The Fund can only guarantee 50 per cent of project costs, and cannot commit more than 10 per cent of its capital to a single project.

- *European Investment Bank.* This was established at the conception of the European Union in 1958 to fund, on a non-commercial basis, projects towards European objectives. It can provide longer-term loans than most commercial financial institutions and is prepared to lend up to half of the costs of a single project. The loans that it provides are equally separated between public and private borrowers, with transport, energy and telecommunication projects accounting for approximately 30 per cent of all lending. Regional development is a primary objective and a considerable proportion of lending goes towards the poorer regions. There are strict criteria that need to be satisfied for finances to be released by the Bank, but it is a very important source of transport investment, accounting for more annual transport investment than the Structural and Cohesion Funds together.

- *The Trans-European Networks.* This has been a controversial policy of the European Commission but is one that is still being evolved. In the early 1990s the Commission drew up plans to integrate European transport networks that covered 58,000 kilometres of road, 70,000 kilometres of rail, 2000 kilometres of inland waterways and 250 airports. These plans are continually changing, as are the individual projects within them, as member states change their priorities. The funding responsibility for the projects ultimately lie with national governments, although the European Commission has brought together funding from the other sources outlined above. An important role is also envisaged for the private sector.

The plans have been criticised for paying little attention to ways in which more capacity and improved services can be drawn from the existing infrastructure. The European Commission has recently been concentrating on more cost-effective ways of developing the networks, namely through better cross-border links, strengthening of weak links within countries, promotion of common standards for equipment and support of projects that benefit third-party member countries.

14.3 | Private investment and public–private partnerships

Private investment and public–private partnerships can be viewed as an extension of privatisation, and as such have been a growing focus of policy-makers over recent decades (although private investment is still relatively small in many European countries). Private investment shifts part of the investment risk from the public sector onto private individuals and groups. It increases the drive for the project to succeed as private investors have greater liability than public bodies which can be rescued by government. It is in this way that the encouragement of private investment is intended to give projects an increased potential for success.

Farrell (1999) states that the role of the private sector in transport investment varies hugely across the continent, depending on historical experience, the nature of the transport sector and government policy.

France has been successful in arranging public–private partnerships, helped by the considerable experience of private involvement in industry in the past and the close links between the authorities and private entrepreneurs. Private investment has played a role in motorway construction since the 1970s. However, the French story is not one of complete success in this regard, as the OrlyVAL light-rail scheme highlights. The 7-kilometre link between Orly Airport and the Paris RER network, financed by a private company, was opened in 1991. Within just a year, it had failed due to over-optimistic traffic forecasts and uncompetitive fare levels. Since the transfer to the public sector the link has prospered, but it had a damaging effect on private investor confidence.

Sweden and Belgium have had much more limited private involvement in the transport sector. The Swedish experience in this regard being largely a result of low traffic volumes on most routes making it difficult for any proposal to be commercially viable, and the Belgian a result of the dense motorway network with frequent interchanges making it unsuitable for toll roads.

The governments of the UK and Germany have pursued private investment much more actively. Both countries have done this because of the realised need for greater finance in the sector, especially in Germany after reunification. The UK has also pursued it as part of the economic reforms initiated by the Major government in the 1990s, leading to toll roads such as the M6 and water-crossings such as those at Dartford on the Thames.

Farrell (1999) also explains how private investment in transport also varies hugely across the different modes of transport. Private investors generally prefer projects in which the success factors largely lie within their control. Ports are more favoured than railways. Private investors also prefer to invest in terminals rather than links because it is easier to capture the revenue and because the land can be used for other complementary projects as well. In this way, airports are more favoured than roads.

Traditionally, roads have not been the investment of choice for private investors because of difficulties with collecting the revenue. However, recent technological developments with road-pricing are potentially going to overcome this problem, opening up the door to increased private investment in this mode. Dense road networks with numerous interchanges, such as those in Belgium, create further difficulties for private investors in terms of revenue collection, and the roads are generally subject to considerable government interference (see Section 10.4 for a further discussion about the provision of roads).

Rail projects have also struggled to attract private investment because the returns are lowered by stringent safety standards and maintenance costs, and because train operating companies absorb part of the revenue stream.

Ports and airports have attracted most private investment for a number of reasons. First, as they are terminal projects it is easier for the revenue to be collected. Secondly, the land can be used for complementary purposes such as retail shopping centres and housing, the latter being especially the case in seaports. Finally, as the owners of these terminals have a close relationship with the users of the facilities, they are able to employ price discrimination effectively and lucratively. The downside to these investments, especially in the case of airports, is the high level regulation that is imposed.

Private investment and public–private partnerships are becoming more prevalent across the European transport sector, especially where governments are actively promoting it through the absorption of part of the commercial risk involved. It is likely to continue to grow as governments and the European Commission seek to reap the potential efficiency gains that it offers and as technological developments make it more feasible.

14.4   The Channel Tunnel

Gerondeau (1997) has claimed that the Channel Tunnel has been a huge technical success, but an equally huge financial and private investment disaster. Contrary to popular belief, the construction of a link between Britain and mainland Europe has been a consideration since the early nineteenth century. However, it was not until 1985 that serious plans were put in motion, with an international competition for the design. The winning proposal was a rail-only project, but one that would transport vehicles as well as passengers.

The work began in 1986 and, on the whole, proceeded successfully. The first link-up was completed on 30 October 1990, and the boring was completed on time. It was at this point that the problems struck. The equipping of the tunnels and the vehicles that would use them ran hugely over schedule, in both time and money. It was only in December 1993 that Eurotunnel, the company responsible for the financing and operations of the tunnel, took possession of it; and it was not until 1995 that the tunnel became fully operational.

By mid-1995, Eurotunnel's financial situation was desperate. The final construction bill was twice that estimated at the outset of the project, and the investors, all of whom were from the private sector, were never to recoup their investment.

In May 1995, the tunnel accounted for a quarter of the trucks and one-eighth of the cars that travelled on an average day between the two land masses. Competition remains very strong for this traffic from the ferries that have developed port infrastructure and their ships to speed up their service. In fact, high-speed ships can now complete the journey faster than the service offered through the tunnel.

The passenger services from London have been more successful, though, and are continuing to expand. However, this is largely a result of the uneven competition that Eurostar, the passenger-train element of Eurotunnel, exerts. The ferry companies and airlines must balance their books, but Eurotunnel is unable to repay its debts and the railway companies receive varying degrees of state subsidisation.

The project has been a financial disaster and as such has dented private investor confidence in such schemes in the future. Gerondeau (1997) suggests that one of the reasons for this failure is the degree of competition that faced the new enterprise from the outset.

General Forms of 15 Government Intervention

15.1 Introduction

There are three broad approaches that can be taken by governments to tackle market failure: command and control; taxes and subsidies; and tradable permits. In this chapter each is explained and analysed on three counts: the market failures that they suit; their effectiveness; and their political acceptability. The last of these is vitally important as the implementation of any solution needs to be viable. Examples from the transport sector will be provided for each to illustrate the conclusions that the theory leads to.

The objective of authorities should be to rectify market failures in the most efficient manner; or in other words, to minimise both the economic and the political costs of achieving the solution. In order to help analyse this in terms of the economic costs it is useful to introduce a new diagram, which is shown in Figure 15.1.

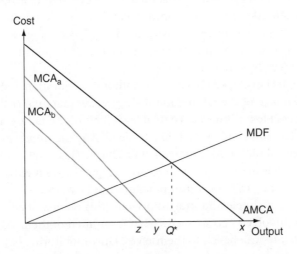

Figure 15.1 The costs of correcting market failure

It can be assumed that any solution incurs a marginal cost, which shall be termed the 'marginal cost of abatement', and that this rises as the failure is increasingly rectified. These extra costs rise as increasing amounts of market failure (pollution, congestion, market power and the like) are eliminated. There is no reason why different producers should have identical marginal costs of abatement and so in Figure 15.1 it is assumed that there are two producers A and B, and that they have different marginal cost of abatement curves, namely MCA_a and MCA_b respectively. Together, these combine to form the 'aggregate marginal cost of abatement (AMCA)' curve by horizontal summation. It can also be assumed that there is a marginal cost generated by the pollution itself, which shall be termed the 'marginal damage of the failure (MDF)', and that this increases as the failure worsens. This can be assumed to be the same across all producers as there is no reason why a unit of pollution, for example, from one producer should cause a different amount of damage to that caused by a unit of pollution from a different producer. This means that in cost–output space, where output represents the output of the production process that generates the market failure, the MCA curve will be downward-sloping and that of the MDF will be upward-sloping.

The efficient level of market failure is, therefore, that at which these two curves intersect, denoted as Q^*. At levels of failure lower than this the MCA exceeds the MDF and so society would be better off by allowing further damage; and at levels higher than this there is too much damage and society would benefit from reducing it. This is the logic as to why the notion that all damage should be eliminated is not economical. If the market is left to itself, though, each individual producer would produce an output at which its marginal cost of abatement is zero: a unit of y for producer A and of z for producer B. Overall, therefore, the total output would be x.

15.2 | Command and control solutions

Command and control solutions have been the approach used for many years now. The authorities simply use legislation and enforcement to achieve the desired outcome. This can take numerous forms dependent on the nature of the market failure: monopolies can be forced to divide or to share technology with competitors; demerit goods can be made illegal; and negative externalities can be limited by penalising any over-production.

Using the model developed above, if the authority in question is able to calculate the marginal damage of the failure and the aggregate marginal cost of abatement correctly it is possible for it to set the total legal limit of the failure at Q^* units: the efficient level. This total limit would then be divided by the number of producers to calculate the legal limit for each individual producer. This is shown in Figure 15.2. If the legal sanctions are large enough to discourage over-failure by the individual participants then the desired amount of failure can be achieved.

Such schemes are simple and straightforward. This is a major advantage as all of the participants involved know exactly what is required of them. Also once established, such schemes can be left to themselves. Only monitoring of the participants

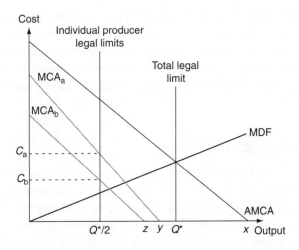

Figure 15.2
Command and control
intervention

will be needed to keep them functioning correctly. Consequently, schemes such as these are likely to be inexpensive to set up and maintain.

It is unlikely that authorities can ever calculate the efficient level of failure accurately, especially immediately. To attain the optimal failure reduction a number of alterations to the laws will probably be required as greater understanding of the processes involved become established. Such changes are likely to involve cumbersome and politically difficult processes and so schemes are more rigid than perhaps one would like.

Command and control schemes treat every participant exactly the same. The desired aggregate failure is calculated and then divided amongst all of the participants. This means that each one has to reduce their failure to the same amount, despite the fact that some will be able to do so more cheaply than others. In Figure 15.2, producer A has to pay a marginal cost of C_a in order to achieve the limit that has been set, whereas producer B only has to pay C_b. This is inefficient as the marginal costs of abatement should be equalised across all participants. If they are not, producers that can reduce failure most cheaply should make further reductions, thus receiving compensation from those that find it more costly to do so. If the compensation is at a level between the difference in marginal abatement costs, all parties will be better off and the total costs of achieving the reductions will have been reduced.

Once the targets are reached, there is no incentive for further reductions in failure by reducing the marginal abatement costs through technological progress. Consequently, whatever level is set initially is going to be the level of failure that results in the long run.

In terms of political viability the targets are likely to be set by politicians in consultation with the major participants, and so the scheme is going to be politically feasible from that standpoint. The obvious potential danger with this is that of political capture. In order to establish the scheme, the targets will fail to go far enough and so the optimal reduction will not be achieved. This is a real danger, but one that faces all of the possible approaches.

Such an approach is suitable in cases where the authorities deem it necessary to eliminate a critical level of damage caused by the failure; for example, the mandatory introduction of certain safety features in transport vehicles, which can be seen as being merit goods. In all other market situations, however, such approaches are inefficiently expensive and unreliable and so market-based solutions are preferable.

15.2.1   Price ceilings and floors

Non-economists often call for authorities to take a command-and-control approach to setting maximum prices within the transport sector. The most frequent demand is to overcome the trend of increasing fuel prices by enforcing a centrally determined price, above which fuel companies are not allowed to go. Fuel companies may see their profit margins squeezed, but consumers would be better off and would be able to use their savings in other sectors of the economy. This proposed solution is known as a *price ceiling* and is analysed in Section 7.4 and illustrated in Figure 7.6. As in the taxi market case, a price ceiling in the fuel market would cause a shortage. It is not feasible to compel a private company to supply fuel and so the lower price means that less will be supplied, Q_s rather than Q_1 (see Figure 7.6). At the same time, the lower price stimulates vehicle owners to demand more, Q_d rather than Q_1. In terms of welfare, consumer surplus will be increased but producer surplus and that of the whole market would fall. A shortage inevitably emerges, which in the market for fuel would manifest itself in queues of frustrated drivers being turned away from the pumps. Such frustration is likely to outweigh any monetary gains that consumers experience and creates a situation that would certainly not be politically desirable.

A similar analysis can be applied to *price floors*, in which the centrally determined price is higher than the price that had prevailed in the market previously. The argument for such legislation is to ensure that producers are receiving higher prices, but analysis shows that it simply leads to surplus stocks being produced and wasted, and another deadweight welfare loss. There is not an important example of a price floor in the European transport sector, but the European Common Agricultural Policy (CAP) does take this form.

15.2.2   The Austrian Ecopoints Scheme

Due to European economic growth there has, for a long time, been a growing volume of traffic using routes through the Austrian Alps. This has been particularly true of heavy goods vehicles. It was in response to this, and to the damaging environmental effects it was having, that in May 1992 the then European Community signed an agreement with the Austrian government to allow these volumes to be regulated. The Ecopoints Scheme was born.

The intention was to reduce the emission of nitrous oxide from heavy goods vehicles by 60 per cent between 1991 and 2003. Ecopoints were created so that one ecopoint equated to one unit of nitrous oxide and then an appropriate number of them were made available to users of the regulated routes. It was legislated that in order to use these routes, a driver of a heavy goods vehicle had to possess the correct number of ecopoints to cover the amount of nitrous oxide it would emit during the course of the journey. Cleaner vehicles would, therefore, be charged fewer ecopoints and so an incentive to drivers to use cleaner vehicles was created. Each year the number of ecopoints would be reduced until the target values had been achieved by 2003.

The available ecopoints were allocated to the different member states of the European Union so that it was then the responsibility of national authorities to determine their allocation to hauliers. A European Community reserve was also created. These ecopoints were not tradable amongst member states or amongst individual hauliers and so the scheme was very much of a command-and-control nature.

As the decade in which it was in operation wore on, shortages of ecopoints became increasingly regular and severe. Towards the end of 1999 Danish hauliers began to run out of ecopoints and so had to reduce their exports to countries south of Austria, particularly Italy. These wider trade effects have been a serious drawback of the regulation, but it was agreed that the scheme would be extended, in a more stringent form, in 2004 for a further two years at the most.

The total number of ecopoints allocated to member states of the European Union in 2004 was approximately 6.5 million. Over the remaining potential two years this number was to be reduced by 5 per cent each year. The accession states were allocated ecopoints, for example 80,078 to the Czech Republic and 500 to Cyprus. Heavy goods vehicles which were categorised as being particularly harmful to the environment were no longer allowed to use the routes.

The Ecopoints Scheme has now been drawn to a close. In its place there is now a series of motorway tolls that adhere to the Eurovignette Directive. The revenue from these tolls is being hypothecated, or earmarked, to co-finance the planned 50-kilometre Brenner railway tunnel.

15.2.3 Demotorisation

Across the European Union there are cases of *demotorisation*: the prohibition of vehicles in a certain area, sometimes during a certain time of the day. In the City of Cambridge, as in many other European cities, the central area is pedestrianised to avoid the negative externalities of congestion, noise, pollution and accidents. Since 1992, Italian cities have been able to introduce entrance checks and to levy a charge to protect the cultural and historical values of a city. In Rome, for example, the central area is protected between 6:30 AM and 6:00 PM during the week and between 2:00 PM and 6:00 PM on Saturdays. A part of the city is completely closed to all vehicles that are not in possession of a special permit. Similar systems exist in Bologna and Genoa.

Mountainous areas are particularly susceptible to environment damage during night times. The topography and the stable weather conditions slow down the removal of exhaust fumes from mountain valleys. As such, local vehicle bans have been introduced in these areas. In 1999, in the lower Inn Valley, the Austrian government introduced a night-driving ban between 8:00 PM and 5:00 AM for lorries above a certain weight. Even environmentalists criticised this measure, though, because it simply caused these vehicles to drive longer distances around the regulated area, thereby worsening the overall environmental impact. The European Court of Justice stopped this particular ban because it would contradict the right of the free movement of goods within the European Union.

15.2.4 A key lesson from these examples

Two examples of command-and-control measures in the European transport sector have been outlined. There are an uncountable number of others that could be analysed: weight limits, speed limits, technical and environmental standards, the list goes on. They are all introduced to correct a particular market failure, usually a negative externality, but they all have unintended side effects. The Austrian Ecopoints Scheme may have helped to correct the excess damage that nitrous oxide was causing to the fragile environment of the Alps, but it did so at the cost of reduced trade across the European Union. The demotorisation of the lower Inn Valley may have reduced the nocturnal damage caused by the build-up of reservoirs of exhaust fumes, but it simply shifted the damage to alternative routes and hampered the goals of the Single European Market. It is vital that authorities carefully consider all the possible costs and benefits of a policy before its implementation.

15.3 | Taxation

Taxation is a market form of intervention as it simply changes the market conditions and then allows participants to make their own decisions based upon these, leading to new market equilibria. A *tax* is an extra cost levied upon the participants. In the transport sector taxes take the form of *indirect taxes*, meaning that they are levied upon the suppliers, who then pass it onto the consumers, rather than *direct taxes* (such as income tax), which are levied on the consumers. Taxes aim to reduce a failure by increasing production costs, thereby shifting the supply curve inwards. Taxes are potentially applicable to demerit goods and negative externalities.

A tax is intended to shift the supply curve in such a way that the resulting quantity of the good or the pollution produced is equal to the efficient level, in terms of the damage that it causes, which is denoted by Q^*. If this can be calculated accurately by the authority then theoretically the rate can be set so that the efficient output is reached.

In terms of the model here, a common tax rate is set throughout the market for every unit of the output that causes failure. This is denoted by T in Figure 15.3. The producers will then reduce their output of the failure until their marginal cost of abatement is equal to the tax rate. Reducing output by less than this would mean

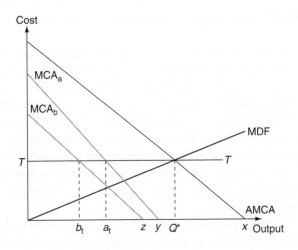

Figure 15.3 Taxation

that they are paying a tax on some units that would be cheaper not to produce; and reducing output more than this would mean that it would actually be cheaper to produce more and pay the tax on the additional units.

Producers will reduce their output by different amounts, according to how costly it is for them to do so. In Figure 15.3, producer B is able to reduce its output more than producer A: from z to b_t rather than from y to a_t. As they all have the same marginal cost of abatement this is an economically efficient way to achieve the desired overall total reduction, from x to Q^*, as there is no way of reallocating the reductions and using compensation payments to reduce overall costs. Tietenberg (1995) has estimated that use of taxes or tradable permits (see below) can reduce the compliance costs by 50 per cent or more; a significant saving.

The problem in reality is that it is highly unlikely that authorities will be able to estimate the actual effects of a tax. There is always going to be considerable uncertainty regarding how sources will respond to a given tax rate. Calculating the response of sources requires knowledge of the price elasticity of the existing processes to the output that is the focus of the intervention: to know how an increase in the *price* of the output will affect the quantity of it produced. It also requires knowledge of the cross-price elasticities of the current production processes to alternatives, and the targeted production that each of these alternatives has. All of this is problematic to calculate and so it will be extremely difficult to properly calculate the marginal cost of abatement for each of the sources. Consequently, there is always going to be considerable doubt as to what effect a given tax rate will have. The major advantage of the command and control scheme is that the output could be established clearly. This is not the case with a tax. As authorities are cautious not to harm their political constituents, it is likely that any taxes will simply fail to go far enough.

In their favour, taxes have the advantage that they are a continual irritant to participants. As they have to pay the tax on each unit produced, there will always be an incentive to search for ways to reduce production. Taxes are also more easily adjusted than a command-and-control regulation, which allows greater flexibility for future responses to new scientific understanding and as the effects of the scheme become clear.

Taxes correct a distortion in the economy by reducing the excess damage caused by a market failure. As well as doing this in the most efficient way, they also raise revenue for authorities that can then be used to reduce other taxes in the economy, thereby reducing the distortions that these other taxes cause. For example, income tax is distortionary because it reduces the incentive that people have to work hard in the economy and so serve to reduce economic effort. With the revenue raised from taxation aimed at correcting market failure, such income tax distortions can be reduced. In this way there is a *double dividend* effect from market failure taxation: it corrects the market failure whilst simultaneously reducing other economic distortions as well.

This double dividend feature of market failure taxation makes it much more politically feasible as it can be promoted not just as an extra tax, but as part of a package of taxes, in which the population is actually made better off. It does, however, shift the incidence of the taxation away from consumers and towards producers (unless the revenue is used in such a way that producers are left no worse off) and may be resisted by producers.

15.3.1 Taxation using demand-and-supply analysis

As noted above, there are two general types of tax: indirect taxes, which are levied on producers, who then decide how much of it should be passed onto consumers; and direct taxes, which are levied directly on consumers. The latter of these simply causes the disposable income of consumers to fall, and so shifts the demand curve inwards to the left, thereby causing price and quantity traded to fall.

Figure 15.4 illustrates the impact of an indirect tax. First, it causes the supply curve to shift inwards to the left, from S to S_2, because producer costs have increased

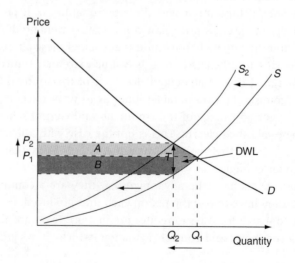

Figure 15.4 Tax analysis using demand and supply

and so they are willing and able to supply less to the market at any given price. As the demand schedule has not changed, consumers will compete for the fewer products and so the price will rise from P_1 to P_2.

It would initially appear that the tax rate is simply the difference between the original price and the resulting price. This is too simplistic, though, because producers do not necessarily pass the whole tax rate onto consumers. In Figure 15.4 the actual tax rate is represented by T: the difference between the two supply curves at the final equilibrium. Producers pass the difference between the two prices onto consumers, who consequently bear a tax burden equal to the shaded area A. Producers decide to absorb the rest of the tax rate themselves, and so bear a tax burden equal to the shaded area B.

In this example, the producers actually pay more of the tax than consumers. The reason for this is the price elasticity of demand. In this situation, the demand is price elastic and so it would be unwise for producers to pass on more of the tax rate in the form of higher prices, because that would lead to a greater reduction in quantity demanded and so a greater reduction in revenue. The producers actually maintain higher overall revenue, in this case, by paying more of the tax themselves, but this is not always the case. When demand is price inelastic, producers will pass on more of the tax in the form of higher prices, because the quantity demanded by consumers is relatively unresponsive to the resulting increase in price. When demand is perfectly inelastic, all of the tax will be passed on to consumers in this way. Conversely, when demand is perfectly elastic, the producers will pay all of the tax themselves.

The tax, causing the quantity of the product traded to fall and the price of it to rise has inevitably caused consumer surplus to fall. Similarly, producer surplus has also fallen because producers are selling fewer units at a lower price (P_2 minus T). Much of this reduction in consumer and producer welfare has been transferred to the government in the form of tax revenue, shown by areas A and B in Figure 15.4. There is some welfare, however, that has been lost as a result of the tax. This is shown by the shaded area denoted DWL in Figure 15.4, because it is known as the deadweight welfare loss of the tax.

This reduction in overall welfare is an argument against government intervention in the economy. Many economists argue that the market should be left to function freely, without any interference from the government. However, the question needs to be raised, which is worse: the initial market failure or the subsequent government failure?

15.3.2 Examples of taxation

Taxation is used throughout the transport sector of Europe: fuel taxes for motor vehicles and airliners, road taxes and corporation taxes. These can all be analysed using the tools developed above. A specific form of taxation which is growing in popularity and importance is that of road-pricing, which we analyse in detail in the next chapter.

15.3.2.1 Fuel taxation in the European Union

Since the Single European Act of 1987, the European Commission has been promoting and developing economic integration across the Union. The intention has been to allow producers of all member nations to compete with one another on a level playing field, thereby reaping the efficiency benefits that competition can bring. A key, but at times contested, part of this integration has been the harmonisation of tax rates so that producers from no single nation are at a particular competitive advantage or disadvantage.

Directive 99/62/EC, which was then revised by Directive 2006/38/EC, stipulates common rules on annual taxes for heavy goods vehicles. It stipulates a set of maximum charges that can be applied to vehicles of 12 tonnes or more with three or four axles. It also prohibits the imposition of a toll in addition to these user charges, except if the toll is for more specific physical structures such as bridges, tunnels and mountain passes. The specific structure and administration of the charge is then left to national authorities.

As a consequence of these directives, Belgium, Germany, Denmark, Luxembourg, the Netherlands and Sweden agreed on the introduction of a common system of user charges for such heavy goods vehicles. According to this system the payment of a specified amount confers to hauliers the right to use motorways of any of the participating countries for a given period, usually a year. This has become known as the *Eurovignette*, and so the initial directives above have become known as the *Eurovignette Directives*. Germany withdrew from the system on 31 August 2003 so that it could introduce its own motorway tolls.

A similar thing can be said of fuel taxes as well. The minimum rates of excise duty since 1 January 2004 are as displayed in Table 15.1.

The actual fuel charges levied in the different member states of the European Union vary hugely, as shown in Figure 15.5. Fuel duty is particularly high in the UK – in April 2005, total taxation (which includes fuel duty and VAT) represented 69.9 per cent of the pump price for unleaded petrol and 67.3 per cent of the pump price for diesel. As Figure 15.5 illustrates, in December 2004 the UK had the 14th highest pre-tax petrol price amongst the European Union members. However, because the UK has the highest total tax of all these countries, it has the second highest post-tax petrol price, slightly behind the Netherlands.

Fuel taxation has two objectives: first, to correct the negative externalities caused by its usage; and secondly, to raise revenue for the government. Fuel is

Table 15.1 Minimum rates of fuel duty as stipulated by EC directive

	Leaded petrol	Unleaded petrol	Diesel fuel
Minimum rate (EUR/1000 litres)	421	359	302

Source: EUROPA Transport; *Road Charging: Annual vehicle taxes and fuel taxes (excise duties)*; http://ec.europa.eu/transport/road/policy/road_charging/charging_vehicle_fuel_taxes_en.htm

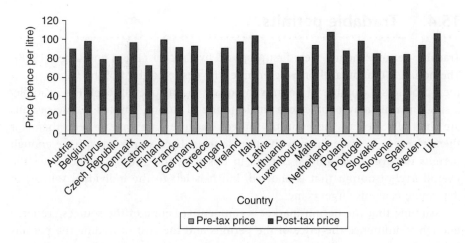

Figure 15.5 Fuel prices and duties in the European Union, December 2004

Source: Leicester (2006)

an ideal commodity for this latter purpose because it is highly price inelastic and so quantity demanded is unresponsive to a rise in its price, therefore leading to significant revenue hauls from seemingly small tax rates. Fuel taxation is certainly an important contributor to government revenue in the UK: in 2004–2005, it is estimated that it raised around £23.5 billion, or 5.2 per cent of total revenue. Only income tax, National Insurance, VAT and corporation tax raise bigger shares of the total.

15.3.2.2 Carbon taxation in Europe

In the 1990s Norway, Sweden, Finland and Denmark all introduced carbon taxes. Norway did so in order to not only reduce the negative externalities caused by carbon dioxide emissions (see Section 9.4) but also to use the generated revenue to reduce the distortions created by labour taxes.

The Norwegian tax initially covered 60 per cent of its domestic energy-related carbon dioxide emissions. The cement, foreign shipping and fishery industries were all exempt, along with natural gas and electricity production (virtually all of Norway's electricity is produced as hydroelectric power). Partial exemptions were also granted to Norway's domestic aviation and shipping, and pulp and paper industries.

The Norwegian tax generates substantial revenue. In 1993 the tax represented 0.7 per cent of total tax revenue, and by 2001 this had increased to 1.7 per cent (Stern, 2007). It has been estimated that the tax reduced carbon dioxide emissions by approximately 2.3 per cent in the final decade of the twentieth century. It has also created an incentive for technological advancement. Norway is now a world leader in the capture and storage of carbon dioxide. Statoil, Norway's state oil company, has implemented large-scale capture of the carbon dioxide it emits, which it then pumps into subterranean caves and lakes, thereby preventing it rejoining the carbon cycle and adding to atmospheric carbon dioxide concentrations.

15.4 | Tradable permits

Tradable permit schemes were first proposed by Crocker (1966) and Dales (1968). The notion is that an authority determines the desired output of the failure, Q^*. It then produces a number of permits to equate to this overall level. For example, a single permit may equate to a single tonne of carbon emitted. These permits are then allocated to the emitting sources and they are free to keep them for themselves, or to trade them with other sources. Each source must have enough permits to cover their annual output. In this way, the authority determines the overall *level* of output that is allowed, but it is left to the individual sources to determine *how* this target is met.

Assuming that the permit market is competitive, none of the sources are large enough to influence the price of the permits and the cost of trading the permits is low, the outcome will be as that shown in Figure 15.6. Under these conditions, the effect is exactly the same as with taxation but the way in which it achieves this result is different, as the analysis below shows.

As can be seen from Figure 15.6, such schemes encourage individual producers to equate their marginal costs of abatement to one another and to the permit price, P. If the market-given permit price exceeds the marginal cost of abatement, there is an incentive to reduce output and to sell the surplus permits, generating revenue. If, on the other hand, the permit price is less than the marginal cost of abatement, it makes sense for producers to increase output and purchase the necessary permits, thus making a saving. These processes continue until the marginal costs of abatement across the system are equal to the market-given permit price and hence to one another. This is economically efficient as it means that those who can reduce their emissions most inexpensively do so to a greater extent (source B, for example). Conversely, those who cannot reduce their emissions as easily pay the price of greater permits (source A). The efficient reduction in output, x to Q^*, is achieved

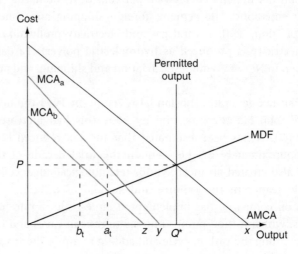

Figure 15.6
Tradable permits

in the cheapest way possible. The reduction in compliance costs is the same as that of the carbon tax scheme discussed above: savings of some 50 per cent or more compared to a command-and-control alternative (Tietenberg, 1995).

With taxation the costs incurred by the sources are known with a fair degree of certainty but the resulting reduction in output is unknown. With tradable permit schemes the resulting reduction in output is known with certainty but the actual costs incurred by producers are unknown. This is a drawback which may lead to greater resistance from the producers, but in terms of tackling market failure it is perhaps the more desirable option.

It needs to be remembered, however, that this result arises if the permit market is competitive and if the transaction costs of trading them are low. If it is not competitive, there will be sources large enough to influence the permit price: they could withhold permits from the market and so drive up the permit price, increasing the revenue that they generate from the permits they sell; or they could purchase fewer permits so as to keep the price low, saving money on the permits they do buy. Either of these strategies would reduce the efficiency gains as the permit price would not be set at P as above.

As with taxation, tradable permit schemes also act as a continual incentive to sources to reduce their output. If sources can make further reductions they can then sell their surplus permits, generating for themselves additional revenue.

Tradable permits also afford the system much more flexibility than both of the two previous alternatives. If it becomes clear that greater reductions are necessary, which is possible as scientific understanding of damages becomes clearer, permits can simply be purchased by authorities, thereby lowering the total amount in circulation. This is much less cumbersome and time-consuming than altering legal regulations or the rate of tax.

Depending on how the permits are initially allocated, a revenue could be raised (the permits could be auctioned off, for example) as with taxation. This revenue could similarly be used to reduce distortions and inefficiency elsewhere within the economy and so potentially generate a double dividend.

The political considerations are similar to those discussed in the context of taxation. The double dividend feature will help to make it more politically feasible and the revenue can be used to offset any undesired effects it may cause.

Tradable permit schemes are being increasingly used across the world. The first, in 1995, was that in America to reduce sulphur dioxide and nitrous oxide emissions that cause acid rain. Norway introduced emissions trading in January 2005 for major energy plants and heavy industry, and Switzerland plans to do so in order to help it achieve its Kyoto goals. Currently, there is only one example of a tradable permit scheme that directly concerns the transport sector (outlined in Section 15.4.1), but in a study on behalf of the European Commission (2004) there is a thorough analysis as to how one could be designed and implemented for freight transport in environmentally sensitive regions.

15.4.1 The European Union's carbon-trading scheme and the airlines

The European Union's carbon-trading scheme was introduced on 1 January 2005 and is arguably now the world's largest and most advanced example of a tradable permits system. It comprises around 11,000 power stations and industrial installations across the Union, which together account for approximately 45 per cent of the Union's entire carbon emissions.

Member states decide on the quota of permits to be allocated during each phase of the scheme (phase one ends on 31 December 2007; phase two runs from 2008 to 2012; and further phases will be implemented thereafter) and how those permits are to be allocated amongst their domestic producers. Their plans have to be approved by the European Commission, which ensures that they are in line with the broader reduction targets. The majority of permits are currently allocated free of charge, with only 0.2 per cent of permits being auctioned during the first phase. Most countries have also prevented the banking of permits between the first two phases, although it is allowed between years within either phase.

A sophisticated and effective permit market has developed, particularly based in the City of London, and trading volumes have increased steadily. Participants in the scheme have also been able to offset their carbon dioxide emissions by investing in cleaner production processes in developing countries, thereby developing cleaner technologies across the world.

The scheme has been a significant step forward in environmental policy, but it has not been a complete success. As member states have been able to determine their own quota and allocation of permits, it has been estimated that the resulting carbon dioxide emissions in phase one will only be 1 per cent lower than that had no intervention been made (Stern, 2007). It is necessary for quotas to be determined centrally. The costs of administration have also been high, particularly for small participants that have had to pay for their reports to be independently verified in the same way as their larger counterparts have. There has also been uncertainty regarding the price of permits and so of the economical emission reductions required. This could be overcome by the introduction of larger central permit auctions.

Currently, climate change policies do not require any significant contribution from the aviation sector, and kerosene, or jet fuel, has historically been exempted from taxation. This situation – coupled with the fact that already the sector accounts for approximately 3 per cent of the Union's total greenhouse gas emissions; its emissions are increasing rapidly (by some 87 per cent since 1990); and its emissions are expected to continue to rise, so that by 2020 it may have doubled from the present level – has compelled the European Commission to act. At the end of 2005, the Commission proposed that the sector should be brought into the carbon-trading scheme.

Aviation is to be grafted into the scheme in two stages. From the start of 2011, emissions from all domestic and international flights within the European Union will be covered. At the start of 2012, emissions from all international flights globally that involve a European airport will be included as well. All airlines will be treated equally and the following will be exempt: very light aircraft, military aircraft, police aircraft, customs aircraft, rescue flights, government flights and training or testing flights.

As with the producers that are already within the trading scheme, airlines will receive tradable permits to emit a certain level of carbon dioxide per year. At the end of each year, operators must surrender a number of permits to cover all of their emissions that year. Any surplus permits that they have may then be traded or *banked* for use in subsequent years. The number of permits will be capped at the average level of emissions in the years 2004–2006 up until the end of 2022, although this would be reviewed if international aviation is brought into a global climate agreement. Each airline will be allocated a number of permits on the basis of its share of overall passenger and cargo traffic on the routes to be covered. Up to 10 per cent of the permits will be auctioned, and from 2013 there will be no limit on auctioning.

Each airline is to be responsible for calculating its own emission levels based on its fuel consumption multiplied by a standard emission factor. Their reports will then be checked by an independent verifier. If an operator fails to surrender sufficient permits to cover its emissions for a given year, it will be fined 100 EUR for every tonne of carbon not covered and it would no longer be able to sell its permits. It may even have its operating licence revoked.

The European Commission expects there to be a reduction of 183 million tonnes of carbon per annum, some 46 per cent, by 2020 compared to the *business-as-usual* approach. The Commission states (20/12/2006) that this is equivalent to twice Austria's annual emissions from all sources. It also expects there to be little effect on the profitability of the airlines, as they will be able to pass on the costs to their passengers. Assuming this, by 2020 the price of a return ticket within the European Union could rise by between 1.8 EUR and 9 EUR. The price of long-haul flights, because of their higher environmental impact, is expected to rise substantially more.

15.5 | Case studies of the three options

In a study on behalf of the European Commission (2004) the three general policy options have been tested using simulations of two case studies. The first case study is along the Lyon–Turin corridor, connecting France and Italy across the Alps. The corridor is 4 kilometres wide, and only the tunnel of Fréjus, with a total length of 12.9 kilometres, is considered. The second case study is a region in the southern part of the German Black Forest between Freiburg, Titisee-Neustadt and Donaueschingen. It is also a corridor 4 kilometres in width but with a total length approaching 57 kilometres.

The studies do not estimate the total costs of the different policies; they simply look at their environmental impacts. In the Lyon–Turin case study, road-pricing (taxation) has only a small effect on traffic volumes, whereas a total ban of heavy goods vehicles leads to the greatest environmental benefits. This is perhaps to be expected, particularly as there are no close alternatives to using this corridor and so the demand for its use is price inelastic and drivers will simply pay any charges to keep using the route. The authors of the study state that the environmental effect of a tradable permits scheme would be determined by the number of permits allocated.

Similar conclusions are reached in the second case study, although the effectiveness of taxation is much improved because of the existence of close alternatives to using the regulated route. Consequently, taxation and tradable permits schemes lead to traffic relocation around the regulated area.

Overall, the choice of which policy to implement largely depends on the initial intention of the policy. If it is intended to achieve a specific reduction in the output in question, then a command-and-control approach is the most certain to succeed. If it is to generate revenue for use elsewhere, then taxation is the most effective option. If it is to reduce negative externalities in the most socially efficient and least costly way for producers, then tradable permits schemes are the most effective. It should be noted, however, that this latter policy is not always practically feasible.

15.6 | Bureaucratic rent-seeking

Svendsen (2003) has analysed the political economy within unelected bureaucracies such as the European Commission, civil services and the British Traffic Commissioners. He has found that rather than there being a drive for cost minimisation, there is actually a push towards budget maximisation. By pressing for larger and larger budgets and greater responsibility, each department within a political body can create a cushion against politicians who would seek to cut the size of the bureaucracy. This affords the department more power in subsequent decision-making. Bureaucracies can achieve this aim because they are monopoly suppliers of public services and because they are the beneficiaries of asymmetric information in relation to the budget-setting authority regarding the resources necessary to fulfil their responsibilities: another example of the principle-agent problem.

Bureaucratic departments within an authority compete with one another to secure the greatest share of the authority's budget, placing a fiscal pressure on the authority. Eventually this is likely to lead to higher taxation and a reduction in the volume of production as entrepreneurs migrate to the jurisdiction of authorities with looser fiscal policies. Flags of convenience in the shipping industry provide an example of this. It does not pay a single department to unilaterally reduce its demand of resources because the benefits will simply be captured by competing departments rather than leading to gains for all. The departments within authorities that are going to be implementing solutions to market failure in the transport sector will be caught up in this competitive environment. This means that they will be likely to want to establish the system that is going to require the most work by its members and the largest budget from the central authority.

Tradable permit schemes are likely to require the most bureaucratic involvement as it is necessary to allocate the permits, which may involve the organisation of auctions or the calculation of how many permits each producer is entitled to under grandfathering; monitor and record the output of each producer; sanction any punishments that may be required if there has been any over-production; and allocate the revenue that has been generated. Taxation is likely to require the second most bureaucratic involvement with the monitoring of output, collection of taxes and allocation of the revenue. This means that command-and-control measures come at the bottom of this scale, simply requiring the monitoring of output and the imposition of any sanctions as necessary. As such, it is likely that there will be pressure within bureaucratic authorities to introduce tradable permit schemes to tackle market failure in the transport sector, making these a more politically viable option from within the authority.

Tackling Traffic 16 Congestion

16.1 | The situation

In the UK, and across Europe, the provision of roads and the management of their use is one of the few remaining market-free, centrally administered sectors of the economy. There are no explicit charges for the use of the road system, and expenditure on maintenance and new capacity is ultimately controlled by Whitehall. When a user purchases fuel, well over half of the price at the pump is accounted for by taxation. This could be argued to be a road charge but nobody thinks in those terms. Unlike in a properly functioning market, the price of fuel to the user bears no relation to the direct costs of the roads, the costs imposed on others, the benefits they enjoy or their willingness to pay for better service.

Nor does the total tax revenue bear any relation to public expenditure on transport: Coates (1999) notes that in 1975 road taxation totalled £12.8 billion and spending on local roads, local public transport and national roads totalled £11.5 billion (both figures in 1998 prices). By 2005 this tax revenue had risen to £44 billion but spending had fallen to under £7 billion.

The outcome of centralised planning and a lack of market signals has been what one would expect: under-provision in some places with the limited capacity being rationed by queuing in the form of traffic congestion; over-provision in other places with expensive infrastructure offering excessive capacity of little economic value; commerce and the general public paying a great deal for their use of the roads but with no mechanism through which they might express their preferences for paying more (or less) for better (or worse) standards of service.

Traffic growth in Britain is placing an increasingly heavy burden on the road infrastructure capacity. If present policies are maintained, England could have 25 per cent more traffic by 2010 than it did in 2000 (DETR, 2000, DfT, 2003). Relentlessly worsening traffic congestion reminds many voters on a daily basis that there is a transport problem. The announcement in December 2002 (DfT, 2002) of a carefully targeted and modest increase in road building may have been a response to this. There was recognition by the Secretary of State for Transport in July 2003 (DfT, 2003) that under current policies things will inevitably continue to deteriorate and that road-user charging should be seriously investigated as one of the practical ways of dealing with the problem.

The areas of stress are London and the motorway corridors into London, the West Midlands conurbation and some other urban centres including Tyneside. There is also an important medium stress band stretching from Manchester to Leeds and Bradford. There will be little speed reduction due to increased congestion elsewhere due to spare capacity outside the large towns.

Glaister and Graham (2004) illustrate how things might look if there was over 20 per cent traffic growth over the next few years but no change in fuel prices or road capacity. First, as speeds are reduced so much in London due to increased congestion, time costs of travel are increased and the traffic growth is held to less than 5 per cent. Higher time costs due to traffic congestion *choke off* part of the underlying growth in traffic demand and, as a result, traffic growth is less in the capital and the South-east than in other areas. Secondly, there is an increase of more than 20 per cent in rail patronage as travellers switch to this alternative mode of transport. The financial position of the railways consequently improves. Thirdly, the Exchequer receives over £4 billion per annum in additional fuel tax revenues. Finally, there is an increase in environmental damage costs of over £1 billion per annum.

16.2 | The principles behind road-user charging

The economic principles underlying road-user charging are those outlined in Chapters 9 and 15: long run marginal social cost pricing. Road congestion and pollution from vehicles are typical examples of negative externalities which lead to market failure because those making the decisions to use the roads do not take proper account of the costs that their decisions impose on others. They lead to over-consumption of road travel which is, therefore, allocatively inefficient.

One way to deal with this is by imposing an appropriate additional charge. These were initially proposed by Pigou, and so have become known as *Pigouvian taxes*. For roads the theory was completely specified in Sir Alan Walters' (1961) seminal article 'The Theory and Measurement of Private and Social Cost of Highway Congestion'. An official UK committee under the chairmanship of Ruben Smeed (1964) thought road-pricing both timely and technologically practical.

Panel A in Figure 9.1 is pertinent for the analysis of traffic congestion and road-user charging, although it does require some new definitions.

■ The vertical axis should be considered to measure the *generalised cost* of road transport, in a particular place at a particular time of day.

- The marginal private cost is a measure of the monetary value of the total of all the costs faced per person-kilometre: the cost of petrol and vehicle wear and tear, plus the costs of time moving and stationary, plus the cost of any charges paid, plus any other relevant costs. In other words, it is the cost to a particular individual of making an extra 1-kilometre trip.

- The marginal social cost is a measure of the marginal private costs plus the external costs, such as infrastructure wear and tear; atmospheric pollution and the health effects it brings; noise pollution; accidents; and, crucially, travel delays. In other words, this is the cost to all individuals in society of one particular individual making an extra 1-kilometre trip.

- The vertical distance between the marginal private cost curve and the marginal social cost curve, therefore, represents the difference between the costs borne by the individual user and costs imposed on everybody else.

- The marginal social, and private, benefit curve can be considered to be the demand curve for road transport. This is dependent on the generalised cost of using the roads and on the generalised cost of using all other alternative modes. This represents the propensity to switch between modes in response to changes in relative money charges or congestion.

- The horizontal axis represents the flow of passenger kilometres per hour.

The analysis is then the same as that in Section 9.1 for a general negative externality. The free market equilibrium is where the flow of passenger kilometres per hour is Q_1, because travellers only consider their own private costs and not the total costs to society of their actions. From a social point of view, which fully considers all of the costs of road travel, the optimum flow of passenger kilometres per hour is Q^*. The free market leads to over-consumption of road transport, which is allocatively inefficient. This could be achieved by imposing a unit charge represented by the distance between the marginal private cost and the marginal social cost at the socially efficient passenger flow, Q^*.

16.3 | Experiences and types of road-user charging

Road-user charging schemes take on a variety of forms and it is important that the definitions are clear from the outset:

- *Point-pricing* schemes charge a vehicle for passing a certain physical position, such as the entrance to a main trunk road.

- *Cordon-pricing* schemes charge a vehicle for entering into a specified geographical area, such as a central business district.

- *Area-pricing* schemes charge a vehicle for driving within a specified geographical area during certain times. The subtle difference between these and cordon schemes is that with these the vehicle does not have to cross the boundary of the area; it will be charged even if it is already within the area.

- *Distance-pricing* schemes charge a vehicle according to the distance that it travels within an area.
- *Congestion-charging* schemes charge a vehicle according to the level of congestion and, therefore, the reduction in traffic flow speed that it is contributing to.

Such charging schemes have been implemented across the world, becoming more theoretically and practically sophisticated over the years. Four key examples are outlined below, but in addition to these Hungary has a nationwide heavy-goods vehicle charging scheme, which is an example of a distance-pricing scheme; and Italy and France have had tolled motorways since 1925 and 1955 respectively, these latter examples being cases of point-pricing schemes.

Whether or not schemes such as these are ultimately judged to have been successes, they have already achieved a most important change: they have demonstrated to the general public and to politicians that charging for the use of roads is a practical policy that can make a real difference to behaviour and to congestion levels.

16.3.1 Singapore

The Area Licensing Scheme, an example of cordon-pricing and the first modern road-pricing system, was introduced in Singapore in June 1975. It was implemented in a designated restriction zone of about 7 square-kilometres, covering the central business district. At first it was a paper-based scheme, but since 1998 it has used electronic road-pricing technologies.

The intention behind the system has always been to regulate traffic in order to overcome the problems caused by congestion. In practice, this is done by the system aiming to achieve a target speed for the traffic flow between the hours of 7:30 AM and 6:30 PM during weekdays and up to 2:00 PM on Saturdays, except on public holidays. As it falls beneath this desired speed, the charge is increased and vice versa. The charges are reviewed every three months and are displayed on electronic billboards at every gate. From 2001 the charges have also included an environmental element and so electric and hybrid vehicles pay a lower charge.

Since 1990 there has also been a quota system for the number of vehicles that can be owned on the island. It requires anyone wanting to own a vehicle to bid for a Certificate of Entitlement. This, along with efficient public transport systems, has helped the success of the Area Licensing Scheme.

16.3.2 Oslo

The Oslo electronic road toll was introduced in 1990 and was intended to generate revenue that could be used for new infrastructure. A ring of 19 toll stations was set on all roads leading into the central business district, forming a cordon-pricing scheme. From the outset, payments could be made electronically, manually or through coin-drops, but now the majority of vehicles pay electronically. Charges are made throughout the day by drivers of all vehicles, except emergency vehicles, scheduled buses and motorcycles.

16.3.3 Trondheim

The Trondheim system was very similar to that of Oslo and was introduced a year later. It was an electronic road-pricing system for entering the central business district, consisting of eight toll zones. The intention behind its introduction was to generate revenue to finance new infrastructure projects. The majority of vehicles involved paid through a transponder, but there were also payment machines and a few manned stations. The major difference between this system and that in Oslo is that the charge was only operational between the hours of 6:00 AM and 6:00 PM. The peak rate applied between 6:00 AM and 10:00 AM, and a charge of roughly half of that was applied between 10:00 AM and 6:00 PM. Larger vehicles were also charged more than smaller ones. As the charge was lower during off-peak hours, this system took traffic volumes into account.

16.3.4 London

The London Congestion Charge was introduced in February 2003 in response to the growing congestion problems that residents and workers within the capital experienced. The charge is levied upon all vehicles that are moving within central London between the hours of 7:00 AM and 6:30 PM during weekdays, and so is an example of an area-based congestion charging scheme. The fee is for a single day and remains the same irrespective of how far one actually travels within the area during that day. Buses, taxis, motorbikes and emergency vehicles are exempted from the charge; residents have the opportunity to purchase discounted weekly passes; and there are low annual or one-time charges for the disabled and environment-friendly vehicles.

The system is implemented using vehicle-recognition cameras that compare passing registration-plates with a register of vehicles that have paid in advance. Cameras are placed at the boundaries of the areas as well as within it.

Transport for London has issued a series of impact-monitoring reports (for example, Transport for London, 2006) which record the beneficial effects on traffic and congestion and give estimates of the overall economic benefits created. Figure 16.1 clearly shows that the introduction of the congestion charge in February 2003 had a marked effect on traffic flows within the charging area. Almost overnight, the volume of cars, vans, lorries and others fell by over a quarter and has since stabilised at that level; whereas that of taxis, buses, coaches, motorcycles and pedal cycles has continued to gradually increase.

16.4 | The methodology of road-user charging

This methodology is based upon that of Glaister and Graham (2004), who take the situation in the UK in 2000 as a base set of flows of vehicles and people. They establish this as an equilibrium in which: traffic flows, demands, speeds and

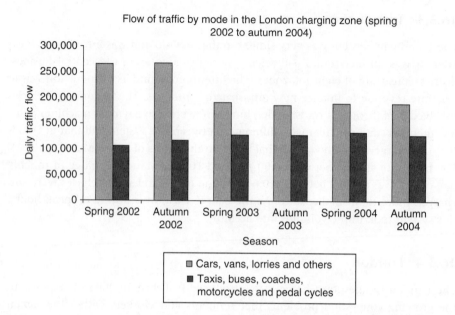

Figure 16.1 The effects of the London congestion charge upon traffic volumes

generalised costs are mutually consistent. That is, equilibrium speeds are taken to imply a set of generalised costs, which in turn implies a set of demands for the use of the network, which in turn implies a level of traffic, which in turn, finally, implies the equilibrium speeds. They then estimate new equilibria following changes in generalised costs brought about by the imposition of new charging regimes.

This approach recognises three fundamental linkages. First, varying prices will change volumes which, in turn, will lead to variations in important dimensions of quality, such as speed, as congestion changes. Secondly, varying prices and times will affect the mode of travel used. Thirdly, varying prices, taxes and subsidies will change the burden on the public purse and may change the funding available for new infrastructure from both public sources and privately funded investment. Differing pricing regimes will create changes in patterns of demand, and consequently changes in the case for investment in infrastructure.

16.4.1 The method and its theoretical issues

The steps for computing the movement from the free market equilibrium to the socially efficient equilibrium are as follows:

1. Establish a base equilibrium in which speeds, traffic flows, demands and generalised costs are mutually consistent.
2. Set up the appropriate responses of demand to price (the elasticities of demand) and the relationships between changes in traffic flow and changes in speeds (the speed–flow relationships).
3. Make a change to a policy variable such as public transport fare, tax on fuel or road-user charge per vehicle-kilometre.

4. Calculate a new equilibrium with a new mutually consistent set of speeds, generalised costs and demands.

This last stage involves an iterative process of calculation because of the many interdependencies.

Suppose that in the free market equilibrium, as shown by Q_1 in Panel A of Figure 9.1, the uncharged road is carrying 100 vehicle-kilometres per hour and the time and money cost to the vehicle users amount to £0.10 per vehicle-kilometre. Then, to reflect external costs an additional charge of £0.03 per vehicle-kilometre is imposed. The demand relationship indicates that traffic must fall: by construction, the *last* vehicle onto the road was willing to pay a maximum of £0.10, so some traffic will be deterred by the new charge bringing the total cost to the user to £0.13. As the cost to users has been increased, the marginal private cost curve will shift inwards to the left, perhaps taking us to a point to the left of the socially efficient equilibrium, Q^* in Panel A of Figure 9.1, say to a traffic flow of 90.

But there is now less traffic and congestion will be less severe, so the £0.03 is now too high a charge to reflect the external costs imposed by each user on all the others. So the user charge should be reduced from £0.03 to, say, £0.025. The marginal private cost curve will shift back out to the right and traffic will increase, perhaps to a point to the right of the socially efficient equilibrium, say to 96, which is shown by Q in Panel A of Figure 9.1.

And so the process continues until it converges to point Q^* in Panel A of Figure 9.1, where traffic is, say, 95. At this point a new equilibrium is established in which the *last* vehicle onto the road is just willing to pay its own costs and the user charge and that user charge just balances the costs the *last* vehicle (and any other vehicle) imposes on society. Marginal private cost is now equal to marginal social cost at that traffic flow, and so each vehicle is paying the full marginal social cost of its decision to use the road, which is allocatively efficient.

A common mistake that students make is to assert that the charge, or the tax rate, should be set equal to the difference between the marginal private cost and the marginal social cost at the free-market output, Q_1. This is incorrect, and the exposition above demonstrates that it should be set equal to the difference between the two curves at the socially efficient output, Q^*.

Having found the equilibrium set of charges corresponding to the socially efficient equilibrium, this also yields estimates of the revised volumes of traffic and hence the changes to tax revenues and public transport costs, revenues and subsidies. Thus an estimate is produced of the overall net effect on the public finances.

At the new equilibrium traffic level, congestion and pollution have all fallen and the road-user charge has generated revenue. Road users generally are made worse off because they are either paying more or have been deterred from travelling. But it can be demonstrated that, in principle, there is more than enough revenue to compensate them so that everyone can end up better off: there has been a Pareto improvement. This is a reflection of the fact that the facility is being more efficiently used so that the overall economic value of the system is increased.

This is one reason for the crucial importance of the issue of what happens to the revenues from road-user charging. If, as may well be the case in practice, the revenues are not used to compensate those paying the charge in some way, then those groups will be disadvantaged. That is why the decision to legislate to ensure that London congestion charging proceeds must be applied to transport purposes in London was crucial to securing public support. At the very least, the net revenues must remain in the transport sector and in the relevant geographical area. At a national level charges can be returned by reducing vehicle excise duty (see below).

This desire to use net revenues to compensate the losers in the transition from one method of levying taxes for road use to that of another raises the issue of the costs of charge collection and enforcement. If they are too high there will not be enough net revenue left to compensate the losers, even in principle. The economic value created through efficient pricing would be more than consumed by the scheme administration.

This exposition is over-simplified because charged roads will be used by individuals with a range of values of time saving. When charges are introduced, those with the higher values will be more inclined to stay on the road, pay the charge and enjoy the benefit of higher speed. Therefore, the scarce and valuable resource, road space, is reallocated to those who gain the greater value from using it. This is a further source of allocative efficiency. Even without compensation, road users as a group may gain overall. There might also be economic welfare benefits that go beyond the benefits arising purely in the transport sector. For example, the overall costs of living in a congested area (say, the South-east of England) will be more closely matched by the costs the individuals that live there pay. Individuals can take more economically efficient decisions about where they live and where they locate their businesses.

Bus users will also benefit from higher speeds and greater reliability, and bus-operating companies will enjoy reduced operating costs. This will ultimately be reflected in lower demands for subsidy from the taxpayer.

Not surprisingly, a propensity to switch time of day makes an important difference to the outcomes of road-pricing. Time switching allows pricing to achieve a more efficient use of existing capacity by encouraging some trips out of the most congested times to periods when there is spare capacity. It also generates benefits by allowing those with the highest valuations of the peak capacity to use it and pay for it whilst those who do not mind switching so much can respond to the financial incentive to do so.

Similarly, quite modest propensity to increase average car occupancy (to *car share*) in response to road-pricing in congested conditions makes an important difference. The higher it is, the less the overall disbenefit to road users from road-user charging, the greater the environmental benefits, the less the revenues (because congestion is relieved with lower charges) and the greater the overall net benefit from the scheme.

16.4.2 The actual data of the analysis

A full presentation of the technicalities of the models and data sources is in Glaister and Graham (2003a). The data used came primarily from two sources.

- Detailed road traffic flow data were provided by the UK Department for Transport (DfT) and were used to create a *base* set of figures. The data represent flows of private cars, buses, LGVs, heavy goods vehicles and articulated goods vehicles. The data for private cars were further disaggregated by six journey purposes. England was divided into the nine English Government Office Regions, Wales and Scotland and the data were further divided by type of road, a variety of different urban and rural area types and 19 different times of the week.
- Public transport demand data were derived from published sources, principally *Transport Statistics for Great Britain* (DTRL 2001a) and *Regional Transport Statistics* (DTLR 2001b). Estimates for bus and rail passenger-kilometres by region and for average bus and rail fares paid were derived. Whilst bus fares varied by region, rail fares did not because satisfactory rail receipts data by region could not be secured. A national average was used for rail.

Since a primary objective of road-pricing is to reduce delays it was necessary to find a way to impute a money value to the time saved. There are well-established techniques, based, as usual, on the principle of estimating how much people would be willing to pay to enjoy the benefit. The detail of the methods developed over many years by the UK government, together with the recommended values, can be found on the Internet at www.webtag.org.uk. Vehicle-operating cost formulae can also be found there. These show how costs vary with vehicle type and speed.

For each road type and area type in the road traffic data there was information that facilitated the estimation of speeds. Speed–flow relationships are crucial to the computation of the costs of congestion because they represent the way that speeds reduce as traffic increases. The ones used by Glaister and Graham (2004) were suggested by the DfT.

For the private and social costs of vehicle trips, Glaister and Graham (2004) used the figures given in the study of road and rail transport costs in Britain by Sansom *et al.* (2001). They provide estimates of the external costs of road and rail travel specifying costs related to infrastructure operation, accidents, air pollution, noise and global warming. Some of the values used are shown in Table 16.1. Separate estimates are presented for different vehicle types, area types and infrastructure types. Glaister and Graham (2004) estimated the marginal social costs of congestion, computed numerically using the traffic data in conjunction with the speed–flow relationships.

The elasticities represent the propensities of the various types of traveller to change their volume of travel or to switch mode of travel in response to changes in travel costs and journey times. The elasticities used were derived from a variety of

Table 16.1 Road costs (pence per vehicle-kilometre), Great Britain, 1998 prices and values

Cost category	Low	High
Infrastructure operating costs and depreciation	0.42	0.54
Accident costs	0.82	1.40
Air pollution	0.34	1.70
Noise	0.02	0.05
Global Warming	0.15	0.62

Source: Sansom *et al.* (2001)

sources. Graham and Glaister (2002a; 2002b; 2004) provided a survey of evidence on price elasticities of car traffic and freight traffic. The most important of these was a long run elasticity of car traffic with respect to fuel price of −0.35. Bus elasticities were taken from Dargay and Hanly (1999) and rail elasticities from ATOC (2001). London-specific elasticities were provided by Grayling and Glaister (2002).

16.4.3 The limitations of the analysis

No model can be a complete and accurate representation of the real world: the whole point of modelling is to find a simplified representation which is easier to analyse and understand. In implementing the model, Glaister and Graham (2004) have used the best evidence they could find, but many simplifying assumptions were necessary and the approach does have important limitations: it is best thought of as a rough sketch of how things might turn out.

The model has no explicit transport network and makes no attempt to represent origin-to-destination trip patterns. Consequently, it is not possible to distinguish between changes in numbers of trips and changes in average trip length. The historically observed responses to changes in costs and prices (the elasticities) are measures of a combination of both phenomena.

The modelling works throughout in terms of costs and charges per vehicle-kilometre and average traffic flows (passenger car units per hour). The model is not capable of accurately representing certain types of charging schemes, such as workplace parking charges, cordon or area schemes. In cordon schemes, vehicles are charged at the moment they cross a cordon bounding a designated area and not for the distance they may travel inside the designated area. In area schemes, a vehicle is liable for a charge if it is used in the designated area at the designated times (whether or not it crosses a cordon), like the London scheme. Again, the charge may not be related to distance travelled. Proper modelling of these schemes requires a different approach at a finer grain of geographical detail.

The representation of public transport is less satisfactory than that for road travel. This is because the available public transport statistics are simply not as good as those that were available for road traffic.

The costs that are to be imputed for environmental damages such as air pollution and global warming are uncertain but they are important determinants of the pricing policies considered in this study. Glaister and Graham (2004) accept the estimates of Sansom *et al.* (2001) of the several external and environmental costs of transport, summarised in Table 16.1. They recognise that making these estimates is difficult and different people will come to different conclusions. They use values at the *low* and the *high* ends of the ranges to give an indication of how sensitive the policy conclusions might be to different assumptions made about the level of costs that should be imposed upon motorists in respect of environmental externalities. There are also some important factors that have not been, or cannot be, quantified. Some of these omitted factors may be detrimental to the environment or create social costs, for example severance of communities by roads. Others are beneficial or create social benefits; for example, better accessibility to family, leisure pursuits or employment opportunities. It is not apparent that they have necessarily either under-estimated or over-estimated the external costs and benefits of transport.

As a simplification, the modelling in the remainder of this study abstracts from the complication of future growth and analyses the way road-user charging policies might have looked had year 2000 conditions been imposed on them.

16.4.4 Adding user charges to existing taxes (revenue additional scheme)

Glaister and Graham (2004) have modelled a range of road-user charging policies. These include *revenue raising* and *revenue neutral* charging options and economically efficient pricing. More detailed results and in-depth discussion can be found in their other works (2003a, 2003b) and (2003).

Table 16.2 shows the extent of the change in usage of different modes of transport, arising from the imposition of congestion charges followed by changes in costs and subsidies. The transport usage figures are defined as ratios so that 0.5, for example, would illustrate that usage had reduced by 50 per cent.

Table 16.3 Column (1) shows an estimate of the total reduction in environmental costs as a result of the user-charging policy. Column (2) shows benefits accruing to car, bus and rail passengers and to road freight operators (the total of charges paid net of any benefits such as faster journey times arising from the reduced traffic flow). Column (5) shows the direct revenue gain to the Exchequer in terms of the user charges net of any rebates paid to vehicle users. There are additional financial implications for the Exchequer. It is assumed that changes in bus and rail subsidies ultimately pass to the Exchequer in full (a positive number in columns (3) and (4) indicates a reduction in subsidy) and there are changes in fuel tax receipts (above changes in VAT on fuel) because of changes in the volume of fuel purchased (column 7). Column (8) summarises the overall Exchequer position.

First Glaister and Graham (2004) take current fuel duty and other charges as fixed at today's level and assume that new road-user charges are *additional* to them. It is assumed that charges are added to reflect the environmental costs of road use only. Then they consider the impact of road-user charging when an element reflecting the cost of congestion is added.

Table 16.2 Result of adding charges to existing taxes: England, 2000 traffic levels

Scenario	Traffic	All passenger-kilometres	Car-kilometres	Commercial vehicle-kilometres	Bus passenger-kilometres	Rail passenger-kilometres	Car cost (£/km)	Bus subsidy (£m p.a.)	Bus fare (ex London) (% change)	Rail subsidy (£m p.a.)	Rail fare (% change)
		Ratio of flow to the current value									
Current (2003)	1	1	1	1	1	1	0.104	1408	–	1597	–
				Low environmental costs							
Environmental charge	0.94	0.95	0.95	0.94	1.014	1.015	0.116	1403	0	1547	0
Environmental charge plus congestion charge	0.91	0.92	0.91	0.90	1.07	1.02	0.132	1358	0	1520	0
				High environmental costs							
Environmental charge plus congestion charge	0.81	0.87	0.82	0.77	1.09	1.06	0.152	1390	0	1447	0

Table 16.3 Economic evaluation: adding charges to existing taxes (£b p.a., 2003 prices): England, 2000 traffic levels

Scenario	Saving in environmental cost	Passenger and freight benefit	Reduction in bus subsidy	Reduction in rail subsidy	Environmental tax, congestion charge revenue & rebates	Net benefit	Tax revenue correction	Net gain to the Exchequer	Benefits net of all costs to the Exchequer	Weighted average marginal congestion costs (£/vehicle-km)
Column reference	(1)	(2)	(3)	(4)	(5)	(6) = (1 + 2 + 3 + 4 + 5)	(7)	(8) = (3 + 4 + 5 + 7)	(9) = (1 + 2 + 8) = (1 + 2 + 3 + 4 + 5 + 7)	
					Low environmental costs					
Environmental charge	0.54	−4.66	0.01	0.05	5.8	1.7	−1.3	4.56	0.4	0.080
Environmental charge plus congestion charge	0.91	−7.99	0.05	0.08	11.9	4.9	−2.2	9.83	2.8	0.075
					High environmental costs					
Environmental charge plus congestion charge	5.04	−15.57	0.05	0.18	19.13	8.83	−4.36	15.0	4.47	0.082

16.4.4.1 Environmental charges only

Under this policy an additional charge is made to reflect environmental costs alone (which depend somewhat on vehicle type and location). There are no congestion charges and low environmental costs are assumed to determine the charge. In this case, where user charging is added to existing road taxes and charge, traffic and travel are reduced by 5 and 6 per cent respectively. There is some increase in bus and rail travel.

Table 16.3 shows an environmental cost saving of about £0.5 billion per annum and an increase in the Exchequer revenues of about £4.5 billion per annum. This illustrates how a charge can be used to address concerns about environmental damage. Of course, the critical issue is the set of estimates used for the per-vehicle-kilometre environmental damage costs. But it is not the case, of course, that the existence of environmental damage should lead policy towards reducing traffic at all costs, unless one believes that the environmental costs are unbounded. Note that the environmental charges also achieve benefits through reducing congestion because they reduce overall traffic flow.

16.4.4.2 Environmental charges and congestion charges

Glaister and Graham (2004) now make a further addition of a charge to fully reflect the incremental congestion cost that each vehicle inflicts on all others. In this scenario every type of road user bears an additional charge per vehicle-kilometre matching the estimated environmental damage it causes and a congestion charge corresponding to the total congestion costs that each additional vehicle-kilometre imposes on all other traffic.

Table 16.3 shows that using the low environmental damage costs to determine the charges, this set of charges would yield extra direct revenue of £11.9 billion per annum, some improvement of bus and rail finances and an overall increase in the Exchequer position of £9.8 billion per annum.

In some congested places the charges are high and the reduction of traffic is substantial. But in many places and for much of the time there is little congestion so the increase in charges is only the relatively small environmental tax. The net result is that this level of charges, which reflect all the costs of road use, can be achieved with a reduction of only 9 per cent in overall traffic levels, indicating the extent to which congestion is a localised problem.

Figure 16.2 shows a map of how the traffic changes vary across the country with a revenue additional scheme. It should be noted that the results reported in Tables 16.2 and 16.3 relate to England and to 2000 traffic levels, taken from Glaister and Graham (2004); whereas Figure 16.2 relates to England, Wales and Scotland and to 2010 traffic levels, taken from Glaister and Graham (2006).

In the Greater London Area the inner and outer areas are a shade darker than the central area. This feature is also to be found in the maps in the work by Glaister and Graham illustrating other policy scenarios. It indicates that traffic congestion and the benefits of congestion charging are greater in

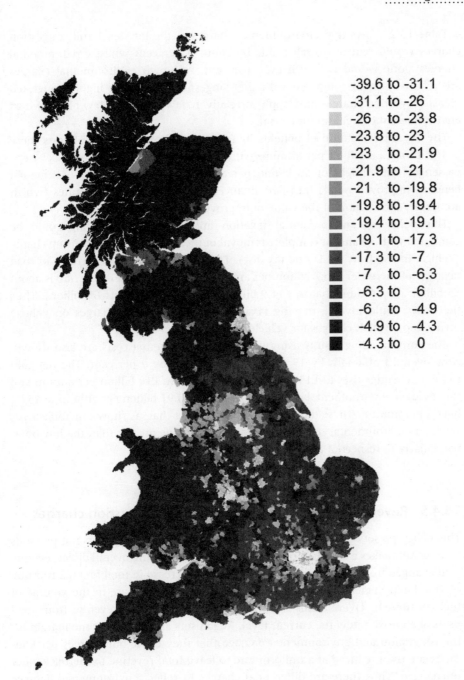

-39.6 to -31.1
-31.1 to -26
-26   to -23.8
-23.8 to -23
-23   to -21.9
-21.9 to -21
-21   to -19.8
-19.8 to -19.4
-19.4 to -19.1
-19.1 to -17.3
-17.3 to -7
-7   to -6.3
-6.3 to -6
-6   to -4.9
-4.9 to -4.3
-4.3 to   0

Figure 16.2 Average percentage traffic changes by census ward: Great Britain, 2010 (revenue additional)

those inner and outer areas than in the central area where congestion charging was actually introduced in February 2003. This reflects the common experience of London conditions and it does suggest that, if a way can be found to achieve it, the strongest case in England for congestion charging would be inner (as opposed to central) London, or possibly the whole of the Greater London Area.

Table 16.2 shows that environmental charges at the low level and congestion charges would reduce overall traffic by about 9 per cent whilst environmental charges alone would reduce it by 6 per cent. Although environmental charges are relatively small compared with the congestion charges in highly congested areas, congestion charges only apply at relatively few times in a few places whilst environmental charges are universal.

The overall evaluation of benefits in Table 16.3 shows that net of costs there is a gain of £2.8 billion per annum, with the overall disbenefit to vehicle users, passengers and freight of £8 billion per annum being offset by environmental benefits, improved public transport finances and increased tax revenues (which are largely a reflection of the value of improved travel conditions).

This policy of environmental taxation and congestion charging could be combined with an almost complete removal of the annual vehicle licensing charge (Vehicle Excise Duty, VED, the tax disc). That would leave a net increase of road taxation of the order of £7 billion per annum because total VED revenue is about £5 billion per annum (that is, £11.9 billion in Table 16.3 minus £5 billion). Thus the policy could involve moving taxation away from fixed charges on vehicle ownership towards charges for vehicle use.

The corresponding results using the high environmental costs are also shown. Now overall traffic falls by 19 per cent rather than by 9 per cent. The net gain to the Exchequer rises to £15 billion per annum from £10 billion per annum and the saving in environmental costs increases from £0.91 billion per annum to £5.04 billion per annum. These differences reflect the fact that, as shown in Table 16.3, the high environmental cost estimates are significantly greater than the low ones, particularly in respect of air pollution and global warming.

16.4.5   Revenue-neutral environmental and congestion charges

This policy preserves the same structure of taxes and charges as in the previous section, but makes a rebate per vehicle-kilometre so that the overall direct revenue is unchanged from today's level (and there is an increase in total fuel tax revenue of £0.6 billion per annum because there is an overall increase in the volume of fuel consumed). Overall, this has the effect of maintaining revenue from road users at approximately the current level. Road users are charged at the margin for the congestion and environmental damage that they cause but charges per kilometre are then reduced at a uniform rate to leave total revenue to the Exchequer unchanged. Thus there are differential charges to reflect environmental damage and congestion because the rebate paid to motorists is based only on total distance travelled. Glaister and Graham (2004) assume that VED is left unchanged.

The results are displayed in Figure 16.3. The effects are quantified in Tables 16.4 and 16.5. This scenario is particularly interesting in that it achieves a redistribution of traffic away from congested times and places and away from those areas where environmental damage is greatest, whilst leaving total tax revenues largely unchanged and accommodating a slight increase in overall traffic.

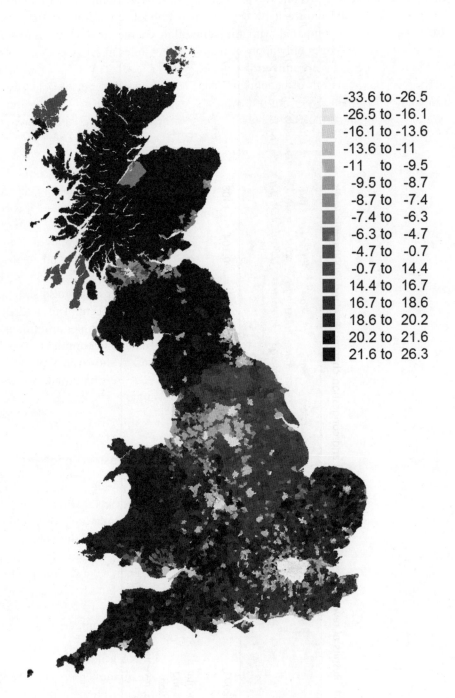

-33.6 to -26.5
-26.5 to -16.1
-16.1 to -13.6
-13.6 to -11
-11   to   -9.5
-9.5 to   -8.7
-8.7 to   -7.4
-7.4 to   -6.3
-6.3 to   -4.7
-4.7 to   -0.7
-0.7 to 14.4
14.4 to 16.7
16.7 to 18.6
18.6 to 20.2
20.2 to 21.6
21.6 to 26.3

Figure 16.3 Average percentage traffic changes by census ward: Great Britain, 2010 (revenue neutral)

Table 16.4 Results of revenue-neutral environmental and congestion charges: England, 2000 traffic levels

Scenario	Traffic						Car cost (£/km)	Bus subsidy (£m p.a.)	Bus fare (ex London) (% change)	Rail subsidy (£m p.a.)	Rail fare (% change)
		All passenger-kilometres	Car-kilometres	Commercial vehicle-kilometres	Bus passenger-kilometres	Rail passenger-kilometres					
		Ratio of flow to the current value									
Current (2003)	1	1	1	1	1	1	0.104	1408	–	1597	–
					Low environmental costs						
Environmental charges and congestion charges, revenue neutral	1.01	1.04	1.01	1.01	1.05	0.99	0.103	1371	0	1633	0

Table 16.5 Economic evaluation: revenue-neutral environmental and congestion charges (£b p.a., 2003 prices), England, 2000 traffic levels

Scenario	Saving in environmental cost	Passenger and freight benefit	Reduction in bus subsidy	Reduction in rail subsidy	Environmental tax, congestion charge revenue & rebates	Net benefit	Tax revenue correction	Net gain to the Exchequer	Benefits net of all costs to the Exchequer	Weighted average marginal congestion costs (£/vehicle-km)
Column reference	(1)	(2)	(3)	(4)	(5)	(6) = (1+2+ 3+4+5)	(7)	(8) = (3+4+ 5+7)	(9) = (1+2+8) = (1+2+3+ 4+5+7)	
				Low environmental charges						
Environmental charges and congestion charges, revenue neutral	0.28	0.88	0.04	−0.04	0	1.2	0.6	0.6	1.8	0.068

Table 16.4 shows how the overall effect on traffic volume is broadly neutral. There is, of course, a considerable dispersion about the average. Whilst many cases (that is, times and places) would experience only a small increase or decrease in traffic, there are substantial numbers that would enjoy a 20 or 30 per cent reduction, the more congested times and urban areas, and substantial numbers that would experience 10–15 per cent increases, the less congested times and rural areas. The drivers in these latter areas would benefit from the rebate designed to ensure revenue neutrality but would pay very low user charges. The overall effect on commercial vehicles is less variable than that on private cars, but it is interesting to note that the lighter classes of commercial vehicle are more likely to enjoy a cost reduction than the heavy, articulated lorries. This is because the heaviest vehicles, which consume a great deal of fuel, suffer more from the environmental charge and also use the more congested roads on average. There is a broadly neutral overall effect on rail travel with small reductions at many times and places balanced by larger increases over a wide range of times and places. There is an overall 5 per cent increase in bus travel.

Figure 16.3 shows the geographical distribution of traffic reduction. Traffic is reduced greatest in the big conurbations and it increases most in the country areas most notably in the North of England. Much of the central part of England outside the big cities experiences little traffic volume change. The big cities enjoy a substantial speed improvement. Interestingly, many of the places that have the biggest traffic volume increase (such as the North of England) have little or no speed reduction, because they are areas with spare capacity and therefore little congestion. Thus many motorists will have a substantial speed improvement, there will be very little reduction in traffic speeds in other areas and motorists as a whole are not financially worse off. The redistribution of traffic from congested to non-congested areas, facilitated by this charging scheme has clear economic benefits. This scenario illustrates the proposition that at today's overall rates of fuel tax motorists in city areas are under-charged for the congestion and environmental damage they cause, whilst those in country areas are significantly over-charged.

From Table 16.5 we see that, compared with the policy that is not tax revenue-neutral the overall net economic benefit is reduced from £2.8 to £1.8 billion per annum. This is mainly because traffic is reduced less so there are fewer environmental benefits. The rebate ensures that many motorists are not quite paying the full marginal social cost of making journeys, although if the rebate were in a different form (for example, through reducing vehicle excise duty) the overall economic benefits would be greater. However, the use of the per-passenger-kilometre rebate has the advantage of leaving passengers and freight users as a whole better off by £0.9 billion per annum, whilst generating a small improvement to the Exchequer finances. Further, the costs arising from the pressure to provide more road capacity would be significantly reduced.

Thus, here we have a set of road-user charges that are clearly not optimal from an economic point of view. Road-user charges that reflect all the costs of road use are imposed. However, existing charges are retained, which should not happen in an optimal system, and a uniform rebate is offered, which also should not happen in an optimal system. Nevertheless, even with this system, there are considerable economic benefits. If politicians feel the need to buy off affected groups through other tax changes, even if this undermines some of the economic objectives of the policy, there can still be considerable economic benefits compared with the current situation.

16.4.6 Fully efficient taxes and subsidies

The current set of taxes has developed over the decades and has no economic rationale. There is no reason to expect that the total tax revenue over and above that which would result from the standard rates levied on other sectors of the economy has any justification in terms of external costs. The various taxes imposed upon motorists have not been developed to ensure that the total costs of motoring reflect the marginal social cost of vehicle use. In this section we look at the derivation of a set of taxes and subsidies built upon fundamental economic principles that has been conducted by Glaister and Graham (2004).

From Tables 16.6 and 16.7 we see that if environmental charges are set at a low level, compared with today's levels it costs the Exchequer £7.9 billion per annum in rebates of fuel duty, and so on, and overall Exchequer revenues are reduced by £3.8 billion per annum after considering the revenue from user charges. Traffic increases by 12 per cent, private car use by 6 per cent and commercial vehicles use by 16 per cent. The subsidy to the bus industry falls from £1408 to £793 million per annum and that for the rail industry falls from £1597 to £914 million per annum. Overall, as shown in Table 16.7, there is a benefit to passengers and freight of £6.8 billion per annum, although there is an environmental damage cost of £0.4 billion per annum.

These results illustrate the proposition that, on these assumptions, if charges were to be set in accordance with economic efficiency principles, rather than continuing charges that have come about largely by historical accident, then road users might pay less than they do today. Average monetary costs per car-kilometre would fall from 10.4 pence to 9.3 pence and there would be a net increase in economic efficiency. Indeed, there would be a general increase in traffic speeds which would be substantial in some areas. The impacts on traffic speeds and volumes are far from equally distributed geographically. Traffic is reduced in areas where vehicles impose a high marginal cost currently and increased in other areas. The redistribution of traffic is one aspect of the increased economic efficiency from this set of charges.

In Tables 16.6 and 16.7 it is shown that the outcome would be different if the high environmental costs are focused upon. Rather than a net loss to the Exchequer of £3.8 billion per annum there would be a net gain of £4.61 billion. Of course, this reflects the more aggressive stance towards charging for environmental effects: there is an estimated environmental gain of £1.6 billion per annum against the current base compared with a £0.4 billion per annum loss using this set of charging principles but with low environmental costs. Average monetary costs per car-kilometre would rise from 10.4 pence to 11 pence.

Therefore, in terms of this model, the answer to the question 'were road users paying too much or too little in the early twenty-first century?' depends

Table 16.6 Fully efficient taxes and subsidies: England, 2000 traffic levels

Scenario	Traffic	All passenger-kilometres	Car-kilometres	Commercial vehicle-kilometres	Bus passenger-kilometres	Rail passenger-kilometres	Car cost (£/km)	Bus subsidy (£m p.a.)	Bus fare (ex London) (% change)	Rail subsidy (£m p.a.)	Rail fare (% change)
				Ratio of flow to the current value*							
Current (2003)	1	1	1	1	1	1	0.104	1408	–	1597	–
				Low environmental costs							
Efficient environmental charges and congestion charges	1.12	1.06	1.09	1.16	1.12	0.67	0.093	793	+20	914	+80
				High environmental costs							
Efficient environmental charges and congestion charges	1.01	0.98	1.0	1.0	1.14	0.69	0.111	783	+20	807	+80

* For example, a ratio of 1.2 would normally be interpreted as a 20 per cent increase and a ratio of 0.94 as a 6 per cent reduction.

Table 16.7 Economic evaluation: Fully efficient taxes and subsidies (£b p.a., 2003 prices), England, 2000 traffic levels

Scenario	Saving in environmental cost	Passenger and freight benefit	Reduction in bus subsidy	Reduction in rail subsidy	Environmental tax, congestion charge revenue & rebates	Net benefit	Tax revenue correction	Net gain to the Exchequer	Benefits net of all costs to the Exchequer	Weighted average marginal congestion costs (£/vehicle-km.)
Column reference	(1)	(2)	(3)	(4)	(5)	(6) = (1+2+ 3+4+5)	(7)	(8) = (3+4+ 5+7)	(9) = (1+2+8) = (1+2+3+ 4+5+7)	
				Low environmental costs						
Efficient, environmental charges and congestion charges	−0.40	6.81	0.62	0.68	−7.9	−0.2	+2.8	−3.80	2.6	0.062
				High environmental costs						
Efficient environmental charges and congestion charges	1.60	−1.92	0.63	0.77	3.03	4.11	+0.18	4.61	4.29	0.065

upon what view is taken about where the *correct* environmental charges lie. Nevertheless, whichever set of environmental charges are deemed appropriate, there are economic benefits from changing the charging structure for motorists.

It is also worth noting that, although the simulations have not been done for this case, it would appear that using a mid-range estimate for the environmental costs would probably produce a set of charges that are approximately revenue neutral. Whilst not having any particular economic significance, it may be of political significance that a change in the structure of road-user charges could, in fact, be engineered so that it is approximately revenue neutral yet, at the same time, brings about significant economic advantages.

In the future, when there will have been traffic growth, the average congestion charges, and the revenues they generate, will be higher.

16.5 | How widely should charging be implemented?

It is easy to see that there may well be a case for considering a scheme that does not attempt to cover the whole country. As a charging scheme is extended progressively to less dense areas, the administrative costs are likely to rise whilst the traffic affected and the economically efficient prices that traffic should pay, and hence the revenue, are likely to rise much less rapidly.

The issue of initial investment and ongoing administration costs is crucial, as illustrated by the experience with the scheme introduced in London in February 2003. A substantial part of the revenues are consumed by the capital and operating costs of the scheme. This does not necessarily mean that the London scheme is not worthwhile, but it does suggest that a sensible scheme covering a wider and less congested area would have to have much lower costs if it were to remain worthwhile.

The spread of costs and economies of scale will depend on the technology used. This in turn will have implications for the coverage. With camera-based technology the case for limited geographical coverage may be stronger than with technology involving satellite-based geographical positioning systems. With the latter, the marginal cost of extending the charging area to cover areas with less dense traffic may be considerably reduced, even though cameras and other roadside equipment will be essential in support of any satellite-based system and for enforcement.

16.6 | The case for building more road capacity

For a variety of reasons Conservative and Labour governments alike have found it difficult to construct new road capacity, despite the fact that any conventional appraisal demonstrates that some road schemes offer unbeatable value for public money. Suppose a proper system of national road-pricing is put in place; would there still be an argument for building new road capacity? Clearly, the demands would be less, because the prices are designed to reduce the demand to match the available capacity at the peak times.

In the present system, prices charged for use of the system, the level of capacity provided and the sources of funding are all decided independently of one another under a centralised, administered system. But for a rationally managed infrastructure enterprise these three things should be determined simultaneously. If *proper* road-pricing were in place then the revenues generated by any piece of road infrastructure in relation to the costs of providing extra capacity would provide a clear signal about the justification for making the expansion.

Current research aims to estimate the costs of expanding capacity under certain circumstances and then to throw light on the extent to which new capacity might be justified if road-pricing were in place.

16.7 | Issues to be resolved to make road-pricing a practical national policy

What would be the relative roles of national and local government in deciding precisely which roads should be charged; at what times of day the charges would apply; what rates should be charged; how charge collection should be enforced; who should be accountable for the revenues; and who should be responsible for how those revenues should be spent? One view is that *national* implies that all of these things would become the responsibility of Whitehall, just as, in essence, they are now. It seems more likely that considerable powers and discretion would be left with local government in view of the large amounts of money involved; the bitterness of road users concerning the mismatch between what they currently pay through duties and the government expenditure on roads; the general lack of trust that the electorate now has in government promises on the new systems of taxation and charging; and the general move towards devolution of powers away from Whitehall.

But if, in a national scheme, local authorities are left in control of substantial amounts of road-charging revenues, consideration of the local government finance regime will be inevitable. What adjustments should be made to the grants made by Whitehall to local authorities if they start to collect this new money? This question would be particularly acute under a revenue-neutral package because large city regions would stand to lose several billions of pounds a year. On the other hand, if the city regions were allowed the use of a substantial part of these revenues, they could become a crucial contribution towards the portfolio of new locally generated incomes that devolutionists see as vital to the future democratic viability of city regions (see Glaister, Travers and Wakefield, 2004 and Travers and Glaister, 2006).

But this raises another issue: are the current local governance arrangements appropriate? The geographical coverage of a sensible road-pricing scheme must correspond to a suitable set of traffic patterns. Apart from Greater London, few local authorities are suitably configured. It was only possible to introduce congestion charging in London because the directly elected mayor can be held to account for the charges, the budgeting is transparent and the net revenues are manifestly applied for transport purposes within the authority.

There are several possibilities to deal with this. Perhaps trunk roads and motorways could be handled by Whitehall under arrangements similar to the present Highways Authority. These are strategic roads, many of them with serious congestion problems, and the more important ones may not fall naturally to any local authority. But the vast majority of roads could be administered by local highway authorities. The government is discussing the possibility of replicating the London system in other city regions and that could solve the problem in those regions. A less radical change would be to capitalise on the existence of the Passenger Transport Authorities (see Travers and Glaister, 2006). When first created in 1968 they were envisioned as powerful bodies responsible for passenger transport in the metropolitan areas. But over the years their power has diminished. They could be reinvigorated as all-embracing transport authorities with such highways powers as they would need in order to implement road-pricing. New authorities might be created to serve cities such as Bristol, Southampton and Portsmouth.

Other solutions could have the advantage of removing these decisions from national and local politics and establishing the required trust of those who would be paying the charges. One would be to create public trusts – as with the US Federal roads, some British ports and the institutions that funded many roads in the first place – which would be legally accountable for the revenues and for spending them in accordance with defined objectives. Once properly priced, roads would be little different from other infrastructure utilities such as gas, water and electricity. It would be possible to think in terms of creating a similar regulatory regime.

Successful introduction of national road-pricing would have profound implications for other areas of government policy although there is no sign that these are being considered. Although the effect on public transport patronage would not be great at the national level, it could be an issue in certain local markets. Buses would need to carry more people, but would gain capacity because of higher road speeds. The passenger demand for railways in the commuter markets in London and other big cities would be increased. But these are situations where crowding is already severe. Conversely, if a revenue-neutral package made road use cheaper in rural areas, then the competitive position of railways and other public transport would be further weakened in markets where they are already weak.

Planning and land use policy would also be affected. Some planning policies are used to prevent excessive road congestion, for instance restrictions on new shopping centres. If congestion had been dealt with directly by road-pricing then this motive for planning restrictions would fall away. In the long term road-pricing would inevitably affect densities because the costs of transport are one of the main determinants of density. Those parts of government seeking to influence densities should have an interest in the policy on road-pricing.

Would road-pricing be *fair*? This issue is discussed in Glaister and Graham (2006). Who might gain and who might lose plainly depends crucially on a number of characteristics of the policy. In the case of a revenue-additional policy, road users as a group would be worse off. If these revenues were returned to the local communities from which they came then road-pricing could lead to important overall gains for the communities, though the net effect on road users or transport users generally clearly depends upon what the money is spent on. As long as the costs of collection do not consume too much of the revenues, there would be a new and significant stream of annual income that local authorities could use either for revenue support or to service borrowing. That could be used for capital finance for some of the items they cannot fund presently.

The revenue-neutral policy would generate somewhat less overall net benefit. But it would make road users as a whole better off because the revenues are returned to them and the road network is more efficiently used. A major feature of the revenue-neutral policy is that it would transfer considerable sums of money from urban areas to rural areas, particularly from London. Unless compensation is made, such as a change in the local government finance regime, the residents of the urban areas would, as a group, be made worse off. Since a majority of the population lives in or near the urban areas, a consequence could be that a large number of people would be made worse off and a small number would be made better off.

These average calculations need to be treated with caution because they conceal important variations. For instance, under a revenue-neutral scenario, car users in urban areas at un-congested times would be paying less, even though, averaged across the week, car users in urban areas are paying more. The revenue-neutral proposal has important presentational attractions. However, there would be no net revenue to defray the costs of the scheme or to spend on the "complementary measures" that are important in winning general support.

The revenue-additional policy does more to reduce accidents, fuel consumption and vehicle emissions because, in effect, it increases the average monetary cost of using roads compared with the revenue-neutral policy.

To what extent would road-pricing benefit disadvantaged people? To represent spatial variation in disadvantage, Glaister and Graham (2006) use the deprivation measures which form the components of the official Indices of Deprivation. Road-pricing would definitely involve higher average charge rates in large urban areas where there are also concentrations of deprivation, so they had expected to find a relationship between the rates of charge and the levels of deprivation. There is indeed such a relationship, but across England as a whole it is not a very marked one. This is because high deprivation is to be found in most types of area, in the remote parts of the country as well as in the large urban areas.

Employment, housing and education deprivation all show a significant positive relationship with traffic change. Thus wards showing high deprivation on these measures will, other things being equal, tend to have smaller traffic reductions, because of smaller price increases. Indeed, in the case of the revenue-neutral policy they are more likely to enjoy price reductions. To the extent that reduced travel costs by car are helpful in mitigating these types of deprivation road-pricing will be less damaging on these measures than on the other measures of deprivation.

Not everybody is a car user and those that are not would stand to benefit from the clearer roads and improved bus services. Car use in London is much lower than the national average because of the superior public transport. But road charges would, on average, be substantially higher in London.

This case study has illustrated that basic microeconomic principles are helpful in analysing problems that affect many people's daily lives. They can point to ways of improving things. But economics is not enough. Few politicians understand or care about pure economic theory, important though it is. To influence improvements in real policy one has to be willing to understand and debate technological and engineering realities and also the *political economy* of the situation.

The Future

Concluding Remarks 17

17.1 The major challenges ahead

The transport sector has undergone large-scale change over the last century. The single most significant change has been the revolution on the roads. Since the Second World War the volume of traffic on European roads has increased at an astounding rate. As well as this, a second, perhaps equally significant, change has begun in Europe – the revolution of the skies. Only two decades ago air travel was the exclusive domain of the affluent. Now there are over 80 low-cost airlines in Europe, opening up air travel to the masses.

As incomes rise, both of these trends are set to continue into the foreseeable future. As the volumes of traffic on the roads and also of passengers passing through airports continue to rise, two major problems are going to increase in severity. The first is that of pollution and the second is that of congestion. Both of these negative externalities will need to be addressed if society is to maximise the welfare of the population, both now and in the future.

Up until recently, European airlines have largely been exempt from environmental regulations. This has been rectified by their incorporation into the European Carbon Trading Scheme, but this will need to be reviewed to cope with the environmental effects that the growth of the airline market is likely to cause. However, it is the growth of road traffic that is likely to cause the most serious environmental damage. This is especially true as increasing conventional oil prices will lead to a shift towards synfuel, which causes greater environmental damage in its production. Authorities need to use economic policies to increase the marginal private costs of driving so that they are in line with the marginal social costs it creates, thereby internalising the negative externalities it generates. Authorities also need to act immediately if the worst damages, such as those of global warming, are to be avoided.

Increasing congestion on European roads and at European airports will lead to increasing time costs of transport, which on the roads is also likely to increase the risks of accidents. It has been realised by authorities that the solution is not simply building more capacity; a policy which has been relied on in the past. In a similar way to tackling environmental damage, authorities need to implement policies that will bring the marginal private costs of travel in line with the marginal social costs it creates. In road transport, the solution appears to lie with road-pricing schemes, which will inevitably become more numerous across the European Union.

17.2 Other trends

The growth of the low-cost airlines is likely to continue unless there is a dramatic change in taxation policy towards the airlines. Rather than using the heavily congested main international hub airports, such as London Heathrow, these airlines have been exploiting the opportunities offered by the smaller airports along the periphery of European cities. This behaviour is likely to continue, leading to the airlines almost joining the dots between these smaller airports across the continent.

Shipping has always been an important part of the European transport system, accounting for 90 per cent of the goods imported into the European Union. There are currently no signs that this is likely to change as shipping still has significant advantages compared to airfreight.

The inland waterways are still heavily employed in freight transport in some European countries, the Netherlands and France in particular. In the UK, where networks of canals were first constructed for industrial purposes, the usage of the canals has all but ceased because of decisions made regarding their construction in the second half of the nineteenth century. There have been signs recently that UK producers are beginning to turn to the inland waterways again, but there are serious doubts as to whether this is the start of a significant and continued trend.

17.3 Words of perceived wisdom

Over the last quarter of the twentieth century, the market failure in the European transport sector that has been focused on the most has been that of market power. There has been a determined effort, by both individual national governments and the European Commission, to promote competition throughout the sector in order to reap the efficiency gains it promises. This has led to widespread deregulation and privatisation. This battle has largely been won and so the focus of transport policy needs to shift towards that of correcting the growing market failure of negative externalities.

History clearly demonstrates that policies always have unintended, and perhaps unforeseen, effects. The Railway Mania in the UK that led to infrastructure that would be unsuitable for modern locomotives at the end of the twentieth century and the narrow construction of British canals that would lead to their industrial demise are just two examples of this. Policy-makers need to be careful to consider all of the possible effects of their decisions, or of the decisions that they do not make, and to assess all of the policy options fully. This requires the techniques of cost–benefit analysis to be further developed and refined. This should be a priority for economists working within the field.

The future holds significant opportunities for the European population, and the transport sector is to play an important role in their realisation. The sector needs to be guided carefully to ensure that it helps social welfare to be maximised, and so the role of transport economists is just as important now as it has ever been.

Mathematical Appendix

M.1 | A straight-line demand curve

As explained in Section 3.2, there are many determinants of transport demand. Mathematically this means that demand is a function of these factors, which is represented by

$$Q_d = f\,(P,\,Y,\,P_s,\,P_c,\,R,\,S\,...)$$

where Q_d is the quantity demanded of the product, P is the price of the product, Y is the income of consumers, P_s is the price of substitute products, P_c is the price of complementary products, R is the reliability of the product and S is the speed of the product.

These are a few of the main likely determinants, but in reality there are many more that should perhaps also be included.

For simplicity, this can be shortened to solely include the price of the product, with the other variables held constant, so that it can then be plotted on a diagram with price and quantity space; or in other words, with these as the axes. An example equation for a straight-line demand curve is shown below, where the number 30 is the vertical intercept and –2 is the gradient. This means that at zero price there will be 30 units of the product demanded and that, as the price increases, the quantity demand falls, in accordance with the law of demand:

$$Q_d = f(P)$$

$$Q_d = 30 - 2P$$

This is written so that the price is the independent variable and quantity demanded is the dependent variable, meaning that it should be plotted with price along the horizontal axis and quantity along the vertical axis. This is how the true demand curve should be drawn but it is not the form that economists use, as it is more informative to have price as the dependent variable along the vertical axis. To obtain this, it is necessary to calculate the inverse demand curve, which is generally termed 'the demand curve' by economists and throughout the main body of this text for simplicity. This transformation for the example above is shown as follows:

$$2P = 30 - Q_d$$

$$P = 15 - 0.5Q_d$$

A straight-line demand curve can, therefore, be written in the form of the equation:

$$P = x - yQ$$

where x is the vertical intercept and y is the gradient.

Any change in the price of a product causes a movement along the demand curve and so the quantity demanded changes. A change in any of the other determinants causes a shift of the demand curve and so can be modelled mathematically by a change in the intercept value.

M.2 | A straight-line supply curve

The same analysis applies to the supply curve. The supply of a product is also a factor of a range of variables and so can be represented by the following equation:

$$Q_s = f(P, C, \pi_a, N, G ...)$$

where Q_s is the quantity supplied of the product, P is the price of the product, C is the cost of the necessary factors of production, π_a is the profitability of alternative products that could be produced with the same factors of production, N is the number of producers in the market and G is the government spending or taxation.

Again, in reality, many more determinants should perhaps be included.

As with demand, this can be simplified so that supply is only a function of price, thereby holding all the other determinants constant. This gives the supply curve which can then be inverted so that price is the dependent variable and quantity supplied is the independent variable. An example of this is shown, in which the gradient and the vertical intercept are simply assumed:

$$Q_s = f(P)$$

$$Q_s = 2P - 10$$

$$2P = Q_s + 10$$

$$P = 5 + 0.5Q_s$$

A straight-line supply curve can, therefore, be formulated by

$$P = w + zQ$$

where w is the vertical intercept and z is the gradient. The intercept and the gradient are both likely to be positive, the first because producers will produce zero units even at a positive price if it is below that required to earn normal profit, and the second because of the law of supply.

Any change in the price of the product causes a movement along the supply curve, and so the quantity supplied changes and a change in any of the other determinants will cause it to shift and so will cause the intercept value to change.

M.3 Equilibrium

With formulae for both the demand and the supply curves, it is possible to calculate the equilibrium price and quantities. In equilibrium, the quantity demanded will be equal to the quantity supplied and so the formulae are simultaneous equations. Solving these will generate the equilibrium market conditions. An example of this procedure, using the example demand and supply curves above, is worked out below:

$$Q_d = Q_s = Q$$

$$P = 15 - 0.5Q$$

$$P = 5 + 0.5Q$$

$$15 - 0.5Q = 5 + 0.5Q$$

$$Q = 10$$

$$P = 15 - (0.5 \times 10)$$

$$P = 15 - 5 = 10$$

In this example, therefore, the price is £10 and the quantity traded is 10 units. Checking this result in the supply curve formula proves that it is correct.

M.4 Substitute and complementary products

This analysis can be made slightly more complicated to involve substitute and complementary products. Two substitute products x and y will have demand curves in the following form, assuming that they are straight lines for simplicity:

$$Q_x = a - bP_x + cP_y$$

$$Q_y = d - eP_y - fP_x$$

The vertical intercepts are denoted by a and d; the coefficients of their own prices are denoted by b and e, and are negative because of the law of demand; and the coefficients of the price of the alternative product are denoted by c and f, and are positive because an increase in the price of one will cause an increase in the demand for the other.

It is possible to use such equations to calculate the equilibrium price and quantity for both products. This is first done by including the supply curve equations for both products and then rearranging them so that there is a single equation for the price of each product. This can be done, as in equilibrium the quantity demanded of each product will be equal to the respective quantity supplied (for example, the quantity demand of product x, Q_{dx}, will be equal to the quantity supplied of product x, Q_{sx}). These are then simultaneous equations that can be solved to calculate the equilibrium conditions for both. An example is worked out below:

Product x	Product y
$Q_{dx} = 50 - 2P_x + P_y$	$Q_{dy} = 200 - 5P_y + 4P_x$
$Q_{sx} = 10P_x - 20$	$Q_{sy} = 5P_y - 50$
Equalising these to create a simultaneous equation:	Equalising these to create a simultaneous equation:
$Q_{dx} = Q_{sx}$	$Q_{dy} = Q_{sy}$
$50 - 2P_x + P_y = 10P_x - 20$	$200 - 5P_y + 4P_x = 5P_y - 50$
$12P_x = 70 + P_y$	$10P_y = 250 + 4P_x$

$$12P_x = 70 + P_y$$

$$10P_y = 250 + 4P_x$$

$$10P_y = 250 + 4P_x$$

$$P_y = 25 + 0.4P_x$$

$$12P_x = 70 + P_y$$

$$12P_x = 70 + 25 + 0.4P_x$$

$$11.6P_x = 95$$

$$P_x = 8.19$$

$$12P_x = 70 + P_y$$

$$12 \times 8.19 = 70 + P_y$$

$$P_y = 28.28$$

$$Q_{dx} = 50 - 2P_x + P_y$$

$$Q_{dx} = 50 - (2 \times 8.19) + 28.28$$

$$Q_{dx} = 61.9$$

$$Q_{dy} = 200 - 5P_y + 4P_x$$

$$Q_{dy} = 200 - (5 \times 28.28) + (4 \times 8.19)$$

$$Q_{dy} = 91.36$$

Checking these results in the supply equations of the two products proves that they are correct. The price in the market for product x will be £8.19 and 62 units will be traded; and in the market for product y the price will be £28.28 and 91 units will be traded.

M.5 | Elasticities

In Section 3.4.1 of the text, the general formulae for calculating elasticities were outlined. However, there are actually two mathematical approaches to calculating them. There is the calculation of point elasticity and then that of arc elasticity.

M.5.1 Point elasticity

This is the calculation of elasticity at a specific point on the demand or supply curve or indeed on the income expansion path (when calculating income elasticity of demand).

Given a demand curve of the form

$$P = a - bQ$$

The point elasticity of demand (P_{ed}) can be calculated for any point P_1 and Q_1 by

$$P_{ed} = \frac{\Delta Q}{\Delta P} \frac{P_1}{Q_1}$$

This can be rewritten as

$$P_{ed} = \frac{1}{-b} \frac{P_1}{Q_1} \text{ because } \frac{\Delta Q}{\Delta P} = \frac{1}{-b}$$

The point elasticity depends solely on the price, P, and the vertical intercept, a. This is shown by rearranging the initial demand equation and then dividing through by $1/-b$:

$$P = a - bQ$$

$$-bQ = P - a$$

$$P_{ed} = \frac{1}{-b} \frac{P}{Q} = \frac{P}{P - a}$$

As such, if two straight lines are drawn to the same scale the point elasticity at any given price will be the same if the curves have the same vertical intercept even if they have different gradients.

M.5.2 Arc elasticity

This is the approach of calculating the elasticity over a given range by using the averages of the prices (or incomes) and quantities at the two extremes of the range.

The formula for income elasticity of demand (Y_{ed}) is shown below, but it is easily adapted for the other elasticities:

$$Y_{ed} = \frac{\Delta Q}{\Delta Y} \frac{\frac{1}{2}(Y_1 + Y_2)}{\frac{1}{2}(Q_1 + Q_2)}$$

$$= \frac{\Delta Q}{\Delta Y} \frac{Y_1 + Y_2}{Q_1 + Q_2}$$

M.6 | More sophisticated demand-and-supply analysis

M.6.1 Equilibria

It is unlikely that demand and supply curves will be completely straight, but the same analysis as above can be used to calculate the equilibrium conditions. An example of doing this for quadratic inverse demand and supply curves is outlined below, along with the graphical solution in Figure M.1.

$$P_d = Q^2 - 20Q + 30$$

$$P_s = Q^2 + 10Q + 15$$

$$P_d = P_s$$

$$Q^2 - 20Q + 30 = Q^2 + 10Q + 15$$

$$15 = 30Q$$

$$Q = \frac{15}{30} = 0.5$$

$$P_d = Q^2 - 20Q + 30$$

$$P_d = 0.5^2 - 20(0.5) + 30$$

$$P_d = 0.25 - 10 + 30 = 20.25$$

Solving for the equilibrium conditions for these curves generates a price of £20.25 and a traded quantity of 0.5 units, which, in this case, are 500 units. This result can be checked by substituting $P_s = 20.25$ and $Q = 0.5$ into the supply equation (that for P_s) above; and also by plotting the demand (the equation for P_d) and supply (the equation for P_s) curves on the same graph and locating the point of intersection.

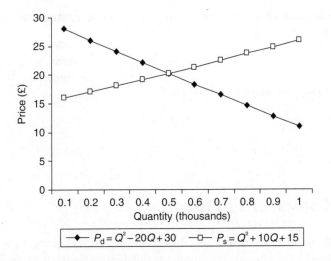

Figure M.1 Demand and supply analysis

Caption for graph legend: $P_d = Q^2 - 20Q + 30$ $P_s = Q^2 + 10Q + 15$

M.6.2 Elasticity of demand

It is possible to calculate the point elasticity of demand of a more sophisticated inverse demand curve by using an adaptation of the point elasticity of demand formula. Instead of using the inverse of the gradient in the formula, as in Section M.5.1, it is necessary to use the first derivative with respect to the price:

$$P_{ed} = \frac{dQ}{dP} \frac{P}{Q}$$

This derivative can be generated simply by using the following formula, which makes it easy to obtain from the inverse demand curve:

$$\frac{dQ}{dP} = \frac{1}{\frac{dP}{dQ}}$$

For example, calculating the point price elasticity of demand at $Q = 1$ for the more sophisticated demand curve above,

$$P_d = Q^2 - 20Q + 30$$

$$\frac{dP}{dQ} = \frac{d(Q^2 - 20Q + 30)}{dQ}$$

$$= 2Q - 20$$

$$\frac{dQ}{dP} = \frac{1}{\frac{dP}{dQ}} = \frac{1}{2Q - 20}$$

$$Q = 1$$

$$P_d = 1^2 - 20(1) + 30 = 11$$

$$P_{ed} = \frac{dQ}{dP} \frac{P}{Q}$$

$$= \frac{1}{2(1) - 20} \frac{11}{1}$$

$$= -0.61$$

The demand at this quantity for this demand curve is, therefore, price inelastic.

A useful demand function is one that has the same elasticity at all prices and quantities. It has the form

$$Q = kP^e$$

where k is a positive constant. Thus

$$Q = kP^{-2}$$

always has an elasticity of –2.

M.7 | Consumer surplus

It is possible to calculate the value of consumer surplus using integration. An example is worked out below. For simplicity the demand curve is a straight line, and since we know that the area of a triangle is half the base multiplied by the height, formal integration is unnecessary in this simple case; but the same technique can be used for more irregular functional forms as well.

Figure M.2 shows a demand curve, and a market price and quantity of £80 and 60 units respectively. To calculate the value of the consumer surplus it is first necessary to calculate the whole area beneath the demand curve from a quantity of zero to one of 60 units:

$$\int_{Q=0}^{Q=60} (200 - 2Q)\, dQ = \left(200Q - 2\frac{Q^2}{2}\right)_{Q=0}^{Q=60}$$

$$= \left[200(60) - 60^2\right] - \left[200(0) - 0^2\right]$$

$$= £8400$$

This is the total amount that consumers are willing and able to pay for the product, and so the final stage is to subtract the amount that they actually pay in order to

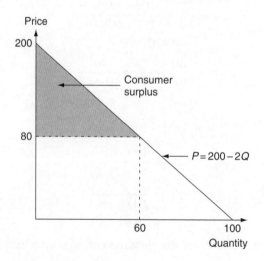

Figure M.2
Consumer surplus

arrive at the consumer surplus. As consumers pay £80 for every unit and 60 units are bought, this is simply

$$P \times Q = 80 \times 60$$

$$= £4800$$

It is the area of the rectangle formed by the market price and the quantity consumed. Consequently, the consumer surplus is

$$8400 - 4800 = £3600$$

Note that using the rule for the area of a triangle, the consumer surplus is $(1/2) \times 120 \times 60 = £3600$.

The general rule for calculating consumer surplus is therefore

$$\int_{Q=0}^{Q=Q_m} (equation) \, dQ - (P_m \times Q_m)$$

where *equation* is the equation of the demand curve, P_m is the market price and Q_m is the quantity traded at this price.

M.8 | Producer surplus

It is similarly possible to calculate the value of producer surplus using integration as well, but the technique is slightly different. An example is again worked out below, and for simplicity the curve is again a straight line.

Figure M.3 shows a situation where the market price is £120 and 80 units are traded at that price. It is first necessary to calculate the total revenue that the producers are earning. This is simply the area of the rectangle formed by the market price and quantity.

$$P \times Q = 120 \times 80$$

$$= £9600$$

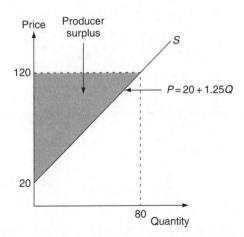

Figure M.3 Producer surplus

The producers are, therefore, earning £9600. The next step in the calculation is to calculate the minimum amount that they would be willing to produce the 80 units for. This can then by subtracted from what they actually earn to leave the producer surplus. This is found by calculating the area underneath the supply curve from a quantity of zero up to one of 80 units:

$$\int_{Q=0}^{Q=80} (20+1.25Q)\,dQ = \left(20Q+1.25\frac{Q^2}{2}\right)_{Q=0}^{Q=80}$$

$$= \left[20(80)+0.625\left(80^2\right)\right]-\left[20(0)+1.25\left(0^2\right)\right]$$

$$= £5600$$

Subtracting this from the producers' revenue gives a producer surplus of £4000, which is confirmed by calculating the area of the triangle directly.

In general, producer surplus can be calculated by

$$P_m Q_m - \int_{Q=0}^{Q=Q_m} (equation)\,dQ$$

where *equation* is that of the supply curve, P_m is the market price and Q_m is the quantity traded at that price.

M.9 | Total, marginal and average costs

M.9.1 Moving from one to another

The average cost curve is likely to be of a U shape and so the total cost curve is likely to have a cubic form; for example,

$$TC = \frac{1}{3}Q^3 - 13Q^2 + 170Q$$

To calculate the marginal cost function from this, it is necessary to differentiate it with respect to the quantity:

$$MC = \frac{d(TC)}{dQ} = \frac{d\left(\frac{1}{3}Q^3 - 13Q^2 + 170Q\right)}{dQ}$$

$$= Q^2 - 26Q + 170$$

The average cost function is generated by dividing the total cost by the quantity:

$$AC = \frac{TC}{Q} = \frac{\frac{1}{3}Q^3 - 13Q^2 + 170Q}{Q}$$

$$= \frac{1}{3}Q^2 - 13Q + 170$$

These average and marginal cost curves are displayed in Figure M.4.

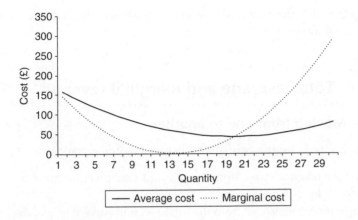

Figure M.4 The relationship between average and marginal costs

M.9.2 That the MC curve passes through the AC curve at its minimum point

This shows that the marginal cost curve passes through the average cost curve at its minimum point. To prove this mathematically, one first needs to differentiate the average cost curve with respect to quantity and then to solve this for zero. This generates the quantity at which the slope of the average cost curve is zero; or in other words, the quantity at which the average cost curve is flat:

$$AC = \frac{1}{3}Q^2 - 13Q + 170$$

$$\frac{d(AC)}{dQ} = \frac{1}{1.5}Q - 13$$

$$\frac{1}{1.5}Q - 13 = 0$$

$$Q = 13 \times 1.5 = 19.5$$

If there are multiple such turning points, the minimum is found by calculating the second derivative for each with respect to quantity. The minimum point on the curve will be where this is positive:

$$\frac{d^2(AC)}{dQ^2} = \frac{1}{1.5}$$

As this is positive, the minimum point of the average cost curve is at a quantity of 19.5 units. It is then necessary to calculate the average and marginal costs at this quantity to see if they are equal:

$$AC = \frac{1}{3}(19.5)^2 - 13(19.5) + 170$$

$$= 43.25$$

$$MC = (19.5)^2 - 26(19.5) + 170$$

$$= 43.25$$

As they are equal, the marginal cost curve must pass through the average cost curve at its minimum point.

M.10 | Total, average and marginal revenue

M.10.1 Moving from one to another

In the same way as for the cost curves, to generate the equation of

- an average revenue curve from the relevant total revenue curve it is necessary to divide it by quantity;
- a marginal revenue curve from the total revenue curve it is necessary to differentiate it with respect to the quantity.

M.10.2 Revenue curves under perfect competition

A perfectly competitive producer has a completely elastic demand curve. It can be formulated as

$$P_d = Z$$

Z is a constant price because a perfectly competitive producer has to take this price irrespective of the output it supplies to the market.

The total revenue is

$$TR = P \times Q$$

$$TR = Z \times Q$$

The average revenue is

$$AR = \frac{TR}{Q} = \frac{ZQ}{Q} = Z$$

The marginal revenue is

$$MR = \frac{d(TR)}{dQ} = \frac{d(ZQ)Q}{dQ} = Z$$

This is the mathematical proof that for a perfectly competitive producer the average revenue is equal to the marginal revenue. Abnormal profit will be zero.

M.10.3 The MR curve has twice the slope of the AR curve under imperfect competition

Under the other market structures the demand or average revenue curve is downward-sloping. Assuming, for simplicity, that it is a straight-line curve, it takes the form

$$AR = a - bQ$$

This is the same as the simple demand curve in Section M.1 and so is also the formula for price at every level of quantity. The total revenue curve, therefore, is this multiplied by the quantity:

$$TR = (a - bQ)Q$$

$$TR = aQ - bQ^2$$

The equation for the marginal revenue curve is generated by differentiating that for the total revenue:

$$MR = \frac{d(TR)}{dQ}$$

$$= \frac{d\left(aQ - bQ^2\right)}{dQ}$$

$$= a - 2bQ$$

The gradient of the average revenue curve is $-bQ$ and that for the marginal revenue curve is $-2bQ$. As such, the marginal revenue curve falls at twice the rate of the average revenue curve. This result only holds for a straight-line demand curve, though.

M.11 | Profit-maximising condition

It was explained in the text that for a producer to maximise profit it is necessary for it to produce a level of output at which its marginal cost is equal to its marginal revenue. This can be proved mathematically by using differentiation, starting with the equation for profit (total revenue minus total cost):

$$\pi = TR - TC$$

$$\frac{d(\pi)}{dQ} = \frac{d(TR)}{dQ} - \frac{d(TC)}{dQ}$$

$$= MR - MC$$

It is then necessary to solve this for zero in order to show the rule for where the profit function has a zero gradient and so is at a turning point:

$$\pi' = MR - MC = 0 \rightarrow MR = MC$$

This is, therefore, the profit-maximising condition. However, if there are multiple turning points in the profit function, the one for profit maximisation is found by finding the second derivative of each with respect to quantity. The profit-maximising output will be that where this is negative:

$$\frac{d^2(\pi)}{dQ^2} = \frac{d(MR)}{dQ} - \frac{d(MC)}{dQ} < 0$$

Bibliography

General references

These are references that have been used in more than a single chapter.

Aldcroft, D.H., 1974. *Studies in British Transport History: 1870–1970*. David and Charles Ltd.

Button, K.J., 1993. *Transport Economics*. Second edition. Edward Elgar Publishing Ltd.

Calder, S., 2006. *No Frills: The Truth Behind the Low-Cost Revolution in the Skies*. Virgin Books Ltd.

Commission for Integrated Transport, June 2004. *The Bus Industry: Encouraging Local Delivery. Advice from the Commission for Integrated Transport*.

European Commission, Directorate-General for Energy and Transport in Co-operation with Eurostat, 2006. *Energy and Transport in Figures. Part Three: Transport*.

National Economic Research Associates, December 1997. *The Effectiveness of Undertakings in the Bus Industry*. Research Paper 14, prepared for the Office of Fair Trading.

UK Office of National Statistics (ONS) and the Department for Transport (DfT), 2004. *Transport Statistics Bulletin, Road Traffic Statistics*.

Quince, T. and Whittaker, H., September 2003. *Entrepreneurial Orientation and Entrepreneurs' Intentions and Objectives*. ESRC Centre for Business Research. Working Paper Number 271. University of Cambridge.

Stern, N., 2007. *The Stern Review: The Economics of Climate Change*. Cambridge University Press.

Varian, H.L., 1999. *Intermediate Microeconomics: A Modern Approach*. Fifth edition. Norton Publishing Ltd.

Introduction

Harcourt, G.C., September 1995. *Joan Robinson, 1903–1983. The Economic Journal*, 105 (Reprinted in: Harcourt, G.C. 2001. *50 Years a Keynesian and Other Essays*. Palgrave MacMillan, pp. 91–113).

Robinson, J., 1960. *Exercises in Economic Analysis*. London: MacMillan, p. 17.

1   The History of Transport in Europe

Burton, A., 1995. *The Great Days of the Canals*. Tiger Books International.

Heap, C. and Van Riemsdijk, J., 1980. *The Pre-grouping Railways: Their Development and Individual Characters. Part Two*. The Stationary Office Books.

Heilbroner, R., 2000. *The Worldly Philosophers*. Penguin Books.

Henshaw, D., 1994. *The Great Railway Conspiracy: The Fall and Rise of Britain's Railways Since the 1950s*. Second edition. Leading Edge Press.

Lewis, M.J.T., 1970. *Early Wooden Railways*. Routledge Keegan Paul.

Ransom, P.J.G., 1989. *The Victorian Railway and How It Evolved*. Heinemann.

Rolt, L.T.C., 1950. *The Inland Waterways of England*. George Allen and Unwin Ltd.

Savage, C. I., 1966. *An Economic History of Transport*. Hutchinson & Co. (Publishers) Ltd. Third impression (Revised edition).

White, H.P., 1986. *Forgotten Railways*. David St. John Thomas.

There is also a range of websites with excellent information about the history of transport, including: http://www.historyworld.net and http://www.en.wikipedia.org

3 The Demand for Transport

Cole, S., 2005. *Applied Transport Economics: Policy, Management and Decision Making*. Third edition. Kogan Page Limited.

Nash, C.A., 1982. *Economics of Public Transport*. Longman Group Limited.

Oum, T.H., Waters II, W.G. and Yong, J.S., January 1990. A Survey of Recent Estimates of Price Elasticities of Demand for Transport. *Policy, Planning and Research Working Papers: Transportation*. Infrastructure and Urban Development Department. The World Bank, WPS 359.

Quinet, E. and Vickerman, R., 2004. *Principles of Transport Economics*. Edward Elgar.

UK Department for Transport (DfT), May 2005. (Amended June 2006). *Traffic Speeds on English Urban Areas: 2004*.

UK Office of National Statistics (ONS), 2007. *Retail Sales Index*. (Up-dated: 11 June 2007), http://www.statistics.gov.uk

Van de Voorde, E. and Meersman, H., 1997. The Effect of Economic on Future Freight Transport; In *Which Changes for Transport in the Next Century?* Fourteenth International Symposium on Theory and Practice in Transport Economics (Innsbruck – 21/23 October); Topic 1: What is the Future for Transport? Paris: CEMT.

Vienna International Airport, 2006. *Business Report*. Second quarter.

4 Markets, Costs and Revenues

Anderson, W.L. and Ross, R.L., 2005. The Methodology of Profit Maximisation: An Austrian Alternative. *The Quarterly Journal of Austrian Economics*, 8(4), Winter.

Baumol, W., 1959. *Business Behaviour, Value and Growth*, New York and London: The Macmillan Company.

City Sprint Ltd, http://www.citysprint.co.uk

Cyret, R.M. and March, J.G., 1963. *A Behavioural Theory of the Firm*. Englewood Cliffs NJ: Prentice Hall Inc.

Fitzpatrick, G.D., 1986. *Microeconomics: New Theories and Old*. Oxford University Press.

Friedman, M., 1953. The Methodology of Positive Economics. *Essays in Positive Economics*. Chicago: University of Chicago Press.

Griffiths, A. and Wall, S., 2000. *Intermediate Microeconomics: Theory and Applications*. Second edition. Pearson Education Limited.

Marris, R., 1964 June. *The Economic Theory of Managerial Capitalism*. London: Macmillan.

Simon, H.A., 1959. Theories of Decision-making in Economics and behavioural Science. *The American Economic Review*, XLIX(3), 253–283.

Williamson, O.E., 1963. Managerial Discretion and Business Behaviour. *The American Economic Review*, 53(5), December.

Williamson, O.E., 1975. *Markets and Hierarchies: Analysis and Structural Implications*. New York: Free Press.

5 | Competition and Contestability

Baumol, W.J., 1982a. Contestable Markets: An Unsurprising in the Theory of Industry Structure. *The American Economic Review*, 72(1), March, 1–15.

Baumol, W.J., Panzar, J.C. and Willig, R.D., 1982b. *Contestable Markets and the Theory of Industry Structure*, San Diego: Harcourt Brace Jovanovich.

Baumol, W.J. and Willig, R.D., 1986. Contestability: Developments Since the Book, *Oxford Economic Papers*, 38, Supplement: Strategic Behaviour and Industrial Competition, November pages 9–36.

6 | Monopoly

Air Scotland, http://www.air-scotland.com

European Commission, Directorate-General for Competition 2004. *EU Competition Policy and the Consumer*.

Go Skills. *Skills Needs Assessment: Bus and Coach Industries*. Solihull: Go Skills: www.goskills.org/UploadedDocs/Publications/1147944122.pdf

7 | Monopolistic Competition

UK Department for Transport, June 2006. *Road Freight Statistics 2005*.

9 | Externalities

European Commission, June 2003. *Europe at a Crossroads: The Need for Sustainable Transport*.

European Conference of Ministers of Transport, 12–13 March 1998. The Spread of Congestion in Europe: Conclusions of Round Table 110. Paris.

European Union Road Federation, 2006. *European Road Statistics*, p. 52.

Eurostat, 2005. *European Business: Facts and Figures*, p. 321.

Hardin, G., 1968. The Tragedy of the Commons. *Science*, pp. 1243–1247.

Intergovernmental Panel on Climate Change (IPCC), 2001. *Climate Change 2001: Synthesis Report, Summary for Policymakers*, Figure 2-7.

Intergovernmental Panel on Climate Change (IPCC), 1999. *IPCC Special Report: Aviation and the Global Atmosphere*.

Rutter H., 2000. Modal Shift: Transport and Health. *A Policy Report on the Health Benefits of Increasing Levels of Cycling in Oxfordshire*, October; www.modalshift.org/reports.tandh/print_version.htm

Webber, M., 14 October 2002. BBC News, http://www.news.bbc.co.uk

World Commission on Environment and Development (more commonly known as the Brundtland Report), 1987. *Our Common Future*. Oxford University Press.

10 | Public and Demerit Goods

Amos, J., 28 December 2005. Europe's Galileo Project. *BBC News*.

Button, K. and Pitfield, D., 1991. More Private Sector Provision of Roads in Europe? In K. Button and D. Pitfield (eds). *Transport Deregulation: An International Movement*. Macmillan Academic and Professional Ltd.

Crime Concern and the Social Research Associates of the Department for Transport; Personal Security Issues in Pedestrian Journeys; First published 8 November 1999 and then modified January 2006.

Oc, T. and Trench, S., 1992. *How Can We Make Cities Safer For Women?* Symposium Paper, University of Florida.

UK Department for Transport (DfT), 2005. Road Casualties in Great Britain 2004. *Annual Report*. September, London.

11 | Inequality, Poverty and Asymmetric Information

Eurostat. *Inequality of Income Distribution*, http://epp.eurostat.ec.europa.eu

Eurostat. *At-risk-of-poverty rate after social transfers, by gender*, http://epp.eurostat.ec.europa.eu

12 | Privatisation and Deregulation

Barrett, S., 1987. *Flying High: Airline Prices and European Regulation*. Avebury.

Barrett, S., 1998. The Importance of State Enterprises in the Irish Economy and the Future for Privatisation. In D. Parker (ed.). *Privatisation in the European Union: Theory and Policy Perspectives*. Routledge.

Barrett, S., 2006. Privatisation in Ireland. In M. Köthenbürger, H.W. Sinn and J. Whalley (eds). *Privatisation Experiences in the European Union*. MIT Press.

Begg, D., Fischer, S. and Dornbusch, R., 1991. *Economics: Third Edition*. McGraw-Hill Book Company Europe, pp. 327–329.

Dodgson, J., 1991. The Bus Industry: The Cases of Australia, the USA and the UK. In K. Button and D. Pitfield (eds). *Transport Deregulation: An International Movement*. Macmillan Academic and Professional Ltd.

Esser, J., 1998. Privatisation in Germany: Symbolism in the social market economy? In D. Parker (ed.). *Privatisation in the European Union: Theory and Policy Perspectives*. Routledge.

Glaister, S., 2004. *British Rail Privatisation: Competition destroyed by Politics; Centre for the Study of Regulated Industries*. University of Bath School of Management. Occasional Paper 23.

Go Skills. *Skills Needs Assessment: Bus and Coach Industries*. Solihull: Go Skills: www.goskills.org/UploadedDocs/Publications/1147944122.pdf

Gómez-Ibáñez, J.A. and Meyer, J., 1993. *Going Private: The International Experience with Transport Privatization*. Washington: Brookings Inst.

Haarmeyer, D. and Yorke, P., April 1993. Port Privatisation: An International Perspective. *Executive Summary*. Reason Foundation Policy Study No. 156.

Hensher, D.A. and Wallis, I.P., 2005. Competitive Tendering as a Contracting Mechanism for Subsidising Transport: The Bus Experience. *Journal of Transport Economics and Policy*, 39(3), 295–321.

Knieps, G., 2006. Privatisation of Network Industries in Germany: A Disaggregated Approach. In M. Köthenbürger, H.W. Sinn and J. Whalley (eds). *Privatisation Experiences in the European Union*. MIT Press.

Leaman, J., 1994. Regulatory Reform and Privatisation in Germany. In M. Moran, and T. Prosser (eds). *Privatisation and Regulatory Change in Europe*. Open University Press.

National Prices Commission, 1972. Occasional Paper 10. Government Publications (Ireland).

Pearce, M. and Stuart, G., 1996. *British Political History 1867–1995: Democracy and Decline*. Second edition. Routledge.

Yarrow, G., 1986. Privatisation in Theory and Practice, *Economic Policy*, 1(2), April, 323–377.

13 Project Appraisal: Cost–Benefit Analysis

Bamford, C.G., 2006. *Transport Economics*. Fourth edition. Oxford: Heinemann Educational Publishers.

Boardman, A., Greenberg, D., Vining, A. and Weimar, D., 2006. *Cost-Benefit Analysis: Concepts and Practice*. Third edition. Pearson Prentice Hall.

Cairncross, F., 1992. *Costing the Earth: The Challenge for Governments, the Opportunities for Business*. Harvard Business School Press.

Markandya, A., Harou, P., Bellù, L.G. and Cistulli, V., 2002. *Environmental Economics for Sustainable Growth: A Handbook for Practitioners*. Edward Elgar Publishing Limited.

Perkins, F., 1994. *Practical Cost Benefit Analysis: Basic Concepts and Applications*. MacMillan Education Australia PTY LTD.

UK Department of Transport, May 2004. *The COBA Manual*, http://www.dft.gov.uk/pgr/economics/software/coba11usermanual

14 Transport Investment

Farrell, S., 1999. *Financing European Transport Infrastructure: Policies and Practice in Western Europe*. MacMillan Press LTD.

Gerondeau, C., 1997. *Transport in Europe*. Artech House INC.

15 General Forms of Government Intervention

Crocker, T.D., 1966. The Structure of Atmospheric Pollution Control Systems, In Wolozin, H. (ed.) *The Economics of Air Pollution*, New York: W.W. Norton.

Dales, J.H., 1968. Land, Water and Ownership, *The Canadian Jouranal of Economics*, 1(4), November, 791–804.

European Commission, Directorate C – Environment and Health, November 2004. *Transport-Related Impacts and Instruments for Sensitive Areas: Final Report*. Part two: Policy instruments to reduce transport impacts in sensitive mountain areas.

Leicester, A., 2006. *Fuel Taxation*. The Institute for Fiscal Studies. Briefing Note No. 55.

Svendsen, G.T., 2003. *The Political Economy of the European Union: Institutions, Policy and Economic Growth*. Edward Elgar Publishing Limited.

Tietenberg, T.H., 1995. Transferable Discharge Permits and Global Warming. In D.W. Bromley (ed.). *The Handbook of Environmental Economics*. Blackwell Publishers.

UK Parliament, 1 March 2007. *Emissions Trading Scheme must improve robustness and transparency*. EAC 28.02.07a, http://www.parliament.uk

16 | Tackling Traffic Congestion

Association of Train Operating Companies (ATOC), 2001. *Passenger demand forecasting handbook*.

Coates, J., 1999. *Roads to Accountability*, AA policy. Automobile Association, April.

Dargay, J. and Hanly, M., 1999. *Bus Fare Elasticities: Report to the Department of Environment, Transport and the Regions*. ESRC Transport Studies Unit, ref. 1999/26, UCL.

Eliasson, J. and Lundberg, M., 2003; *Road Pricing in Urban Areas*; Vägverket, Swedish National Road Administration: http://www.transport-pricing.net/download/swedishreport.pdf

Glaister, S. and Graham, D.J., 2003a. *Transport Pricing and Investment in England: Technical Report*. Working Paper. Imperial College London, http://www.cts.cv.ic.ac.uk/html/ResearchActivities/publicationDetails.asp?PublicationID=307

Glaister, S. and Graham, D.J., 2003b. *Pricing our Roads: Vision and Reality*, Research Monograph 59, Institute for Economic Affairs.

Glaister, S. and Graham, D.J., 2004. *Pricing Our Roads: Vision and Reality*. London: Institute of Economic Affairs.

Glaister, S. and Graham, D.J., October 2006. *National Road Pricing: Is It Fair and Practical?*, Social Market Foundation.

Glaister, S., Travers, T. and Wakefield, J., April 2004. *Investing in Cities*. Development Securities.

Graham, D. and Glaister, S., 2002a. *Review of income and price elasticities of demand for road traffic;* UK Department for Tansport.

Graham, D. and Glaister, S., 2002b. The Demand for Automobile Fuel: A Survey of Elasticities, *Journal of Transport Economics and Policy*, 36, 1–26.

Graham, D. and Glaister, S., 2004. Road Traffic Demand Elasticity Estimates: A Review, *Transport Reviews* 24(3), May.

Grayling, T. and Glaister, S., 2002. *A New Fares Contract for London;* Institute for Public Policy Research.

Kian Keong Chin, 2002. *Road Pricing: Singapore's Experience*. Imprint-Europe.

Sansom, T., Nash, C.A., Mackie, P.J. and Shires, J., 2001. *Surface Transport Costs and Charges: Final Report* for the Department of Transport Environment and the Regions. Institute for Transport Studies. Leeds: University of Leeds.

Smeed, R., 1964. *Road Pricing: The Economic and Technical Possibilities*. HMSO.

Transport for London, October 2003. *Congestion Charging: Six Months On*, http://www.TfL.gov.uk

Transport for London, February 2004. *Congestion Charging: Update on Scheme Impacts and Operations*, http://www.TfL.gov.uk

Transport for London, June 2006. *Congestion Charging: Impacts Monitoring, Fourth Annual Report*, http://www.TfL.gov.uk

Travers, T. and Glaister, S., May 2006. Improving Local Transport: How Small Reforms Could Make a Big Difference. *Local Government Association*. London.

UK Department for Transport (DfT), 2000. *Transport Ten Year Plan 2000: Background Analysis*. DETR. London.

UK Department for Transpor (DfT), 2002. *Delivering Better Transport*. HMSO.

UK Department for Transport (DfT), 2003. *Traffic in Great Britain*. HMSO.

UK Department for Transport (DfT), 2004a. *Feasibility Study of Road Pricing in the UK: A Report to the Secretary of State for Transport*. London.

UK Department for Transport and Local Regions (DTRL), 2001a. *Transport Statistics for Great Britain*. HMSO.

UK Department for Transport and Local Regions (DTRL), 2001b. *Regional Transport Statistics*. HMSO.

Walters, A.A., 1961. The Theory and Measurement of Private and Social Cost of Highway congestion. *Econometrica*, 29(4).

Index

accidents
  aviation 279
  buses 169–70
  COBA 220, 222, 223, 235
  external cost 251, 257
  nationalisation 279
  rail 194, 198
  regulation 235
  road 217
  road charging 235, 275
  valuation 257
  see also safety
acquisitions, *see* takeovers
addictiveness 54
adverse selection 181
agglomerations 9, 30–2
Air Scotland 104
asymmetric information 177–8, 181–2,
auctions 201, 243, 244–7
Australia 58
Austria 226, 235, 241, 245
Austrian school of economics 84
automobiles
  anti-competitive behaviour 117
  business objectives 83–5
  Channel Tunnel 229–30
  costs 69, 79
  demerit goods 149
  derived demand 36
  development 7–8
  importance 21–30
  income elasticity of demand 57–8
  industry 147–8
  international comparisons 26–9
  niche markets 126
  peak demand 42–6
  price elasticity of demand 50–3
  privatisation 192–3

regulation 8–9, 121, 123, 208–9
rural demand 64–5
second-hand markets 181–2
sharing 256
see also buses; COBA; congestion, road;
    cost–benefit analysis; externalities;
    inequality; investment; road
    haulage; road provision; street
    lighting; sustainable
    development; taxis
aviation
  barriers to entry 103–5
  charter 15, 141
  contestable markets 101–2
  costs 69, 103–4
  cross elasticity of demand 58–9
  demerit goods 175
  development 13–15
  economies of scale 73–4
  external costs 151–2, 163
  Galileo 168–9
  hub-and-spoke structure 143
  importance 21–4, 279–80
  international comparisons 26–9
  investment 228–9
  liberalisation 15, 142–6
  low-cost 15, 63–4, 104, 142–6, 280
  market structure 141–6
  peak demand 47–8
  price discrimination 115
  price elasticity of demand 83
  pricing and booking strategies 146–7
  privatisation 188–9
  regulation 229
  scheduled flights 141
  yield management 115–6
  see also cost–benefit analysis

barriers to entry/exit
    anti-competitive behaviour   105–7
    aviation   103–4, 141–3
    brand loyalty   104–5, 126
    buses   202–6
    contestable markets   101–2
    economies of scale, *see* economies
        of scale
    initial capital costs   103
    licences, *see* licences
    monopolistic competition   125–6
    monopoly   103–8, 123
    oligopoly   137–8
    perfect competition   91–3, 95
    privatisation   103, 197–9, 201–3
    road haulage   104, 127–32
    shipping   97
    sunk costs, *see under* costs
    taxis   132–5
    see also regulation
basic economic problem   211
Belgium   4, 58, 128, 226, 228, 229,
        240, 241
benefits   151
    see also cost–benefit analysis; demerit
        goods; externalities
bicycles   57, 64, 88, 172
Britain, *see* UK
British Airways   15, 63, 104, 141–2,
        145–6, 210
British Rail   183, 188, 193–6
budget maximisation   187, 246
Bulgaria   14
bulk buying, *see* economies of scale,
        marketing
bureaucracy   39, 41, 122, 131, 246–7
buses
    costs   76, 83
    cross elasticity of demand   58–9
    deregulation   189–90
    development   8, 19, 189
    factors of production   67–8
    hub-and-spoke structure   142
    importance   24–7, 33
    international comparisons   29–32
    London   8, 19, 202–3
    market structure   119–22
    peak demand   48
    price discrimination   112–16
    price elasticity of demand   53–5
    privatisation   197–8, 202–3
    road charging   254, 256, 259–62,
        272, 274
    rural demand   64–5
    yield management   115–16
business objectives   85–9, 212
    altruistic   88
    behavioural theories   87–8, 90
    environmental   87–9
    growth maximisation   86–7
    managerial utility maximisation   864
    profit maximisation   83–5, 90, 295
    sales revenue maximisation   85–6

cabotage   141, 209
callable flights   147
canals
    and cross elasticity of demand   58–9
    development (520BC–1960s)   16–17
    freight   23–4
    future   280–1
    and income elasticity of demand   58–9
    international comparisons   26–9
    and privatisation   201–2
capital   67
    and normal profit   92–3
    and privatisation   186–7
    and sustainability   166–9
    see also barriers to entry/exit;
        cost–benefit analysis; investment
carbon dioxide   88, 157–60, 241,
        244, 245
carbon trading, *see* tradable permits
cars, *see* automobiles
cartels, *see* collusion
Channel Tunnel   229–30
charter services
    aviation   15, 142
    buses   120–2
    shipping   98, 99
China   10, 16, 31, 161
City Sprint   88–9
clusters   31
    see also agglomerations
coach transport, *see* buses
Coase theorem   155–6
COBA   220–4
    see also cost–benefit analysis
cobweb model   100–1
collusion   19, 106, 107, 117
command-and-control policies   234–7,
        243, 246, 247
    compare taxation; tradable permits
    see also regulation
commons   156–7

competition policy 95, 106, 116–19, 183, 186
complementary goods 38, 40, 49, 59, 168, 229, 285
  mathematical exposition 287, 293–5
  compare substitute goods
composite units 26
conference system 11, 20
congestion
  aviation xiii, 164
  charging, *see* road charging
  rail 163, 274
  road xiii, 7, 163–4, 262–3, 274
  see also COBA; externalities; road provision
consignment consolidation 75–6
  see also transhipment
consumer surplus 62–3, 290–1
  and monopolistic competition 126
  and monopoly 116–23
  and oligopoly 137
  and perfect competition 91–3
  and price ceilings 133–4, 234
  and taxation 236–9
  and terrorism 63
  and valuation 217–8
  compare producer surplus
  see also welfare
contestable markets
  buses 189–90
  efficiency 94–6
  model 96–7
  privatisation 189, 203
  on the spectrum of competition 90
  tramp shipping 97, 99, 102
contract of affreightment 99
costs
  abatement, marginal 232
  average 70–8, 292–4
  common 80, 172
  external 151–3
    see also cost–benefit analysis; externalities; road charging
  fixed 68–72, 75–8
  inventory 39–41
    see also costs, time
  joint 80
  marginal 76–8, 292–3
    and supply 106
  opportunity 79–80, 216

  private 151–3
    marginal 151–3
    see also demerit goods; externalities; road charging
  semi-variable 68
  social 151–3, 255
    marginal 151–3
  specific 80
  sunk 104, 196
  time 79
    see also costs, inventory
  total 70, 292–3
  variable 68–75, 78
  see also cost–benefit analysis; externalities; road charging
cost–benefit analysis 211–24, 281
  COBA 221–4
  limitations 219–20
  methodology 212–15
  types of 211–12
  valuation 216–19
cross-subsidisation 48, 105, 147, 197, 202
crowding out 187–8
cycling, *see* bicycles
Cyprus 235–41
Czech Republic 179, 235, 241

demand
  average revenue 81–2
  curves 36–7, 40–1, 60–3, 82
  derived 36, 57
  determinants 36–41, 283
  effective 35, 37
  Hicksian 41
  kinked 137–8
  law of 36–8, 283
  markets 36
  Marshallian 41
  mathematical exposition 283–95
  notional 35
  peak 42, 43, 47, 48
  rural 64–5
  Say's Law 35
  Slutsky 41
  see also cost–benefit analysis; elasticity; regulation, valuation
demerit goods 167–8, 232, 236
demotorisation 235–6
Denmark 12, 208, 240, 241

deregulation 185–210
  arguments against 189–90
  arguments for 186–9
  aviation 14–15, 144, 209–10
  buses 202, 208–9
  rail 194–6
  road-haulage 209–10
  shipping 201–2, 209–10
destructive pricing, *see* predatory pricing
discounting 215
diseconomies of scale 72, 75
double dividend effect 238
duopoly 141, 142, 143

ear-marking, *see* hypothecation
early start thesis 20
economic appraisal, *see* cost–benefit
  analysis
economic development 27, 39, 148,
  189, 208, 211, 240
economies of density 76, 84–5
economies of scale 34–6, 79–83, 119
  external 31–2
  financial 72–3
  managerial 74
  marketing 74
  technical 73–4
economies of scope 75–6
Ecopoints scheme 234–5
Eddie Stobart 104, 131
Edgeworth box analysis 155–6
education 180, 190, 275
efficiency
  allocative 30, 94–6, 108
  Pareto 29–30, 95, 109, 126
  productive 72, 94, 100, 118, 126
    see also cost–benefit analysis;
      deregulation; investment;
      market failure; privatisation;
      regulation
elasticity 54–5
  cross elasticity of demand 58–9
  income elasticity of demand 37, 57–8,
    287
  mathematical exposition 283–4,
    293–5
  price elasticity of demand 50–6
    actual estimates 57–9
    determinants 60–1
    and perfect competition 93–4
    and price discrimination 112–15
    and revenue 53, 80
    and road charging 256, 258–9, 262

and taxation 239, 241–2, 244–5
  uses 52–3
Elf Aquitaine 119
employment xiii, 21–24
  automobile industry 147–8
  aviation 209–10
  bus industry 120–1, 204
  and inequality 180–1
  and nationalisation 185, 189, 199
  and rail privatisation 193–6
  shipping 201–2
  and street lighting 169–71
  see also business objectives, managerial
    utility maximisation; economies of
    scale, managerial
entrepreneurial capitalism 84
entrepreneurship 67, 68, 89, 92, 165
  see also business objectives
envelope theorem 72
environmental regulation
  and road charging 253–6, 273
  road haulage 127
  types 231–47
  see also cost–benefit analysis; global
    warming; pollution; valuation
Estonia 241
Eurostar 114, 230
Eurovignette Directive 235, 240
excess capacity pricing, *see* price
  discrimination, second-degree
expenditure
  household xiii, 21–3, 50, 170
    see also valuation
  public xiii, 188, 203, 249, 273
    see also infrastructure; investment,
      public; public sector
externalities 151–66, 279
  and demerit goods 173–5
  and nationalisation 185
  regulation 234-6, 243, 246, 252
  and road charging 253–6, 273
  and road provision 172–3
  see also accidents; global warming;
    noise; pollution; sustainable
    development

factors of production 67–8
  mathematical exposition 283
  see also capital; entrepreneurship;
    labour; land
fashion, *see* popularity effects
ferries 38, 230
financial appraisal 211–12

Finland   12, 208, 241
flag carriers   11, 141–2
flags of convenience   12, 246
flight amalgamation   147
forecasting   52, 214
France
    automobiles   8, 148, 173
    aviation   141–2, 164
    canals   16–17, 280
    elasticities   49, 56
    investment   172–3, 228–30
    rail   114
    regulation   235–8
    shipping   10, 19
free riding   169
    see also public goods
Friedman thesis   90
fuel
    and costs   68, 264
    derived demand   36
    and global warming   157–63
    income elasticity of demand   57–8
    kerosene   63, 244
    mergers   118
    and price discrimination   110–11
    price elasticity of demand   249–50
    regulation   234, 239–41, 244,
        254, 258
    see also externalities; pollution; synfuel

Galileo   168–9
game theory   191, 200
Germany
    automobiles   8
    aviation   142
    canals   17, 209
    deregulation   109
    investment   228
    privatisation   209–10
    rail   3, 209
    regulation   240–1
    road haulage   210
    shipping   17
Giffen goods   37
global warming   157–63, 166, 279
    and road charging   250–2, 257–8
    see also externalities
goods of conspicuous consumption   37
grandfather rights   142, 209
Greece   104, 128, 179, 227, 241
greenhouse gases   157–8, 160, 162, 166
    see also global warming

hackney carriages   7, 132, 135
    see also taxis
health   162, 164–5, 180, 190, 194, 217,
    251, 299
    see also accidents; externalities; safety
Hicks–Kaldor assertion   219
horizontal summation   92, 232
hub and spoke structures   143
    see also transhipment
Hungary   241, 252
hypothecation   235

importance of transport
    international comparisons   26–29
    statistical importance   21–4
    theoretical importance   29–30
income effect   36, 37
index numbers   42
India   161
indifference curve analysis   37, 154–5
inequality   177–82
inferior goods   57–8
information   32, 98–101, 106, 117,
    177–8
    see also asymmetric information;
        cost–benefit analysis; valuation
infrastructure
    agglomerations   30–2
    bus   207–8
    costs   79–80
    international comparisons   26–9
    peak demand   47–8
    privatisation   185–6, 188–92, 197–206
    rail   192–201, 208
    road   169–75, 249–76
    rural areas   64–5
    see also COBA; congestion; cost–benefit
        analysis; externalities; investment;
        sustainable development; tolls;
        valuation
insurance   69, 111–12, 121, 128, 223
investment
    EU   225–28
    income elasticity of demand   57
    private   169, 173, 187, 188, 225,
        228–9
    public   65, 183, 187, 188
    public-private partnerships   227,
        228–9
    see also business objectives;
        infrastructure; privatisation;
        research and development; *separate
        modes of transport*

Ireland
    aviation   115, 209–10
    buses   203
    deregulation   209
    investment   209, 226
    privatisation   209
    rail   209
    regulation   241
    road haulage   210
    shipping   210
    wealth   197
Italy
    agglomerations   30–2
    automobiles   117–18
    aviation   114–15
    canals   16–17
    investment   163–4
    regulation   229, 234, 236, 237, 243

Japan   27–29, 178

Kyoto agreement   158, 243
    see also global warming; regulation

labour   31, 67, 68
land   67, 68
Latvia   178, 241
legal lettering   122
legislation, see regulation
Leicester taxi market   132–5
leniency policy   107, 117
liberalisation, see deregulation
licences   107, 127
    aviation   104, 143
    bus   5, 69, 121–2
    and price discrimination   110–15
    rail   4, 197–9
    and road charging   273–6
    road haulage   127–32
    sunk costs   104
    taxi   103, 132–5
    compare command-and-control policies;
        tradable permits
    see also regulation
Lithuania   241
location decisions   139–41
London congestion charge   172, 253–6
long run   67, 72–5
    compare short run
loss-leader pricing   146
lower Inn Valley   235–6
Luxembourg   178, 179, 240–1

Malta   241
managerial capitalism   84
marginal rate of substitution   155
market failure   149–82, 280
    see also asymmetric information;
        demerit goods; externalities;
        inequality; market power; poverty;
        public goods
market power   103–23, 149, 280
    compare perfect competition
    see also competition policy;
        deregulation; privatisation;
        regulation
markets   33–4
    clearing price   60–1
    fluctuations   99–101
    for lemons   181–2
    missing   153–6, 181
    niche   127, 141
    second-hand   98, 100, 131, 143,
        181–2
    see also regulation
mass production   8, 148
    see also economies of scale
merger control   118–19
metro   4, 25–6
Michelin   117–18
microeconomics   33, 60, 276
minimum efficient scale (MES)   72
monopolies
    and barriers to entry   103–7
    buses   120–2, 202–6
    and competition policy   116–19
    efficiency   108–9
    model   96–97, 107–9
    and price discrimination   110–15
    and privatisation   183, 185, 186–7,
        193–201
    rail   183
    on the spectrum of competition   90
    welfare   108–9
    see also natural monopoly
monopolistic competition
    automobile industry   130
    competition   126–7
    efficiency   125–6
    model   125–6
    road haulage   130–1
    taxis   132–5
    on the spectrum of competition   90
    welfare   133–4
motorbikes   25, 167, 253
motorisation   28–9

multidivisional structures 89
myopia 18–19

narrow boats, *see* canals
nationalisation 123, 185, 189–90, 199
   arguments against 186–9
   arguments for 189–90
   canals 16
   rail 3–4, 20
   shipping 10
   World War One 4, 11, 18
   compare privatisation
natural monopoly
   model 122–3
   and nationalisation 207
   and privatisation 192, 194, 199
   rail 194, 199
   on the spectrum of competition 90
   compare monopolies
necessities 54, 56–7
negative branding 105
neoclassical economics 83–5, 90
Netherlands 16–17, 163, 226, 240–1,
   280
noise 235, 251, 257–8
   see also externalities
normal goods 57–8
Northern Ireland 122, 203
Norway 12, 179, 208, 241, 243

oligopoly
   automobile industry 147–8
   aviation 107, 141–3
   buses 120
   efficiency 138–9
   model 137–41
   shipping 153
   on the spectrum of competition 90
   welfare 134
   see also price discrimination; product
      differentiation
Open Skies legislation 142, 168
   compare regulation
   see also deregulation
Oslo road charging 252
output effect, *see* scale effect
overbooking 147

park and ride schemes 208
patents, *see* licences
peace dividend 188
peak pricing 48
pedestrianisation, *see* demotorisation

penetration pricing 146–7
perfect competition
   efficiency 95–6
   mathematical exposition 293–4
   model 93–7
   road haulage 4–5
   on the spectrum of competition 90
   tramp shipping 97–101
   welfare 95
   compare contestable markets
petrol, *see* fuel
pipelines 23–4
planned obsolescence 147–8
Poland 12, 241
policy risk 200
political capture 19, 233
   see also rent-seeking
political economy xv, 246
political risk 190–2, 200–1
pollution
   and nationalisation 185
   regulation 232, 235, 250, 251, 255,
      258–9
   road 164, 170
   see also externalities; global warming;
      regulation
popularity effects 39, 41
population 39, 41
   see also demand, rural; inequality;
      poverty
Portugal 227, 241
poverty 177–8
powered two-wheelers, *see* motorbikes
predatory pricing 105, 117, 146
   see also competition policy
price ceilings 133–5, 234
   compare price floors
price discrimination 48, 110–15, 229
   perfect 110
   second-degree 111–12
   third-degree 112–15
   compare yield management
price fixing 106, 117
   see also barriers to entry/exit,
      anti-competitive behaviour;
      collusion
price floors 234
price stickiness 137–8
price wars 101, 137, 145
private goods 167
   compare public goods
private hires 132, 135
   see also taxis

private sector   185, 187,
   211, 228
privatisation   183, 185–210, 280
   arguments against   189–90, 204
   arguments for   186–9
   British Rail   103, 193–201
   buses   201, 202–8
   competitive tendering   192, 196,
      204–9
   employee buyouts   188, 192, 201
   methodology   192–3
   shipping   10, 209–10
   compare nationalisation
   see also private sector
producer surplus   62–3, 291–2
   and monopolistic competition   125
   and monopoly   103–9
   and oligopoly   137
   and perfect competition   90
   and price ceilings   133–4, 234
   and taxation   242–3
   and terrorism   63
   compare consumer surplus
   see also welfare
product differentiation   127, 131, 132,
      140, 141, 148, 209
   compare perfect competition
   see also barriers to entry/exit,
      brand loyalty
production possibility frontiers   187
profit
   abnormal   92–3
   accountancy   92
   marginal   83
   -maximisation   83–5, 89–90, 295
      compare business objectives
      see also price discrimination; yield
         management
   normal   92–3
   operating   63–4
   see also financial appraisal
project appraisal   211–24
property rights   155
protectionism   17, 107, 127, 190,
      195–7, 210
   see also competition policy;
      deregulation; privatisation;
      subsidisation
public goods   167–75
   compare private goods
   see also cost–benefit analysis;
      investment, public

public–private partnerships   169, 227,
   228–9
public sector   171–2, 185, 187, 188–9,
   201

Quality Bus Partnerships   207
Quality Contracts   207, 208
quasi-public goods   167, 171–2

rail
   barriers to entry   103–4
   Channel Tunnel   229–30
   costs   69, 103
   cross elasticity of demand   58–9
   development   3–4
   external costs   164
   importance   25
   income elasticity of demand   57
   international comparisons   26–9
   investment   229, 230
   nationalisation   5, 6
   natural monopoly   123
   peak demand   55–6
   price discrimination, *see under* Eurostar
   price elasticity of demand   50, 52–3
   privatisation   103, 114, 194–5, 209–10
   regulation   4–5
   road charging   273
   rural demand   64–5
   sustainable development   165
   underground, *see under* metro
   yield management   115–16
   see also cost–benefit analysis; inequality;
      investment
regulation   255–72
   arguments for   189–90
   automobiles   8, 18, 117, 249–76,
      279–80
   aviation   141–3, 144, 244–7, 279–80
   buses   8, 116, 189, 204, 207
   fuel   111, 240, 258
   rail   3–4, 10, 20–1, 194–5
   road-haulage   19, 121–2, 210
   taxis   103, 132–5
   see also command-and-control policies;
      cost–benefit analysis; licences;
      nationalisation; price ceilings; price
      floors; public sector; subsidisation;
      taxation; tradable permits
Reliant Robin   127
rent-seeking   246–7
   see also political capture
reputation   31, 121, 182

research and development   117, 127
revenue
  average   81–2, 294–5
    and demand   82
  marginal   82–3, 294–5
    see also profit, -maximisation
  -maximisation   85–6
  price elasticity of demand   50–1
  total   80–1 294–5
  see also privatisation; road charging;
      taxation; tradable permits
road charging   172, 250, 251–6, 273–4
  experiences and types   251–3, 272
  methodology   253–72
  principles of   250–1
  taxation   249
road haulage
  barriers to entry   103, 137–8
  costs   83
  cross elasticity of demand   58–9
  development   5, 9–10, 24
  importance   24–5
  income elasticity of demand   57
  international comparisons   26–9
  market structure   141–3
  peak demand   41–9
  price elasticity of demand   50–1
  regulation   129–30, 209–10
  see also automobiles; buses; COBA;
      congestion, road; cost–benefit
      analysis; externalities; investment;
      road provision; sustainable
      development; taxis
road provision   80, 172, 173
Russia   1, 168

safety
  automobiles   148
  bus   122, 218
  command and control policies   234
  demand   33
  investment   228–9
  nationalisation   189–90
  public goods   167–9
  regulation   189
  road   164
  valuation   218
  see also accidents
satisfaction, see utility
satisficing   87
Say's Law   35
scale effect   37, 50
security   40, 41, 61

sensitivity analysis   215, 219
shipping
  bulk   12, 97–8, 102
  carbon taxation   241
  costs   68, 70
  development   1, 10
  external costs   151–2
  freight   10–14, 24, 80, 99, 128, 280
  hub-and-spoke structure   143
  international comparisons   26–9
  investment   228
  liner   10–11, 12, 97, 100
  passenger   13, 28–9
  privatisation   201, 210, 228
  specialised   12, 97, 102
  tramp   11, 12–13, 97–101, 102
  see also flags of convenience
short run   67, 70–2, 75–6
  compare long run
Singapore   74, 252
Slovakia   241
Slovenia   241
South America   161
Spain   142, 173, 226, 227, 241
state-aid, see protectionism
street lighting   33, 169–71
subsidiarity   116–17
subsidisation
  aviation   12, 103, 104, 107
  bus   202, 203, 205–7
  and cost-benefit analysis   211
  and natural monopolies   122–3
  and price elasticity of demand   50
  and privatisation   191
  rail   200, 208, 230
  and road-charging   273
  shipping   10
  see also investment, public;
      expenditure, public
substitute goods   37, 38, 40–1, 49,
    55, 217
  mathematical exposition   285–7
  compare complementary goods
substitution effect   37, 50
supply
  constraints   134–5
    see also licences
  curves   63–64
  determinants   283
  effective   60
  law of   60, 285
  and marginal cost   76–9
  and markets   38

supply – *continued*
  mathematical exposition 283–95
  and Say's Law 35
  see also cobweb model; regulation
survival 87–8
sustainable development 165–6
Sweden 12, 208, 228, 240–1
Switzerland 13, 142, 226, 243
synfuel 159, 279

takeovers 84, 118, 148, 186, 199
taxation 201, 221, 236, 280
  and bureaucratic rent seeking 246–7
  carbon 241
  direct 236, 238
  fuel 240–1
  income 38
  indirect 238
  mathematical exposition 283
  and price elasticity of demand 50
  road 69, 249–76
  and welfare 239
taxis 42–43, 44, 253
terrorism 39, 40, 63
third-party logistics companies 128
time period 42, 54, 67
  see also long run; short run
tolls 56, 235, 240
TotalFina 119
tradable permits 231, 237, 242–5, 246
tragedy of the commons 156–7
trains, *see* rail
Trans-European Networks 227
transhipment 59, 75–6
  see also hub and spoke structures
transport (definition) 1
Trondheim road charging 253
turnpikes 7, 8, 172, 173
  compare road charging

UK
  agglomerations 31
  automobiles 6–9, 58, 213
  aviation 12, 63, 103, 104, 107, 158, 159–60
  buses 8, 9, 19, 76, 132, 202–3, 252, 256
  canals 16–17, 20, 24, 280
  COBA 220–4
  congestion 164, 250–1
  demotorisation 235–6
  deregulation 183, 212–21, 222–8
  employment 21

income elasticity of demand 57
investment 225, 228–9
monopoly 103
peak demand 41–9
private expenditure 21
privatisation 185, 193–10
public expenditure 188, 203, 249
rail 3–4, 20–23, 103, 115–16, 193–201, 274
road charging 273
road haulage 5, 9–10, 19, 24, 54, 96, 104, 121, 209–10
road provision 80, 172, 173
rural demand 64–5
shipping 10–13, 19–20
street lighting 169–71
taxation 236–8, 264, 273
taxis 144
wealth 179
unionisation 148, 188–9
unitary business structures 89
urbanisation 64
USA 27–29
  automobile industry 80, 163
  aviation 69–70, 112, 158
  cost-benefit analysis 220
  global positioning system 168
  rail 217
  roads 274
  shipping 100
  tradable permits 231
  wealth 179
utilitarianism 219
utility 29, 41, 45, 68–9, 94, 95, 96, 151
  marginal 86
  see also consumer surplus; producer surplus; welfare

valuation 166, 167, 193
  hedonic pricing 218
  revealed preference direct proxy methods 216–17
  revealed preference indirect proxy methods 217–18
  stated preference contingent methods 218–19
  willingness-to-pay 214, 218–19, 221, 249
vertical restraints 105, 117
  see also automobiles, anti-competitive behaviour
Virgin Atlantic 106–7, 144
Volkswagen AG 117–18

walking   64, 170–1, 180
waterways, *see under* canals
welfare   61–3
    see also consumer surplus; *general forms
       of government intervention*; market
       failure; producer surplus; utility
welfare state   189

winner's curse   200
work, *see* employment

x-inefficiency   94

yield management   115–16
    compare price discrimination